THE ARMY AND VIETNAM

The Army and Vietnam

ANDREW F. KREPINEVICH, JR.

The Johns Hopkins University Press • Baltimore and London

The Johns Hopkins University Press, 701 West 40th Street, Baltimore, Maryland 21211
The Johns Hopkins Press Ltd., London

∞

The paper used in this publication meets the minimum requirements of American
National Standard for Information Sciences—Permanence of Paper for Printed Library
Materials, ANSI Z39.48-1984.

The views expressed in this book are those of the author and do not necessarily represent those of the Department of Defense, the United States Army, the United States
Military Academy, or the United States Naval War College.

Library of Congress Cataloging-in-Publication Data

Krepinevich, Andrew F.
  The army and Vietnam.

  Includes index.
  1. Vietnamese Conflict, 1961–1975—United States. 2. United States. Army—
History—Vietnamese Conflict, 1961–1975. 3. Strategy. I. Title.
DS558.K74   1986   959.704'33'73   85-45865
ISBN 0-8018-2863-5 (alk. paper)

To those who went, and who served,
in the finest tradition of duty, honor, and country

Contents

Illustrations

Foreword

Armies frequently are accused of preparing for the last war instead of the next. This charge, regardless of its validity, implies that the institution as a collective has learned from its most recent conflict. Dr. Andrew Krepinevich raises serious questions concerning the learning ability of the U.S. Army, particularly in the realm of tactical doctrine, during its long Vietnam experience. The careful and well-documented manner in which the inquiry proceeds permits the work to be read on two planes. First, the student of organizational behavior and institutional learning will find the work to be an excellent case study in large-scale bureaucracy. Second, the practitioner or scholar of war will discover an engaging and scholarly critique of the U.S. Army and its ability to fit tactics, doctrine, and strategy to the fog-shrouded terrain of a people's war under modern conditions. I shall comment on the latter of these two dimensions.

Doctrine, in a sense, is a distillation of collective wisdom or collective will that the institutional leadership uses to condition the ways in which the people who make up the institution execute and plan present and future training and operations. For the U.S. Army, the doctrine of the past thirty-five years or so emerged from the experience of World War II, or more accurately, from a set of assumptions based on that experience and was codified in field manuals, service-school curricula, training programs, and the like, largely in the first five years following the war. The future war that the Army was to be prepared to fight was, above all, one rather like World War II in the European Theater of Operations (especially the sector of Bradley's Twelfth Army Group) from the breakout at St. Lô to the end of the war. Changes in organization and weaponry, slight

The views expressed herein are those of the author alone and do not necessarily reflect those of the U.S. government or any of its agencies.

modifications or refinements in doctrine, and experience in combat in such places as Korea, Vietnam, and elsewhere did not contribute in any important way to changing the fundamental assumption that the future war, what Krepinevich rightly terms the "Army Concept," was to be World War II from July 1944 to May 1945 in Western Europe *mutatis mutandis* because of nuclear weapons (sometimes) and helicopters (increasingly) added to the battlefield. Indeed, the combats and battles of Korea, Vietnam, and other campaigns were treated in retrospect as if each were *sui generis,* so that whatever adjustments to doctrine had to be made in the course of each could be relegated to the "special-case" category and thus required no permanent adjustment or modification of the Army Concept or the doctrine based on it.

Doctrine became dogma. The institutional paradigm was fixed. Over time, moreover, dogma had a pernicious effect on the relationships between strategy, the operational art, and tactics. Tactics, based on doctrine derived from the Army Concept, dominated the operational art, and in turn, strategy was dominated by the operational art and tactics. Success in tactical operations, that is, victory in individual battles, replaced the accomplishment of a campaign plan based on strategy intended to attain the objectives of the war. The latter were assumed to be attainable through additive victories in battles. The effect of this approach to war, standing Clausewitz on his head, is obvious in Col. Harry Summers's *non pareil* statement to his Vietnamese counterpart in 1975: "You know you never defeated us on the battlefield."[1]

In mitigation it must be said that the commitment of the United States to the North Atlantic Treaty and to the structures based on that agreement, along with the military threat to the alliance posed by the forces of the Warsaw Pact, especially in the Central Sector in Europe (essentially the area of responsibility assigned to Allied Forces Central Europe), contributed both to causing and reinforcing the Army Concept. Yet, it is the clarity of the commitment of both the North Atlantic and Warsaw alliances to the maintenance of the status quo in Central Europe and the mutual commitment of forces in and to that theater that make interalliance war there unlikely. Ironically, one hopes not tragically, additional or new commitments of U.S. military forces and all of the actual combat over the next decade or two are likely to occur *outside* Central Europe.

It is here that the relevance of Dr. Krepinevich's book comes to the fore. He shows us how little the U.S. Army as an institution anticipated

1. Col. Harry Summers, *On Strategy* (Novato, Calif.: Presidio Press, 1982), 1.

and prepared for the kind of war it found itself engaged in in mainland Southeast Asia and, what is most important, how little impact that long engagement had on the doctrine controlling the way in which the Army prepares for future engagements outside Central Europe. To be sure, the establishment of Delta forces and the (re-)creation of Ranger and region- ally oriented Special Forces formations do provide some capability to intervene in so-called extra-European, special cases. Similarly, the orga- nization of "light" divisions could contribute to a capability to engage in what we now call low-intensity conflict. However, without some major changes in doctrine and training, one may be permitted to question the efficacy of organizational fix. One might add that the lack of agreement on the definition of what low-intensity conflict may be could be as much a reflection of doctrinal blindness or confusion as anything else—presently the term tends to mean whatever the user wants it to mean.

Dr. Krepinevich illuminates both the dangers that accompany the process of doctrine becoming dogma and, worse, when such tactical dogma influences the predominance of methodism in the campaign and in strategy. Just as Capt. (now Maj.) Timothy T. Lupfer demonstrated some years ago, in his splendid little study "The Dynamics of Doctrine: The Changes in German Tactical Doctrine During the First World War,"[2] the doctrinal flexibility of the German army at the tactical level in the face of the realities of war on the western front in World War I, Dr. Krepinevich here demonstrates the doctrinal rigidity at all levels of the U.S. Army in the face of its experience of the last thirty-five years and, what is more serious, its lack of doctrinal preparedness or its failure to break the shackles of methodism for the future.

Dr. Krepinevich refrains from prescribing any simple solution to the syndrome he describes and analyzes with such clarity. Perhaps he is unwilling to venture from what he knows and understands so well into the uncharted. He does, however, give us much to think about if we wish to ponder the uncertainties as well as the probabilities that may arise in the campaigns of the coming decades.

George K. Osborn III
COLONEL, U.S. ARMY

2. Leavenworth Papers, No. 4 (Fort Leavenworth, Kans.: U.S. Army Command and General Staff College, July 1981).

Acknowledgments

This book could not have been written without the help of a great many people. It was my extraordinary good fortune to have the guidance of two exceptional soldier-scholars throughout my research. Colonel George K. Osborn, Department of Social Sciences, and Colonel Paul A. Miles, Department of History, U.S. Military Academy, both provided enthusi astic support and invaluable expertise. Each patiently listened to my many ruminations on the Army's Vietnam experience and provided guidance that greatly facilitated my research effort. The genesis of this project occurred during my years as a graduate student where I received guidance from two excellent scholars and teachers in the field of national security studies: Dr. William W. Kaufmann and Dr. Michael L. Nacht. Their critical assessment of my early research efforts proved to be of immeasurable assistance. I am especially grateful to both the Army's Center for Military History and the Military History Institute for assisting me during my research visits. Vincent Demma, in particular, went well beyond the call of duty in providing both archival assistance and scholarly insight at the Center for Military History.

Both Professor Douglas Kinnard (then at the University of Vermont) and Professor Alvin H. Bernstein of the U.S. Naval War College kindly consented to take time from their busy schedules to read several drafts of the book and provided useful comments and much encouragement. I owe a debt of gratitude as well to Dr. William J. Taylor of Georgetown University's Center for Strategic and International Studies, who was instrumental in helping me frame my initial approach to the subject and who provided useful comments on the book in its final stages of development. A colleague during my years of teaching at West Point, Major Stephen Bowman, generously shared the fruits of his ongoing research, saving me considerable time and effort and eliminating many "dead end" paths of research. Many thanks are also owed to Lieutenant Commander Michael Uebelherr, Shirley Bonsell, Gail Rainey, and Judy Dubaldi for teaching me the rudiments of word processing, a necessary skill in this kind of endeavor. A word of gratitude is also in order for Joanne Allen, my editor, who provided much advice, assistance, and friendly prodding over the project's final months. To the extent that the reader finds this book useful, these people deserve much of the credit. Naturally, any short-comings associated with this book are attributable to the author alone.

Finally, a much deserved acknowledgment of my parents, whose encouragement and personal sacrifices laid the foundation for my education. I also want to acknowledge the support and sacrifice of my wife, Julia, and my children, Jennifer, Andrew, and Michael, who willingly gave up many hours of family time to allow me the chance to complete this project, and who shared with me the joys and frustrations this effort has brought us.

Abbreviations and Acronyms

ACTIV   Army Concept Team in Vietnam
BLT   Battalion Landing Team
CAP   Combined Action Platoons
CCP   Combined Campaign Plan
CDC   Combat Developments Command
CG   Civil Guard
C&GSC   Command and General Staff College
CIA   Central Intelligence Agency
CIDG   Civilian Irregular Defense Groups
CINCPAC   Commander-in-Chief, Pacific Command
COMUSMACV   Commander, U.S. Military Assistance Command, Vietnam
CONARC   Continental Army Command
CORDS   Civil Operations and Revolutionary Development Support
CPSVN   Comprehensive Plan for South Vietnam
CTZ   Corps Tactical Zone
DA   Department of the Army
DOD   Department of Defense
DRV   Democratic Republic of Vietnam
FM   Field Manual
FWMAF   Free World Military Assistance Forces
GVN   Government of Vietnam
HES   Hamlet Evaluation System
ISA   International Security Affairs (DOD)

JCS	Joint Chiefs of Staff
JCSM	Joint Chiefs of Staff Memorandum
JGS	Joint General Staff
MAAG	Military Assistance Advisory Group
MACOV	Mechanized and Armor Operations in Vietnam
MACV	Military Assistance Command, Vietnam
MAF	Marine Amphibious Force
MAP	Military Assistance Program
MATA	Military Assistance Training Advisors Course
MATT	Mobile Advisory Training Team
NCP	National Campaign Plan
NSAM	National Security Action Memorandum
NSC	National Security Council
NSSM	National Security Study Memorandum
NVA	North Vietnamese Army
ODCSOPS	Office of the Deputy Chief of Staff, Operations
OSA	Office of Systems Analysis
PAVN	Peoples Army of Vietnam
PF	Popular Forces
PROVN	Program for the Pacification and Long-term Development of South Vietnam
RF	Regional Forces
ROAD	Reorganization Objectives Army Division
ROE	Rules of Engagement
ROK	Republic of Korea
RVN	Republic of Vietnam
RVNAF	Republic of Vietnam Armed Forces
SACSA	Special Assistant for Counterinsurgency and Special Activities
SEATO	Southeast Asia Treaty Organization
SGCI	Special Group, Counterinsurgency
SFG	Special Forces Group
STRICOM	Strike Command
SWC	Special Warfare Center
TAOR	Tactical Area of Responsibility
USIA	United States Information Agency
VC	Viet Cong
VCI	Viet Cong Infrastructure

THE ARMY AND VIETNAM

One

THE ADVISORY YEARS
1954–1965

1
Brushfires on a Cold Dawn

In early June 1965 the United States Army had been in South Vietnam in one capacity or another for nearly fifteen years. Arriving on the scene in 1950, the Army spent a decade overseeing the flow of U.S. military assistance, first to the French and then to the South Vietnamese, aimed at blocking Communist Vietnamese insurgents' efforts to topple the Saigon government. During the Truman and Eisenhower years the number of Army observers and advisers grew from a mere handful to well over three hundred. With the advent of the Kennedy administration came a sharp rise in the level of the insurgency, progressively limiting the authority of President Ngo Dinh Diem. This was met by steady increases in American troop strength, the numbers climbing to over sixteen thousand by the time of Kennedy's assassination, and material assistance designed to stabilize the situation.

This outpouring of aid from the United States appeared to have an adverse effect upon the fortunes of the South Vietnamese. The more assistance that was given, it seemed, the less hopeful the prospects of defeating the insurgents became. In February 1965, Gen. William C. Westmoreland, Commander, United States Military Assistance Command, Vietnam (MACV), or COMUSMACV, requested that the first of a number of Army and Marine combat battalions be dispatched to South Vietnam to provide security for U.S. support bases, such as Da Nang, and to free those South Vietnamese forces guarding them for offensive action.

Now, in June, Westmoreland could see no alternative but to commit large numbers of American combat troops. In a cable to Washington on 7 June, Westmoreland requested that forty-four U.S. and allied combat battalions be deployed to South Vietnam for military operations designed to defeat Communist Viet Cong (VC) guerrillas and their North Viet

3

namese brethren, who had deployed several regiments into the country. The general's request found broad support at both the Pentagon and the White House, and by month's end Army airborne troops were engaged in direct clashes with Viet Cong guerrillas as part of MACV's concept of operations for winning the war.

As the powerful war machine that is the United States Army swung into action during those weeks in the late spring and early summer of 1965, few, if any, military leaders thought to ask, What kind of Army are we sending to war? What has the Army done these past fifteen years to prepare itself for a war quite unlike those "traditional" wars—World Wars I and II and the Korean War—that it had become accustomed to waging? What will the Army do to eliminate the insurgent movement that has not been done these past fifteen years?

For the Army, the Vietnam War still represents a series of unanswered questions, the foremost of which is, How could the army of the most powerful nation on Earth, materially supported on a scale unprecedented in history, equipped with the most sophisticated technology in an age when technology had assumed the role of a god of war, fail to emerge victorious against a numerically inferior force of lightly armed irregulars? The answer to this question is to be found by examining those questions, mentioned above, that the nation's civilian and military leadership failed to address during those critical months of 1965. It is in answering these questions that the story of the United States Army and the Vietnam War can be told.

The Army Concept

To paraphrase General of the Army Omar Bradley, the United States can look back on Vietnam as the wrong war—at the wrong place, at the wrong time, with the wrong army. Simply stated, the United States Army was neither trained nor organized to fight effectively in an insurgency conflict environment. To understand why, it is necessary to examine the evolution the Army has undergone over its history, particularly in this century—an evolution that has provided the United States with a superb instrument for combating the field armies of its adversaries in conventional (or "mid-intensity") wars but an inefficient and ineffective force for defeating insurgent guerrilla forces in a "low-intensity" conflict.

The key to understanding this condition is a recognition that the Army's approach to war, referred to here as the Army Concept, is the product of an organizational character that has evolved over time and that, because of its high regard for tradition, has become deeply imbedded in the service's psyche, or memory.[1]

The Army Concept of war is, basically, the Army's perception of how wars *ought* to be waged and is reflected in the way the Army organizes and trains its troops for battle. The characteristics of the Army Concept are two: a focus on mid-intensity, or conventional, war and a reliance on high volumes of firepower to minimize casualties—in effect, the substitution of material costs at every available opportunity to avoid payment in blood.

Unfortunately, the Army's experience in war did not prepare it well for counterinsurgency, where the emphasis is on light infantry formations, not heavy divisions; on firepower restraint, not its widespread application; on the resolution of political and social problems within the nation targeted by insurgents, not closing with and destroying the insurgent's field forces. Although the Army received its baptism of fire in the Revolutionary War, where it often found itself forced to play the role of guerrilla against superior British forces, the memory of that experience had long since dissipated by the mid-twentieth century. Similarly, the skirmishes against the Indian tribes on the American frontier during the nineteenth century and the Army's role in suppressing the Philippine Insurrection rapidly faded as the Army leadership maintained the focus of its study on the great battles in Europe, while ignoring the colonial wars in which the Great Powers of the Continent were engaged. World Wars I and II, along with the Korean War, solidified the service's focus on conventional war, which has become a comfortable, familiar frame of reference in which to approach conflict. The imprint of these great conventional wars had become so pervasive that by the dawn of the post–World War II era the advice of Army advisers to U.S. allies faced with insurgencies, such as the Greeks and the Filipinos, was generally counterproductive or, at best, irrelevant.[2]

Contributing to the hardening of the conventional mindset within the Army was the emergence shortly after the end of World War II of a war against the Soviet Union in Europe as the Army's primary contingency. Thus, the "worst-case" threat that the Army had to deal with was also the "preferred" threat, and it contributed to the service's persistent ignorance of counterinsurgency warfare, even though the emerging Third World was smoldering in brushfire wars as the old empires of Europe crumbled, to be replaced by new and unstable regimes—easy marks for insurgent movements, fueled, in many cases, by Chinese or Soviet military assistance.

Another prime contributor to the formation of an Army Concept of war was the recognition by the brass of the political necessity which demanded that every possible measure be taken by American commanders to minimize U.S. casualties. This concern was to reach new heights in limited wars such as Korea and, especially, Vietnam.[3] In this century, as the United States has had a resource advantage over each of her adversaries, firepower and technology have evolved as substitutes for precious manpower. Indeed, the Army even has a statement for it: "It is better to send a bullet than a man." This philosophy was in vogue particularly during limited wars, when resources were not as constrained as in a general war. As I shall discuss directly, however, counterinsurgency operations place a premium on the protection of the population, and this often conflicts with the axiom of massive firepower liberally applied.

Furthermore, at the time of Vietnam the Army Concept of war had become entrenched in the minds of the military hierarchy simply because it had been so successful. Up until Vietnam the Army had never lost a war. In this century it had emerged victorious in two world wars and had conducted a successful limited war in Korea employing conventional "general-purpose" forces and enormous quantities of materiel. Defeat often leads a vanquished army to question its methods and change its approach to conflict, but the United States Army had never had to undergo such a soul-searching process. Repeated success in war had had the effect of strengthening the Concept in the Army's thinking as the way in which wars should be fought.

Finally, we are talking about a question of resource allocation. Given the expansion in the number and complexity of America's security interests and obligations in the postwar era, the Army has had to prepare for a seemingly infinite number of contingencies with a finite amount of resources. The question, What kind of war (or threat) do you prepare for when you cannot prepare for them all? was easily answered in the early years of the cold war owing to the overwhelming strategic importance of Western Europe and the absence of any major threat to U.S. security other than the Red Army. The Army quickly established a precedent for the first large standing American army in peacetime: it would be organized and trained for war against the Soviet Union, that is, for a conventional war in a familiar conflict environment.

This, then, was the Army's approach to war as it became increasingly entangled in the growing insurgency in Vietnam. While throughout its Vietnam experience the Army encountered a number of signs indicating that a change in its Concept was required in order to combat the insurgency more effectively, the Army leadership persisted in approaching the war within the framework of the Concept. The reason for this rigidity was best expressed by Bernard Brodie when he wrote: "The fact that the military have to practice only intermittently the function for which they exist means that a doctrine that is congenial can be adopted and cherished and given a dominant place in strategic planning. . . . One must remember too . . . that people wedded to dogmas will often continue to cherish them undiminished despite ongoing experience that to any detached observer would prove these dogmas wrong. Awkward events can be explained away as being due either to special circumstances not likely to recur or to a misreading of the evidence."[4]

In sum, the Army's pre-Vietnam experience in low-intensity conflict in general and in counterinsurgency in particular represented a trivial portion of the service's history as compared with the three conventional wars that it had fought over the previous half-century. It was the Army's experience in these conflicts—the two world wars and the Korean War—that formed the basis for its approach to the war in Vietnam.

Any understanding of why the Army Concept represented such a gross mismatch with the needs of an effective counterinsurgency strategy, however, requires an appreciation of how and why insurgent movements succeed, as well as what steps can be taken to defeat them.

Guerrillas: Why They Are There

An insurgency is a *protracted struggle* conducted methodically, step by step, in order to obtain specific intermediate objectives leading finally to the overthrow of the existing order.[5] Insurgencies typically follow the prescription laid down by such revolutionaries as Mao Zedong and General Vo-Nguyen Giap. As developed by Mao in China and adapted by Giap in Vietnam, contemporary insurgency is a Third World phenomenon comprising three phases: first, insurgent agitation and proselytization among the masses—the phase of contention; second, overt violence, guerrilla operations, and the establishment of bases—the equilibrium phase; and third, open warfare between insurgent and government forces designed to topple the existing regime—the counteroffensive phase.[6]

Specifically, phase I involves the creation of a party. The insurgent seeks to develop a close-knit political cadre and to recruit new members to the cause. During phase 2 the insurgent expands his base of support through attacks on the local government leadership and efforts to gain control over villages located in remote or nearly inaccessible areas. Guerrilla units are formed utilizing the base of support that has developed among the population. The link with the population becomes crucial at this stage of the insurgency. As Mao noted, guerrilla warfare without a base of support among the people is nothing but "roving banditism." Unless they can maintain their access to the population, insurgent forces cannot extend their control and are bound to be defeated. During this stage there are attacks on the government structure at the district level, as well as hit-and-run assaults on vulnerable government forces.

In phase 3 the government witnesses the formation of main-force, or conventional-style, maneuver battalions, regiments, and even divisions of insurgent forces and the initiation of open warfare with government troops. Insurgent lines of communication at the province (state) level are put into place, and a regional command structure is initiated to coordinate efforts on a large scale. The aim is to create an irresistible momentum that will make an insurgent victory appear inevitable. Furthermore, the activities conducted at the lower stages do not cease; they continue to reinforce the overall insurgent effort to topple the regime in power.

In this, the final stage, all insurgent forces are committed to a general offensive conducted in coordination with a massive popular uprising against the government. Full-scale, set-piece battles occur, possibly with the help of large-scale, external, main-force units. The end result of this stage is the insurgents' victory and their assumption of power.

Time is an ally of the insurgent, allowing him to forge a strong organization and consolidate his strength. Furthermore, the longer the insurgency continues, the greater the sense of futility and frustration on the government's part, a frustration that can lead to ill-advised attempts at shortcuts in trying to defeat the insurgents.

If time is essential to the accumulation of insurgent strength, the people are the foundation upon which that strength is built. Political mobilization, said Mao, "is the most fundamental condition for winning the war."[7] Since the insurgent is initially too weak to openly challenge the government, he must pursue an indirect approach. The target of that approach is the population. If the insurgent can gain control over the population through fear, popular appeal, or, more likely, a mixture of both, he will win the war. He will win because the support of the people, be it willing or unwilling, will provide him with manpower for his guerrilla units, the food, medicine, and shelter to support them, and the intelligence on government forces necessary to his safety. At the same time, the inability of the government to control the people will sap away its strength, denying it replacements for the armed forces, making taxes difficult or impossible to collect, and drying up its sources of information about insurgent cadres and guerrillas.

Thus, to eventually control the country, the insurgent must control the people. The people enable the insurgent forces to survive and grow. As Mao noted, "The people are like water and the army is like fish."[8] The support of the people does not, however, necessarily imply their support for the aims and goals of the insurgent, although this is, of course, desirable. Rather, the support of the people is a measure of the insurgents' ability to *control* the people, whether through their willing cooperation or as the result of threats, acts of terrorism, or the physical occupation of their community. T. E. Lawrence recognized this when he stated that "rebellions can be made by two percent active in a striking force, and 98 percent passively sympathetic."[9] Thus, the insurgent need not possess the hearts and minds of the population, only the minds—the peoples' acquiescence, willing or unwilling, in the revolutionary cause.

Insurgent control of the population explains why an insurgent movement can expand as a whole even while heavy casualties are inflicted on its guerrilla units. The ability of the insurgent to draw on the population for replacements and the expansion of insurgent control over the people through subversion, persuasion, or terror not only will serve to replace losses but will likely result in an increase in strength. The population, therefore, serves as the indispensable base of the insurgent forces.

Until the insurgents' strength can be built up, military operations will be planned and executed, not primarily against government forces, but with an eye toward how well they will extend control over the population. Furthermore, the protracted nature of the conflict allows the insurgent to refuse to give battle with government forces in the event that losses would be unacceptably high.[10]

The bottom line for a successful guerrilla warfare operation, then, is a primary support system anchored on the population. Sir Robert Thompson, the noted British expert on insurgency warfare, viewed this support system as running in the *opposite* direction from that of a conventional army.[11] In a conventional war, supplies and support are brought up from the rear to support combat operations focused on the destruction of the enemy's armed forces. In an insurgency, supplies and support are *at the front, among the people,* and the direction of the logistical flow is *opposite* that of the line of advance (it flows from the "front lines"—the people—to the insurgents' rear base areas). Combat operations focus on controlling the population to drain the government of its strength and to pave the way for the move to the general counter-offensive. A common error on the part of "conventional" military people has been to view the interruption of infiltration or external support for the guerrillas as the key to isolating and defeating the insurgents. External support for guerrilla forces, however, at best performs the role of a secondary support system during phase 1 and phase 2 operations. Such external support achieves primacy only during the phase 3 counter-offensive, if then.[12] It is important to recognize that even as the insurgents move from guerrilla warfare to phase 3 operations, the conflict is never transformed into a purely conventional war. The process of transformation is a gradual one in which the principles of regular warfare gradually appear and increasingly develop but still bear a guerrilla character.[13]

While time, access to the people, and guerrilla warfare are the tools the insurgent uses to build a successful strategic framework, two essential elements make up the foundation of that structure: a cause around which to rally popular support and a weak governmental administrative and law enforcement apparatus. They allow the insurgent to survive and expand in the early stages of the insurgency, when his forces are weakest and most vulnerable. A cause provides the insurgent leadership with the means to attract that dedicated core to form the revolutionary cadre that is essential if the revolution is to succeed. Ideally it embodies something that the government cannot espouse without risking loss of power (anti-colonialism/nationalism and land reform are two examples). Inefficient police methods and the absence of effective administrative control allow the insurgent cadre the freedom of movement necessary to recruit new followers. The absence of a well-run police force also provides fertile ground for the employment of terror by the insurgents against those individuals who persist in supporting the government.

Guerrillas: How to Beat Them

Just as insurgents have their own set of principles, maxims, or "rules," so must the government develop a set of rules apart from those of con-ventional warfare if it hopes to prevail. In conventional warfare, military action focused on the achievement of the military objectives set by the policymakers assumes priority, while political, social, and economic considerations are consigned to a secondary role. Yet, if the insurgents are to be defeated, these "secondary" considerations must achieve equality with military goals and objectives. In conventional wars, strategy pre-scribes the conquest of the enemy's territory, yet this rarely occurs prior to the destruction of the enemy's forces in battle. These rules do not apply, however, against an enemy that refuses to fight for territory.

In an insurgency, the way to destroy the insurgent is to attack him at the source of his strength: the population. If the counterinsurgent forces can minimize insurgent access to the population, the insurgent's access to manpower, supplies, and intelligence will be curtailed. Guerrillas can adjust their tempo of operations and remain inactive during periods when ammunition and/or weapons are in short supply, but they must eat. They therefore cannot maintain sizeable forces over a protracted period of time without access to a rather substantial food supply. The intelligence information that the insurgents derive through their ability to inspire or intimidate the people also provides a key link in the chain of factors that enable the guerrillas to survive and prosper. For the insurgents, loss of intelligence means that they can no longer determine with any degree of certainty the whereabouts and movements of government forces. Furthermore, the problem is compounded if the people, feeling secure from insurgent retribution, begin to provide the counterinsurgent forces with information on the activities of the guerrillas.

If denied the ability to move quickly and easily among the population, the insurgent will become, to paraphrase Mao, like a fish out of water. He will be forced to stand and fight to reassert control over the population, in which case he can be identified and destroyed by the superior counterinsurgent forces; or he can retreat to his remote base areas, where isolation from the people will diminish his strength and render the movement increasingly irrelevant in the eyes of the people.

Should government forces attempt to defeat the insurgency through the destruction of guerrilla forces in quasi-conventional battles, they will play into the hands of the insurgent forces. Insurgent casualties suffered under these circumstances will rarely be debilitating for the insurgents. First, the insurgents have no need to engage the government forces—they are not fighting to hold territory. Second, as long as the government forces are out seeking battle with the guerrilla units, the insurgents are not forced to fight to maintain access to the people. Therefore, *the initiative remains with the guerrillas*—they can "set" their own level of casualties (probably just enough to keep the government forces out seeking the elusive big battles), thus rendering ineffective all efforts by the counterinsurgent forces to win a traditional military victory.

As a result of these circumstances, the conventional forces of the government's army must be reoriented away from destroying enemy forces toward asserting government control over the population and winning its support. Government forces should be organized primarily around light infantry units, particularly in phases 1 and 2 of the insurgency. These forces must be *ground*-mobile in order to patrol intensively in and around populated areas, keeping guerrilla bands off guard and away from the people. The counterinsurgent must eliminate the tendency, fostered by conventional doctrine, to cluster his forces in large units. Only when the insurgency moves into phase 3 will the need for substantial numbers of main-force conventional units arise. Of course, even in phase 3 the counterinsurgent will require a force of well-trained light infantry to combat guerrilla and subversive activity that occurs in the shadow of the big-unit war.

Winning the hearts and minds of the people is as desirable for the government as it is for the insurgent. This objective can only be fully realized, however, after control of the population is effected and its security provided for. Developing popular support often involves political participation (at least on the local level), public works (irrigation ditches, dams, wells), and social reform (land reform, religious toleration, access to schools). These actions are designed to preempt the insurgent's cause, as, for example, in the case of land reform in the Philippines during the Huk Rebellion or the timetable established for the end of British rule in the Malaysian insurgency.[14] Nevertheless, even though attempts to co-opt the insurgents may prove successful in winning the hearts of the people, they will be for naught unless the government provides the security necessary to free the people from the fear of insurgent retribution should they openly support the government.

While it is a relatively easy matter for government forces to drive guerrilla bands away from a given area, it is far more difficult for the military to work hand in hand with the local police and paramilitary forces over a prolonged period to complete the destruction of insurgent forces that have mixed with the population. Yet this is exactly what must be done, and every military move must be viewed with an eye to how it will promote the achievement of this objective.

The support of the population is conditional in that the government must prove to the people that it has the resources to defeat the insurgency and the will to do so. The people who have watched the insurgents painstakingly construct their political infrastructure and punish those who oppose them will not expose themselves to support the regime merely because government forces have temporarily occupied the area and dug a well. The insurgent infrastructure within a village must be eliminated and there must be a long-term government presence in order to create an atmosphere free from fear of reprisal before the people will openly associate themselves with the regime. The people can weather an oc-casional guerrilla assault on their village, even when the loss of life is involved, far better than they can endure a string of assassinations indicating that insurgent agents are living among them. The former implies a relatively high degree of security, while in the latter case security is nonexistent. Without this degree of security, civic action programs designed to win the support of the people are irrelevant. Such civic action programs in the absence of government control over the area merely increase the resources available to the people for reaching an accommodation with the guerrillas.[15] Finally, the government must execute its actions as part of a well-planned strategy executed by forces trained and organized for counterinsurgency.[16] There must be a unity of effort and a unity of command among the government agencies involved. In combating an insurgency, a government has no resources to waste.

The elements of a successful strategy for the counterinsurgent involve securing the government's base areas, separating the guerrilla forces from the population, and eliminating the insurgent infrastructure. In an area infested by insurgency, the army must concentrate enough force to either destroy or expel the main body of guerrillas in clear-and-hold operations to prepare the area for pacification, that is, for those actions taken by the government to assert its control over the population and to win its willing support.

After the army has driven off or killed the main guerrilla forces, its units must remain in the area while local paramilitary forces are created and the influence of the police force is reestablished. The paramilitary forces should be drawn from among the inhabitants of the area and trained in counterinsurgency operations such as small-unit patrolling, night operations, and the ambush. Resurrection of the local police force is equally important. Properly trained, the police can make an invaluable contribution to the defeat of the insurgents by weeding out the political infrastructure, thus preventing the reemergence of the insurgent movement once the army departs.

Thus, if the paramilitary forces can perform the local security mission, and if the police can extinguish the embers of the insurgent movement through suppression of its infrastructure, the people will begin to feel secure enough to provide these forces with information on the movements of local guerrilla forces and on the individuals who make up the cells of the insurgent movement. But before any of this can occur, it is necessary for the government's main-force army units to demonstrate that they will remain in the newly cleared area until such time as the people are capable of assuming the bulk of the responsibility for their own defense. Should the army depart the area before the paramilitary units and the police force are capable of effective operation, it will have accomplished nothing. The insurgent infrastructure will quickly reemerge from hiding, and the guerrillas will return to reassert their control. The temporary control established by the government must be followed by the implementation of measures designed to achieve permanent control. Thus, the counter-insurgent must direct his efforts, not toward seeking combat with the insurgent's guerrilla forces, but at the insurgent political infrastructure, which is the foundation of successful insurgency warfare. Keep the guerrilla bands at arm's length from the people and destroy their eyes and ears—the infrastructure—and you can win.

To this end, the police force resurrected in the aftermath of the army's clear-and-hold operation in step 1 must, in coordination with military intelligence, seek to focus its information-gathering operations on the infrastructure, not the guerrillas. This activity has traditionally been a difficult one for the military, which traditionally focuses intelligence efforts on the enemy's order of battle. The key is to maintain a unified intelligence operation concentrated on the insurgent's political cadre. If the intelligence organization is targeted on the infrastructure, it will get the order of battle as well, but if it is targeted on the order of battle, it will not get the infrastructure.[17]

The process of rooting out the insurgents' political cells is necessarily a long one. Obviously, the army cannot position several battalions of troops in every village and town over a prolonged period to prevent the guerrillas from reasserting themselves; it would have nowhere near the forces required for such an undertaking. What the government can do, however, is train and equip paramilitary forces comprising people indigenous to the area. These forces should receive their training while regular army units provide local security. As the local forces acquired skill and confidence, the army units would be phased out of local security operations. The ultimate objective would see the paramilitary forces assuming the entire local security mission, calling upon a mobile quick-reaction force of regular troops only when under attack by main-force guerrilla units.

Emphasis must be placed on mobile, light infantry operations, pri-marily in a nocturnal environment. When enough small, friendly units are roaming the countryside, it will be both difficult and dangerous for the insurgents to mobilize their forces into main-force units for attacks upon the towns and hamlets. They will no longer have the ability to move within a large geographical area for an extended period of time without being detected and intercepted.[18]

A locally recruited force will have an advantage over even the govern-ment's regular units in that it has a better knowledge of the people and the terrain. This increases the likelihood that counterinsurgent operations will be based on intelligent anticipation, not blind swipes at the enemy. The effect of this kind of patrolling is to break down the communication between the insurgent infrastructure that exists among the people and the guerrilla bands that lie in wait just outside the populated areas. What is equally important, saturation patrolling keeps guerrilla bands small and fragmented, denying them the ability to concentrate in large groups and robbing them of the element of surprise should they mass for large-scale attacks.[19]

Once the security of the population and its attendant resources is accomplished, the initiative in the war will pass from the insurgent to the government. The insurgent will either have to fight to maintain control of the people or see his capabilities diminish. If the insurgents decide to fight, they will present themselves as targets for government mobile reaction forces.

To be successful, counterinsurgency requires coordination among many government organizations, of which the military is only one, albeit the largest. Because of the political and social nature of the conflict and the myriad nonmilitary institutions involved, a unified approach that orchestrates the multidimensional elements of the government's counterinsurgency strategy is essential.

If this strategy is carried out effectively, more and more areas will be pacified, the source of insurgent strength will abate, and guerrilla attacks will become increasingly rare. Kidnappings and assassinations will dwindle, while insurgent defections will increase. Here the efforts of the government have been compared to an oil drop that upon striking a cloth gradually seeps outward. So, too, the government forces, once they secure their bases, gradually seep outward to pacify more regions and transform them into secure, government-controlled areas. At this point the insurgent will be forced to retreat to phase 1 operations. If the insurgent is receiving assistance from outside the country, he will eventually have to relocate to remote areas near or across the national border in order to keep the aid flowing and the revolution from being extinguished. Years may pass before these small, isolated bands are eliminated and the insurgency stamped out; however, the insurgency will have ceased to threaten the government's existence.

Thus, both insurgency and counterinsurgency represent major departures from "conventional" war. For the United States Army, an army that "won its spurs" through winning conventional wars, the reorientation of thought and process, of doctrine and organization, to acclimate itself to what was, for it, a "new" conflict environment in Vietnam presented a major challenge. Prior to entering into the quagmire that was Vietnam, however, a brief look at the Korean War—the Army's first taste of limited war in the nuclear age—is in order.

The Impact of the Korean War

The Korean War was waged by the Army, in congruence with its Concept, within limits set by the political leadership. With the exception of MacArthur's brilliant assault at Inchon, American Army commanders placed their emphasis on massive firepower and attrition of North Korean and Chinese forces.[20] Attrition in Korea was essentially a strategy adopted by default, the result of the Truman administration's limiting the military's ability to horizontally or vertically escalate the war to execute a campaign of annihilation against the North Koreans and the Chinese.[21] The reality was that the parameters of war were modified through the advent of nuclear weapons and the emerging balance of terror between the Superpowers. The potential costs of a full-scale land war with China, coupled with the possible intervention (in Europe, it was feared) of America's budding nuclear rival, the Soviet Union, mandated a limit on U.S. objectives.

For the Army leadership, accustomed to being given its objective (usually total victory) by the political leadership and then having a relatively free reign in achieving it, Korea proved a frustrating experience. After three years of fighting, these self-imposed limitations on troops and weaponry left the Army in a stalemate along roughly the same lines as those that existed when the war began. At the time of the armistice in July 1953, the U.S. commander, General Mark Clark, told newsmen, "I cannot find it in me to exult in this hour."[22] There was a strong feeling among the upper echelons of the Army that Korea was, to quote General Bradley, "the wrong war, at the wrong place, at the wrong time." This belief was reflective of an Army accustomed to winning its wars and waging them to a successful conclusion. A "Never Again" attitude developed in the Army, fortified by the negative reaction of the American people to the idea that limited wars were neither desirable nor acceptable.[23]

The American public's disenchantment with limited war was in part responsible for the failure of Truman's Democratic party to maintain its twenty-year hold on the White House in the 1952 presidential election. Truman's successor, Dwight Eisenhower, adopted a strategy that reflected his concerns about America's willingness to pursue limited wars to a successful conclusion and the high costs of maintaining an army capable of intervening in such conflicts at a moment's notice.

According to Eisenhower's strategy, Massive Retaliation, the United States would not necessarily respond directly to Communist attacks such as the one in Korea but would reserve the right to respond massively, with nuclear weapons, at a place and time of its choosing.[24] Using the marked U.S. superiority over the Soviet Union in nuclear forces, the proposed strategy would avoid American involvement in unpopular limited wars by threatening to escalate the conflicts immediately to a nuclear exchange.

Massive Retaliation placed a premium on nuclear delivery systems, particularly the bombers of the Air Force's Strategic Air Command. The Army was to maintain a capability for nuclear combat and to be available for any minor contingencies that might arise. Within the parameters of Massive Retaliation, the Army struggled to maintain a role for itself in its traditional sphere of mid-intensity conflict.[25] Indeed, after their retirement, Generals Ridgway, Taylor (former Chiefs of Staff), and Gavin (former Deputy Chief of Staff for Operations) all wrote books criticizing the administration's strategy for failing to give enough consideration to the possibilities for conventional war.

During the era of Massive Retaliation the Army had neither the mandate nor the inclination to examine the more esoteric force structures and doctrines required for low-intensity conflicts. Given the absence of pressure from above to force Army consideration of this "new" conflict environment so prevalent in the nuclear age, the only avenue that existed to force organizational awareness of low-intensity warfare was direct involvement. The Army would experience just such an involvement during the 1950s in Vietnam.

Early Involvement in Indochina

The insurgency that began in French Indochina in 1946 was the result of France's attempt to reassert its influence in the area after the departure of the Japanese, who had seized the territory from Vichy France in 1941. The Communist insurgents, led by Ho Chi Minh and known as the Viet Minh, had fought against the Japanese occupation during the war years and had actually received some U.S. assistance. Having fought to expel the Japanese, the Viet Minh were not about to allow a reascension of French influence in the area. Thus, when French military forces were reestablished in Indochina in September 1945, it was only a matter of time before the two groups were at odds with each other. The insurgency began in earnest shortly after the pullout of Allied occupation forces in April 1946.

In the four years that followed, the U.S. policy regarding the insurgency was one of neutrality; however, with the defeat of the Nationalist Chinese by Mao in 1949 and the initiation of war in Korea by the Communists in June 1950, the struggle between the French and the Viet Minh took on a new light. Moscow and Beijing had both recognized Ho's movement in January 1950. Several weeks later Secretary of State Dean Acheson had noted that this action removed "any illusions as to the 'nationalist' nature of Ho Chi Minh's aims and reveals his true colors as the mortal enemy of native independence in Indochina."

Less than a month after the Communist attack on South Korea, the Joint Chiefs of Staff (JCS) held that Indochina was now the key to Southeast Asia.[26] In August a Military Assistance Advisory Group (MAAG) was authorized for that region. Although at first there were only 4 members in MAAG, its strength grew rapidly to some 342 advisers by 1954. It is evident from the experience of MAAG that the Army had neither a good appreciation for the unique conflict environment of insurgency warfare nor a feel for how the war was really going for the French. After his visit of August 1953, Army representative Lt. Gen. John W. O'Daniel reported that the new French command in Indochina would accomplish the "decisive defeat" of the Viet Minh by 1955 and that "additions other than in divisional organization would be in error since it is the divisional team, with its combat proven effectiveness, which is sorely needed in Indochina."[27] This faith in the ability of conventional forces to achieve success was disputed in a Central Intelligence Agency (CIA) report filed only a few months later, which concluded that "even if the U.S. defeated the Viet Minh field forces, guerrilla action could probably be continued indefinitely."[28]

In April 1954, less than a year after O'Daniel's visit, a full-blown crisis erupted when Viet Minh forces surrounded the French base at Dien Bien Phu. The French, unable to break the siege and finding their defense perimeter becoming progressively smaller in the face of the Communist attacks, petitioned the United States for assistance.

In their evaluation of the situation, the JCS viewed the conflict in conventional terms. The options that they envisioned were two: waging another Korean War or implementing the administration's new policy of Massive Retaliation. The Chiefs implicitly rejected the Korean War alternative. Building up bases would take too long and too many troops would be employed for too long a period. Instead, the Chiefs leaned toward taking the offensive against Communist China, the source of the aggression in the minds of the military. Using the erroneous rationale that would later drive the bombing campaign against North Vietnam, the Chiefs argued that the principal sources of Viet Minh supply lay outside Indochina. They therefore contended that "the destruction or neutralization of these sources in China proper would materially reduce the French military problems in Indochina."[29]

The JCS plan called for employing atomic weapons wherever advantageous; ground offensives by Franco-American forces to destroy the insurgents; blockading the China coast; seizing or neutralizing Hainan Island; and attacks by the Nationalist Chinese against mainland China. A notable dissenter from this approach was Army Chief of Staff Gen. Matthew B. Ridgway. In an unsolicited report, Ridgway held that victory could not be achieved solely by the use of nuclear weapons, air power, and sea power. He cautioned that the use of U.S. ground forces would seriously affect the country's ability to meet its NATO commitments. Between seven and twelve U.S. divisions, said Ridgway, would be required to achieve victory in Indochina.[30]

While Ridgway brought the high costs of intervention to the attention of the political leadership, he nevertheless believed that victory could be achieved (albeit a costly victory in an insignificant area) if the administration was willing to commit a sufficient number of Army divisions trained and equipped for mid-intensity warfare. The decision by President Eisenhower in May not to intervene laid the issue to rest. It also sealed the fate of the defending French forces, who surrendered to the Viet Minh shortly thereafter. At this point the French people, wracked by dissension at home, ineffective commanders abroad, and the musical-chair governments that were the trademark of the Fourth Republic, were unwilling to continue the struggle. A conference was arranged at Geneva to negotiate a peace between the French and the Viet Minh. The Geneva accords, signed on 20 July, broke Indochina up into four countries: Cambodia, Laos, and the two Vietnams, with Ho Chi Minh in control of North Vietnam, now the Democratic Republic of Vietnam (DRV).

The United States Assumes Responsibility

As the French began phasing out their forces, and with them French influence, the Americans assumed a greater measure of responsibility for the security of non-Communist Indochina, South Vietnam in particular. Even though the French pullout left the door open for the United States to assert its influence in South Vietnam, the JCS were initially reluctant to assume responsibility for organizing that nation's defense program. On 15 June 1954, before the Geneva accords had been finalized, Lieutenant General O'Daniel, now the MAAG chief, sought and received French permission for U.S. participation in the training of Vietnamese soldiers. The JCS, however, expressed their reservations. Among the conditions they considered necessary to provide for an environment under which U.S. assistance would be effective were a reasonably strong, stable civil government in Saigon and the complete withdrawal of the French from the country.[31]

JCS concerns were raised again in the Chiefs' memorandum of 22 September, in which they recommended against assigning training responsibilities to MAAG. Nevertheless, they were directed by the National Security Council (NSC) to determine the necessary force levels to insure South Vietnam's basic security needs. The Chiefs found that a 234,000-man army would be necessary, at an annual cost of $420 million.[32] The proposal quickly drew fire from Allan Dulles, at the CIA, who contended that "the mission of the Vietnamese National Armed Forces should be to provide internal security." Seen in this light, said Dulles, the JCS manpower and cost estimates, designed to produce a full-blown conventional army, were "excessive."[33]

The Chiefs objected to Dulles's conclusion, particularly since the Vietnamese army had the dual mission of providing both internal security and deterrence from external aggression. They also reaffirmed their position that the United States should not get involved in the training of Vietnamese forces. Despite these objections, the NSC initiated a crash program in October to establish internal security for South Vietnam, and the Chiefs were directed to define the force levels necessary for this more narrowly defined mission. The military's response, submitted on 17 November, called for a force level of 89,085, at a cost of $193.1 million for fiscal year (FY) 1956. In the report, the Chiefs restated their reservations concerning South Vietnam's political weakness and the program's lack of emphasis on forces designed to repel external aggression à la Korea.

On 11 December, Lieutenant General O'Daniel met in Saigon with Vietnamese Defense Minister Ho Thong Minh and informed him that the United States would train and fund a force of approximately 100,000 men for internal defense. The bilateral agreement provided for three territorial divisions with a total of 13 security regiments of three security battalions each. As a hedge against invasion from North Vietnam, three field divisions were to be formed. The field divisions would hold off a North

Vietnamese attack until forces of the newly formed Southeast Asia Treaty Organization (SEATO) could intervene.[34]

Two months after the U.S. commitment to assist the Diem regime, an agreement was worked out with the French whereby the two nations agreed to undertake a joint training effort until the departure of the French expeditionary force in April 1956. The combined training effort went under the name of the Franco-American Training Relations and Instructions Mission (TRIM) and was headed by Lieutenant General O'Daniel.[35]

Once TRIM was in place, a shift in emphasis occurred. The U.S. Mission viewed its role primarily in terms of creating a *conventional* army of divisional units and supporting forces. Basically, MAAG was working off the initial JCS force structure blueprint submitted to the NSC in September 1954, which had supposedly been blocked by Dulles. At the same time, MAAG was soft-pedaling the commitment to organize forces for internal defense against insurgency. It was easier for the Army to envision a Korea-type threat in Vietnam—a cross-border invasion of the Republic of Vietnam (RVN) by North Vietnam—than the insurgency threat which posed a dramatically different conflict environment than the Army was used to and which it was unprepared to address.

The Birth of the ARVN

Throughout its early years the Vietnamese National Army (VNA) was dominated by the French. Although the Vietnamese ministry of defense was established on 2 July 1949, the French maintained a Mission Militaire Française, which controlled the Vietnamese forces. Infantry battalions, *bataillons Vietnamiens* (BVNS) were commanded by French officers and noncommissioned officers (NCOs) transferred from the French army, as were local National Guard units.

An officer training school for the Vietnamese was not established until late 1951, nor was a general staff for Vietnam's army created until May 1952. The Chief of the General Staff was a former member of the French air force; his executive officer was a French captain. This obviously retarded the development of South Vietnamese military leaders, a fatal shortcoming in the days ahead when South Vietnamese officers would have to match wits against the veteran commanders of the Viet Minh.

At the time of the Geneva accords, in July 1954, the VNA comprised 82 BVN battalions, 81 light infantry battalions, 5 airborne battalions, 6 imperial guard battalions, and 9 artillery battalions, for a total of 167,700 regulars. Most conspicuous, however, was the absence of that prime ingredient of successful armies—capable leadership. It was this force, basically light infantry with a bit of artillery, that TRIM was to work with. From an organizational point of view, it was not incompatible with the configuration of forces required for internal defense. Training in the techniques of counterinsurgency operations and the kind of equipment needed to wage such a war—light weapons, communications gear, helicopters—was lacking, as was a sturdy corps of officers and NCOs. However, if these formidable challenges could be met, then the new nation would have a chance of survival.

In April 1955 MAAG proposed a timetable for demobilizing a large portion of the VNA to reach the 100,000-man level imposed by funding limitations. The Vietnamese government (GVN) preferred a drawdown that allowed for a volunteer professional army with the ability to secure areas, as well as engage in mobile defense. The Americans, on the other hand, opposed the idea of regional units for internal defense because they would not be "strategically mobile."[36] Although there was some compromise (each province was to have a territorial battalion), the Americans won. Troops with specialized training, the kind useful in conventional operations, were retained, while over 6,000 veteran NCOs were hastily discharged. Considering the shortfall of leadership that the Army of the Republic of Vietnam was to experience throughout the war, this proved a grievous error.

Further negotiations between the two countries culminated in a more favorable force level of 150,000 troops to be organized into 10 divisions, 4 field (heavy) and 6 light.[37] The thrust of the force structure decision was clearly designed to increase the ARVN's ability for conventional, or mid-intensity, warfare. The light divisions were essentially a concession to Vietnamese concerns over internal defense. The force structure would be "light," but it would be organized into division formations capable of dealing with a Korea-style invasion from North Vietnam. The JCS were worried about an attack from North Vietnam and, possibly, China. In that event, the Communists would come down the coast, and the Vietnamese forces' likely mission would be to hold the coastline. Although the French had just been defeated after an eight-year struggle against Vietnamese insurgents, the Chiefs were generally oblivious to the guerrilla threat.[38]

The man appointed to take charge of the American training operation as MAAG chief was Lt. Gen. Samuel "Hanging Sam" Williams. According to Major General Ruggles, Williams's deputy, just before Williams arrived he received instructions from the Army brass at the Pentagon to "organize a military establishment in Vietnam that would be capable of fending off attacks from the North."[39] Ruggles watched as Williams stuck with the idea of big units even as evidence accumulated that the primary danger to South Vietnam was an internal, insurgent threat. "He was bound that he was going to terminate his assignment out there with corps maneuvers," recalled Ruggles, "because that was what he was sent out there to do—organize an army that could resist aggression from the North. And he had those maneuvers before he left, and . . . the units did very, very well."[40]

The Vietnamese General Staff was not enthusiastic over American proposals to standardize Vietnamese forces along American lines, believing that smaller, more flexible units than divisions would be required in any likely future conflict. General Williams, however, gave only lip service to the idea.[41] The training program for the Vietnamese forces under TRIM generally ignored instruction on counterinsurgency operations. The advisers assigned to MAAG had little or no information about Vietnam, its culture, or its people prior to their arrival in Saigon. The subject of teaching U.S. advisers Vietnamese or French was never brought up.[42] Owing to the short tour of duty for advisers, those assigned felt that it simply was not worth it to try to learn the language, a problem that increased as U.S. involvement deepened. This cultural hubris on the Army's part conflicted with a basic tenet of counterinsurgency that holds that in order to be successful, you must be as familiar as possible with the people and the area that you are trying to win over and control. The training program itself was nothing more than a mirroring of the instruction that American soldiers received in the United States. Programs of instruction were almost exact copies of corresponding U.S. Army training courses.[43] As one general officer later reflected, "We had the TO&Es (Tables of Organization and Equipment) of the U.S. translated into Vietnamese and issued through the Vietnamese army, and I don't recall any major variations."[44]

These efforts to Americanize the ARVN often produced some absurd situations; for example, the Americans insisted that twenty-mile marches with fifty-pound packs would be good training. This might have been the case for six-foot, 200-pound Americans, but for a five-foot, 120-pound Vietnamese the results proved less than optimal. Yet another problem was the American insistence that training programs culminate in regimental and divisional maneuvers. Not only were these maneuvers irrelevant but they diverted troops away from active combat responsibilities.

By April 1956 the French had essentially left Vietnam, and General Williams, having received his marching orders from the Pentagon, was in control of the advisory effort. From that point until 1961 the emphasis in both training and force structuring was almost totally in line with the Army Concept. A two-year program of extensive field tests began in search of an optimal force structure for ARVN divisions. Williams reported to Washington in November 1956 that "a long range plan is being developed with a view towards the possible future conversion of existing ARVN field and light divisions into standard-type infantry divisions."[45] Little consideration was given to preparing Vietnamese forces for counter-insurgency warfare. The result was inevitable: over the next three years all light ARVN divisions were disbanded because MAAG thought that they would be no match for regular North Vietnamese Army (NVA) divisions. In the words of the deputy chief of MAAG, "We found that light divisions were so light that they were practically worthless."[46] Over two hundred TO&Es were developed to determine an optimal ARVN force structure. Yet when the dust cleared, what came out, to no one's surprise, was a force structure of seven ARVN divisions based on the U.S. Army divisional force structure.

The transformation of the ARVN was completed in September 1959. In addition to seven "standard" divisions, it boasted four armored cavalry regiments. Several months prior to the completion of the reorganization, the United States Commander-in-Chief, Pacific (CINCPAC), directed MAAG to provide American advisers for all levels, down to Vietnamese infantry regiments and armor, artillery, and marine battalions. The final product was a conventional army. It did not have the heavy firepower associated with the field armies of Western Europe and the United States, but that was more a result of funding limitations than anything else. Looking at the ARVN divisional structure, one senior MAAG officer commented that it was "a very close parallel on a considerably lighter scale of the division as we knew [it] in World War II."[47]

With MAAG developing the ARVN into a force that could block external aggression, the Diem government took steps to provide for internal security. Indeed, Diem's approach to combating the insurgent threat is hard to fault in general terms. It called for implementation of all the elements of counterinsurgency strategy: clear-and-hold operations, political indoctrination teams, civic action, paramilitary security forces, and land reform. The implementation of Diem's programs, however, often left a great deal to be desired. They were often the victims of poor leadership, half-hearted execution, and corruption. For instance, less than 10 percent of South Vietnam's farmers benefited from Diem's land reform programs of the 1950s.

The paramilitary forces also fared poorly. Both the Self Defense Corps

(SDC) and the Civil Guard (CG) were "poorly trained and equipped, miserably led, and incapable of coping with insurgents."[48] The SDC and CG forces actually alienated the population with their thievery and lack of discipline; and they provided weapons and ammunition to the VC—the result of losses in battle and in some cases outright collaboration.

As late as November 1959, MAAG had yet to involve itself in supporting the SDC, the CG, the Municipal Police, or the Sureté (the Vietnamese FBI), the paramilitary units whose performance would either sustain or render irrelevant anything the ARVN might do to defeat the insurgents. The CG, 53,000 strong, received some training from the United States Operations Mission (USOM), which contracted for civilian police specialists from Michigan State University to travel to Vietnam to give instruction.[49] The SDC, or village militia, numbering about 43,000, was generally ignored. The Municipal Police comprised 8,722 men, a force totally insufficient for a country of some 14 million people. The police were stationed only in cities whose population exceeded 15,000, leaving the countryside uncovered. Finally, the Sureté counted a mere 7,700 plainclothesmen in its compliment. The ARVN, designed to counter the threat of overt invasion, viewed pacification and population control as outside its assigned mission and rarely assisted the paramilitary forces in security operations.

As much as it may have wanted to, however, the Army could not ignore the growing insurgency within South Vietnam. When the VC began intensifying their activities in early 1957, a team from the newly activated 1st U.S. Army Special Forces (USASF) Group began training fifty-eight Vietnamese at the Nha Trang training center. Ironically, the training focused, not on counterinsurgency operations, but on unconventional warfare, which concerned itself with *organizing* guerrilla and partisan forces. If the Vietnamese were good students, they would learn how to start an insurgency, not stop one.[50]

Quite unintentionally, MAAG became concerned about the SDC and CG forces. These paramilitary forces, it seems, were so ineffective that ARVN units had to be sent to assist them. This diversion of units threw a monkey wrench into MAAG's training cycle for the ARVN, giving the Americans an incentive to try and help buck up the paramilitary units. Thus, provincial training centers were established to provide at least four weeks' training to SDC and CG personnel. The results, however, were unencouraging, and the insurgents grew in strength.

In December 1960 the formation of the National Liberation Front (NLF), the political arm of the VC, was announced in Hanoi. The NLF, which had been operating since 1958, now felt strong enough to openly challenge the Diem regime. Yet, despite the growth of the insurgent movement, MAAG had either played down its significance or ignored it entirely. In a narrative statement at the end of 1959, MAAG headquarters contended that "operations are being conducted against remnants of dissidents and Viet Cong guerrillas." The Army asserted that "successful operations against these anti-government forces has facilitated the release of the majority of Vietnamese military units from pacification missions and has permitted increased emphasis on unit training."⁵¹ Gen. Samuel L. Myers, the MAAG deputy chief, announced in testimony before the Senate Foreign Relations Committee that April that the guerrillas in South Vietnam had been "nibbled away until they ceased to be a major menace to the government."⁵²

While the men running MAAG were not incompetent, the conflict environment of insurgency warfare was alien to them. Once the force structure of seven standard divisions had been put in place and exercised at the corps level, American military advisers felt that they had accomplished their mission. South Vietnam, it was believed, could now hold off a North Vietnamese invasion across the 17th parallel long enough for SEATO forces to be rushed to the scene. The problem was that North Vietnam had no intention of conducting an overt invasion or of waging war according to the preferences of the American generals.

With the formal activation of the NLF, MAAG could no longer ignore the situation. ARVN units were increasingly committed in counterinsurgency operations. Field exercises at regimental and division levels were temporarily suspended. At the same time, unit training programs were revised to involve only battalion and smaller units. The ARVN and MAAG no longer had the luxury (if they ever did) of waiting around for the "real" war to start. The paramilitary forces, so long neglected, were being chewed up by their Communist adversaries.

Finally, the Army took some belated steps to adapt the Vietnamese armed forces (VNAF) to the kind of war they now faced. In March 1960 the JCS began drawing up a comprehensive plan for counterinsurgency (it would take nearly a year to complete). In May, thirty USASF instructors were sent from Fort Bragg to Vietnam to set up a training program for Vietnamese Special Forces. In June MAAG approved Diem's formation of Ranger companies. Finally, MAAG began assuming the mission of training and equipping the CG, reflecting the greater priority now being given these forces.

2

The Revolution That Failed

The Kennedy Administration: Revolution from Above

Throughout the 1950s, neither the budding insurgency in South Vietnam nor the Eisenhower administration's focus on high-intensity conflict provided the U.S. Army with an incentive for thinking about wars of national liberation, let alone developing a capability to successfully combat them. With the coming of the Kennedy administration, however, the Army experienced strong pressure for change from the Commander-in-Chief himself. How the Army responded to Kennedy's efforts to engineer a "revolution from above" in its approach to war says a lot concerning how strongly the Army Concept was embedded in the organizational psyche.

The election of John Kennedy in 1960 brought about a change in administrations and a change in national strategy as well, from Massive Retaliation to Flexible Response. In contrast to Eisenhower's Massive Retaliation, which threatened the use of U.S. nuclear forces in response to any act of Communist aggression, Flexible Response proposed to meet such aggression at the level of violence at which it was initiated.

Kennedy, and many defense experts, felt that Massive Retaliation had not provided the nation with a credible deterrent against Communist adventurism. As Soviet nuclear might grew throughout the 1950s, the costs that the United States would incur by resorting to nuclear war increased. These costs reached such a high level that they undermined the credibility of Massive Retaliation's nuclear threat in all but a few areas where America's vital interests were at stake. Thus, the Communist victory in Indochina, the shelling of Quemoy and Matsu by Communist China, and the Soviet suppression of Poland and Hungary were all effected without Massive Retaliation's being invoked.

President John F. Kennedy and the new administration's defense leadership, 25 March 1961. *From left to right*: Secretary of the Navy John B. Connally, Jr.; Deputy Secretary of Defense Roswell Gilpatric; Secretary of Defense Robert S. McNamara; Vice-President Lyndon B. Johnson; Secretary of the Army Elvis J. Stahr, Jr.; and Secretary of the Air Force Eugene Zuckert.   *courtesy U.S. Army*

And yet, containment of communism remained U.S. policy. The problem was imposing a credible deterrent against Communist expansionism, one where prospective American costs would be more in line with the anticipated benefit of communism restrained. The answer, Kennedy felt, was Flexible Response. The United States would maximize its options for responding to aggression and increase the credibility of its threats to employ force by generating forces capable of meeting the Communists at any level along the spectrum of conflict, from subversion and insurgency, up through conventional and tactical nuclear war, all the way to a full-scale nuclear confrontation.

Kennedy's philosophy found its roots in the writings of General Maxwell Taylor, Army Chief of Staff from 1955 to 1959. In *The Uncertain Trumpet* Taylor laid out the parameters for this new strategy and actually coined the term *flexible response*. As Taylor put it, Kennedy read *The Uncertain Trumpet* and made Flexible Response his slogan, "just as Ike had made Massive Retaliation his."[1]

Taylor's interpretation of Flexible Response focused primarily on creating an army with the ability to wage a mid-intensity conflict, where the practitioners of the Army Concept would feel most at home. The new president would try to stretch Taylor's concept to cover low-intensity conflict as well. By and large, the Army welcomed Kennedy's commitment to Flexible Response as a reprieve from the lean budget years of the Eisenhower administration.[2] However, Flexible Response also implied the generation of forces and doctrine capable of addressing threats to U.S. security at the lower end of the conflict spectrum—wars of insurgency. This strategy quickly ran into conflict with an Army bent on preparing for conventional war in Europe, not brushfire wars in the emerging nations of the Third World. The question soon became one of how quickly and to what degree of magnitude the president could get the Army to modify its operational concept.

John Kennedy came into office only a fortnight after Nikita Khrushchev proffered his country's support for "wars of national liberation." The president was so impressed by Khrushchev's hurling down the gauntlet before the new administration that he read excerpts from the speech at the first meeting of his National Security Council. Kennedy directed all members of his administration involved in the setting of national security policy to read and ponder the speech.

Of course, the president's concern regarding wars of national liberation predated the Khrushchev speech. As a congressman and senator, Kennedy had made several trips to Indochina during the Viet Minh insurgency. He had spoken out in the Congress on the shortcomings of French efforts to combat insurgency, both in Indochina and in Algeria. To Kennedy, insurgencies—or wars of national liberation, as the Communists referred to them—were what the Chinese and Soviets were counting on as the wave of the future. Nuclear war was out of the question; even Khrushchev realized that. In Korea the United States had shown the Communists that limited wars of overt aggression did not pay. Thus the new approach—insurgency.

For the Army, which would have to bear the brunt of administration efforts to counter insurgencies, insurgency warfare implied dramatic changes in traditional military operations. The president said as much in an address to the graduating class at West Point in 1962: "This is another type of war, new in its intensity, ancient in its origins—war by guerrillas, subversives, insurgents, assassins; war by ambush instead of by combat; by infiltration, instead of aggression, seeking victory by eroding and exhausting the enemy instead of engaging him. . . . It requires in those situations where we must counter it . . . a whole new kind of strategy, a wholly different kind of force, and therefore a new and wholly different kind of military training."[3] In the words of General Taylor, "It came through loud and clear that he saw a new kind of threat coming for which conventional armies, navies and air forces weren't ready to fight."[4] Kennedy's problem, and his challenge, was to effect a revolution in the Army's organizational perspectives, a revolution from above in which the service would be forced to stretch its limited resources to cover the counterinsurgency option of Flexible Response, in addition to the familiar contingency of war in Europe.

During his first year in office, the president made strong efforts to get the Army moving in this area. One of his first questions to his principal advisers after the inauguration was, "What are we doing about guerrilla warfare?" National Security Action Memorandum (NSAM) 2 instructed Secretary of Defense McNamara to look into the matter of "increasing the counter-guerrilla resources." Kennedy also examined Special Forces equipment and manuals. Dissatisfied on both counts, he called a special meeting to confront the JCS. When the president queried General Taylor about the Army's efforts to develop a capability for low-intensity conflict, Taylor informed him, "We good soldiers are trained for all kinds of things. We don't have to worry about special situations." "That," Taylor later said, "didn't satisfy him a nickel's worth."[5]

Brig. Gen. William P. Yarborough, commander of the Special Warfare School at Fort Bragg, observed that Kennedy could not "find any military chain of command that was aware of this phenomenon in depth."[6] Despite his absence of concern over insurgency warfare, Taylor was held in high regard by the president, who saw him as a soldier-scholar who understood the nuances of this "new" form of conflict. Taylor was recalled to active duty shortly after the president took office and became Kennedy's Special Military Representative, a duty that required the general to monitor the ongoing counterinsurgency programs.

Kennedy continued to push. He singled out the Special Forces for attention, authorizing them, over the objections of the Army brass, to wear the green beret as a mark of distinction, while approving a 5,000-man increase in the size of the force as well. His goal was to create a big enough shock in the Army that it would be forced into a revision of its priorities and a reorientation of its Concept. On 28 March 1961, in his special message to the Congress on the defense budget, the president argued that the nation needed "a greater ability to deal with guerrilla forces, insurrection, and subversion."[7] And in his State of the Union address to Congress on 25 May 1961, the president declared his intention to expand "rapidly and substantially" the existing forces for the conduct of "nonnuclear war, paramilitary operations and sub-limited or unconventional wars."[8]

Kennedy pushed his approach through the national security structure. In NSAM 52, dated 11 May 1961, he directed the military to examine its force structure in light of a possible future commitment to Southeast Asia.[9] Yet the president realized that for all his prodding, and for all his authority, the Army could not be forced to adopt his concern for counterinsurgency. This led to an extraordinary session in the Oval Office on 30 November, when the president summoned in all the Army's major commanders. So far as anyone could determine, it was the first session of its kind.

Elvis Stahr, then secretary of the Army, was present. He found the president very much on a "counterinsurgency kick." Kennedy said, "I want you guys to get with it. I know that the Army is not going to develop in this counterinsurgency field and do the things that I think must be done unless the Army itself wants to do it."[10] This appeal had a minimal impact on the Army brass. The Army would do it if the president wanted, but the service itself was not behind it. Over a month later, many of the presidential queries concerning Army preparation for low-intensity conflict were still being ignored. Kennedy's frustration was evident in a memo to Robert McNamara in which the president bluntly informed his secretary of defense that he was "not satisfied that the Department of Defense, and in particular the Army, is according the necessary degree of attention and effort to the threat of insurgency and guerrilla war."[11] Responding quickly to the direct pressure exerted by the president, the JCS designated Marine Maj. Gen. Victor H. Krulak as Special Assistant for Counterinsurgency and Special Activities [SACSA]. The Army appointed Brig. Gen. William B. Rosson to be in charge of Special Operations.

That same month, on 18 January, Kennedy set up the Special Group, Counterinsurgency (SGCI), with General Taylor as its chairman. Other members included Robert Kennedy, the president's brother (and attorney general), U. Alexis Johnson (undersecretary of state), Roswell Gilpatric (undersecretary of defense), Gen. Lyman Lemnitzer (chairman of the JCS), John McCone (director of the CIA), McGeorge Bundy, and Edward R. Murrow (USIA). By placing in the group individuals who held positions

President John F. Kennedy gets a close look at STRAC (Strategic Army Corps) airborne troops during a visit to Fort Bragg, North Carolina, in October 1961.

courtesy U.S. Army

of high responsibility in the administration, the president hoped to prod the Army on a more frequent basis than he himself had been able to do.

In addition to applying pressure from above, Kennedy sought to indoctrinate the Army from within. In his blistering note to McNamara, Kennedy informed the secretary of defense that he wanted counter-insurgency training added to the curricula of military schools at all levels, from West Point all the way up to the Army War College. The president also dropped a broad hint that future promotions to general officer would depend on the individual's demonstrated competence in the field of counterinsurgency. To get the indoctrination program moving, Kennedy directed that topnotch Army colonels and brigadier generals be sent to the Special Warfare Training Center at Fort Bragg for a course on counterinsurgency.[12]

Problems with the Kennedy Approach

Although the president felt that there was something special and out of the ordinary about wars of national liberation and the Communist insurgency threat, he did not have the time to oversee directly the administration's counterinsurgency program; nor did he have the time to become an expert himself on the nature of protracted conflict and counterinsurgency warfare. Like other presidents in postwar America, Kennedy relied heavily on his aides to carry out his directives and ensure that the bureaucracies complied with them. Unfortunately, the individuals chosen by Kennedy to perform this role were not well suited for the task. Their lack of expertise in the realm of low-intensity conflict hampered the ability of the administration to hold the Army's feet to the fire over counterinsurgency; thus, the Army could give lip service to requirements placed on it by the administration or ignore them entirely. The Army was not intentionally frustrating the formulation of national security policy but was, rather, acting out of its convictions that its first priority was in Europe and that if you could win a big war, you could certainly win a little one.

One of the administration's leading "experts" on counterinsurgency was Walt W. Rostow, deputy to McGeorge Bundy, the president's special assistant for national security. Rostow, a graduate of Yale and a Rhodes scholar, had served in the Office of Strategic Services (OSS) during the war and was an economist long associated with the government. Rostow felt that "communism is best understood as a disease of the transition to modernization" and that "a guerrilla war must be fought primarily by those on the spot . . . [because] it is an intimate affair, fought not merely with weapons but . . . in the minds of men who live in the villages and in the hills."[13] Simply stated, insurgency was a threat to emerging Third World nations that revolved essentially around the need of the indigenous government to obtain the support and control of the population. Rostow also posited, quite correctly, that the best way to defeat an insurgency was to nip it in the bud, before it had an opportunity to develop into its guerrilla warfare phase. Rostow felt, however, that once the guerrilla warfare phase had been reached, the vulnerable state might well have to "seek out and engage the ultimate source of aggression."[14] This Massive Retaliation mentality, rooted in his earlier World War II days, when he had served as a target selector during the bombing of Germany, led Rostow to conclude that strategic bombing of North Vietnam would provide a way out of counterinsurgency operations for the United States. This great faith in air power led Rostow to focus more on the concept of a traditional state-to-state military confrontation between the United States and the DRV than on the insurgency in South Vietnam.

To a certain extent, Rostow was the protégé of General Taylor, perhaps *the* key individual involved in translating into action the president's anxieties over the Army's inertia on the counterinsurgency front. During the early 1960s, Taylor served as the president's Special Military Representative, chairman of the SGCI, chairman of the JCS, and ambassador to South Vietnam. Kennedy also sent Taylor to South Vietnam on a number of special missions to get the facts on the insurgency. The only problem with Taylor's serving in so many key positions was that he advocated preparing for limited war, not sublimited war (as counterinsurgency was then referred to). What Taylor had fought for in *The Uncertain Trumpet* was the regeneration of the Army's capability to wage mid-intensity conflicts in accordance with its Concept. Down the road, as U.S. involvement in Southeast Asia grew, Taylor's solution to the insurgency problem coincided with Rostow's: the execution of an American strategic bombing campaign against North Vietnam. Taylor could accept no more than most other generals the proposal that in order to deal effectively with the VC, the Army, which had fought to modernize and improve in terms of mobility and firepower, must become not more sophisticated but more primitive.[15] Ironically, the effect of placing Taylor at so many of the junction points between the political leadership and the Army was not so much the application of pressure from above on the military as it was the insulation of the service from the very pressure that the president was trying to generate.

Kennedy's secretary of defense, Robert McNamara, a graduate of the Harvard Business School and former president of the Ford Motor Company, possessed a background geared more to the managerial aspects of defense policy than to its doctrinal or operational elements. McNamara was indeed to effect a revolution at the Pentagon, but it was to be a managerial revolution inspired by the introduction of his Planning Programming Budgeting System (PPBS). PPBS, as implemented by the young, talented, civilian Whiz Kids that McNamara had brought to the Pentagon with him, was to challenge the Army's procurement policies far more than its doctrine. Cost-effectiveness became the byword in the development of new forces. Thus, the battles waged between McNamara and the JCS were primarily over the technological and logistical elements of strategy. With few exceptions, the operational approach to counterinsurgency was left to the Army. McNamara was strictly out of his element when forced to look beyond the technical and managerial dimensions of the counterinsurgency problem and examine its operational nature. He felt more at ease referring to the "tremendous increases, percentagewise" in counterinsurgent force levels than he did when dealing with the strategy and tactics involved in such a conflict.[16] Finally, the secretary of defense was an extremely busy individual. The directive from the president to implement the strategy of Flexible Response, coupled with the introduction of PPBS into the Pentagon's procurement system, among other things, was enough to tax even a man of McNamara's energy. There just was not sufficient time for McNamara to become closely involved in the development of counterinsurgent forces.

In examining the men who sat on Kennedy's oversight board, the SGCI, one fairs no better in the search for someone versed in the field of low-intensity conflict. Indeed, one wonders why a president so intent on forcing the Army to develop a new approach to this form of warfare would opt for so conventional a group of men to bring about that change. It has been noted that the group's chairman, General Taylor, had his focus on the problems of limited war, not counterinsurgency. Robert Kennedy, the president's brother, was a member of the group primarily as JFK's watchdog. This notwithstanding, his knowledge of doctrinal and force structuring requirements was minuscule. Taylor recalls that the attorney general once asked, "Why can't we just make the entire Army into Special Forces?"[17] Roswell Gilpatric, representative for the Department of Defense (DOD), was an individual whose Air Force background was largely irrelevant to the problem at hand. U. Alexis Johnson, at the Department of State, was viewed by the president simply as a fellow "who gets things done."[18] Murrow, McCone, and Bundy represented agencies or organizations that would be needed if a counterinsurgent capability were to be developed; none, however, came near to being an expert in counterinsurgency. Army Gen. Lyman Lemnitzer, chairman of the JCS, was not enthusiastic regarding the administration's push on low-intensity warfare.

Compounding the flaws within the membership of the group were structural defects. Despite the top-heavy nature of the SGCI, its staff was not sufficiently large to monitor the initiatives that it attempted to undertake. This was particularly crucial, since the senior composition of the membership offered little opportunity for personal follow-up. But the problem ran deeper. The record of the SGCI shows a good deal of activity dealing with organizational and programmatic detail but relatively little concerning the more profound problem of doctrine and the need for an integrated interagency approach. As in DOD, the emphasis was on the technical and logistical aspects of the problem rather than on development of a governmentwide approach to insurgency. When General Taylor departed in October 1962 to become chairman of the JCS, the SGCI declined. By 1966 its influence had so diminished that it was quietly absorbed into the NSC system of senior interdepartmental groups.

Ironically, such "experts" as the administration had were not at the center of the policy process but on the periphery. Roger Hilsman, initially director of intelligence and research at the State Department, had fought with guerrillas in Burma during World War II. He was a West Point graduate and had a close relationship with R. K. G. Thompson, the noted British expert on guerrilla warfare. Despite these credentials, Hilsman was never given a major role in the administration's counterinsurgency program. The same fate befell Air Force Brig. Gen. Edward Lansdale, who had worked with Magsaysay in the Philippines and in the special military mission in Saigon. Lansdale, not a favorite of Taylor's, quickly found himself relegated to a minor role in the policy process. Furthermore, the administration, while upgrading the status of the Special Forces, did not see fit to challenge the Army's designation of MAAG chiefs or, later, the commander of MACV, yet the officers assigned were quite ill-suited for supervising counterinsurgency operations. General officers with training in the field, such as Major General Rosson and Brigadier General Yarborough, remained on the sidelines.

The Army's Response

The administration's emphasis on developing a counterinsurgency capability shook the Army brass. They were, in effect, being told to alter radically the Army's method of operation, a method that had been eminently successful in recent conflicts. The notion that a group of novice civilians (Kennedy, McNamara, and the Whiz Kids) should require the Army to de-emphasize its strong suits (heavy units, massed firepower, high technology) in favor of stripped-down light infantry units was bound to encounter strong resistance from the Army leadership.

Attitudes within the Army hierarchy bore out both the service's disinterest in Kennedy's proposals and its conviction that the Army could handle any problems that might crop up at the lower end of the conflict spectrum. For instance, General Lemnitzer, chairman of the JCS from 1960 to 1962, stated that the new administration was "oversold" on the importance of guerrilla warfare. Gen. George H. Decker, Army Chief of Staff from 1960 to 1962, countered a presidential lecture to the JCS on counterinsurgency with the reply, "Any good soldier can handle guerrillas." Gen. Earle Wheeler, Army Chief of Staff from 1962 to 1964, stated that "the essence of the problem in Vietnam is military." At the time, General Taylor felt that counterinsurgency was "just a form of small war" and that "all this cloud of dust that's coming out of the White House really isn't necessary." Taylor later recalled the Army's reaction to Kennedy's program as being "something we have to satisfy. But not much heart went into [the] work."[19]

Indeed, in the Army's perception counterinsurgency operations were lumped with conventional-style military operations like those undertaken in the Korean War. A *Newsweek* interview with a Pentagon staffer reflected this sentiment. The United States, said the spokesman, ought to commit troops to the Asian mainland only on the conditions that no "privileged sanctuary" be granted the enemy, that U.S. power be applied "without any limitation" against the enemy's military resources, and that the United States not undertake a prolonged land war. The article noted that "many competent soldiers" believed in this approach. The prescription for victory in a limited war in Southeast Asia, he said, would center on a strategic bombing campaign and on mobile tank warfare on South Vietnam's "savannah grasslands and open plains, just like in Europe or west Texas."[20]

The Army's response to the administration's call for a reevaluation of its doctrine and force structure was a negative one. In the Army's thinking, there was scant difference between limited war and insurgency. The service's response was unidimensional, reflecting a traditional approach to the conflict, while ignoring its social and political dimensions. All would be solved if the president and his people would just let the Army alone. Unable to fit the president's prescriptions into its force structure, oriented on mid- and high-intensity conflict in Europe, the Army either ignored them or watered them down to prevent its superiors from infringing upon what the service felt were its proper priorities.

Doctrine, basically, is an authoritative, approved statement of how to perform a task. Current doctrine within the Army has often been described as what 51 percent of the Army thinks it is. In the Army, doctrine is developed in several ways. Service schools (such as the Command and General Staff College [C&GSC] and the Army War College), certain service commands (such as the United States Continental Army Command and the Combat Developments Command), and professional journals (such as *Parameters, Military Review,* and *Armor*) all contribute formally or informally in the production and dissemination of doctrine. The schools and commands are particularly important, since they contain the service's doctrinal memory and present the approved way of doing things to the Army's officer corps.

Service schools, through their instruction of officers, are of crucial importance in propagating doctrine. The higher the rank an officer achieves, the more times he will have returned to one of these schools to be "grounded" in the proper Army methods of war. Nearly all general officers have attended their respective branch's basic course (for newly commissioned officers) and advanced course (primarily for captains), as well as the C&GSC (for majors) and the Army War College (for colonels). Doctrine is also developed and disseminated through training given in field exercises and evaluations. This allows the doctrinal guidance presented in manuals and in the classroom to be put into practice, making "real" what had formerly been abstract. Finally, ideally, the actual employment of doctrine under wartime conditions provides the positive reinforcement necessary to validate the doctrine or negative feedback leading to modification in the Army's approach to the problem. Thus, the military reversals in Vietnam during the early 1960s ought to have resulted in the Army's modifying its approach to insurgency warfare.

Development of Doctrinal Literature for Counterinsurgency

In the years following World War II, the Combat Developments Organization within the Army Field Forces proved inadequate for developing doctrine for future conflicts. Responding to this shortcoming, the G-3 (Operations) section of the Army Field Forces organized the Combat Development Group in October 1953. This arrangement was short-lived, however. In June 1954 an Army reorganization plan established the United States Continental Army Command (USCONARC), which replaced the Army Field Forces in February 1955. USCONARC was responsible for commanding all Army forces in the continental United States, as well as developing doctrine and materiel. Within this structure, the C&GSC was charged with "the development of doctrine for all of the combined arms and services."[21]

In 1961 the system was further restructured with the arrival of Robert McNamara as secretary of defense. USCONARC was divided into three commands: the Continental Army Command (CONARC), which retained responsibility for training; the Army Materiel Command, responsible for procurement; and the Combat Developments Command (CDC), charged with the development of doctrine. While this purportedly removed the service schools, particularly the C&GSC, from their primacy in the area of doctrinal development, they remained influential in the doctrinal formation process. The new system, activated by General Decker on 7 March 1962, provided the basis for doctrinal development prior to U.S. intervention in Vietnam in 1965.

In spite of efforts to generate a forward-looking approach to doctrinal development through various changes and refinements in the organizations responsible for it, the Army failed to create a coherent body of doctrinal literature for counterinsurgency. An examination of Army field manuals (FMs) during the period reveals that counterinsurgency warfare was ignored almost entirely during the Eisenhower era. While this changed with the advent of the Kennedy administration, doctrinal literature on counterinsurgency during the early sixties was slow to materialize, and when it did, it reflected the service's tendency to fit all forms of conflict within the familiar framework of the Concept.

Any discussion of FMs must begin with FM 100-5, *Operations*, also referred to as the bible on how to fight. Editions of this manual were published in 1944, 1954, 1956, 1958, and 1962. Until the 1962 edition, there was no discussion in the manual concerning counterinsurgency warfare or how to organize guerrilla units in support of conventional operations (as was done in World War II and Korea).[22] As a result of the Kennedy administration's push in 1961, the 1962 edition contained two chapters relating to "counterinsurgency." Chapter 10, "Unconventional Warfare Operations," dealt basically with disrupting the enemy by organizing friendly guerrilla forces in a mid-intensity conflict environment. Chapter 11, "Military Operations against Irregular Forces," was fraught with overtones of the Concept. For example, the manual held that "operations to suppress and eliminate irregular forces are primarily *offensive in nature*. Thus, the *conventional force* must plan and seize the initiative at the outset."[23]

In addition to FM 100-5, the Army produced a number of manuals in the 31 series that were intended to address counterguerrilla operations. FM 31-20, *Operations against Guerilla Forces*, published in 1951, called for conventional forces to deal with guerrilla or partisan forces. In 1953, FM 31-15, *Operations against Airborne Attack, Guerilla Action and Infiltration*, discussed the provision of rear area security from partisan forces. Again, the framework for discussion was conventional war. Later published as *Operations against Irregular Forces*, the manual was adequate as an expression of general principles but did not provide guidance at the implementation level.[24] When the manual came out in 1964 retitled *Special Warfare Operations*, it included specific chapters on counterinsurgency operations. FM 31-21, *Guerrilla Warfare*, issued in 1955, called for the execution of counterguerrilla operations with conventional forces as part of a general war. Surprisingly enough, when the manual was revised in 1958, all mentions of counterguerrilla operations were deleted.[25] A 1963 edition, written by the Special Warfare Center, included a chapter on counterinsurgency, but only as it related to the Special Forces.[26] In 1963, FM 31-22, entitled *U.S. Army Counterinsurgency Forces*, was issued. Like FM 31-21, it was written by the Special Warfare Center and directed at Special Forces troops, *not* the Army as a whole.[27]

The result of this small but highly publicized surge in counterinsurgency doctrinal literature was not a little organizational confusion. In May 1962 Major General Rosson characterized the Army's progress in this area as "short term in nature, that is, designed to meet immediate requirements" (that is, pressure from the administration).[28] General Depuy, then a colonel serving as the director of special warfare at the Pentagon, recalled that "we were rather mechanistic about the whole thing" and that the doctrinal effort was perceived to be in response to a "fad" originating during the Kennedy administration.[29] By 1964 the Army had yet to publish a manual dealing specifically with counterinsurgency at the Army level. An Army evaluation of doctrinal literature for special warfare in January 1964 reported that "nowhere is there a definitive listing of doctrinal requirements for special warfare." The report observed that "except for some tips for individual advisors in FM 31-22, doctrine for the organization, employment, and support of an advisory organization, other than the Special Forces, does not exist."[30] Counterinsurgency doctrine was categorized overall as "defective" at the national level, the host country level, and the combined arms level.

As late as November 1964 the Army was still involved in a review and reevaluation of its role "in the entire field of counterinsurgency."[31] In February 1965, CDC was still working on an adviser handbook and on plans for the integration of counterinsurgency doctrine into the service schools and training programs of the Army.[32] Army doctrine, as reflected in its patchwork formulation, reflected the activity of the service going through the motions of churning out a response for a contingency that it did not really understand, out of a desire to satisfy the requirements of the civilian leadership. The result of this lack of motivation on the Army's part was that as late as 1966 most American unit commanders and division staff officers were not familiar with the standard doctrinal literature contained in Army field manuals.[33] Indeed, in 1967, CONARC would note that "there is insufficient doctrine on area warfare."[34]

Even if U.S. troop leaders had been familiar with counterinsurgency doctrine, there is strong evidence that the Army Concept persisted even after U.S. ground forces became involved in Vietnam. For example, the Army's FM 31-16, *Counterguerrilla Operations*, published in 1967, framed counterinsurgency doctrine within the borders of the Concept. Counterinsurgency was a duty added to the regular combat mission of divisions and brigades; the Army prescribed no changes in organization nor any scaling down of the firepower to be used in fighting an insurgency.[35]

In addition to Army field manuals, the service's professional journals were being used to disseminate doctrine. These journals are, for the most part, associated with service schools and, as such, reflect the doctrinal emphasis given counterinsurgency by the school and the officers who attend it. By and large, the journals remained indifferent to the proliferation of insurgency warfare in the 1950s and early 1960s, exhibiting but a minor reaction to the counterinsurgency "fad" created by the Kennedy administration. For instance, in nineteen issues of *Army* magazine, from January 1959 through July 1960, there was not a single comment on insurgency in the letters section. One searches in vain for the professional strategists who might have conducted analyses of insurgencies that either were ongoing or had been recently concluded in Greece, the Philippines, Cuba, Malaysia, Indochina, and Algeria. A fall 1960 issue of *Military Affairs* devoted to unconventional warfare was as close as the professional journals were to come to a discussion of insurgency warfare prior to the Kennedy "revolution."

Kennedy's call for an Army counterinsurgency capability slowly created an increase in the journals' consideration of the subject. An examination of *Military Review* published by the C&GSC revealed that despite a noticeable increase in 1962, as the administration's program began to impact on the Army, the overall share of insurgency-related articles quickly stabilized at slightly above 10 percent of the total, notwithstanding the increase in the American involvement in Vietnam and the designation, in 1962, of counterinsurgency as a primary Army mission, coequal with nuclear and conventional war contingencies.

Given the general quality of the articles purporting to deal with counterinsurgency, it is just as well that the exposure remained low. One finds in many of them an author attempting to fit counterinsurgency doctrine into something approximating traditional Army operations. One contributor to *Armor* magazine, for example, assured his readers that if armored personnel carriers (APCs) and light tanks were substituted for heavy armor, "standard doctrine becomes applicable."[36] In fact, to fully develop Army counterinsurgency capabilities in Vietnam, the author concluded, what was necessary was the deployment of more APCs, to "kill more VC," or better yet, more light tanks, to "kill VC more efficiently." Another armor officer baldly stated armor's need to find a niche in counterinsurgency warfare lest the branch lose influence within the Army: "The future of armor lies in its officers and noncommissioned officers, developing new concepts for its employment in limited war and counter-guerrilla operations. If armor is not able to be deployed in this type of role, it will find itself becoming less and less 'THE COMBAT ARM OF DE-CISION.' "[37]

An artilleryman faced with much the same dilemma called for the employment of "lean" artillery in counterinsurgency operations, such as 105 mm howitzers. The use of artillery, said the contributor, was justified by its "tremendous killing power."[38] Articles such as these are disturbing not only in and of themselves but also as a reflection of the service schools that screened such articles and then offered them up as representative of new doctrinal development.

Army Efforts to Address Counterinsurgency

Part of the Army's response to President Kennedy's directive to generate counterinsurgency forces was the proliferation of various conferences, boards, offices, and teams, ostensibly instituted to assist the leadership in coming up with an Army program of action. By March 1960 the insurgency in Vietnam had progressed to the point where the Army Chief of Staff, General Lemnitzer, recommended that MAAG in Saigon shift its emphasis to antiguerrilla warfare training. The JCS also began work on a Counterinsurgency Plan (CIP) for South Vietnam. The plan progressed slowly, however, and was not approved until after President Kennedy assumed office in January 1961. At Kennedy's prompting, the Army increased the resources devoted to the formation of counterinsurgency forces and doctrine. As previously mentioned, both the JCS and the Army set up special staff sections to oversee the development of the counter-insurgency program. A Remote Area Conflict Office (RACO) was es-tablished within the Army's Office of the Deputy Chief of Staff for Operations (ODCSOPS). RACO, which was to coordinate and expedite development of special warfare doctrine and materiel requirements, suffered from a lack of personnel familiar with special warfare, which minimized its effect on the development process.[39] Brigadier General Rosson, the Army's special assistant for special warfare, attempted to establish a special warfare program for the Army but received little encouragement or guidance from ODCSOPS. Despite the appearance of placing emphasis on the generation of a counterinsurgency capability, the effect was the creation of staff positions of high visibility but little real power.

Brigadier General Rosson's experience as head of the Special Warfare Directorate is a case in point. Rosson was intended to be Army Chief of Staff General Decker's eyes and ears on special warfare activities within the service and to recommend changes in doctrine and force structure as he saw fit.[40] General Decker, however, informed Rosson that he opposed the creation of Rosson's position as special assistant as an intrusion visited upon the Army by the Kennedy administration and the "New Frontiersmen."[41] Decker told Rosson that while he would have access to both the Chief of Staff and the Vice Chief of Staff, he would not be permitted to develop his own staff but would be required to work through the DCSOPS.[42] Rosson was to focus only on the Army's "special" assets—the Green Berets and the Psychological and Civil Affairs units, along with special warfare curricula at the service schools and work being done at test and development facilities. The bulk of the Army's forces were considered to be outside of Rosson's purview.[43] Decker told Rosson that he, Decker, and Lt. Gen. Barksdale Hamlett would handle special warfare requirements affecting Army main-force units, such as infantry and armor divisions, the implication being that the Army would retain the "purity" of these units and their orientation on the "big war" in Europe. That Rosson would control the Special Forces was bad enough; the Army leadership was not going to stand idly by while their standard units were engulfed by the president's counterinsurgency "fad." Thus, Rosson and his unwanted directorate were quickly crowded out of the picture, reinforcing the point that the Army leadership assessed its participation in developing a counterinsurgency capability in purely negative terms, that is, in terms of how much it would detract from optimum readiness for limited or general war.[44] Nonetheless, service efforts at doctrinal development were affected significantly by several internal reports, of which two became known as the Stilwell Reports, and another, the Report of the Howze Board on Special Warfare.

One Stilwell Report, entitled "Army Activities in Underdeveloped Areas Short of Declared War," was the product of Brig. Gen. Richard G. Stilwell, a brilliant officer serving on the Army Staff. The report dealt with Army counterinsurgency capabilities and was highly critical of Army doctrine and force structuring. Submitted to the secretary of the Army and General Decker on 13 October 1961, the report stated that Army efforts to date had been marked by a "failure to evolve simple and dynamic doctrine." It went on to say that the average military man was not accustomed to thinking within the "conceptual framework" of counterinsurgency. Criticism of the JCS was strong. They were cited as having no in-house capability for generating doctrine or forces and being indifferent and sluggish in their response to directives from the administration to give such matters high priority.[45]

The report recommended upgrading the Special Warfare Division in DCSOPS to a directorate, establishing a direct command line between the Army Staff and the Special Warfare Center, and initiating a "comprehensive informational/education program throughout the Army." What was more important, the report called upon the Army *as a whole* to accept counterinsurgency as its mission rather than as a contingency limited to the Special Forces.

General Decker's response to the Stilwell Report and the queries that followed from Secretary Stahr consisted in adopting the report "as a primary reference" for use by the Army Staff.[46] The Chief of Staff dispatched briefing teams to provide senior officers with information on Army special warfare activities and developed a counterinsurgency course at the Special Warfare Center. The idea of a special warfare directorate would be "studied." There was, however, no commitment to make counterinsurgency an Army-wide responsibility. As Brigadier General Rosson had discovered, the Army leadership was in no hurry to implement any real changes, particularly changes that implied diverting appreciable resources away from standard Army operations.

Following on the heels of the Stilwell Report came the findings of the Howze Board on Special Warfare, issued on 28 January 1962. Formation of the board had been directed by General Powell, commanding general of USCONARC.[47] Although the board was not directed to examine the Army's doctrinal proficiency for counterinsurgency, it did address some doctrinal issues. The board concluded that the Army had "a latent potential" for counterinsurgency operations but that "neither its indoctrination nor training is now altogether satisfactory for this mission" and that "much of this concept is foreign to fundamental Army teaching and practice."[48]

Echoing the Stilwell Report's critique of Army doctrinal shortcomings, the Howze Board concluded that "the tactical doctrine for the employment of regular force against insurgent guerrilla forces has not been adequately developed, and the Army does not have a clear concept of the proper scale and type of equipment necessary for these operations."[49] The implications of the board's findings were best expressed by Lieutenant General Howze himself: "If the board's recommendations are approved the Army will experience a very considerable reorientation of its outlook and effort, particularly as respects training."[50] The question to be answered was whether the Army was willing, or able, to effect these proposed changes.

Prompted in large measure by the findings of the Howze Board and the Stilwell Report, as well as by a letter from the Chief of Staff, General Powell called a special conference on counterinsurgency in CONARC for 23–24 March 1962. The two-day conference produced a recognition that there was fragmentation in development of doctrinal manuals, with as many as three separate agencies developing field manuals on counter-insurgency.[51] It also produced USCONARC pamphlet 515-2, *Counterinsurgency,* published in April 1962. The pamphlet was compiled from presentations made at the conference and was intended to serve as a two hour orientation course of instruction for Army personnel.[52] While it addressed, albeit briefly, the nature of protracted warfare and counter-insurgency, insurgency was still portrayed as an abnormal, or "special," situation for the Army. Counterinsurgency was viewed as something in which the Special Forces were involved, "in addition to their normal 'hot' war capability." The presentation itself, replete with lists of civilian needs, cold war weapons, and the like, characterized the Army's effort as one to satisfy a requirement rather than effect a change in attitude and behavior. As a first step in a vigorous program of indoctrination it might have succeeded; by itself, it was just another slide show for the troops. Brigadier General Yarborough sensed that "the Army was getting tired of being booted from the highest level to get with the counterinsurgency bit," so the leadership directed that a film be made to explain to all Army personnel just what counterinsurgency was. According to Yarborough, the film was the Army's way of saying, "Everybody's going to understand this. You guys understand me, you're all going to understand counter-insurgency, every damn one of you." Ironically, Yarborough and the others at the Special Warfare Center quickly realized that because of such quick-fix efforts, the Army brass blithely assumed that everyone really did understand counterinsurgency and that therefore the problem was solved.[53]

On the surface, one had the impression that in terms of organizational commitment to the president's directives the Army was moving rapidly: studies were being done, boards were convening, the troops were being briefed, and staff sections were being created and/or expanded. Yet these actions represented simple, inexpensive responses requiring little diversion of time or resources. In fact, the Army was not taking the difficult and expensive steps to indoctrinate and train its soldiers to fight insurgents.

Training for Counterinsurgency

Training is an important element of doctrinal development. Even if the Army managed to produce doctrinal literature (through FMs, professional journals, and so on) and even if it generated studies and conferences on what was to be done, there remained the task of training its officers and men in the new *modus operandi,* both in the classroom and in the field. Much of this classroom training is conducted at the Army's service schools, branch schools (such as the Infantry School at Fort Benning, Georgia), the C&GSC, and the Army War College. If the Army were going to adapt itself to counterinsurgency operations, it would have to orient its officers on a doctrine that was alien to standard Army operations. A look at the curricula at these schools, however, indicates that the Army modified its training only slightly, if at all.

Indeed, in the period prior to the Kennedy push on counterinsurgency the Army paid little attention to training for low-intensity conflict. The president's strong desire for increased training emphasis on counterinsurgency found the Army in a bit of a dither in its early efforts to respond to his orders. The result was a slapdash reaction, as was borne out in Lieutenant General Hamlett's June 1961 status report to the JCS. In the report, Hamlett noted that the Army's service schools had added from six to twelve hours of instruction on insurgency warfare under "common subjects"; furthermore, the Special Warfare School was sending an Unconventional Warfare Operations Traveling Team out to brief key personnel on the topic.[54] Unfortunately, most of the counterguerrilla warfare training was standard training redesignated to demonstrate the Army's "prompt" response to the president's interest. For instance, interior guard duty, map reading, organization of strong points, crosstraining of individual and crew-served weapons, civil defense training, challenging, and the use of countersigns were all labeled "counterguerrilla operations."[55] Obviously, these subjects are part of military training for *any* kind of war. Counterguerrilla training, such as it was, focused on searching out and destroying guerrilla bands in situations more reminiscent of partisan warfare in World War II and Korea than of the protracted warfare of insurgency.

Responding to pressure generated by the SGCI, the Army directed its service schools to increase counterinsurgency instruction.[56] This directive was implemented on 30 March 1962 under the direction of CG CONARC, who also mandated an increase in unit training in counterinsurgency operations. The goal as advocated in the Stilwell Report was to give counterinsurgency "equal prominence" with other forms of warfare. Henceforth counterinsurgency training would no longer be considered "special" but would be a part of the Army's normal mission, on a par with conventional and nuclear warfare operations.[57]

One result of the Army's training program was the compilation of statistics showing how the Army had "accomplished" the mission. The data, it was hoped, would dispel any presidential misconceptions regarding the service's support for its low-intensity contingency. A JCS report to the NSC in July 1962 claimed dramatic increases in the hours devoted to counterinsurgency instruction at all the service schools.[58] Corresponding to the Army's counterinsurgency effort was its designation by the JCS as the organization responsible for the development of doctrine, tactics, and equipment for counterinsurgency to be employed by both the Army and the Marines.[59] Yet these actions were, in reality, only so much fluff. The real issue was how well the Army would translate its mandate for action into meaningful training programs for its troops. Predictably, the Army training program did not go much beyond the initial organizational drill of coughing up the data necessary to mollify its critics.

Training to Defeat Guerrillas

Just what was the Army teaching at its service schools? Was counterinsurgency being treated as a coequal with mid- and high-intensity conflict? How well were the courses on low-intensity conflict structured? Did they really address the problems facing the Army in developing an approach to combating insurgent forces? The best place to begin a search for the answers to such questions is in the schools that were highly focused on counterinsurgency, such as the Special Warfare Center at Fort Bragg.

The Special Warfare Center (SWC) was a newcomer to the Army school system. Established in 1952 as the Psychological Warfare Center, it was responsible for psychological warfare operations, as well as operations relating to unconventional warfare. The latter was a new role that reflected the creation of the Special Forces that same year. Indeed, unconventional warfare remained the "major objective" at the SWC up until the Kennedy administration.[60] The training conducted at the SWC was oriented overwhelmingly toward foreign nationals. As late as 1961, 95 percent of the students at the SWC were from foreign countries. With the administration's push to develop a counterinsurgency capability within the Army, the SWC quickly found itself with greatly increased resources and obligations. The center was charged with supporting the buildup of the Army's Special Forces and developing a senior officers' counterinsurgency and special warfare orientation course and a "national interdepartmental seminar."[61]

The SWC quickly ran into difficulty. By attempting to accommodate these requirements, the school became too big too fast.[62] This, combined with the short period of instruction involved, particularly in the senior officer's course, led to little in the way of productive instruction. As Brigadier General Yarborough remembered, the course "was obviously an attempt to give the president what he kept demanding of the military." The general felt that it "wasn't done properly" and that it was definitely "not a success."[63] The Seminar, very popular at first, proved to be too generalized to be of much use and was quietly shelved after the president's assassination.

Yet another "special" course conducted by the SWC was the Military Assistance Training Advisors (MATA) course, intended to provide officers and NCOs going to Vietnam with a working knowledge of what they could expect to encounter in their role as advisers. It was proposed by the Department of the Army and was approved by the Defense Department in January 1962. The program of instruction called for a four-week course including 25 to 30 hours of conversational Vietnamese, as well as the study of counterinsurgency operations in Greece and Malaya but, curiously enough, not Indochina. Students attending the course gave the program very low marks early on, citing as major shortcomings the absence of qualified instructors and the lack of any good definition of just what an adviser's duties were. The program was assembled so rapidly that CONARC had to authorize the school to hire Berlitz language instructors. Indeed, the lack of qualified language personnel was so acute that a conversational class in Vietnamese consisted in a single instructor's reciting phrases in front of an auditorium filled with students, who would then try to repeat them.[64]

The men sent to this school for training as advisers reflected the value that the service placed on its counterinsurgency contingency. Many of the early attendees were on their last duty assignment prior to retirement—which is evidence that men had to be pressured into accepting the assignment—or were viewed as "expendable."[65] Many came from backwater assignments as ROTC or service school instructors or National Guard advisers. The course also remained too small—at the end of 1963, with roughly sixteen thousand servicemen in Vietnam, the Army had trained less than three thousand of its officers and NCOs in the MATA program.[66] Many key personnel, such as pilots, never attended the course, receiving waivers because of the shortage of such personnel in Vietnam.[67]

If the Army did not train its people in these courses on counter-insurgency, where, then, did they receive their training? One possibility is that they obtained it while attending the Army's branch schools. Since counterinsurgency is primarily a light infantry war, one would expect the instruction offered by the Infantry School at Fort Benning, Georgia, to have placed strong emphasis in this area. A look at the program of instruction, however, reveals that the infantry got into the counter-insurgency game late and departed early. In the Infantry Officer Basic Course (IOBC), the course given to new lieutenants in the branch, little instruction on counterinsurgency was given until 1963, when it jumped to 21 percent of the total. Of this, only *2 percent* of the instruction was directed *primarily* at counterinsurgency.[68] The Infantry School remained basically indifferent to counterinsurgency until 1965, when it became evident that the Army was going to Vietnam. At that point, insurgency-related instruction jumped to 56 percent of the total, yet only 16 percent of the instruction focused primarily on counterinsurgency.

Nineteen sixty-five was the peak year for counterinsurgency training. As it became more and more evident that the Army was going to fight in Vietnam using only variations of its standard operational repertoire, interest in counterinsurgency quickly abated. By 1969 less than 28 percent of the instruction in IOBC concerned insurgency, a drop of over half the instruction presented four years earlier. Compounding this lack of effort was the fact that many hours of instruction supposedly dedicated to low-intensity conflict were actually more related to traditional infantry operations. For instance, over 20 percent of the "pure" counterinsurgency training given in 1965 concerned the infantry company in search-and-destroy operations.

The Infantry Officers Advanced Course (IOAC), given to Army captains, had more hours available for instruction but employed fewer hours teaching counterinsurgency doctrine. The pattern was the same as in the basic course, peaking in 1965 with 15 percent of the instruction being "counterinsurgency-related" and rapidly dropping off to 7 percent in 1969.[69] In no year was the level of purely counterinsurgency instruction above 6 percent. How the doctrinal instruction was weighted in favor of standard operations can be seen by examining the discussion devoted to big-unit operations (battalion and above) as opposed to small-unit, counterinsurgency operations. In 1964, on the eve of U.S. intervention, the former was given six times as much attention as the latter. Clearly, there was no great effort to dilute the doctrinal precepts of the Concept and provide counterinsurgency doctrine the coequal status called for by the administration.

An even more striking trend occurred at the Armor School at Fort Knox, Kentucky. Although the Army was to claim an ever-increasing need for armor units and armor officers in Vietnam, the school never took counterinsurgency seriously. Rather, it tried to fit its current operational doctrine into an insurgent conflict environment. A study of the Armor Officer Basic Course (AOBC) for the years 1959–69 provides remarkable insight into the attitude of the armor branch toward low-intensity conflict. From 1959 to 1967 there was *no instruction* on counterinsurgency doctrine. In 1968 five hours of instruction were classified as pertaining to counterinsurgency, yet a closer examination reveals that none of the instruction directly addressed the topic.[70] The trends for the Armor Officer Advanced Course (AOAC) were much the same; insurgency related doctrine never exceeded 5 percent of the total course offering.[71] The armor branch simply rejected the notion that it should change its doctrine.[72] This notion was supported by Army Chief of Staff and later chairman of the Joint Chiefs of Staff Gen. Earle Wheeler. In addressing the 2d Armored Division, the general observed, "Our division is not a stranger to guerrilla-type warfare. In fact, some historians credit troops of the division with originating and perfecting the armored ambush—and the ambush is certainly basic to guerrilla warfare."[73]

Despite the armor branch's sanguine outlook concerning its ability to cope with the counterinsurgency mission, many of its junior officers did not feel that their indoctrination at Fort Knox prepared them for what they found in Vietnam. One young officer wrote back that the courses taught at the Armor School did not even "scratch the surface of the efforts, techniques and methods which can be directed towards the insurgency."[74] Another officer, citing his branch for "what I believe is the unbalanced thinking of armor and its preoccupation with fighting a nuclear war in Europe," charged the branch with "tying itself to a conventional war in the training of its officers."[75]

Perhaps even more important than the training being given the Army's junior officers was that imparted at the C&GSC. The C&GSC had been a prime influence in the formation of Army doctrine. Attendance at the college was not "automatic," as in the case of the branch schools for junior officers. Only the brightest young field grade officers (majors) attended. It was generally assumed that owing to its reputation as a doctrinal fount for the Army, the C&GSC would be "out in front" of the Army's counterinsurgency program. In reality the college remained a model of dedication to the Army Concept. Dr. Ivan Birrer, a senior official at the C&GSC from 1948 to 1978, recalled that the Army brass showed little interest in whether the college modified its program of instruction or not, so long as it produced statistics showing that it was operating in compliance with Army directives. "All we had to do," said Birrer, "was certify that each officer had X number of hours of counterinsurgency. There were some efforts by the CONARC staff to at least review what was in our instruction, but we were too far from Washington for anyone to really come down and bother us. . . . For the most part, the tactical problems continued to be concerned with land warfare as we had customarily thought of it—on a large land mass."[76]

As with the programs of instruction offered at the Infantry and Armor schools, the C&GSC curriculum provided officers little in the way of a counterinsurgency education. Instruction ostensibly devoted to the topic was frequently skewed to reflect a conventional war environment. In any event, the attention given to counterinsurgency studies was paltry.[77] For example, in 1959–60 and 1960–61 the three hours of instruction devoted to insurgency warfare consisted of a class on how to defeat partisans in the Army's rear area during conventional operations. In 1961–62 this instruction was expanded, with an additional six hours being devoted to airborne unit operations against irregulars.

The impact of the administration's push on counterinsurgency started appearing at the C&GSC in 1962–63. Even so, twenty-seven of the forty-four hours devoted to insurgency that year dealt with corps- and division-level operations; the remainder included heavy doses of unconventional warfare doctrine. Such creative labeling of conventional topics as counterinsurgency-oriented continued in 1963–64. In one case, a counterinsurgency planning exercise called for the insertion of a two-division corps into a country resembling Ghana to clean out insurgents. The instruction was categorized as counterinsurgency training, yet in form and in substance it was right in step with conventional Army operations.

This form of labeling of course offerings continued throughout the war. According to Dr. Birrer, "It became expedient for Leavenworth to appear to be immersed with unconventional and insurgent warfare. We solved this problem . . . by a careful definition. Into the setting of our problems we would include a sentence or two suggesting that there might be the possibility of some irregular forces. . . . This permitted us to count the entire subject as unconventional warfare and it was by such a device that we ran the hours up to 437. But the point to be made is that at *no time* . . . did unconventional warfare really occupy any substantial place in the College Program." Thus the C&GSC "stridently supported the teaching of conventional warfare."[78]

Finally, a look at the Army War College—a school for "the best and the brightest" that the service has to offer—is in order. Here the Army trains its future general officers. During the Vietnam era the course of instruction ran approximately forty weeks and was divided into a series of seven to ten study blocks. These blocks of instruction reflected broad interest areas, such as "The United States and the North Atlantic Community" and "Management of United States Military Power." A rundown of the curricula throughout the 1960s finds the War College strikingly indifferent to insurgency conflict and to the growing conflict in Vietnam itself. From 1959 through 1964 *none* of the study blocks at the War College dealt with low-intensity conflict as either a primary or a related concern for the Army. Beginning in 1964–65 a one-month block of instruction on "The Developing Areas" was offered, yet it was not until 1968, *seven years* after President Kennedy's call for the Army to get moving on counterinsurgency and *three years* after the introduction of U.S. combat troops into Vietnam, that the War College adopted a short (three-week) block of instruction on "Army Internal Defense and Development Operations."[79]

Even in instances where the Army's senior leadership had the opportunity to acquire an understanding of insurgency warfare they balked. While the British sent their *senior* officers and NCOs to the British jungle warfare school in Malaya, the Americans persisted in sending their *junior* officers. To British officers this made no sense, since a junior officer who had attended the school was unlikely to have a great impact on his senior commander, who had not.[80]

In other service schools, Army indoctrination for counterinsurgency was also inadequate. Even while the schools ignored the directives of the political leadership, they dutifully compiled statistics showing that they were complying, in form if not in substance. One civilian observing the events at the time recalled that "word went out from the Chief of Staff of the Army that every school in the Army would devote a minimum of 20 percent of its time to counterinsurgency. Well, this reached the Finance School and the Cooks and Bakers School, so they were talking about how to make typewriters explode . . . or how to make apple pies with hand grenades in them."[81]

The problems inherent in operating in an alien culture whose people spoke a strange language was, to a large extent, ignored by the Army. Only a few dozen soldiers a year received comprehensive training in Vietnamese; a six-week crash course in Vietnamese was given to a few hundred more men bound for Vietnam.[82] The vast majority received only a smattering of instruction; even the MATA course relied on contracted (Berlitz) instruction for its prospective advisers.[83] A number of internally generated reports during the early 1960s, including one by Major General Rosson, noted that the language barrier continued to present a major bar to optimum exploitation of U.S. assistance in this area.[84] Yet the Army failed to produce significant numbers of individuals whose understanding of the language and culture of Vietnam would have made them invaluable contributors to the success of the mission. One senses a belief within the Army hierarchy that if the Army were going to fight in Vietnam, it would fight as it had in Korea and as the war plans of the early sixties called for—with heavy units in a mid-intensity war not unlike that which they expected to find in Europe.

Field Training

The Army's training exercises suffered from the same problems as did the instruction at its service schools: they were generally *pro forma* in nature, and even when serious attempts were made to train, they were often more a bastardized form of conventional operations than a reflection of counterinsurgency doctrine. Again, the statistics generated were impressive. By FY63 most enlisted men had received some form of counterinsurgency training. Many, however, had only been given the Army's two-hour slide show.[85] Beginning in FY64, the goal was to have battalion-sized units of all combat arms (infantry, armor, and artillery) conduct six weeks of counterinsurgency training, capped by a two-week field exercise, each year. Yet given the general lack of understanding in the Army of what counterinsurgency was, these efforts were bound to fail. For example, among the topics considered as part of counterinsurgency training were underwater demolition, air rescue operations, and guerrilla warfare.[86] The essence of counterinsurgency—long-term patrolling of a small area, the pervasive use of night operations, emphasis on intelligence pertaining to the insurgent's infrastructure rather than his guerrilla forces—proved both difficult to simulate and easy to ignore. Mock Vietnamese villages were set up but were of limited utility. Units were primarily taught how to enter a potentially hostile village, search it for booby traps and enemy hiding places, question the villagers about local enemy forces, and then move on.

A few examples of the training undergone by Army units highlight this confused and ineffectual approach. Of particular interest are the exercises conducted at Fort Bragg by the 82d Airborne Division and Special Forces units. The former performed the role of counterinsurgents, the latter that of the insurgents. The mission of the counterinsurgents was to search and destroy: to find, fix, and eliminate all guerrilla forces in the area. In these exercises, the heart of successful counterinsurgency operations was not population security but helicopter availability.[87] A large U.S. Strike Command (STRICOM) exercise in July and August 1963 purported to train participating forces in counterguerrilla operations; however, the exercise consisted in the U.S. XVIII Airborne Corps' going up against an enemy corps of two divisions. The role of U.S. "counterguerrilla" forces was not to combat insurgents but to *organize* them behind enemy lines, a useful unconventional warfare adjunct to mid-intensity conflict but of small relevance in counterinsurgency.[88]

Another special warfare exercise that year pitted a unit of the 82d Airborne against insurgent forces. The training consisted of an airdrop (a "counterguerrilla assault"), followed by the occupation of a town of one hundred Spanish-speaking individuals and the guarding of three supply dumps. Although short in duration, the exercise presented the unit with some real problems in population control. In summing up its experience, the battalion noted that during the operation, "it became increasingly obvious that a large gap exists in both doctrine and training concerning the handling of civilians and unarmed insurgents."[89]

Finally, let us look at an example of Army counterinsurgency training in Europe as described by Col. John K. Singlaub. The colonel reported that each American soldier received seven hours of instruction in counter-guerrilla operations, while a ten-day orientation was provided for colonels and above.[90] In addition, the U.S. Seventh Army had dispatched several mobile training teams to units able to engage in some special tactical training. As in the United States, the "special warfare" instruction covered such conventional topics as "instinctive" firing, demolitions, combat in cities, and "ranger-type" (that is, commando) training. The most effective training provided, according to the colonel, occurred when Bundeswehr troops led by detachments of the U.S. 10th Special Forces acted as insurgents, opposed by Army regulars acting as the counterinsurgent force. In order to obtain intelligence on the guerrillas from the local population, Singlaub reported, U.S. commanders constructed a soccer field near one village, whereupon the entire population proceeded to abandon their support of the insurgents and come over to the government's side!

Even if the Army had achieved its goal of six weeks' training each year, and even if it had managed to make that training truly reflective of counterinsurgency operations, the time involved would have been relatively trivial compared with the overwhelming preponderance of time spent on "traditional" conflict contingencies (that is, Europe). Add to this the misplacement of training emphasis, the confusion over just what doctrine called for, and the frequent rotation of unit personnel, and it is easy to understand how the Army entered the war so unprepared in 1965.

3

Into the Quagmire

With the introduction of U.S. advisers into Vietnam in 1959 and the buildup of U.S. support strength from 1961 to 1964, the Army witnessed firsthand the growth of the insurgency during its phase 2 period—guerrilla warfare. Despite the ARVN's deteriorating position during this period, the U.S. Army successfully insulated itself against reports of the failure of its counterinsurgency efforts. This allowed for a remarkable continuity in the service's approach to the war. The Army's attitude on Vietnam was one of general disinterest in applying counterinsurgency principles, particularly when they conflicted with more traditional military operations. Feedback to the brass indicating that MACV's methods were working was eagerly accepted; reports portraying a picture of failure were, for the most part, ignored. Priority was given to the destruction of guerrilla forces through large-scale operations that inevitably alerted the VC in advance of their execution. As time passed, the Army's reliance on technological solutions (helicopters, increased airpower, electronic barriers, defoliants) would increase in an attempt to make up for its strategic shortcomings.

December 1960 witnessed the formal establishment of the NLF and the People's Liberation Armed Forces (PLAF), an indication that the insurgency was progressing to phase 2 operations. MAAG chief Lt. Gen. Lionel C. McGarr assumed his position upon the departure of Lieutenant General Williams in September 1960. Prior to his assignment, McGarr had been head of the Army's C&GSC, the source of much of the Army's doctrine.

McGarr proved to be an eccentric MAAG chief; nevertheless, his erratic views on counterinsurgency were quite representative of the Army's during the advisory years. As a commander, McGarr was extremely aloof. At times he would not go to the headquarters for two or three days, staying in his quarters and making recordings, then sending them over to the MAAG staff. In the recordings were supposed to be instructions for the staff, but they were often so garbled that the staff had to call McGarr to find out what he wanted done.[1] McGarr rarely went to the field to visit either U.S. advisers or Vietnamese forces during his stint as MAAG chief, which ran until the establishment of MACV in February 1962. In the words of one senior Army officer, the brass "couldn't get McGarr out fast enough. He was a very poor MAAG chief, a stuffed shirt."[2] Despite this harsh criticism of McGarr, no steps were taken to remove him. Despite the fact that successful counterinsurgency requires intimate knowledge of the target nation's culture, its people, and its terrain, as well as the operations being conducted, the Army Staff was content to have as its eyes and ears an officer who was a recluse from his own staff.

McGarr did in Vietnam what the Army leadership was doing in Washington: he gave lip service to counterinsurgency doctrine, while operating in accordance with the Concept. One has only to look at the pamphlets, memoranda, and policy papers issued by MAAG under McGarr's stewardship to see a dual philosophy in action. A reading of these documents uncovers many statements in agreement with traditional counterinsurgency doctrine. For example, one of McGarr's missives read:

We cannot hope to match vc *foot* mobility with *mechanical* mobility alone. In an area characterized by a lack of roads our primary lines of communication for carrying the fight to the vc must be jungle trails, inland waterways and air transport—both fixed and rotary wing. Otherwise, the result will be that even though the RVNAF take the *offensive,* the all-important initiative will remain with the Viet Cong.

There is only one way he [the vc] can survive—capitalize on the conventional concept by taking advantage of the inherent relative weakness of its built-in inflexibility . . . even its conventional type thinking! A thinking which is *too often* geared to highly sophisticated weapons systems, complex logistics, stylized or rigid tactics, and vulnerable lines of communications.[3]

While lip service was given to counterinsurgency, the bottom line was that traditional Army doctrine and force structure applied. The objectives, as McGarr saw them, were to "find, fix, fight, and finish the enemy," the Army's mission in a conventional war.[4] Despite his warning against "conventional-type thinking," McGarr examined the possibility of establishing a five- to ten-kilometer cordon sanitaire along the entire land border of Vietnam. McGarr also promoted the idea of search-and-destroy operations, which at that time were referred to as "net and spear" operations. Wars, McGarr informed his command, "are won by *Offensive Action.* Therefore, you must . . . 'bring the vc to battle' at a time, place, and in a manner of the RVNAF's choosing—the primary objective of every commander." He summed up his approach by concluding that "*current conditions* which are so favorable to the VC can be *reversed* by OFFENSIVE action—only!" In one memorable closing statement, McGarr exhorted his subordinates with the words, "I know that together with your Vietnamese counterparts, we will 'out conventional' the unconventionalists!"[5] In light of this confusion over what counterinsurgency operations represented, it is not surprising that the MAAG counterinsurgency plan for 1961 reflected the traditional two-up-and-one-back company/platoon approach geared for mid-intensity conflict.[6]

Toward the Creation of MACV

MAAG's counterinsurgency plan was approved by President Kennedy shortly after he took office in January 1961. Although the approval was viewed as a routine action, there were strings attached to the aid portion of the plan requiring Diem to establish a central intelligence organization, a single chain of command for counterinsurgency operations, and other reforms conducive to combating the insurgent threat. Diem proved reluctant to initiate any of these reforms. While the U.S. ambassador, Elbridge Durbrow, wanted to withhold the increase in aid pending South Vietnamese compliance, both MAAG and the JCS quickly grew impatient with his foot-dragging; they wanted to get on with the war. The result was the issuance of a number of meaningless decrees by Diem in exchange for implementation of the increased aid program. Thus did MAAG under McGarr quickly affirm its preference for military action in lieu of political-military reforms that would have strengthened the country's base for counterinsurgency operations.

On 29 April President Kennedy approved, as part of the program, an increase in the ARVN of 20,000 men, bringing its strength to 170,000. The president also authorized MAAG to provide support and training to the SDC paramilitary units, as well as MAP support to the CG. Despite the dramatic growth in insurgent guerrilla operations, the DOD report upon which the president based his decision called for an increase of two divisions in the ARVN as insurance against a conventional invasion of South Vietnam.[7] Finally, a Special Forces Group (approximately 400 men) would be sent to South Vietnam to accelerate the training of South Vietnamese Special Forces.

In light of this increase in U.S. assistance, the JCS were asked for their views concerning possible deployment of U.S. combat troops to Vietnam. The request came from Deputy Secretary of Defense Roswell Gilpatric in response to a JCS task force draft of 6 May 1961 which examined deploying two U.S. battle groups to the Central Highlands to train ARVN troops and deter external aggression.[8] On 10 May the JCS replied to Gilpatric's request for specifics, stating that if "the political decision is to hold Southeast Asia outside the Communist sphere, the Joint Chiefs are of the opinion that US forces should be deployed immediately to South Vietnam."[9] McGarr seconded this recommendation from Saigon, requesting 16,000 troops.[10] McGarr's MAAG study further recommended U.S. support for the development of a fifteen-division–equivalent ARVN force of roughly 280,000 men, an increase that would nearly double the size of the RVNAF. Aside from the increase in Vietnamese forces, the study called for the Army to deploy two battle groups plus 10,000 additional trainers and support personnel. In a letter to General Decker, McGarr recognized the resistance in Washington to such a commitment and proposed as an initial step an increase in the ARVN force levels to 200,000, with no U.S. combat troops involved.[11] There was scant appreciation among the Army leadership for the disutility of sending troops versed in conventional warfare to train ARVN forces for combat against insurgents

In a letter to Kennedy on 9 June, Diem proposed an increase in the RVNAF to 270,000, matching almost precisely the number called for in the MAAG study. A U.S. team headed by Eugene Staley, president of the Stanford Research Institute, went to South Vietnam in mid-June to evaluate the request and returned with two options. Option A would increase the size of the RVNAF to 200,000; option B would support the buildup to 270,000 which Diem had requested. Kennedy adopted the former course of action, despite the absence of an Army plan for utilizing these forces. This time Diem was not even pressured to make the reforms that he had previously promised but had failed to enact. By September McGarr, in his "Outlook For Next Year," observed an "enhanced sense of urgency and offensive spirit" in the ARVN.[12] At the same time that McGarr was filing his optimistic report, correspondent Theodore H. White was writing the White House from Saigon that "the situation gets worse almost week by week." "The guerrillas now control almost all the southern delta," said White, "so much so that I could find no American who would drive me outside Saigon in his car even by day without military convoy."[13]

Indeed, a sharp upsurge in VC activity that began in late summer, along with the deteriorating situation in Laos, led Walt Rostow, then on the Policy Planning Council at the State Department, to propose that 25,000 SEATO troops be sent to Vietnam with the mission of sealing off the Vietnamese-Laotian border and the Demilitarized Zone (DMZ).[14] Yet a national intelligence estimate at the time of his proposal observed that 80–90 percent of the VC were *locally recruited,* their weapons coming almost exclusively from stocks captured from government forces. Nevertheless, as early as 13 July, Rostow had sent a memo to Secretary of State Dean Rusk contending that if diplomacy could not resolve the situation in Vietnam, the United States should contemplate a "counter-guerrilla operation in the north, possibly using American air and naval strength to impose about the same level of damage and inconveniences that the Viet Cong are imposing in the south." If the Viet Minh became involved in the fighting, Rostow advocated "a limited military operation in the north; e.g., capture and holding of the port of Haiphong."[15]

Rostow's proposal was sent to the JCS for comment on 5 October. Owing to the ongoing conflict in Indochina and the president's interest in counterinsurgency warfare, the Army had already formulated plans and studies examining the potential use of American combat forces in the region. Only a week after Kennedy took office, DCSOPS was visualizing the use of combat and logistics troops from the Strategic Army Corps (STRAC) to participate in counterinsurgency operations in Vietnam.[16] Later, in August, the Army came out with a "Limited War Capabilities Study." Purporting to examine "military operations in Southeast Asia," the study was primarily concerned with the Army's ability to deploy two STRAC divisions to Indochina.[17] The study directed most of its focus, not on the insurgency that was threatening Vietnam, but on CINCPAC OPLAN (Operations Plan) 32-59 and CINCUSARPAC (Commander-in-Chief, U.S. Army, Pacific) OPLAN 32-60, both of which concerned themselves with a Korean-style conflict complete with a conventional invasion of South Vietnam by North Vietnam. Discussion of counterguerrilla operations was terse and focused on North Vietnamese partisan forces, not VC insurgents. Both scenarios ended with Army forces conducting a combined airborne/seaborne/ground assault on Hanoi, whereupon the Communists sued for peace. Thus, it was not surprising that the JCS advocated going into Laos to get at the heart of the problem, which they felt was the DRV. If that was not politically feasible, said the Chiefs, then it would be necessary to go into Vietnam with a force of at least three divisions (the maximum found to be initially supportable in the study).[18] The Chiefs also "provided" (but did not recommend) an "interim course" that initially called for 20,000 U.S. troops, with expansion in force levels anticipated. It was felt that "40,000 US forces will be needed to clean up the Viet Cong threat."[19]

The JCS proposal (as well as Rostow's) was quickly parried in a paper entitled "Concept of Intervention in Vietnam," drafted by U. Alexis Johnson, then a deputy under secretary of state. Johnson noted that the JCS plan focused on protecting South Vietnam from an insignificant external threat, while it "would not in itself solve the underlying problem of ridding South Vietnam of communist guerrillas."[20] A national intelligence estimate issued in October revealed that the Chiefs lacked an appreciation of the conflict environment. It noted that the insurgent reaction to any large-scale commitment of U.S. ground forces would be to play upon "SEATO weariness over maintaining substantial forces and accepting losses in South Vietnam over a long period of time."[21]

Before deciding for or against increased U.S. assistance, President Kennedy dispatched General Taylor and Walt Rostow to Vietnam to assess the situation. Upon arriving in Saigon, they were informed that VC strength had increased from 10,000 at the beginning of the year to 17,000. The VC were on the move in the Delta, in the Highlands, and along the country's north-central Coastal Plain.

While in Saigon, General Taylor suggested that Diem utilize his forces in "mobile offensive actions" to cover the frontiers. The fiction that external support was the prime source of insurgent strength persisted despite intelligence reports to the contrary. As an enticement, Taylor held out the possibility that Army and Marine helicopter units might be made available to support ARVN search-and-destroy operations. Meanwhile, Taylor had Brigadier General Lansdale, a member of his team, work up an estimate of the manpower and materiel costs involved in sealing off the Laotian-Vietnamese border. General Taylor found that the MAAG staff "thought of the defense of South Vietnam in terms of a conventional attack down the coast by North Vietnamese divisions to which the introduction of a SEATO force would be the appropriate countermeasure."[22]

Toward the end of Taylor's trip, Lieutenant General McGarr reported a "serious flood in the Mekong delta area . . . [that] could be justification for moving in US military personnel for humanitarian purposes with subsequent retention if desirable."[23] The flood could not have come at a better time for Taylor, who was faced with the predicament of what recommendation to make upon his return to Washington. Taylor recalled leaving the capital "knowing the President did not want a recommendation to send forces." Yet Taylor soon found universal agreement among the American military in Honolulu and Saigon that the South Vietnamese "needed the American flag to buck them up."[24] Taylor felt that U.S.

combat troops could be inserted into Vietnam under the guise of protecting U.S. flood relief operations and withdrawn upon their termination without loss of American prestige if things turned out badly. This, he thought, would satisfy the military's request for troops while at the same time providing Kennedy with a hedge against failure. Thus, Taylor's report to the president called for improving the ARVN's tactical intelligence and increasing its firepower and mobility through the use of helicopters; developing a "frontier ranger force" to block infiltration; and introducing an Army flood relief task force of 6,000–8,000 troops to raise Vietnamcse "national morale," "conduct such combat operations as are necessary," and "support flood relief operations."[25]

Arriving in the Philippines on his way back to Washington, the general filed another report—"Eyes Only For the President"—which expanded upon the possibility of utilizing U.S. ground forces in Vietnam. Although the flood was in the Mekong Delta, Taylor advocated deploying U.S. troops to the Central Highlands and the Coastal Plain, where "the terrain is comparable to parts of Korea." American forces, said Taylor, would fight "large, formed guerrilla bands" but would not engage in "small-scale guerrilla operations."

The threat that Taylor saw to the task force was not the insurgency in South Vietnam but a conventional war with the DRV or China. Adopting a position to which he would cling throughout the war, Taylor contended that "the risks of backing into a major Asian war by way of South Vietnam are present but are not impressive." The reason: "North Vietnam is extremely vulnerable to conventional bombing."[26]

In his final report, submitted on 3 November, Taylor concluded that the insurgency in South Vietnam represented "a new and dangerous Communist technique which bypasses our traditional political and military responses." Reflecting his aversion to dealing directly with the insurgency and his preference for conventional operations of the limited war variety, the general concluded that "it is clear to me that the time has come in our relations to [sic] Southeast Asia when we must declare our intention to attack the source of guerrilla aggression in North Vietnam."[27]

Thus, while admitting that the "new" Communist strategy of insurgency bypassed the Army's traditional approach to war, Taylor offered all the old prescriptions for the achievement of victory: increased firepower and mobility, more effective search-and-destroy operations, and if all else failed, bombing the source of trouble (in thought if not in fact), North Vietnam, into capitulation.

The recommendations of the Taylor-Rostow mission were reviewed by DOD, and a joint DOD-JCS memo was sent to the president on 8 November. The memo supported Taylor's proposals except for the introduction of ground combat forces, which were felt to be insufficient to convince the DRV that "we mean business." If the United States became involved in a ground combat role, the memo stated, the six-division force of 205,000 troops called for in OPLAN 32-59 would be sufficient.[28] In its summary, the memo held that deployment of ground combat troops must be supported by all necessary military actions—there should be no restrictions on the use of military power to achieve victory as there were in Korea. The memo formed the foundation of a joint State-DOD report to the president on 11 November. The report reflected the awareness of McNamara and Rusk that the president was strongly averse to dispatching ground troops to Vietnam and recommended against either the deployment of a small task force or the establishment of a major military presence. Instead it proposed that the JCS "be prepared with plans for the use of United States forces . . . to defend South Viet Nam and to boost South Viet-Nam morale . . . [or] to assist in suppressing [the] Viet Cong insurgency short of engaging in detailed counter-guerrilla operations but including relevant operations in North Vietnam."[29] Clearly, the thinking at the time focused on conventional operations, not counterinsurgency.

Less than a month after Taylor's visit to Vietnam, John Kenneth Galbraith, the U.S. ambassador to India and a friend of the president's, stopped off in Saigon at Kennedy's request. His impression of what was needed in Vietnam stood in stark contrast to that of General Taylor and the Army Staff. In his cables of 20 and 21 November the ambassador observed that the comparatively well-equipped ARVN "number[ing] a quarter million men is facing the maximum of 15–18,000 lightly armed men." "If this were equality," Galbraith dryly observed, "the United States would hardly be safe against the Sioux." The ambassador argued that if the ARVN were "well-deployed on behalf of an effective government it should be obvious that the Viet Cong would have no chance of success or takeover."[30]

The disparity in the conclusions of Galbraith and Taylor must have been disquieting for Kennedy. There is little question, however, concerning which evaluation the president put the most stock in. Yet while he felt obliged to follow Galbraith's logic concerning the deployment of U.S. ground forces, Kennedy nevertheless approved the deployment of helicopters and advisory personnel to Vietnam. He also concurred in the creation of the U.S. Army Support Command, Vietnam (USASCV), to handle the increased signal and logistics support for the Republic of Vietnam Armed Forces (RVNAF). Despite the president's refusal to commit ground combat troops to Vietnam, by mid-1962 the Army's strength in that country was eight times what it had been the previous summer.

Even as the president deliberated on the action to be taken in response to Taylor's evaluation of the situation, the JCS were planning to upgrade MAAG in Saigon. On 23 November, the day after the president made his decision on additional aid to South Vietnam, the Chiefs proposed the creation of a Military Assistance Command, Vietnam—MACV—with a mission to assist and support the RVN in defeating the communist insurgency. The proposal was approved by Kennedy and McNamara, and MACV became operational on 8 February 1962. Owing to the rapidly increasing numbers of U.S. military personnel in South Vietnam and the relatively small number of nonmilitary officials from other U.S. government agencies in that country, MACV quickly established itself as the primary source of information on how the war was progressing.

Prior to the activation of MACV, General Taylor suggested to the president that Lt. Gen. Paul D. Harkins be assigned as COMUSMACV, and Kennedy concurred. In terms of the nature of the ongoing conflict in Vietnam, Kennedy could hardly have chosen a general less qualified than Harkins. In terms of the billet to which he was appointed, Harkins's military career was remarkable in two respects: he had had no experience with insurgency warfare, and he had had a close association with Maxwell Taylor. Harkins and Taylor had known each other from earlier days at West Point. Both had fought in Europe in World War II (Taylor had commanded the 101st Airborne Division, and Harkins, an armor officer, had served under General Patton). When Taylor had returned to West Point as superintendent, Harkins had been his commandant of cadets. When Taylor had commanded the Eighth Army in Korea, Harkins had been his chief of staff. Compounding the problem was the lack of counterinsurgency experience on Harkins's staff. For example, his operations officer, Brigadier General Kelleher, once mentioned to a USIS political officer named Douglas Pike that MACV's mission was to kill VC, pure and simple. When Pike observed that the French had killed a lot of VC and still lost, Kelleher tersely replied, "Didn't kill enough Viet Cong."[31]

Other men were suggested for the job. Among the names mentioned were Brig. Gen. William P. Yarborough, a Special Forces officer and head of the SWC; Col. William R. Peers, who had had experience in guerrilla warfare while in the OSS during World War II; and Brig. Gen.

William B. Rosson, who had been to Vietnam with Lansdale in 1954 as part of the Saigon Military Mission (SMM) and who would soon be tapped as head of the DCSOPS Special Warfare Division. Despite their superior qualifications, it was felt that by reaching down so far "into the ranks" to find the head man for the Army's Vietnam operation the president would be antagonizing the Army brass and upsetting the career expectations of senior officers in the service. The Army leadership held a dim view of giving anyone out of the "mainstream" a prime command slot and would resent the selection of a relatively junior officer for the billet, which would strongly imply that the Army hierarchy was somehow lacking. As General Taylor put it when asked about the incongruous selection of Harkins, "A general is a generalist who knows [how to do] everything"; that is, a general competently versed in the ways of the Army Concept could handle the situation.[32]

If Taylor placed Harkins—and it appears that he did—he certainly placed him well. Since MACV was to provide Washington with most of its information on the war, Harkins was in an extremely important position. What is more important, Harkins, owing to his unfamiliarity with insurgency and his close association with Taylor, was not likely to engage in any revolt from below against the Concept and the Army Staff's notions of how to handle the war.

Once this arrangement was in place, the chances of a shift in the Army's approach to counterinsurgency through the efforts of those in the service's hierarchy were minimized, leaving only a revolt from below on the part of the Army's advisers in the field as an avenue for change. Yet the power and influence of the latter group were relatively insignificant when compared with the senior leadership's, making Army adaptation of its Concept to account for the special characteristics of insurgency warfare a longshot proposition.

MACV and Pacification

When MACV was activated, MAAG in Saigon was still advising the ARVN to operate along traditional Army lines. Roger Hilsman, working in the State Department at the time, reported back after one visit to the RVN that U.S. Army–assisted ARVN operations were "more appropriate to the European fronts of World War II than . . . guerrilla warfare," emphasizing as they did multibattalion operations into areas that had already been hit by air and artillery "prep" fires.[33] The predictable result, given the size of the units involved and the prep fire "calling card," was that the VC were rarely, if ever, brought to battle unless it was of their choosing. These sorts of operations diverted large numbers of ARVN troops away from providing security to the population, which, of course, was exactly what the insurgents wanted. Attempts to operationalize counterinsurgency doctrine were usually poorly and indifferently executed. A case in point was the ill-fated Strategic Hamlets program, which ran from January 1962 until Diem's death in November 1963.

The basis for pacification was MAAG's "Geographically Phased National Level Operation Plan for Counterinsurgency," published on 15 September 1961. The plan provided a three-phase conceptual outline for counterinsurgency. The first, or preparatory, phase involved the training of political cadres, economic and political reforms, and intelligence activities focused on the area targeted for pacification. The second, or military, phase involved clear-and-hold operations where the VC would be cleared from an area and government control established under the Civil Guard. In the final, or security, phase the SDC would take over from the CG force and provide long-term security. First priority in the plan would go to the six provinces around Saigon (Operation SUNRISE) and Kontum Province (1962 operations); second priority would involve pacification of the Mekong Delta and the Central Highlands (1963); the remainder of the country would be pacified in 1964. The plan complemented the Counterinsurgency Plan, drawn up earlier, and was to be initiated by an ARVN sweep through War Zone D, a VC stronghold in the jungles northeast of Saigon.

The plan was subject to criticism on several counts. It was patently overambitious in its assertion that Vietnam could be pacified within three years. The role assigned military forces of sweeping an area and handing it over in short order to paramilitary forces was infeasible, given the poor state of the CG and the SDC at the time. Finally, while the plan postulated political/military reforms as part of an essential first step, matters such as land reform, a crackdown on government corruption, and a unified counterinsurgency command were never pushed hard by MAAG prior to the initiation of pacification operations. The plan itself, in typical staff fashion, was about the size of the Washington telephone directory and presented such a formidable appearance that the ARVN high command was afraid of it.[34] As it turned out, neither the CIP nor the MAAG plan was ever executed by the South Vietnamese.

Rather than focusing on the American plan, Diem's attention was drawn to an approach advanced by the six-man British Advisory Mission in Saigon, headed by R. K. G. Thompson, who had played a major role in the successful British counterinsurgency campaign in Malaya. Thompson presented his approach to Diem in October 1961. In contrast to the MAAG plan, Thompson argued that the focus of operations should be, not on the destruction of VC forces but on the political stability and security of the populated rural areas. The British proposal emphasized many traditional elements of counterinsurgency, particularly the use of stringent security measures by the police, who, in turn, were to be supported by ARVN clear-and-hold operations. The plan's intent was to win control of the population rather than to kill insurgents.

McGarr voiced concern over several aspects of the Thompson approach. The MAAG chief was disturbed that the British plan did not include a sweep through the enemy stronghold in War Zone D, an operation that the Army hoped would help instill an "offensive spirit" in the ARVN and serve as a demonstration of its new-found air mobility.[35] McGarr further objected to what he felt was the downgrading of conventional forces in the British approach, focusing as it did on local security efforts and police operations. Nor was the Army receptive to the slow pace of progress envisioned by Thompson. Essentially, the British advocated operations to secure the most populous region in the country, while the Americans put their stock in an offensive operation designed to destroy enemy forces.

On 3 January 1962, Diem opted for the Thompson approach, although by then Thompson had made certain modifications that helped bring MAAG on board. Gone was the insistence on police and paramilitary primacy over the ARVN, a particularly sore point with McGarr.[36] With the "compromise" in place and the decision by Diem to commit the nation to the idea, the Strategic Hamlets program was born. It envisioned the clearing of VC-infested areas by the ARVN, whereupon citizens would be armed and trained to protect themselves with ARVN assistance. Civic action programs would be initiated, the police would root out the VC infrastructure, the area would become stabilized and pro-government, and the next infested area could be tackled in a manner closely resembling the operations called for in the "oil spot" principle.

The program began on 19 March 1962 with Operation SUNRISE, designed to clear Binh Duong Province north of Saigon. The operation quickly ran into trouble. Rather than choose an area of minimal VC infestation as Thompson had urged, Diem and MACV chose a province heavily infiltrated by insurgents and close to their primary base areas. The choice was prompted by MAAG's interest in building a series of strongpoints along the route from Saigon to Tay Ninh Province in the Ben Cat region. The idea was to cut the flow of recruits to enemy base camp training sites.[37] The operation involved the forced resettlement of large numbers of peasants, resulting in the alienation of many whose support the regime was attempting to win. Major General Rosson, who observed parts of the operation, wrote a critical report to General Decker stating that "there is a tendency in both indigenous and United States circles to regard the enemy as one who can be 'found, fixed, fought and finished' in the tradition associated with conventional field operations."[38]

Although by no means primarily MAAG's fault, the failure of Operation SUNRISE can be attributed in part to its belief that the essence of counter-insurgency warfare consisted of military operations designed to bring the insurgent to battle and attrite his manpower. The broad sweeps conducted by the ARVN, netting no appreciable results, were, however, only a part of the larger problem. The forced resettlement (although tacitly approved by MAAG), gross falsification of data on the condition of fortified hamlets (many were merely designated as such without any fortifications being emplaced), widespread corruption of government officials, and per-version of the pacification objective into one of exploitation of the peasantry by Diem's brother Ngo Dinh Nhu were all causes of failure outside MAAG's capacity to influence. The only potential leverage open to MAAG and, later, MACV was to advise a cessation of U.S. assistance. When the occasion arose (as in the cases of the CIP in early 1961 and the Strategic Hamlets program), the Army preferred to get on with the war, assuming that if more military power were applied more efficiently, the insurgents could be defeated.

Operation SUNRISE was a microcosm of the Strategic Hamlets program, for the shortcomings of this first operation were extended and repeated again and again over the life of the program. With the program only a month old, the GVN claimed that over 1,300 fortified hamlets had been constructed. By August, Saigon contended that 2,500 hamlets had been completed; in September the total reportedly stood at 3,225.[39] Most were shams, fortified on paper only. In under two years in Vietnam 8,000 strategic hamlets were "created," yet no attention was paid to their purpose; their creation became the purpose in itself.[40] The program suffered from an absence of unity in the command structure as well. Priority objectives were assigned at the provincial level, resulting in a crazy quilt of plans that often ignored the provincial border areas—it was always believed that the adjacent province would take care of it—which often left the insurgents free to operate in the "seams" between provinces.[41]

For its own part, MACV continued focusing on the shooting war. There was no discussion of the vulnerability of strategic hamlets to insurgent infiltration. The emphasis on mobile, offensive operations alienated the population and failed to bring the vc to battle. As Diem's brother Nhu admitted, "Since we did not know where the enemy was, ten times we launched a military operation, nine times we missed the Viet Cong, and the tenth time we struck right on the head of the population."[42]

When not engaged in sweeps, ARVN forces found their niche in the pacification program primarily by holing up in selected villages and ignoring the area around them.[43] After the death of Diem in November 1963, it became evident that many of the so-called pacified hamlets were offering only cosmetic resistance to vc recruitment, tax collection, and political organization.[44]

MACV's position was to support the Strategic Hamlets program, provided it did not interfere with the broader role MACV had set for the ARVN—conducting offensive operations designed to destroy vc forces. If the program could be utilized to promote Army goals (for example, siting fortified hamlets astride roads that were considered infiltration routes), so much the better. For the most part, however, MACV's reaction was one of indifference. Despite the presence of U.S. advisers at the province level who observed firsthand the inadequacies of the program, the generals in Saigon preferred the bogus statistics of success offered up by the GVN. It was certainly a convenient arrangement for MACV; so long as strategic hamlets were a success, the Army could continue developing the ARVN into an effective strike force based on firepower and air mobility. Problems in the program would jeopardize this development and force the ARVN to divert more regular army units into the pacification program. MACV saw pacification as less important to counterinsurgency operations than searching for and destroying guerrilla forces and base areas. To see this, one need only examine MACV's handling of the U.S. Special Forces units in South Vietnam.

U.S. Army Special Forces and Operation SWITCHBACK

Special Forces had been involved in unconventional warfare operations in Laos beginning in the late 1950s as part of Operation WHITE STAR, in which they had attempted to organize resistance to the Communist Pathet Lao. Before their deployment to the RVN, Special Forces were involved in training Vietnamese Special Forces units. The training's focus was not on counterinsurgency techniques, however, but on unconventional warfare. The reader will recall that unconventional warfare is concerned with the *organizing* of partisan and guerrilla forces and their employment, often to harass enemy main-force units or as an economy-of-force measure to supplement the activities of friendly conventional forces. This, of course, is quite different from counterinsurgency, whose goal is the *defeat* of an insurgent movement, primarily its infrastructure and guerrilla forces. While operating under the CIA in the Civilian Irregular Defense Groups (CIDG) program, unconventional warfare operations took on a secondary role, albeit temporarily.

Special Forces were initially deployed to South Vietnam in November 1961. At the time, two "A" detachments of twelve men each from the 1st Special Forces Group (SFG), on Okinawa, were assigned to support the CIDG program, which was then under the direction of the CIA.[45] The program had as its goal the pacification of provinces located in the interior of the country and occupied primarily by tribal groups. Although initial results were encouraging, most of the gains made in pacification were lost when the Special Forces reverted to MACV's control. The two "A" teams dispatched in November were soon followed by another eight in May. In July 1962 the CIA requested an additional sixteen teams for the CIDG program to reinforce and expand the dramatic success they had had since the arrival of the Special Forces.

From November 1961 until the end of 1962 the Special Forces concentrated on pacifying villages inhabited by people belonging to several minority tribes in South Vietnam. The initial target area was Buon Enao, a village in Darlac Province populated by members of the Rhade tribe. The methods employed by the Special Forces were straight out of classical counterinsurgency doctrine. The Green Berets worked hand in hand with the people to fortify their village; they constructed shelters and an early-warning system and closely regulated the movement of people in and out of the area. A dispensary was built, and local volunteers were armed and trained to help protect the village from attack by guerrillas. A small group of men from the village were designated as a "strike force."

This strike force was the only full-time military force. They served as the quick reaction force, assisting villages under attack, patrolling and setting ambushes to ward off guerrilla infiltration, and training defenders for each of the villages in their area of operations. The village defenders were equipped with small arms only and were provided with a simple radio to call the strike force for help if their village came under attack. Once a cluster of fortified villages had been prepared and defended, the Special Forces pushed the perimeter further out, embracing even more villages in a slowly expanding "oil spot."

The initial results of the program were very promising, and by April 1962 all forty villages in the Buon Enao area had been voluntarily incorporated into the program.[46] From these forty villages the pacification program slowly spread, just as envisaged by the "oil spot" principle, until in August roughly two hundred villages were in the program operated by five "A" detachments assisted by some Vietnamese Special Forces.[47] The CIA considered the program a rousing success, and for good reason: by the end of 1962 the CIDG political action program had recovered and secured several hundred villages, some three hundred thousand civilians, and several hundred square miles of territory from the VC, utilizing some thirty eight thousand armed civilian irregulars. These people fought well on their home ground without support from conventional Vietnamese armed forces and had a record of almost unbroken success against the VC.[48] By the end of 1962 the GVN declared Darlac Province secure. Yet even as the program was achieving its greatest triumph, it was undergoing a change that would rapidly strip it of its success.

Operation SWITCHBACK

With the growth in size and scope of the CIDG program, the Army began to have misgivings over the use of its Special Forces by the CIA. In April 1962, Generals Rosson and Yarborough were sent to Southeast Asia to evaluate Army special warfare operations. Part of their mission involved an evaluation of the Special Forces' performance in the CIDG program. While their joint report praised the work of the Special Forces, it called for the introduction of additional Special Forces units, not to reinforce the pacification effort, but for *offensive operations* in Laos and North Vietnam.[49] In a private conversation with General Taylor, Rosson was candid in his disapproval of the CIDG program (Yarborough, it will be recalled, was in the Special Forces and was head of the SWC).[50] Both Taylor and Rosson agreed that the Special Forces in Vietnam were being used "improperly" and that changes needed to be made allowing them more participation in offensive operations. Rosson expressed disappointment that General Harkins had not asked DA for help in getting the Special Forces out of the CIDG program and back into more traditional, offensive operations.[51]

Less than a month after Rosson's visit, MACV made an agreement with USOM whereby the CIDG program would be coordinated between them. As previously mentioned, by July 1962 the CIA was requesting a major increase of Special Forces troops to follow up the success of the pacification effort. In meeting this request, the Army would have to expand the Special Forces contingent in South Vietnam to over four hundred men. This placed the Army Staff in a strong position to argue that the CIDG program was no longer covert in nature and that under the provisions of NSAM 57, it should be placed under the control of MACV.[52]

When Secretary of Defense McNamara met with Admiral Felt and General Harkins in late July, he announced an agreement to transfer control of the CIDG program over to DOD. The transfer, code-named Operation SWITCHBACK, was to be accomplished in phases, by regions, with the process completed before July 1963. Although the primary rationale for transferring control of the Special Forces to MACV was the overt military nature of the CIDG program, it quickly became evident that the Army was bent on diverting the Special Forces to more traditional operations than those involved in pacification. An officer working on special warfare in the Pentagon at the time, Col. (later Gen.) William Depuy, said that the Army Staff "thought Special Forces had a role to play but we didn't want them to play it under the CIA." The Army, said Depuy, "wanted to play its own game."[53]

Shortly after the July meeting, the Army arranged for a colonel qualified in unconventional warfare (*not* counterinsurgency) to assume command of the Special Forces in Vietnam. More interesting was a cable of 15 August from Lt. Gen. Barksdale Hamlett to MACV outlining the "party line" for Special Forces in which the DCSOPS, speaking for the Army Staff, said, "We prefer to see special forces personnel used in conjunction with active and offensive operations, as opposed to support of static training activities."[54]

With MACV's assumption of greater control over Special Forces, changes occurred in the CIDG program. These changes can be summarized as a rapid expansion in the program that did not allow for the proper development of local security forces as in the earlier Buon Enao project and a shift in emphasis from the establishment of mutually supportive village defense systems to offensive operations into VC base areas and the development of border surveillance forces.

Owing to MACV's rapid expansion of the CIDG program and the diversion of Special Forces to unconventional warfare operations, it became necessary to turn the CIDG villages over to Vietnamese Special Forces. Unfortunately, the incompetent manner in which the transfer was executed effectively destroyed the pacification gains made under the aegis of the CIA. The Vietnamese Special Forces were ill-equipped to assume the responsibilities of their American counterparts. They were poorly trained, incompetently led, and insensitive to the needs of the population. Compounding the problem was the decision made by the GVN to integrate the CIDGs into the RVNAF, while cutting back on the number of weapons issued them by some four thousand. The result of this bungling was the alienation of the population and the collapse of the program itself. As it spread into other areas, the program was bastardized. Military authorities sited camps in certain areas for military reasons, with no regard for political or demographic considerations. Special Forces teams started to lift companies of trained "strikers" from one place to another in order to accomplish purely *military* missions.[55] One Vietnamese official later claimed that the most serious damage resulting from the transfer of strike forces was that it fostered among the villages "the mentality of dependence upon the army and the tendency to regard the defense of villages against the local enemy as a governmental responsibility, and not their own. The people therefore stood on the sidelines, uninvolved and uncommitted."[56]

Nor was MACV blind to what was going on. Col. Wilbur Wilson, the senior U.S. adviser in III Corps, where Buon Enao was located, informed MACV headquarters as early as January 1963 that if the government persisted in confiscating weapons from the villages, "the effectiveness of the Buon Enao concept will decrease sharply throughout all the highlands with the side effect of destroying the potential success of the Strategic Hamlets program in restoring law and order." Wilson warned that "VC incidents will increase rapidly once the VC learn that their previous sources of food, manpower, and freedom of movement can be obtained without combat against a strongly defended village system."[57]

Other reports indicate MACV's awareness that "grave difficulty" would result if the Green Berets turned the camps over to the Vietnamese before they were properly prepared.[58] Even as MACV was gearing up its border surveillance operations using Green Berets and CIDG forces, the Special Forces Command and other allied missions in Vietnam realized that the CIDG program was "falling apart."[59] MACV's response to this deterioration was to continue the planned shift of Special Forces to unconventional warfare. Indeed, when MACV assumed full control over the CIDG program from the CIA, it declared that enough strike force troops had been trained to allow the Special Forces to concentrate on operations directly against the Viet Cong.

MACV in Charge

In October 1963, as the CIDG program was collapsing, MACV unveiled its plan for support of the Border Surveillance program, which it initiated on 1 November. CIDG strike forces would be utilized with Special Forces to attack VC base camps and interdict the infiltration of men and supplies from North Vietnam.[60] These units would also be employed in "support of

regular ARVN forces engaged in large-scale operations." The remainder of
the CIDG program would be integrated with the Strategic Hamlets program, and CIDG troops would be absorbed into the regular military force
structure. In effect, MACV was getting Special Forces out of the counterinsurgency business and into supporting large-scale operations to combat
the external threat. Reflective of this is the attitude of the Army's DCSOPS
(and soon to be Chief of Staff), Lt. Gen. Harold K. Johnson:

I was always having the Special Forces studied because I was not very happy with
their approach to the problem. Here was a mobile force supposed to be training
guerrillas. That's what the Special Forces' special talent was supposed to be, and
what they did was build fortifications out of the Middle Ages and bury themselves, surrounding themselves with concrete; and simply building little enclaves
in each tribal area would not have very much utility as far as creating an
environment for a free society was concerned.[61]

The preferred Army mission for Special Forces was not counterinsurgency but unconventional warfare, where they could better support
traditional, conventional operations. Johnson made no bones about the
fact that he wanted to see Special Forces operations "consistent with the
unconventional warfare doctrine of mobile, agile forces operating with
minimum combat and logistic support."[62]

The trend away from pacification was reinforced when, on 1 May
1964, operational control of Special Forces "A" and "B" detachments was
transferred to the MACV senior adviser in each corps tactical zone. This
was supposedly effected to better coordinate the nationwide pacification
effort. The upshot was that the Special Forces, the Army's experts on
counterinsurgency warfare, were now working for MACV advisers whose
background in insurgency warfare was generally poor and whose motivation to utilize the Special Forces and their CIDG strike forces in support of
conventional ARVN operations was compelling.

By July 1964, twenty-five border projects employing eighteen Special
Forces "A" detachments and 11,250 strike force troops had been established. They were spread so thin that there was only one camp every 27
kilometers along the border, on the average. The minimum acceptable
limit, however, was 20 kilometers between camps. The result was no
decrease in the infiltration rate of men and equipment into South Vietnam.
At the same time, Special Forces participation in the training of hamlet
militia had for all practical purposes ceased to exist.

The changing roles and missions of the Special Forces in Vietnam had a
negative influence on the Special Forces Command's approach to its role

in counterinsurgency operations. Col. John H. Speers, who took command of the 5th Special Forces in Vietnam during the summer of 1964, recalled, "The detachments were supposed to be performing a counterinsurgency type mission, yet in many cases they understood the CIDG Program to be a type or variation of Unconventional Warfare rather than an adjunctive tool to countering the insurgency."[63] Colonel Wilson agreed that the Special Forces had in fact organized conventional forces. "These forces," Wilson noted, "man 'bases' which are in fact static defensive positions. Operations conducted from these bases are no different than the operations that would be conducted by a typical infantry battalion under the same circumstances."[64]

By early 1965 the change in the Special Forces counterinsurgency mission was complete. In a letter of instructions issued by Colonel Speers on 1 January, Special Forces missions were defined as border surveillance and control, operations against infiltration routes, and operations against VC war zones and base areas.[65] The missions were based on a study directed by the new COMUSMACV, Gen. William C. Westmoreland.[66]

Thus, while working for the CIA, the Army's Special Forces effectively emphasized pacification and population security operations. However, once CIA control over the CIDG program was terminated, MACV quickly reoriented the Special Forces away from their "deviant" behavior into missions viewed by the military hierarchy as more appropriate and more reflective of the Army Concept. The result was a collapse of the pacification program in those areas where Special Forces had been operating and the establishment of an ineffectual border surveillance program far from populated areas, against an enemy who, for the most part, was operating and receiving sustenance from *within* South Vietnam.

Sticking with the Concept, 1962–1964

The Taylor-Rostow mission to the RVN in October 1961 produced a jump in military assistance. The number of American advisers in South Vietnam tripled in 1962, climbing to over three thousand, although as one observer noted, "there was no change in the advice provided by the advisor; there were just more advisors."[67] The number of American-operated aircraft, nearly all helicopters, reached almost three hundred. The initial effect of this American technological "fix" to the problem of insurgency was a short-term boost in ARVN morale and an increase in its operational effectiveness.

At first the VC did not know how to react to the massed use of helicopters supported by attack aircraft. Their efforts to depart an area under observation rather than stand and face superior numbers of government forces afforded the helicopters an opportunity to spot them and, along with attack aircraft, inflict heavy casualties. This initial ARVN success proved illusory, however, as the VC quickly developed tactics to frustrate the helicopter's effectiveness. The insurgents modified their operations, focusing on quick strikes against villages and military outposts, normally withdrawing in less than fifteen minutes.[68] Employing this tactic, the VC avoided rapid reaction pursuit by government forces in helicopters. Again, the point was brought home that there was no substitute for the presence of Vietnamese light infantry on the ground functioning as an advance warning against the movement of insurgent forces in populated areas. Another effective VC countermeasure was occupying a hamlet and digging in along the surrounding tree line. When the helicopters and aircraft arrived, they bombed the hamlet, while the insurgents remained dug in along the periphery. After the strafing runs, the VC retired from the field unscathed, while the government inflicted damage and casualties on its own people. For some reason, the Vietnamese air force could never seem to break the habit of bombing the village in favor of the tree line. "You can never tell our Air Force that," one Vietnamese colonel said. "The Air Force always wants to bomb the hamlet. You tell them, 'Bomb the treeline, the VC are always in the treeline,' and they pay no attention at all. The French were the same way; they always bombed the hamlet too."[69] As the VC took steps to counter the use of helicopters, the Army did not reevaluate the efficacy of such operations; on the contrary, MACV requested *more* helicopters to conduct similar operations at a higher level of intensity. The new emphasis on airmobile operations also affected the ARVN, which became dependent upon helicopters and firepower as a crutch in lieu of sustained patrolling.

It was during the period of increased airmobile operations that the Rosson-Yarborough visit occurred, lasting the major part of April 1962. Rosson was informed by Harkins that the military defeat of the VC was now "at hand." When he went to the field, however, Rosson found "almost universal skepticism on the part of both US and South Vietnamese personnel that the VC could be defeated expeditiously."[70] Upon his return to the Pentagon, Rosson filed a report outlining the differences in opinion between the MACV staff and the advisers in the field. Somewhat to his surprise, the Army Staff generally ignored his report.[71] The negative reports given Rosson by advisers in the field were symptoms of an emerging revolt from below by many Army advisers against the Army hierarchy's view of how well the war was going and how well suited the methods of the Concept were against insurgents. This revolt was not one against authority but one against methods. Yet the advisers, small in number and influence, were doomed to failure when matched up against the Army brass, who viewed the advisers' message as an unwelcome one, challenging as it did the foundations upon which they had constructed their approach to the war.

Overshadowing these developments in the late spring and early summer of 1962 was the agreement reached in Geneva in July to "neutralize" Laos. At the direction of President Kennedy, Secretary of Defense McNamara called a full-dress conference on Vietnam at CINCPAC headquarters in Hawaii to review the Vietnam situation. Rosson's report notwithstanding, optimism was the byword for MACV at the conference. General Harkins, exuding confidence, contended that the VC would be eliminated as a significant force within one year from the time that a long range, concerted program began to upgrade the Vietnamese armed forces. McNamara demurred, stating that a reasonable target date would see the withdrawal of U.S. forces by the end of 1965. On 23 July McNamara directed that yet another victory plan—the Comprehensive Plan for South Vietnam (CPSVN)—be drawn up to provide for the withdrawal of American forces within the time frame that he had stipulated. On 26 July the JCS forwarded the requirement through CINCPAC and MACV.

In developing the CPSVN, MACV planners worked on a National Campaign Plan (NCP) for the Vietnamese. The NCP contained many of the shortcomings found in previous "victory plans" for defeating the Communists. Predictably, it called for "an integrated nation-wide campaign of offensive military operations to eliminate the insurgency."[72] Again the Army proposed to make VC strongholds north of Saigon the top priority, with the densely populated Delta given secondary emphasis. Simultaneously with its offensives against the VC, the ARVN would conduct clear-and-hold operations in support of strategic hamlets. The belief persisted that the ARVN could defeat the insurgents by taking them on at their supposed strongpoints—the war zone and base camps.

The CPSVN was submitted to CINCPAC on 7 December, initiating a long debate among MACV, CINCPAC, the JCS, and OSD (the Office of the Secretary of Defense) over how many Vietnamese could be trained in a given amount of time and over Military Assistance Program (MAP) funding levels required during the anticipated phaseout of U.S. forces. MACV's second draft on the CPSVN, submitted on 19 January 1963, called for a rapid buildup of CG and SDC forces abetted by the demobilization of the CIDG. The ARVN itself would stand at nine divisions, with a total of 204,000 men.[73] The Strategic Hamlets program would continue to receive MACV's support.

The discussions over funding levels during the projected phaseout period take on somewhat of an Alice in Wonderland air when viewed in the context of what was transpiring in South Vietnam between the summer of 1962 and the fall of 1963. Indeed, the CPSVN was obsolete before it was even submitted, its premises invalidated by the course of events. These events ought to have given the Army leadership pause concerning not only the assumptions upon which the NCP and the CPSVN were based but also the manner in which MACV was advising the RVNAF regarding the prosecution of the war. These factors notwithstanding, MACV and the Army brass either chose to ignore the negative reports presented or viewed them in a positive light, their true impact distorted by the conceptual lense with which the leadership viewed the conflict.

In early October, elements of the 7th ARVN Division, located in the Delta region, were on a routine sweep designed to ferret out VC guerrillas. Such operations rarely located any guerrillas, and on those occasions when they did, the VC usually slipped away, often to the relief of their "pursuers." On this occasion, however, the government troops located a band of VC that chose to stand and fight. In the battle that ensued, the guerrillas wiped out an entire platoon of Vietnamese Rangers, reputedly among the best soldiers the ARVN had to offer. The American adviser to the division, Lt. Col. John Paul Vann, had reported to MACV headquarters his conviction that the division conducted operations only in areas where intelligence reported that there were no VC, operations characterized by American advisers as "walks in the sun." Incidents and reports such as these ought to have had a disquieting effect on MACV. If the ARVN could not defeat the VC in a pitched battle, the Army strategy of going after the VC in offensive operations made little sense. Furthermore, if the ARVN refused to accept the Army's advice to seek such engagements, was that not a cause for a reevaluation of the MAP and the Army's approach to its implementation?

A little over two months after the incident, the ARVN was again involved in a pitched battle with the VC, and again the ARVN was found wanting. The battle occurred in the village of Ap Bac. Intelligence reported a battalion of VC operating near the village. The ARVN deployed a battalion of regulars, two CG battalions, and a company of M113 armored personnel carriers complete with air and artillery support, to assault the VC position. Despite their inferiority in numbers, firepower, and mobility, the VC held their position until nightfall, when they slipped away undetected. Government casualties totaled nearly two hundred, with five helicopters shot down. It was a dramatic defeat for the RVNAF. The debacle was compounded by the presence of the American press corps, who portrayed the battle's outcome as representative of the Americans' overall failure to make progress in South Vietnam.

Incredibly, General Harkins claimed that the South Vietnamese had won a victory at Ap Bac because their forces had eventually "taken the objective."[74] The general's statement touched off a furor between the press and the military. Two days after the battle, Adm. Harry Felt, the CINCPAC, arrived in Saigon and told the reporters that they were wrong—the South Vietnamese had won at Ap Bac. Harkins, following up the admiral's assault on the press with one of his own, said, "I believe that anyone who criticizes the fighting qualities of the Armed Forces of the Republic of Vietnam is doing a disservice to the thousands of gallant and courageous men who are fighting so well in defense of their country."[75]

It is impossible to determine whether Harkins actually believed Ap Bac to be a victory. His contention that in occupying a village that the insurgents had abandoned the ARVN had won a victory was absurd. The Vietnamese foot soldier was not the target of the press's criticism. The press focused their unsettling questions on South Vietnamese military leadership and, by implication, their American counterparts in MACV. Here lay the crux of the matter: if after nine years in Vietnam the Army could not train the RVNAF to defeat guerrilla bands in pitched battle, what did this say about the Army's performance in training, indoctrinating, and structuring Vietnamese forces? Even more to the point, what implications did this have regarding the application of the Army's Concept to an insurgency conflict environment?

If Harkins truly believed in the efficacy of the Concept as a prescription for victory in war, then he had every reason to minimize the adverse publicity involved in a few setbacks until the Concept could be effectively applied, either by the South Vietnamese or, if worst came to worst, the Americans themselves. The problem that Harkins was running into was that in his efforts to present the best light on MACV's efforts in South Vietnam, he was short-circuiting the negative data provided by many of its advisers in the field. The advisers, frustrated at not being given a hearing by MACV, turned to the press or, on rare occasions, attempted an end run around MACV to the Army Staff itself in an effort to present the Army Staff with information that it did not want to hear—information critical of the basic premises upon which standard Army operations were founded.

MACV's Adviser Problems

No group of officers worked harder to change the Army's approach to counterinsurgency than the advisers. They were on the "cutting edge" of the conflict, receiving daily input through their own experiences on how well the operations being conducted were working. Indeed, in commenting on the dismal performance of South Vietnamese forces at Ap Bac, David Halberstam observed, "Apparently the only people not surprised are the American advisors in the field."[76]

As it turned out, the advisers were the only group (besides, perhaps, some Special Forces) deeply convinced that the Army was failing in its mission in South Vietnam. In their revolt from below, these officers managed to disturb the Army brass to a small degree, particularly during their heyday, between 1962 and 1964, when they were the "action" in South Vietnam; however, with the introduction of large numbers of American combat troops in 1965, the influence of the advisers, never great, rapidly diminished.

That the advisers disputed the efficacy of MACV's approach to the war is something of a surprise in itself, given their background, training, and incentives. The Army selected its advisers, not on the basis of any particular familiarity with counterinsurgency, but on the principle that generalists rather than specialists were best suited for the role. According to this criterion, practically any officer was qualified to serve as an adviser, and just about every kind did. The training program for advisers left much to be desired. Given MACV's optimistic approach to the war, negative reports on an adviser's province, district, or ARVN unit reflected badly on the adviser's performance and thus his career. The official spirit was one of optimism; pessimism was frowned upon. Too much criticism could show a lack of progress in one's area and result in a poor efficiency report.[77]

Those officers who did not follow the party line found their career jeopardized, reinforcing the tendency in other advisers to tell their superiors what they wanted to hear. Thus, it is remarkable that a number of senior advisers in Vietnam—colonels and lieutenant colonels with a good chance of being promoted to the rank of general—jousted with the Army leadership over the conduct of the war.

On 20 March 1963, COMUSMACV issued a "Summary of Highlights" covering MACV's first year. In it, General Harkins claimed that "barring greatly increased resupply and reinforcement of the Viet Cong by *infiltration*, the military phase of the war can be virtually won in 1963."[78] This claim was made in the face of strong evidence to the contrary provided by both the American press and many of the Army's senior advisers. Men such as Col. Wilbur Wilson (senior adviser, III Corps), Col. Daniel B. Porter (senior adviser, III and IV Corps), Lt. Col. John Paul Vann (adviser, 7th ARVN Division, IV Corps), Lt. Col. Fred Ladd (adviser, 21st ARVN Division, IV Corps), and Lt. Col. Rowland H. Renwanz (deputy senior adviser, II Corps) all had submitted strongly worded, negative reports concerning the conduct of the war.[79]

The Army not only ignored these critical reports but tried to limit the information that the advisers provided to the press. Shortly after the negative publicity surrounding the events at Ap Bac, the Army initiated an orientation on press relations for personnel destined for Vietnam. If an adviser had something to tell the press, he was instructed to do so only insofar as the comments reflected favorably on MACV's conduct of the war:

Your approach to the questions of the press should emphasize the positive aspects of your activities and avoid gratuitous criticism. Emphasize the feeling of achievement, the hopes for the future, and instances of outstanding individual or personal credibility by gilding the lily. As songwriter Johnny Mercer put it, "You've got to accentuate the positive and eliminate the negative."[80]

Reluctant to accept the failure of its approach to combating the insurgency, MACV was trying to mute criticism of its methods in South Vietnam. To admit that major problems existed required a general reevaluation of the Army's approach to the conflict, something it was unwilling to undertake. The result was MACV's acceptance of bogus claims of progress reported by the South Vietnamese and those U.S. advisers who were "on board," while viewing the warnings critical of the MACV approach as the product of a disaffected few.

Even as General Harkins's summary of progress was being drawn up, reports from the field indicated that all was not going well. One submitted by Col. Daniel B. Porter was strongly critical of the methods used to fight the insurgents: "In many operations against areas of hamlets which are considered to be hard-corps [*sic*] VC strongholds, all possibility of surprise is lost by prolonged air strikes and artillery bombardments prior to the landing or movement of troops into the area. The innocent women, children and old people bear the brunt of such bombardments."[81] Porter also noticed that "commanders of regular ARVN units rarely if ever conduct night operations. In fact, only on rare occasions will commanders attempt to contain VC which may have been 'bottled up' after nightfall."[82] Harkins was reputedly so upset by the contents of the report that he ordered all copies collected, "sanitized," and pigeonholed.

Colonel Wilson, successor to Porter as senior adviser in III Corps, was equally pessimistic. Speaking on pacification, the colonel stated that "in as much as population and resources control measures are the very essence of counterinsurgency, currently implemented controls are considered to be only marginally effective and tend to confuse the populace, lend themselves to favoritism and graft and discredit the national government."[83]

Despite such harsh criticism from its advisers, MACV maintained that the GVN's glowing statistics reflecting success were correct and continued doing so until the utter collapse of the Strategic Hamlets program after the fall of Diem.

MACV minimized the problems in II Corps as well, but here they had a willing participant in senior adviser Col. Hal D. McCown. At the end of his assignment in August 1963, the colonel reported that "during 1963 the posture of the VC has clearly deteriorated in II CTZ." He held that 86 percent of the population was living in strategic hamlets and that the pacification program was an "unprecedented success." The American press, not the VC, was cited by McCown as a "major problem area." The colonel believed that "strong action should be taken by appropriate authorities to improve reporting in Vietnam." McCown concluded his report with the statement, "In II CTZ we are winning clearly, steadily, and as far as I can see, inexorably."[84] Colonel McCown's report is interesting because it differs markedly from the account given by his deputy senior adviser, Col. Rowland H. Renwanz. According to Renwanz, the Americans had problems getting the ARVN out in the field on operations, and the ARVN rarely patrolled an area intensively or participated in night operations. The Strategic Hamlets program was not progressing well either, Renwanz said. The colonel observed that while the Vietnamese claimed that two hundred fortified hamlets had been constructed in Phu Yen Province, U.S. advisers could count only fifty. Renwanz went on to say that "some hamlets were built but never occupied (one reason: no water). Others were occupied through the forced resettlement of people, who then abandoned the hamlets as soon as they could."[85] Renwanz reported that American advisers in II Corps estimated that it would take *six years* to pacify the area. Nevertheless, MACV put its faith in the "optimistic" point of view expressed by Colonel McCown.

Perhaps the most outspoken of the army advisers was Lt. Col. John Paul Vann. Vann reported that his division, the 7th ARVN, was doing nothing. On those infrequent occasions when operations were conducted, said Vann, they were "walks in the sun" or "safari operations," since the ARVN had "advance knowledge that the operational area was devoid of the Viet Cong." Vann cited the Strategic Hamlets program as being "the most important program underway in this zone"; however, he criticized the haphazard method of implementation and recommended that the "oil spot" principle be employed lest the current methods "precipitate a communist military victory."[86]

Lieutenant Colonel Vann returned to the United States in June 1963 to find that his final report, like Colonel Porter's, had been pigeonholed by MACV.[87] Undeterred, Vann took his case to Lt. Gen. Barksdale Hamlett, the DCSOPS. Hamlett felt that "Vann had a lot to say about what was going on inside Vietnam which was completely counter to the reports we were receiving through JCS channels [from MACV]; and they were so different that I wanted him to brief the Chiefs." Hamlett set up a briefing for 8 July. It was canceled at the last minute by General Taylor, chairman of the JCS. Hamlett recalled that "Taylor sort of posh-poshed the whole idea, and as I remember, he did agree to talk with Vann, but Vann never did get a chance to brief the Joint Chiefs on the situation in Vietnam."[88] The reason for the cancellation appears to have been a report on Vietnam submitted to Taylor by General Krulak, the "expert" on guerrilla warfare assigned to the JCS staff. Krulak had recently returned from a visit to Vietnam echoing MACV's optimistic view of the war, a view in which the chairman no doubt concurred; therefore, what need had the Chiefs for a briefing from an adviser exposed to but a small part of the big picture in Vietnam? Had the briefing been given (advance copies had been provided to Taylor and Krulak), the Chiefs would have heard a harsh critique of MACV's counter-insurgency operations. Excerpts from the briefing script provide a revealing account of what was transpiring in Vietnam:

In the field of combat operations the 41st DTA [Division Tactical Area] was the most active area in South Vietnam. During the period of May 1962–March 1963, the number of enemy reported killed was approximately equal to all the other areas in Vietnam combined. I use the term "reported killed." Actually, the number is highly misleading. With over 200 advisors in the field, we estimate, and I stress this can only be an estimate, that the *total number of people killed was less than two-thirds of those claimed.* Additionally, *we estimate that from 30 to 40% of the personnel killed were merely bystanders who were unfortunate enough to be in the vicinity of the combat action.*

Aside from the ARVN's inflated body counts, LTC Vann questioned the method by which they maintained low casualties among their own forces:

The fact is, these figures point out the major combat deficiency that was rooted in the 41st DTA, the unwillingness on the part of Vietnamese commanders to have their troops close with and kill the enemy. The small number of friendly killed is due to the desire and practice of Vietnamese commanders to use air, artillery and long range crew served weapons to kill the enemy rather than rifles. I would gladly have endorsed such a policy *if we knew who the enemy was and where he was.* In the 41st DTA we never had intelligence that was good enough to justify pre-strikes by air, artillery or mortars. *Guerrilla warfare requires the utmost discrimination in killing.* Every time we killed an innocent person we lost ground in our battle to win the people. The majority of the Vietnamese population in the 41st DTA is not committed either to the Communists or the government, and indiscriminate killing by either side can be the deciding factor. Next to a knife, a rifle is the most discriminate weapon there is; it is the last one that was preferred for use in the 41st Tactical Area. I believe *we are encouraging this attitude by making too many weapons other than the rifle available.*[89]

Vann also reported an "almost complete lack of night patrolling" and "night raids and ambushes by friendly forces." The VC, said Vann, "controlled all the countryside at night as a result of friendly inactivity."[90]

Vann's briefing and the reports of the other advisers indicated a need for a reevaluation of the Army's approach to the insurgency. The unwillingness of MACV and the Army Staff to give serious attention to this revolt from below indicated that the Army was uninterested in information questioning its approach to the war. Furthermore, to the extent that problems did exist, the Army hierarchy felt that they could be handled through more of the same (more helicopters, more firepower, and so on). In the end, the Army not only blocked or ignored the negative reports submitted by the advisers but eliminated, in part, the source of dissent. Porter retired upon the completion of his tour in Vietnam, and Vann quit the Army in disgust; ironically, McCown retired a major general.

The Situation Deteriorates

While MACV was contending with its fractious advisers, there loomed other challenges to its prosecution of the war. These challenges (actually, they represented little more than annoyances) came primarily from fact-finding missions directed by the civilian leadership at State or DOD. In the end, they were dealt with successfully by the Army, which, as the predominant source of information on the war, was in an excellent position to counter any thesis questioning its operations.

Representative of such external criticism of the Army was a report submitted by Michael V. Forrestal and Roger Hilsman in February 1963. The two had been sent by the president to provide him with a firsthand appraisal of the situation in Vietnam. Their report, filed within a few weeks of MACV's "Summary of Events," provided a strong contrast to the Army's views on the war. It noted the absence of an overall counter-insurgency plan and the excessive use of firepower, particularly in pacification operations, as major shortcomings. Furthermore, Forrestal felt that there was too much emphasis on "elaborate set-piece operations. These large-scale operations provide insurance against defeat, but they are expensive, cumbersome, and difficult to keep secret. From a political point of view, they have the additional disadvantage for the Vietnamese of *maximizing the chances of killing civilians*."[91] In addition to criticizing the Army's use of its operational concept for counterinsurgency, the report concluded that the war would last longer than anticipated, certainly longer than MACV was forecasting.

Hilsman recalled that during the visit, General Harkins had mentioned two plans for dealing with the insurgency: one dealt with the logistical aspects of the war, while the other, the operational plan, called for a "national explosion." The plan's essence was the "launching of simultaneous offensive operations by ground, air, and naval forces on all known VC strongholds." MACV felt that the VC "will not be able to shift its strength to counter many simultaneous probes, raids, and clearing operations, and that this campaign, carried through without giving the VC respite, will succeed where the piecemeal operations of the past have failed."[92] Plan Explosion, as it was called, represented the Army's approach to counter-insurgency, the ultimate solution being the grand offensive to destroy the VC. Overlooked was the fact that the insurgents were drawing their primary support from the villages, not base areas. As long as the government placed primary emphasis on conventional operations, the VC could always seek refuge and anonymity in the villages.

MACV's response to the Forrestal-Hilsman report was submitted in early February.[93] It weakly disputed the report's conclusions. For instance, the criticism concerning the overemphasis on search-and-clear (conventional-style) operations vis-á-vis clear-and-hold (pacification) operations was countered using data from only the previous four weeks (as opposed to an evaluation of such operations from the time when the Strategic Hamlets program was initiated in March 1962). Even in MACV's small sample, search-and-clear operations were in the *majority*. MACV's rebuttal to charges of inefficiency and ineffectiveness in pacification asserted that "strategic hamlets have proven effective regardless of standards or location" and that "improvement is a daily fact." Yet at the same time, Sir Robert Thompson was informing Diem that the Strategic Hamlets program was out of control.[94] The bottom line on MACV's report was that while there might be minor problems here or there, they were all being dealt with, and all in all, everything was proceeding nicely. The Army would continue operating as it had been. In fact, as the year progressed, the ARVN moved even further away from assisting the pacification program. Data from July to December 1963 show that pacification-type operations—clear-and-hold and security—accounted for only 1.2 percent and 8.1 percent, respectively, of the total of the 246 battalion-size or larger operations.[95]

MACV's sunny portrait of the war's progress shone through McNamara's Honolulu Conference in May. General Harkins, no doubt playing to the secretary's preference for quantitative analysis, presented McNamara with mountains of facts and figures showing that the war was being won. Based on such "facts" and on Harkins's assessment that in all likelihood the insurgents would be defeated by Christmas, McNamara was impressed. The secretary of defense directed the JCS to plan for the withdrawal of one thousand U.S. military personnel from South Vietnam by the end of the year.

Three days after the conference, for no apparent reason, GVN forces fired on Vietnamese worshipers celebrating Buddha's birthday, striking off the active opposition of the Buddhist community against the Diem regime. Diem, a Catholic, had a long history of distrust for the Buddhists, and his suspicion was reciprocated on their part. The confrontation would persist, with minor abatement, throughout the summer, culminating in Diem's declaration of martial law in August and his overthrow and assassination in November. Yet throughout the summer and into the fall MACV's posture on the war's progress remained relatively static. At the same time, the civilians in the State Department, increasingly skeptical of the military's sanguine reports from Saigon, were drawing conclusions quite different from those advanced by MACV. For instance, several weeks after the Honolulu Conference some senior officials at State, among them Averell Harriman, U. Alexis Johnson, and Roger Hilsman, met with Col. Francis P. Serong, commander of the Australian Training Mission in South Vietnam. While Serong agreed with COMUSMACV that things had improved somewhat over the past year, he saw major problems in the

Strategic Hamlets program, which in the colonel's eyes was "moving ahead too rapidly, leaving dangerous pockets of Viet Cong strength behind." The result, said Serong, was that "the Viet Cong still have the necessary basis of support among the population in a great many areas."[96] The suspicions of the men at State were further aroused when it was discovered that General Taylor had been "coaching" COMUSMACV on the most effective responses to provide the political leadership in Washington in order that the Army might continue to operate with a minimum of civilian interference.[97]

In light of this growing disparity in viewpoints between State and Defense, President Kennedy dispatched Maj. Gen. Victor H. Krulak and Joseph A. Mendenhall, a senior officer at State who had served in Vietnam, to Vietnam to evaluate the situation. In a hectic five-day trip the two attempted to do just that. They presented their impressions before a meeting of the NSC on 10 September. Once again it was apparent that the military viewed the insurgency from a different perspective than did the civilians at State.

The reports given by Krulak and Mendenhall differed so greatly that President Kennedy was prompted to ask, "You two did visit the same country, didn't you?" The general stressed that the military portion of the conflict was progressing nicely, while his counterpart noted the losses incurred on the political side of the war. Mendenhall also brought back with him Rufus Phillips, director of rural programs for USOM, and John Mecklin, the USIS director. The reports given by these "men on the scene" were greatly at odds with MACV's official line. Phillips reported that the war in the crucial Mekong Delta, the "rice bowl" of Southeast Asia, was going poorly (thus supporting the earlier reports of Vann and Porter). The strategic hamlets in the area were being chewed to pieces by the VC, said Phillips, with fifty having recently been overrun. Mecklin argued, pro-phetically, that "conditions in Viet-Nam have deteriorated so badly that the U.S. would be drawing to a three-card straight to gamble its interests there on anything short of an ultimate willingness to use U.S. combat troops."[98]

Krulak, armed with data provided him by Harkins's staff, maintained that Long An Province, in the Delta, had witnessed a 300 percent increase in the number of strategic hamlets since January 1963. The general held that throughout the RVN there was a huge increase in strategic hamlet construction and a declining trend in VC incidents. He also noted that according to MACV's figures, only 0.2 percent of the strategic hamlets established by the GVN had been overrun by the VC.[99]

Despite the data provided by MACV showing that the war was progressing well, Harkins was not getting a rosy picture of the situation from all his sources. Sir Robert Thompson continued peppering Harkins with reports of his trips throughout the RVN. During 1963 he informed COMUSMACV that there was "no clear strategic direction of the [counterinsurgency] program."[100] Regarding the drop in VC attacks on the hamlets, Thompson thought that it was much more likely that the VC were making a greater effort to penetrate secretly amongst the people in the hamlets—to set up their underground organizations, to spread propaganda amongst the people, and to coerce them into sympathizing with their cause and joining their secret organizations. "These secret threats to the people," said Thompson, "are just as frightening as those from armed terrorist units and, if they are allowed to go unchecked, they can influence the people to support the Vietcong cause even more convincingly than armed might."[101]

COMUSMACV was also aware that estimates of VC strength had gone from 16,000 in early 1963 to 23,000 in September, yet since 1962 there had been 36,368 VC killed and 9,228 captured (according to the GVN). Since infiltration estimates showed only 3,500 recruits coming in from outside of Vietnam since early 1962, the conclusion had to be that the VC were adding to their ranks by recruitment from the rural hamlets. This certainly squares with Thompson's analysis but not with the data that MACV provided for discussion at the NSC meeting. It appears from this disparity that MACV and the JCS either believed the optimistic reports of the GVN and rationalized away the problem areas or perceived the problems as existing but as not so serious that they could not be managed. In either case, the Army avoided an internal review of its approach to counterinsurgency.

The evidence available indicates that in General Harkins's case the former condition applied. Even as the debate raged in the NSC late that summer, the general cited the large number of RVNAF offensive operations in July and August as proof that the National Campaign Plan was on track. Not surprisingly, no figures were cited showing how many of these offensive operations actually resulted in contact with enemy forces. General Harkins's optimism continued into October, when he was visited by Secretary McNamara and General Taylor. The two were in Vietnam to resolve the Krulak-Mendenhall standoff and, once again, to "get the facts." The trip appears to have been McNamara's idea, and Kennedy reportedly approved it to keep the military "on board," the president's fear being that the JCS might seek congressional support to widen the war.

Taylor came away from the trip with his faith in the Army's conduct of the war intact: the National Campaign Plan was, as General Harkins had stated, indeed on schedule; the VC threat could, in fact, be reduced to low-level banditry by the end of 1965; if there were problem areas, they could be resolved by more offensive actions in the field. Echoing Harkins's Plan Explosion idea, Taylor reported that "only a ruthless, tireless offensive can win this war."[102] McNamara, meanwhile, had been targeted by the American ambassador, Henry Cabot Lodge, for a number of briefings to reinforce the picture of a Vietnam in trouble as presented by Mendenhall, Phillips, and Mecklin in the NSC meetings. The effect of these briefings was to place some doubts in McNamara's mind that things were going as well as MACV claimed.

The upshot of the trip was a compromise report that called for "pressure and persuasion" to be applied on Diem to ease his repression of the Buddhists but also maintained that "the tactics and techniques employed by the Vietnamese under U.S. monitorship are sound and give promise of ultimate victory."[103]

Shortly after the submission of the McNamara-Taylor report an independent State Department assessment of the situation was distributed among the civil agencies involved in assisting the GVN in combating the insurgents.[104] Using statistical data compiled by DOD, the document, entitled "Statistics on the War Effort in South Vietnam Show Unfavorable Trends," concluded that the military fortunes of the RVNAF had suffered setbacks. Striving to maintain its monopoly over the interpretation of the "facts" and, by extension, its freedom of action on the prosecution of the war, the military moved to block further evaluations by the State Department. In a talking paper to the JCS, Major General Krulak, whose position had been undercut by the State Department, protested that the State Department had not coordinated its conclusions with DOD and that therefore the assessment "directly contradicts publicly announced Defense Department estimates of purely military matters." The State Department assessment had clearly struck a nerve in the JCS, questioning as it did the basic foundations upon which MACV had set its counterinsurgency program. McNamara complied with the requests of the JCS to preserve their exclusive right to appraise the military dimensions of the conflict in a personal note to the secretary of state in which he told Rusk, "If you were to tell me that it is not the policy of the State Department to issue military appraisals without seeking the views of the Defense Department the matter will die." Rusk complied with McNamara's request, and the

Army's problem of having its own data used against it was laid to rest, at least for the time being.[105]

The Fall of Diem and Its Consequences

Within two months of his visit to South Vietnam, McNamara found himself in Saigon on yet another trip, under radically different circumstances. On 1 November a coup to oust Diem ended in the murder of the Vietnamese president and his brother Nhu. On 22 November President Kennedy was assassinated in Dallas. The results of these two events were the emergence of the first of a succession of unstable governments in the RVN and Lyndon Johnson's ascension to the presidency in the United States. Despite the chaos following the fall of Diem, MACV continued to present an optimistic picture of the war's progress. Now, however, it was evident to McNamara that the situation had taken a turn for the worse. The fiction of a successful Strategic Hamlets program could no longer be maintained. Something needed to be done. An Army talking paper proposed disestablishing MAAG and organizing a new unified command reporting directly to the JCS, increasing the defoliation of crops, initiating covert actions against the DRV, and placing advisers further down the ARVN chain of command, below the regimental level.[106] A reinvigoration of the strategic hamlets was also mentioned, but by and large, the topic was given short shrift.

McNamara accepted the Army's contention that the external threat needed to be dealt with. In his report to the president he stated his belief that the U.S. must "give the Viet Cong and their supporters early and unmistakable signals that their success is a transitory thing."[107] Thus emerged the Army's solution to its frustration over the failure of its efforts to direct the RVNAF to victory: to attack the supposed source of the problem—North Vietnam—in the belief that if the military could conduct operations against the DRV, it would achieve success. North Vietnam would be cowed into submission; the infiltration would cease; and the VC would disappear. That this course of action ignored what was actually occurring in South Vietnam was lost on the Army, which saw its failures to date not as an indicator of inappropriate methods but as a sign that they had not been properly applied. This perspective is reflected in JSCM 46-64, sent to McNamara on 22 January 1964, in which the JCS argued that "the United States must be prepared to put aside many of the self-imposed restrictions which now limit our efforts, and to undertake bolder actions which may embody greater risks." The memo depicted the problem in South Vietnam as a military problem rather than a political one. The war, the brass contended, could be made to fit the framework that they had originally set for a Southeast Asian war: a South Vietnam endangered by an external threat. The solution was a strategy focusing on U.S. material advantages and technological superiority and emphasizing conventional operations. For example, the memo recommended aerial bombing of North Vietnam and commitment of U.S. combat forces "as soon as necessary in direct actions against North Vietnam."[108]

Despite the Army Staff's switch from optimism to pessimism over the war, MACV was sanguine concerning events in South Vietnam. Perhaps the party line had not been spelled out to COMUSMACV. In any event, MACV would fall in line once General Harkins was removed. The Army, unwilling to admit shortcomings in its advice and assistance to the RVNAF, asserted that it was only with the fall of Diem that the situation had worsened. The Army contended that it had been "on track" with the NCP and the CPSVN prior to Diem's ouster (which had been supported by nonmilitary elements in Washington). Once it was established that the war effort had been going nowhere, the Army adopted a pessimistic evaluation of the situation to facilitate its recommendations for widening the conflict and applying its Concept to resolve it.

The situation in Vietnam continued to deteriorate in the early months of 1964. A series of CIA reports found "the tide of insurgency in all four corps areas . . . going against [the] GVN."[109] March found Secretary McNamara and General Taylor back in South Vietnam evaluating the counterinsurgency effort. Prior to their arrival the MACV J-3 (Operations officer), General Stilwell, prepared a staff study detailing an approach for "vitalizing" the war effort.[110] The study proposed that COMUSMACV be designated as the ambassador's executive agent for pacification, that U.S. advisers be placed in paramilitary units, and that joint U.S./Vietnamese tactical operations teams be established as a sort of combined senior staff to run the war.

For McNamara and Taylor, the visit provided confirmation of the negative reports that they had been receiving since the fall of Diem. Lieutenant General Johnson, the DCSOPS, reported that a great number of RVNAF military operations amounted to sweeps through the countryside and a rapid return to secure bases.[111]

This latest mission had several significant results. First, bowing to reality, the administration canceled the planned phaseout of U.S. advisory personnel, and the CPSVN and the NCP were terminated. Second, a list of recommendations by the secretary of defense echoed the MACV staff study proposals, calling for an increase in the RVNAF, increased compensation

Secretary of Defense McNamara and General Taylor on one of their visits to South
Vietnam.   *courtesy U.S. Air Force*

for the paramilitary forces, the creation of an offensive guerrilla force, and
the introduction of more MI13 armored personnel carriers into South
Vietnam. While there was general agreement among the JCS, the Army,
and McNamara that a greater U.S. response was required, McNamara did
not recommend the initiation of reprisal attacks on the DRV as proposed by
the JCS. In an effort to placate the Chiefs, however, he advocated that they
be allowed to begin preparations for such a contingency.

This take-it-slow attitude on McNamara's part was supported by
President Johnson. It found little favor within the military, however,
where the feeling was that "if we couldn't make the high jumps in South
Vietnam, . . . we should pole-vault into the North."[112] In fact, McNamara's
report was strenuously criticized by both the Army and the other services,
who were convinced that the reason that more forceful action was not
being taken was Johnson's upcoming campaign for the presidency. An

internal memo to McGeorge Bundy from Michael Forrestal reflected the anxiety on the part of the military "that the strong forthright actions called for may not be taken because some advisors close to the President are telling him his decisions should be determined by their impact on his chances for re-election, rather than by what is required in terms of the 'national interest.' "[113]

McNamara's recommendations notwithstanding, the JCS and the Army began contingency planning for the implementation of their preferred courses of action. Over the next few months the military updated and formulated deployment plans and target lists. Discussion was effected concerning the introduction of Army brigade-size forces, Marine amphibious assault forces (MAFS), carrier task forces, and Air Force bomber wings.[114] Air strike target lists for the DRV were drawn up.[115] CINCPAC OPLANS 37-64 and 32-64 were reviewed with an eye toward deploying a portion of the eight Army divisions assigned to STRAF into Southeast Asia. Foreshadowing a future complication, the Army was directed to study how the plans could be executed without calling up the reserves.[116] Evident in all these activities was the JCS perception that major U.S. participation in the war would focus on traditional military operations.

In the spring of 1964 events began generating a momentum of their own. President Johnson's decision to continue and expand upon the Kennedy administration's support of South Vietnam (as reflected in NSAMS 273 and 288), coupled with the decline of the GVN's fortunes, offered little time for reflection on the Army's suitability for the conflict environment in which it had been placed by the civilian leadership. With the approach of summer several changes were effected in Saigon that would profoundly affect the conduct of the war. On 20 June, General Harkins was replaced by General Westmoreland as COMUSMACV. Harkins, his perennial optimism now a liability, had been slated to retire in September. He was ordered to depart Saigon three months early. It had become obvious during Secretary McNamara's visit in March that Harkins no longer enjoyed McNamara's confidence. To McNamara, Harkins was a continual reminder of the failure of the Army's efforts over the past three years. To make matters worse, the general continued holding out the prospect of quick progress if only MACV were given more leeway. According to General Westmoreland, when McNamara asked Harkins how long it would take to pacify South Vietnam in the wake of the disasters of the past year, he replied, "Mr. Secretary, I believe we can do it in six months. If I am given command of the Vietnamese, we can reverse this thing immediately."[117] Not even the Army, much less Robert McNamara,

was willing to accept that contention after November 1963. As General
Hamlett said of Harkins's early departure, "It wasn't a retirement, it was a
relief."[118]

Less than a month after Westmoreland assumed command, General
Taylor left his position as chairman of the Joint Chiefs to replace Henry
Cabot Lodge as ambassador to South Vietnam. Thus, career Army
officers occupied the top two positions of the American war effort in
Saigon. Prior to the changeover, McNamara and Rusk met with the
country team at the end of May in Honolulu. Harkins, now willing to
admit that the insurgency would drag on until at least 1966, proposed
extending and intensifying the U.S. advisory effort to improve the
operational effectiveness of the ARVN. Roughly nine hundred more
advisers would be required. They would serve as the steel rods reinforcing
the South Vietnamese military force structure. General Westmoreland
supported this request, and it was approved on 21 July. Another outcome
was the approval of a directive authorizing MACV to begin joint planning
with the Vietnamese Joint General Staff (JGS) for cross-border operations
into Laos, even though the Army's worries over infiltration rates had yet
to be substantiated. As Westmoreland himself acknowledged, most VC
were recruited in the South. According to MACV's own estimates, less than
15 percent of the increase in VC strength during 1964 came from infiltration.[119] Supporting the idea of an incursion into Laos, Westmoreland
soberly observed that unless some dramatic victory could be won by
government forces, the war could drag on indefinitely.

Taylor and Westmoreland in Charge

Ten days after General Westmoreland assumed command of MACV,
Ambassador Lodge left Saigon, and Maxwell Taylor became U.S. ambassador, with U. Alexis Johnson as his deputy. Ambassador Taylor arrived
in Vietnam carrying a letter from President Johnson placing him in charge
of the country team and the entire military effort in the RVN as well. Taylor
quickly established a Mission Council as a mini-NSC advisory body in
which the various mission components and COMUSMACV would meet, with
Taylor as chairman, at least once a week to coordinate policy.

While the council appeared to reflect greater civilian input into military
operations, such was not the case. The reasons for this were twofold: first,
Taylor himself, having just come from his position as chairman of the JCS
with over forty years of military service behind him, was not going to
overhaul the military assistance command in whose organization he had
been a prime mover; second, Taylor, despite his grant of authority over

military matters from President Johnson, felt that it was inappropriate for the ambassador to involve himself in the military dimension of the conflict. Taylor assured MACV that he had no intention of meddling in its day-to-day operations, feeling that "it would have been a grave mistake had I injected my own judgment into those strictly military affairs."[120] The ambassador was content to have General Westmoreland show him any important cables going from MACV back to the JCS. In adopting this approach, Taylor was, in effect, further shielding the Army from a source of potential criticism concerning its approach to the war. As the representative of the president and head of the country team, Taylor was in an ideal position to promote the Army viewpoint to the State Department. While acknowledging a political and social dimension to the conflict, Taylor still "viewed it unlikely that they could ever establish that solid political and military base which we all wanted in South Vietnam before taking military action against the North."[121] That the ambassador viewed military action against North Vietnam as a prerequisite for success in South Vietnam is not surprising if one recalls Taylor's earlier preference for the introduction of U.S. forces and the use of American airpower in lieu of a reevaluation of the Army's unsuccessful assistance program. In the end, Taylor viewed the insurgency as a military problem amenable to a military solution resting in the application of military power against the DRV.

Taylor's search for a military solution was in consonance with the thinking of the Army brass and the president's close advisers. Further emphasis was placed on the external aspect of the conflict when, on 2 August, the destroyer USS *Maddox,* on a DE SOTO patrol in the Tonkin Gulf, off the coast of Vietnam, was attacked by a North Vietnamese patrol craft.[122] Following a second attack on the *Maddox* (then accompanied by the USS *C. Turner Joy*) on 4 August, President Johnson authorized U.S. aircraft to attack North Vietnamese patrol boat bases on 5 August in retaliation. Two days later the U.S. Congress passed, with near-unanimity, the Tonkin Gulf Resolution, granting the president great latitude in fashioning a military response to the conflict in Southeast Asia. The resolution authorized the president "to take all necessary measures to repel any armed attack against the forces of the United States and to prevent further aggression." Indeed, the incident itself appears to have heightened anticipations all around concerning the deployment of American ground troops into the area.

On 15 August, COMUSMACV sent his evaluation of the situation in South Vietnam to CINCPAC and the JCS. In it General Westmoreland stated that an overt attack by the DRV across the DMZ in response to the U.S. air attacks was "unlikely" but that units of the People's Army of Vietnam (PAVN) would probably infiltrate into South Vietnam should North Vietnam decide to take action.[123] He recommended that a Marine Expeditionary Force (MEF) and the Army's 173d Airborne Brigade be prepared for "deployment on call" in the event of an increase in enemy activity that might threaten U.S. base areas in South Vietnam, particularly Da Nang. COMUSMACV also requested that one Marine and two Army air defense HAWK missile battalions be deployed to Saigon, Da Nang, and Nha Trang to help protect U.S. air bases at those locations. From his remarks, it is evident that Westmoreland was deeply concerned that the conflict would "go conventional" as a result of an overt invasion from North Vietnam. At the very least, it appeared that the enemy might contemplate moving into phase 3 insurgency operations. In either case, the general noted, the ARVN could not handle the increased tempo of combat "without serious loss of government control over sizeable areas and their populations." Hence the call to prepare forces for implementation of OPLAN 37-64, which viewed U.S. intervention in Southeast Asia in terms of a mid-intensity, Korea-style conflict.

Westmoreland's recommendations were given serious consideration in Washington. In a memorandum for the president dated 31 August 1964, McGeorge Bundy indicated that the use of U.S. combat troops might be desirable in the near future and observed that "a couple of brigade-sized units put in to do specific jobs about six weeks from now might be good medicine everywhere."[124] Bundy's hawkish stance was nothing new. As early as the spring of 1964 he had recommended that the president adopt a policy providing for the use of graduated military force against the DRV. In a memo dated 25 May, Bundy had proposed a series of steps, to include the securing of a congressional resolution in late summer, preparatory to the initiation of a bombing campaign against North Vietnam. Unlike the military, however, Bundy saw such attacks primarily as "signals" to enhance U.S. deterrence of DRV support for the VC. In this case, both the military and the civilian policymakers misread the nature of the conflict. Both groups were looking, for their own reasons, at a revolutionary insurgency war that they felt could be controlled, through application of the Army Concept or limited war deterrence theory.

With the coming of autumn, Washington waited apprehensively for the Communists to press their advantage. Surprisingly, the situation in Vietnam remained relatively static throughout much of the U.S. presidential election campaign. The JCS, however, sensing that the lull was merely the calm before the storm, continued advocating some form of air/sea attacks on North Vietnam. In a memorandum submitted to McNamara on

21 October, they again argued that the focus of the war effort should be on North Vietnam, not on the insurgency in the South: "Application of the principle of isolating the guerrilla force from its reinforcement and support and then to fragment and defeat the forces has not been successful in Vietnam. . . . The principle must be applied by control of the national boundaries or by eliminating or cutting off the source of supply and direction [i.e., North Vietnam]."[125]

The period of relative calm in South Vietnam was broken on 1 November, only days before the U.S. elections, when the VC launched a mortar attack on the airfield at Bien Hoa, killing four American servicemen and damaging a number of aircraft. The JCS repeated their recommendation for air attacks on Laos and North Vietnam, to include the capital, Hanoi, and the country's primary port, Haiphong. Ambassador Taylor cabled his concurrence, along with MACV's, that retaliatory bombing attacks should be carried out. Taylor's recommendation differed from that of the JCS, however, in that it was more of a tit-for-tat response. The Chiefs, opting for a far stronger riposte, recommended that Army and Marine units be deployed around Saigon, Tan Son Nhut, and Bien Hoa to protect American bases in those areas.[126]

On 3 November an NSC working group was established by President Johnson to study "immediately and intensively" the future courses of action and alternatives available to the United States in Southeast Asia. The group included Assistant Secretary of State William P. Bundy (chairman), Marshall Green, Michael Forrestal (both from the Far Eastern desk at State), Robert Johnson (of State's Policy Planning Council), John McNaughton (ISA), and Vice Adm. Lloyd M. Mustin from the JCS staff. Harold Ford represented the CIA.

Throughout the tenure of the group, the JCS maintained a hawkish stance, minimizing the potential problems presented by other members of the group if the U.S. became directly involved in the war, while maximizing the danger to America's position around the world if it failed to act decisively. In criticizing a section of the group's draft report drawn up by Bundy, Vice Admiral Mustin downplayed the lack of popular support for the GVN, contending that "a resolute United States would ensure, amongst other things, that this lack were cured, as the alternative to accepting the loss [of South Vietnam]."[127]

In pooh-poohing Bundy's concern over the failure of the French to hold Indochina, the admiral stated that the French were defeated by "political delays and indecisions" which "tolerated if not enforced a military fiasco." He remarked that the American military was not the French military and that they would "make sure we don't repeat their mistakes."

(In partial support of his contention, the admiral noted that the French had also tried and failed to build the Panama Canal.) Other than Mustin, most of the working group members favored less intensive measures than those being advocated by the military. Despite a sense of high stakes in Southeast Asia, they did not want the United States to plunge ahead with deeply committing actions as long as there was some doubt about the GVN's durability and commitment.[128]

The working group developed three options in a draft paper circulated on 17 November. Of the three, one (option A) centered on a continuation of present policies in hope of an improvement in the RVN, with strong U.S. resistance to negotiations. A second option (option B) advocated strong U.S. pressure against the DRV, with the U.S. resisting negotiations until the DRV complied with its demands. The third (option C) called for limited pressures against North Vietnam, coupled with vigorous efforts to initiate negotiations and a willingness to compromise on U.S. objectives. The JCS criticized the options as half-measures and outlined five of their own, ranging from a total U.S. withdrawal to a "controlled program" of intense military activity that would "be undertaken on the basis that [it] would be carried through, if necessary, to the full limit of what military actions can contribute toward national objectives; it would be designed, however, for suspension short of those limits if objectives were earlier achieved."[129]

The JCS viewpoint reflected the "never again" attitude of the military leadership. The message was unmistakable: either go all-out to achieve a military victory, using whatever means necessary, or withdraw completely. These were the two options added to the "half-measures" offered up by the working group. North Vietnamese compliance, the Chiefs maintained, must be achieved through military means involving the destruction of their capability to wage war. On the other hand, Walt Rostow, the administration's counterinsurgency expert, was concerned at the time about sending the proper "signal" to Hanoi. He argued to McNamara that U.S. ground forces should be in South Vietnam to show American resolve but that any bombing of North Vietnam should be "as limited and as unsanguinary as possible."[130] There was no reference to the insurgency in Rostow's memo. In the end, Rusk, McNamara, the Bundy brothers, and McNaughton supported the moderate alternative, option C, although in varying degrees of intensity. The Army's General Earle Wheeler, now chairman of the Joint Chiefs, favored option B.

Ambassador Taylor returned to Washington and joined the working group on 27 November, painting a bleak picture of the GVN's weakness, the deterioration of the pacification program, and the growing insurgent strength.[131] For Taylor, "the ability of the Viet Cong continuously to rebuild their units and make good their losses is one of the mysteries of this war." While citing a stronger government in Saigon and a better counter-insurgency effort as necessary to turn things around, Taylor contended that it was essential to "drive the DRV out of its reinforcing role and obtain its cooperation in bringing an end to the Viet Cong insurgency." Yet, by MACV's own admission, infiltration in 1964 accounted for *less than 15 percent* of the increase in insurgent force levels. The insurgency was very much a VC operation. If the ambassador had truly appreciated this, he would have recognized that even if Hanoi could turn the insurgency off and on like a spigot (and that was a big if), it would not do so in response to the controlled bombing campaign that he was advocating. The Communists had fought on after the French had returned to occupy Indochina at the end of World War II; how likely was it, then, that they would cave in before a limited American military action or even, for that matter, a new reoccupation of North Vietnam?

The NSC principals met on 28 and 30 November and recommended a two-phase program for the president's approval. Phase 1 would be a thirty-day period of slightly increased pressure on North Vietnam during which time the United States would undertake efforts at shoring up the GVN. Phase 2 would involve direct air strikes against North Vietnam. Phase 1 would involve armed air recce of the Laotian panhandle, known as BARREL ROLL, along with a provision for naval bombardment of the North Vietnamese coast. Phase 2, an intensive bombing campaign against North Vietnam itself, went by the code name ROLLING THUNDER. In essence, the program proposed a mix of options A and C. Authorization for its implementation was granted by President Johnson at a meeting of the NSC on 1 December.

On the Brink

The late autumn of 1964 appeared to harken the beginning of phase 3 insurgent operations of a quasi-conventional nature best suited to the Army's preference for conventional warfare. Furthermore, North Vietnam was now clearly established in the minds of the Army leadership as the source of aggression in South Vietnam. The emphasis was no longer on "nation building" but on "nation saving." While the disarray of the GVN was to be deplored, and while the crumbling of the pacification program signaled the RVNAF's failure to handle the insurgency at its lower levels, at least the war was approaching an approximation of the mid-intensity conflict on which Army war plans had been oriented since 1954.

4
Gearing Up for Counterinsurgency

As 1964 drew to a close, the American political leadership stood on the brink of deploying Army ground forces to arrest the deteriorating situation in South Vietnam. Looking at the Army's force structuring efforts in the years leading up to U.S. intervention in Vietnam, one is immediately drawn to the Special Forces and the Airmobile Division, both of which reflect the two changes in the Army's traditional force structure with the greatest impact on military operations in Vietnam. Ironically, while force structuring of Special Forces was executed with counterinsurgency in mind, the Special Action Groups (SAGs) they comprised were never deployed to the RVN as such; on the other hand, the airmobility concept had its roots in operations on the nuclear battlefield and was oriented on mid-intensity warfare in Central Europe, yet the airmobile division was the first major combat unit deployed to Vietnam after the decision was made to commit U.S. ground troops. Finally, Reorganization Objectives Army Divisions, or ROAD divisions, the Army's heavy formations trained and equipped to fight in a general war against the Red Army, actually formed the overwhelming majority of the Army's "counterinsurgency" forces during the years of intervention, from 1965 to 1969. It is, therefore, hardly surprising that the Army tried to fight a conventional war in Vietnam.

Background of the Special Forces
The Army's Special Forces trace their origins to a variety of "special" units that fought during World War II and whose primary role consisted of commando-style operations (raids, reconnaissance, and long-range penetration activities). The unconventional warfare role the Special Forces acquired as their primary mission in the 1950s was an outgrowth of a

program tht originated during World War II in the OSS under William Donovan. Donovan organized Operational Groups (OGs), whose primary mission was as guerrilla forces behind enemy lines. Both the unconventional warfare mission of the OGs and their force structure (the OG section of two officers and thirteen enlisted men) were later adopted by the Special Forces. The Army contributed some soldiers to unconventional operations during World War II, for example, in the operations involving Detachment 101 in Burma, which organized and trained Kachin tribesmen to operate as guerrillas against the Japanese, and the guerrilla campaign conducted in the Philippines by remnants of the Army who escaped capture by the Japanese.

The forerunners of the Special Forces, however, were not looked upon kindly by the Army brass. Indeed, the OSS itself was basically a civilian-directed organization that prospered largely as a result of President Roosevelt's personal interest in the agency.[1] At the time, the Army saw no need for an unconventional warfare capability. Its G-2, Major General Strong, considered Donovan's proposal to organize Army guerrilla forces "essentially unsound and unproductive."[2] Army commanders were equally reluctant to utilize such forces once they were created. General MacArthur refused to allow OSS activity in his theater, and General Stilwell initially prevented Detachment 101 from operating in Burma, calling guerrilla tactics "illegal," akin to "shadow boxing."[3]

Thus it came as no surprise that when the OSS was deactivated in October 1945 the Army's unconventional warfare capability ceased to exist. Little thought was given to retaining those officers who had participated in unconventional warfare operations. From 1945 to 1950 the Army dabbled only superficially in unconventional warfare and not at all in counterinsurgency. In August 1948 the JCS, with Army support, went so far as to recommend that a guerrilla warfare school not be established, contending that "agencies for conducting guerrilla warfare can be established by adding to the CIA's special operations functions the responsibility for supporting foreign resistance movements and by authorizing the Joint Chiefs of Staff to engage in the conduct of such operations."[4] The result was the assignment of responsibility for covert paramilitary operations to the CIA, a decision that was to the Army leadership's liking.

With the invasion of South Korea by Communist North Korea in June 1950, the Army was committed to a U.N. "police action" designed to expel the aggressors. The Korean conflict, heightened cold war tensions, and pressure from Secretary of the Army Frank Pace, Jr., all influenced the Army to contemplate the idea of forming a Special Forces Group.

Yet the way was not easy for the few Army officers who were trying to engineer a revolt from below, albeit a very modest one, in favor of this addition to the Army's force structure. At the time, a small number of men were deployed to Korea to organize WOLFPACK units composed of North Korean nationals. These units were originally formed to conduct guerrilla operations behind enemy lines; however, it was not long before they were fighting in ever larger units conducting conventional-style operations.[5] One officer, a veteran of guerrilla operations in the OSS, commented on the reluctance of the Army to consider organizing forces for unconventional warfare, observing that "so many strictly conventional military minds 'flash-red' at the mention of anything 'special' or at the diversion of personnel and equipment to any channel other than conventional regular forces."[6]

When the Army brass agreed to establish the Special Forces, they were organized under the auspices of and were subordinate to the Army's emerging psychological warfare capability. General Collins, the Army Chief of Staff, authorized the formation of the 10th Special Forces Group on 27 March 1952, designating the unit as part of the newly established Psychological Warfare Center at Fort Bragg.[7] The reason for this was that psychological warfare had a formal lineage within the Army and was, therefore, more acceptable to the service than were elite units trained in unconventional warfare. Psychological warfare was accorded a position in the Army staff organization in early 1951 (the Office of the Chief of Psychological Warfare [OCPW]), yet it would take another decade and direct pressure from the president before the Army bestowed equal status on the unconventional warfare and counterinsurgency components of special warfare.[8]

On 20 June 1952 the 10th SFG was activated, and this was followed by the activation of the 77th SFG on 25 September 1953. Despite their availability, few Special Forces personnel were used for unconventional warfare operations in Korea, and no Special Forces operational detachments were requested by the Far East Command (FECOM).[9] In fact, FECOM was not at all enthusiastic about using Special Forces. Although Fort Bragg urged FECOM to requisition Special Forces staff personnel and detachments, this was not accomplished until early 1953, when fifty-five officers and nine enlisted men from the 10th Special Forces Group were deployed during March, April, and May. Many of these men were disillusioned with their assignment, believing that their Special Forces and airborne training were not properly utilized.[10]

The Army's reluctance to promote the use of Special Forces in Korea for unconventional operations would later be paralleled by its unwillingness to use them in a counterinsurgency role in Vietnam. When the Army did employ Special Forces, it chose their unconventional warfare capabilities over counterinsurgency, because unconventional warfare operations were originally designed to support conventional military operations, whereas counterinsurgency activities did not. Thus, until the advent of the Kennedy administration, the focus of the SFGs was the organization, training, and employment of guerrilla forces, not defeating insurgents.

Structuring Special Forces for Counterinsurgency

Special Forces' expanded role for counterinsurgency contingencies was the result of John Kennedy's election as president.[11] Because of his strong beliefs concerning the need for a counterinsurgency capability within the Army and his strong personal affinity for the Green Berets, it was a foregone conclusion that the Army would seek to give the president what he wanted: a counterinsurgency force structure based on the Special Forces. This is not to say that the brass was enthusiastic about developing such a capability—they were not. Rather, it was a case of the Army satisfying a requirement using the "parts on hand" in such a way as to disrupt as little as possible the essence of the organization: the heavy (armor and mechanized infantry) division.

Immediately upon assuming office, Kennedy pushed for an increase in the size of the Special Forces. The Army responded promptly; on 3 February 1961 the DCSOPS recommended an increase of 490 personnel for the 7th SFG.[12] Later that month General Decker was called to the White House to brief the president on the Army's capabilities for guerrilla and counterguerrilla warfare. In his briefing Decker laid out a two-year program to increase the Army's counterinsurgency capability. It called for the expansion of Special Forces into four full-strength SFGs, to be augmented by three psychological warfare battalions, civil affairs personnel, and engineer, medical, and military intelligence detachments.[13]

Through these early proposals the Army mollified, albeit temporarily, the president's desire for action on the counterinsurgency front. In his defense budget message to the Congress on 28 March, Kennedy proposed a 5,000-man increase in the Army for FY 1962, with 3,000 of those troops to be earmarked for Decker's buildup of counterinsurgency forces. Shortly thereafter, on 7 April, Lt. Gen. Barksdale Hamlett, the DCSOPS, informed CG CONARC that the Army would field four SFGs by July 1962, oriented as shown in table 1.[14] Upon receipt of congressional approval, the Army planned to increase its Special Warfare forces by 500 during the summer of 1961. Once the 7th SFG had been built up, it would begin providing cadres for the 5th SFG, which it was hoped would achieve a strength of 940 men by mid-1962. The 10th SFG, located in West Germany, would not achieve full strength until late 1962 at the earliest. In the interim, the 5th SFG would serve as a backup, if needed.[15]

In a speech at the Army War College on 8 June General Decker outlined the concept around which these four SFGs would operate. They would form the core element of U.S. free world liaison and assistance groups, or FLAGS. Each FLAG would include an SFG, a psychological warfare battalion, and civil affairs, engineer, signal, military intelligence, and medical detachments.[16] FLAGS would be deployed at the direction of the president to assist friendly governments threatened with Communist-inspired insurgencies. Once deployed, they would be responsible to the U.S. ambassador through his senior military adviser (presumably the MAAG chief). In the Army study outlining the FLAG concept, an annex focusing on a "mini-FLAG" for Vietnam recommended that if the GVN requested U.S. military assistance, a 311-man force should be dispatched immediately. The mini-FLAG would contain personnel from all the components of the projected FLAG but at reduced levels.[17] The Army also set about drawing up plans for possible deployment of FLAGS to Colombia and Nicaragua.[18]

Decker's presentation was quickly followed by a memorandum from the president's military aide, Brigadier General Clifton, to the Chief of Staff outlining the president's interest in FLAGS. The memo voiced concern that full advantage had not been taken of the Army's capabilities in developing counterinsurgency forces. In his response to Clifton's memo, General Decker further detailed the FLAG concept. The Army Chief of Staff noted that FLAGS could participate in training regular forces or paramilitary forces for counterinsurgency operations, as well as perform psychological warfare operations, train paramilitary police, and engage in civic action operations. Decker also saw the FLAGS as capable of "providing ready response for disaster relief, which in some cases may prove the only ingress into certain neutral countries and which, promptly and efficiently executed, can have far reaching effects in projecting a favorable image of the United States. The nature and presence of US FLAG will contribute to deterrence and provide overt manifestation of U.S. will and determination."[19]

TABLE 1. Projected Army Increases in Special Forces, April 1961–
July 1962

Unit	Current Strength	Projected Strength	Orientation
1ST SFG	364	1,262	Southeast Asia
5th SFG	0	1,262	Africa
7th SFG	0	1,262	Latin America
10th SFG	346	1,262	Middle East

Source: ODCSOPS, letter from Lieutenant General Barksdale Hamlett to CG CONARC, "Requirements and Missions for Special Forces," 11 April 1961, CMH.

To cover the contingency of widespread insurgent activity, General Decker hit on the idea of a strategic attack force (STAF). In his letter to Clifton, Decker contended that a STAF, comprising an airborne brigade complete with artillery support group and aviation assets, should serve as "the main battle element" to be committed in the event that a limited war broke out.[20] There was no evidence presented, however, supporting Decker's contention that if widespread guerrilla operations occurred, an airborne brigade would be sufficient to handle the situation. Nor did Decker clearly define what he meant by a limited war.

On 17 August the president signed the Department of Defense Appropriation Act for 1962 authorizing an additional 3,000 spaces for Army counterinsurgency forces. CG CONARC was notified by DCSOPs that expansion of these forces would be in line with the Chief of Staff's FLAG proposal. On 5 September McNamara signed a memo designating the Army as executive agent for counterinsurgency. From the Army Staff's point of view, everything appeared to be proceeding on track; however, the formation of FLAGs as the Army's force structure for counterinsurgency contingencies was not to be. Less than two months after the directive was issued, the Stilwell Report was submitted to Secretary of the Army Stahr. In addition to commenting on Army counterinsurgency doctrine, the report questioned the FLAG's workability in an insurgency environment.

To begin with, the report noted, there were problems in planning. The entire development of the Army's counterinsurgency concept (to include FLAGs; staffing the 3,000-man increase; related operational contingency and deployment planning for Special Forces, to Laos, Vietnam, and Colombia; and support of the rapid buildup of the Special Warfare Center) had been accomplished by the Special Warfare Division of DCSOPS, operating at strength levels unchanged from the Eisenhower era. Not only was the division grievously understaffed but there was also the "reluctance of other staff sections to perform duties which [were] properly theirs" in order to assist the Special Warfare Division. This was in part attributable to the desire of other staff elements to focus on "normal" Army functions. The report also found that the Special Warfare Division chief, a colonel, was too junior to deal effectively with other staff sections. Instead of designing the FLAG with primary emphasis on its utility in waging counterinsurgency, said Stilwell, the Army staff was engaged in "fierce intrastaff arguments which developed . . . over the size and composition of the various blocks on the organizational chart." The emphasis was on expanding the domain of one's own branch rather than on structuring the FLAG to fit an overall strategy for its use.

Essentially, the Army's approach to force structuring for counterinsurgency was to take what forces were available and dress them up a bit, attempting to satisfy the civilian leadership, while at the same time diverting as few precious resources as possible away from the "real" Army mission of defending Western Europe against the Russians. Indeed, Stilwell wondered "whether the specially designed FLAG organizations were essential or merely administratively convenient." The report noted the Army's failure to get the FLAG structure adopted (the FLAG headquarters elements proposed for FY63 having been deleted from the Army program by the secretary of defense). A prime reason for this "dismal record," Stilwell contended, was the Army Staff's failure to provide a specific instance in which the deployment of FLAGs would actually fit a given requirement.[21]

Having identified the shortcomings of FLAGs, Stilwell offered a series of recommendations to get the Army program back on track. Since there were limits to the numbers of elite Special Forces that the Army could create, Stilwell recommended that the Special Forces be considered an *ancillary* source for meeting the counterinsurgency mission and that henceforth the Army *as a whole* be utilized to cover the contingency. He also advocated development of a special warfare directorate within DCSOPS and the involvement of the Army in interdepartmental planning with OSD, State, CIA, AID, and USIA. The report had a strong impact on Secretary of the Army Elvis Stahr, already under pressure from McNamara and the White House to do more to develop counterinsurgency forces.[22] Stahr directed General Decker and the Army staff to respond to the criticisms leveled against FLAGs.

In his response of 8 December, Decker took pains to assure Stahr that special warfare had not been neglected. In fact, Decker noted, many of

Stilwell's proposals had been adopted by the Army: the term "U.S. FLAG" had been dropped; the Special Warfare Division was being augmented, with consideration being given to making it a directorate; and the Stilwell Report had been adopted as a "primary reference" for use by the Army in "adjusting itself" toward special warfare.

At the same time, the DCSOPS sent a letter to CG CONARC, General Powell, directing him to look into the potential effectiveness of airmobile operations against insurgents. CONARC was directed to set up a counter-insurgency training program, with emphasis on the use of helicopters, for use by a ROAD infantry division. It was felt that the reorganization from Pentomic Divisions into the ROAD structure would permit standard units "to meet the needs of the many variables of limited war."[23] Thus the ROAD division, through use of its brigades, would provide the nucleus for upgrading what had been FLAG.

The letter also outlined, in rough terms, the Army's response to the three phases of insurgency. Phase 1 was to be met by specialized counter-insurgency forces to advise and assist host nation forces; phase 2 would see "operational assistance" provided; phase 3 called for the introduction of U.S. ground combat units (ROAD brigades). In essence, what the Army proposed was to augment the discredited FLAG concept by tacking on one brigade from a ROAD division to the force structure. Yet this was only a small deviation from the airborne, brigade-centered STAF which the Army had worked up for FLAG. Basically, the secretary of the army was informed that the present organization was considered "adequate and effective," which was enough to get Stahr and Decker off the hook for the time being.

By early January the Army had devised the name Cold War Task Force for the forces formerly associated with FLAG. This change represented trivial modifications in the FLAG concept; nevertheless, the Army did add something to its previous plans for employment—operational assistance, a broad range of U.S. advisory and support functions—just in time to provide a mission in the Army's counterinsurgency force structure for the support forces dispatched to Vietnam in the wake of the Taylor-Rostow mission. The mission of these forces was to train and equip indigenous forces, primarily in the execution of search-and-destroy operations.[24] For the most part, the Army continued to embellish the original FLAG approach. On 29 January 1962 DCSOPS forwarded a request for an additional 2,283 spaces in FY63 to flesh out its four SFGs.[25]

The day before the request was submitted a board of general officers convened at the direction of CG CONARC (General Powell) issued its report on special warfare activities. Known as the Howze Board, after its chairman, Lt. Gen. Hamilton H. Howze, the group undertook a study of the Army's counterinsurgency program. The board was a direct result of the Stilwell Report and the directive sent by DCSOPS to CONARC on 7 December 1961 outlining the Army's revised position and calling for action. Indeed, a considerable portion of the board's efforts were directed toward evaluating the Stilwell Report. The Howze Board convened on 18 December at Fort Bragg on only four days' notice and worked over the next month to arrive at recommendations in such areas as force structuring, training, and personnel. The board concurred with the Stilwell Report's finding that the Army's current counterinsurgency capabilities were inadequate. While conceding that the Special Forces provided a sound foundation, the board pointed out that the SFGs had "too many assigned missions and are provided inadequate guidance as to priority of effort." The Army would have to recognize that with worldwide insurgency contingencies, the buildup of Special Forces alone would not provide an adequate force structure. The board therefore recommended that "Special Forces be considered as an ancillary, rather than primary, source for meeting world-wide requirements for counterinsurgency/ counter guerrilla training and operational assistance; that the Army as a whole be considered the main reservoir; and that detailed planning start now with respect to selecting personnel, organizing, training, equipping and readying them for deployment."[26]

The board suggested that three divisions and three battle groups be given counterinsurgency as their top priority and that three other divisions and two other battle groups be given the mission as a secondary priority (see table 2). The scheme of employment would see Special Forces deployed during phase 1 and/or phase 2 of an insurgency, while "main force battle groups and/or divisions would be sent to shore up the situation in either Phase I or III of the insurgency."

In moving toward such a force structure, the Howze Board recommended that each division and battle group assigned a primary counterinsurgency mission organize, train, and maintain appropriately sized adviser teams.[27] These forces, to be organized under a centralized headquarters located at the DA level, would maintain area-oriented personnel in sufficient numbers and in the proper units to facilitate readiness. To this end, it was suggested that new policies of assignment and rotation of personnel be established so that the units involved could build up their depth of expertise. This would help provide a greater understanding of a target nation's people and culture, important elements in counter-

TABLE 2. The Howze Board's Counterinsurgency Force Structure

	Primary Mission	*Secondary Mission*
Divisions	1st Infantry	82nd Airborne
	2nd Infantry	101st Airborne
	25th Infantry	4th Infantry
Battle groups	2 Panama	
	1 Pacific	

Source: USCONARC, Historical Division, "Special Warfare Board Final Report," in *Summary of Major Events and Problems, HQ, USCONARC, 1962,* vol. 1a, enclosure to sec. 5.

insurgency operations. The board recommended as a first step that an experimental force be created out of one of the battle groups of the Army's two airborne divisions.[28]

While the board saw the need for an increased force structure for the Army's counterinsurgency mission, it envisioned changes in the structure of the divisions and battle groups as well. Indeed, the experimental force tests were intended to focus on the introduction of large numbers of helicopters into such units, the rationale being "that the mobility of the regular force would for the first time, in many situations, surpass that of the guerrilla, and perhaps the initiative would pass to us."[29]

The process of structuring airmobile forces for counterinsurgency warfare intersects with that of Special Forces at this point. The Army, having failed to localize force structure development for counter-insurgency within the special warfare units, was now faced with some very unwelcome recommendations and suggestions from the Howze Board. The diversion of over three divisions to the counterinsurgency mission was not what Decker and the DCSOPS had in mind when they drew up the FLAG proposal.[30] The Army Staff was particularly irked by the board's thinly veiled call for the development of three airmobile divisions to meet the threat, since the board's chairman, Lieutenant General Howze, was a prime mover in a group of high-ranking officers calling for the formation of air assault divisions for conventional warfare. In any event, the Howze Board stands at the crossroads of the Army's structuring of forces for counterinsurgency. In the future, as the percentage of Special Forces in Vietnam relative to advisory and support groups diminished, so would their role in Army counterinsurgency plans. Concomitantly, with the introduction of large numbers of helicopters to the RVN in the wake of the Taylor-Rostow mission, the perception of airmobility as a technical-tactical solution to combating insurgents would gain increased currency within the service.

Had the recommendations of the Howze Board been adopted in their entirety, the forces *deployed* to Vietnam in 1965 would have been significantly better organized to deal with the insurgents than those actually sent over. Even so, *employed* as they were according to standard Army doctrine, it is difficult to imagine how this modification in force structure could have made a great difference in the outcome of the war. The Army's reaction to the findings and recommendations of the board was predictable. Many minor recommendations were adopted; the major revisions recommended in the force structure, however, were either watered down or disapproved.[31] The formation of an experimental battle group/brigade was rejected by CONARC on the basis that it would degrade the unit's operational readiness for conventional contingencies in Europe or Korea. Furthermore, CONARC contended, "Southeast Asia was already serving as a proving ground for the development of doctrine, tactics and material in the field of special warfare."[32]

In lieu of the three-plus divisions assigned to support the SFGs, the Army Staff opted for the designation of certain brigades as backups. This refined force structure came out of the "Special Warfare Study and Program, FY63–68" drawn up by Rosson's Special Warfare Directorate. Formulated in the spring of 1962, the program called for CONARC to designate four trained, *brigade-size* forces to back up contingency forces in four geographic areas: one each from the 82d Airborne Division (oriented on Latin America); the 101st Airborne Division (the Middle East); the 2d Infantry Division (Africa, south of the Sahara); and the 4th Infantry Division (Southeast Asia). These brigades would provide support, if needed, to the so-called Army Special Action Forces which in reality were rechristened FLAG units.

Rosson's study noted "real problems relative to creating four Special Action Forces . . . while at the same time, maintaining a mobile Army strategic reserve adequate for contingencies and general war."[33] Establishing the Army's concern for conventional war contingencies over those involving counterinsurgency, the study rejected the Howze Board's force structure suggestion. Support brigades could be allowed only as long as they were drawn "from current minimum essential Army forces . . . [and] provided it does not degrade the capabilities of these forces to respond immediately and adequately to contingency and general war situations."[34] Thus, force structuring for counterinsurgency was viewed as very much a resource allocation problem, pitting the Army's need of and preference for conventional forces for its traditional contingency of war in Europe against the new requirements placed on the service to address the problem of Third World insurgencies. The parameters established in the Army's Special Warfare program implied minimal diversion of "standard" Army units (as opposed to "special" forces) from their preparation for mid-intensity conflict. This is not to say that preparing for mid- or high-intensity conflict was not important—it was. It does demonstrate, however, the Army's emphasis on maintaining conventional forces, to the point where it disregarded the recommendations of the Stilwell Report and the Howze Board, not to mention the wishes of the president, to become fully involved in the counterinsurgency mission. As one colonel at DCSOPS recalled, Decker's attention was focused on Europe and, to a lesser extent, Japan: "He pointed out that our primary emphasis must be in Europe. With the exception of Japan, the areas in the East have nothing to contribute toward our survival. Therefore, we could lose in Asia without losing everything but to lose in Europe would be fatal. . . . he was not willing to reduce capabilities in Europe to improve capabilities for Southeast Asia."[35]

The end result involved little more than Decker's original FLAG organization with the STAF airborne brigade as backup. By October 1962 commands such as CONARC and USARPAC were notified that SAFs were to be created within their organizations and directed to designate a ROAD-sized infantry brigade to support them in line with the Special Warfare program.[36]

From the implementation of the Army Special Warfare program in the fall of 1962 until the commitment of U.S. ground troops in Vietnam in 1965, SAFs with associated brigade backups remained the Army's force for counterinsurgency. By 1965, five infantry brigades served as backup forces for seven SFGs. Plans called for the fleshing out of an additional brigade to provide for six SAFs to carry the Army into the 1970s.[37]

In evaluating the SAFs, two major points stand out. The first is the lack of counterinsurgency training afforded backup brigades. Area/country orientation training comprised only two days of classes per year. Counterinsurgency training was limited to six weeks each year, the culmination of which was a battalion-size field exercise requiring offensive military action designed to destroy a hostile guerrilla force.[38] Thus, only 12 percent of a backup brigade's training was devoted to counterinsurgency (or, more accurately, search-and-destroy) operations; the vast majority was devoted to "normal" conventional operations. Even without taking into consideration the personnel turbulence as troops rotated in and out of the brigade over the course of a year, such a small slice of training time was wholly ineffective in weaning the brigade away from traditional operations and giving it a solid counterinsurgency capability.

The second point, one that says a lot concerning how the Army viewed both the war in Vietnam and the SAFs, is that SAFs were never committed to Southeast Asia. The deployment of properly trained SAFs could have substantially bolstered the pacification program in the RVN. Unfortunately, the Army, its perceptions skewed by its Concept, neither trained nor deployed the SAFs in anything approaching a satisfactory mode for counterinsurgency warfare.

Thus the Special Forces' role in the Army's force structuring for counterinsurgency was not to spearhead an imaginative program designed to generate the counterinsurgency capability necessary if the Army was to meet its assigned mission. Rather, the Special Forces became the Army's only force (and an ill-employed force, at that) dedicated to the newly acquired counterinsurgency mission. More than anything else, they would be cited as proof that the Army was doing something to prepare for low-intensity contingencies. Their primary function, therefore, would be to provide the Army with a front behind which it could continue to develop forces for the familiar European contingency.

Background of the Airmobile Concept

The primary modification to the Army's force structure in the period before the commitment of combat units to South Vietnam was the formation of an airmobile division. The creation of airmobile units, with their great numbers of helicopters affording dramatic increases in mobility, has been cited as the Army's force structuring solution to the dilemma posed by the VC mobile guerrilla units. Evidence of this, it is said, can be found in the early deployment of helicopters to Vietnam and the creation of Army airmobile combat forces, with the 1st Cavalry Division (Airmobile) being the first Army divisional organization sent to the RVN.

In fact, the airmobile concept did not develop within the framework of counterguerrilla warfare. Rather, it was the brainchild of a small group of officers who believed that an Army capability to rapidly concentrate and disperse troops on a nuclear battlefield in Europe was essential to its survival. When the mission to develop forces capable of waging counterinsurgency was given to the Army in the early 1960s, the traditional counterinsurgency doctrinal call for light, mobile infantrymen was modified by the Army Concept. Airmobile forces were "light," but only relative to the standard armor or mechanized infantry division. They were mobile—*air*-mobile; the troops they carried were not necessarily *ground*-mobile. This technical "fix" to the problem of counterinsurgency force structuring extended to airmobility training as well—nearly all of it remained centered on conventional operations.

The Army's first significant addition of airmobile capability came in 1952 when, based on the favorable experience the Marines had with helicopters in Korea, the Army formed twelve helicopter battalions. By 1955 the use of helicopters under certain circumstances as an alternate mode of troop and logistical transportation had achieved a measure of acceptance within the Army.

A primary proponent of an expanded role for the helicopter was Lt. Gen. James Gavin, then serving as the DCSOPS on the Army Staff. In an article in the April 1954 issue of *Harper's,* Gavin offered a vision of helicopters, not as a specialized transportation asset within a few select units, but as combat vehicles for rapidly concentrating and dispersing the Army's forces on the battlefield.[39] Shortly after his article appeared in print, Gavin was successful in establishing the position of director of Army aviation, first filled by then Brig. Gen. Hamilton Howze.[40]

Not long before his departure from the service, Gavin had a detailed study prepared outlining the factors involved in equipping the entire Army with helicopter support units. Barksdale Hamlett, then an assistant to General Lemnitzer, the deputy chief of staff for Plans, Operations, and R&D (Research and Development), took the study to his boss for an evaluation. When Hamlett informed Lemnitzer that the price tag for such a program would be $3 billion, he rejected it out of hand. Lemnitzer said, "They are out of their minds. Just send it back and say, 'We're not ready for this yet.' "[41] It was apparent that with the Army struggling to maintain itself under Eisenhower's "New Look," costly solutions under a budget-conscious administration were not welcomed by the Army leadership. Yet even after Gavin's retirement the movement persisted. The problem, as General Howze recalled, was to convince the Army brass that airmobility would fit into the overall Army Concept. It was important, said Howze, "that whatever we developed by way of concept had to work in the European terrain."[42]

As director of Army aviation from 1955 to 1958, General Howze promoted airmobility through a series of tests at the C&GSC in which an air cavalry brigade was substituted for a U.S. armored division, with the mission of delaying the advance of three Soviet divisions in West Germany. The highly mobile air cavalry brigade did a better job of holding off the Russians. As for the utility of heliborne forces in "small wars," airmobile enthusiasts contended that owing to their superior mechanical mobility, they could apply firepower better than standard divisions:

The forces for the small war do not require the heavy organizations and equipment with which our divisions fought in Korea. This organization and equipment were designed for heavy and sustained warfare in Western Europe, and not for warfare in mountains, jungles, deserts, or other areas of the world (i.e., any place besides Western Europe and the United States) where road systems are limited or missing.

Light forces of high mobility and firepower will answer this requirement. Mobility again becomes the key for the Army's preparation for the contingency of further small wars. This mobility cannot be achieved through minor product improvements in surface vehicles. Only by putting the soldier into a flying machine will we be able to give him superior mobility over indigenous forces, partisans, etc., of the small wars. *The required forces, then, for the small war appear to be much the same as those for the atomic war against the Soviet Union.*[43]

Thus, development of the airmobile concept was accomplished with conventional and nuclear wars, not counterinsurgency, in mind. As one of the Young Turks involved in the movement recalled, "Our first doctrine in all of our thinking in Army Aviation was geared to the sophisticated battlefield, not guerrilla and that type of battlefield. . . . It wasn't geared to Vietnam and the jungle at all."[44]

While the Army brass was unenthusiastic over the prospect of having helicopter units throughout the service, and downright skeptical about their utility in combat, the Army's organizational goals, coupled with some pressure from the political leadership, served to boost the stock of the airmobility advocates. The first factor aiding the cause of airmobility was the Army's enduring dissatisfaction with the close air support provided by the Air Force. The Army's solution was to create its own air force. The 1950s had witnessed the rapid growth of Army aviation. In 1950 the Army inventory comprised 668 light airplanes and 57 helicopters; by 1960 the Army had acquired over 5,000 aircraft of fifteen different varieties. The Air Force watched uneasily as the Army became the acknowledged leader in vertical flight and ground effects machines. Against strenuous Air Force objections, the Army "borrowed" three Air Force T-37 jets for testing, and a number of Army aviators were being qualified in various aircraft from other services and NATO. Adding to its concerns, the Air Force found itself described in front of a congressional committee as the "silent silo sitters of the seventies," a reference to the impending addition of large numbers of ICBMs to the service's force structure.[45]

Thus, the helicopter offered the Army a means of increasing its air support while, at the same time, effecting pressure on the Air Force to enhance its ground support capabilities or risk losing the mission (along with the budget slice) of providing its sister service's close air support.[46] Yet despite the growing enthusiasm for airmobility in some Army quarters, the only unit that attempted a significant structural change during this period was the 101st Combat Aviation Battalion (Provisional), the first such organization in the Army. Ironically, the division commander was Maj. Gen. William C. Westmoreland.

McNamara and Airmobility's Coming of Age

With the arrival of the Kennedy administration came a commitment on the part of the civilian leadership to structure military forces according to Flexible Response. Secretary of Defense Robert McNamara was instructed by the president to "develop the force structure necessary to our military requirements without regard to arbitrary or predetermined budget ceilings. And secondly, having determined that force structure . . . procure it at the lowest possible cost."[47]

Kennedy's approach was rational in that it attempted to tailor forces to meet his chosen strategy instead of the other way around, as was generally the case in the Eisenhower era. This implied a significant boost over time to the military budget, albeit a "cost-effective" boost under McNamara's PPBS approach. The change in both the strategic and the budgetary approach had an unusual effect on Army airmobility. The Army, which had ostensibly rejected the development and testing of airmobile combat forces as being too expensive under the Eisenhower administration, continued to soft-pedal the idea. The airmobile advocates, meanwhile, had to engage in a bit of rethinking. Their original selling efforts had revolved around the need for such forces in the projected nuclear environment of Massive Retaliation. Now the Army was being told to prepare for mid- and low-intensity conflict as well, and the brass was looking at beefing up its heavy divisions, not airmobility. Fortunately for the Army's airmobile advocates, OSD was interested in the idea of airmobile forces. Given a free hand to structure the forces most capable of doing the job, McNamara could afford to opt for airmobility if it proved "cost-effective." Thus, the increased cost of developing an air assault Army force structure would not be rejected out of hand, as in the Eisenhower administration, but would compete with alternative options to determine which force structure could provide the most cost-effective Army under Flexible Response.

McNamara's interest in airmobility was first sparked in late September 1961 when he reviewed the Army's aviation plans. On 4 October he conferred with Gen. Clyde D. Eddleman, Army Vice Chief of Staff, and Brigadier General von Kann, director of Army aviation. The secretary questioned them about what he saw as an Army helicopter procurement program strung out over too many years. Did the Army need these helicopters or not? If the answer was yes, then it made sense to procure them earlier and in large numbers. McNamara directed the secretary of the Army to undertake a study of all Army aviation requirements, with a warning that "I shall be disappointed if the Army's reexamination merely produces logistically oriented recommendations to procure more of the same, rather than a plan for employment of fresh and perhaps unorthodox concepts which will give us a significant increase in mobility."[48] McNamara's concern apparently derived from an OSD report highly critical of the Army aviation program. The report contended that "the Army had adopted a doctrinal concept that modern warfare requires order of magnitude increases in battle area mobility of all military missions involving movement. But the Army research, development, and procurement programs devote most of their resources to improvements in surface mobility which can produce only marginal capability improvements."[49] The report concluded that the Army was reluctant to commit resources to a program to substantially increase its airmobility assets, preferring to concentrate instead on other "vital needs," such as the development of the heavy ROAD divisions.

Indeed, in the early 1960s the Army was obsessed with the restructuring of its heavy divisions. Just as the Army feared that resources in the form of brigades and divisions would be siphoned off to support the counterinsurgency force structure, it also feared that the same would occur (compounded by a major drain in budgetary funds) if the airmobile force structure took hold.

While McNamara was forcing an Army reevaluation of airmobility, the service felt that it was already devising the force structure for the new strategy of flexible response. The forces were built around the ROAD division, and the flexibility was to come from the divisional structure and from the newly organized STRICOM.

The ROAD division was developed beginning in March 1961, at the direction of General Decker. The new force structure for the Army division provided a large measure of flexibility, but not for low-intensity conflict. The ROAD system furnished a heavier division than did the Pentomic system, for the Army viewed its responsibility in terms of how to best prepare for war in a mid-intensity conflict environment. If that requirement could be met, it was felt, then the Army could shift gears without too much difficulty for either a nuclear or brushfire war. This confident attitude was reflected in the statements of the Army Chiefs of Staff during the period in question. For instance, General Decker later remarked, "I am very grateful that we were able to get this reorganization achieved before the action in Vietnam, because I don't believe the Pentomic Division would have been a very suitable vehicle for combat of a sustained nature as it has been in Vietnam."[50] General Wheeler, Decker's successor as Army Chief of Staff, said at the time, "We don't want to use a sledge hammer to drive a tack and, therefore, have created versatile, and flexible general purpose forces which can be tailored to the requirements of emergency situations with the least danger of expanding the conflict into unwanted general war. For these purposes also, the relatively new United States Strike Command, STRICOM, has been provided eight combat-ready Army divisions, a commensurate amount of Tactical Air combat power, and the necessary airlift to cope with a number of limited war situations."[51]

Thus, the flexibility of the ROAD system in the Army's traditional mid-intensity conflict environment was translated into absolute flexibility in any conflict environment. That ROAD divisions were neither trained nor equipped for counterinsurgency was lost on the Army. In fact, in neither the original directive to review the Pentomic structure nor the briefing on ROAD given by CONARC was the use of the new division for low-intensity conflict considered. Wargaming tests of ROAD focused strictly on conventional operations.[52]

Nevertheless, it was decided that eight ROAD divisions would form the Army components of STRICOM, activated on 9 October 1961. The organization was commanded by an Army general (with an Air Force lieutenant general as his deputy, reflecting the Tactical Air Command's contribution to the force). STRICOM was the apotheosis of what the Army was looking for in Flexible Response; indeed, not only was STRICOM the embodiment of the Kennedy administration's drive for a greater number of conventional options but it was the means of bringing the Air Force and the Army back into the formidable air-ground combination that had dominated the land battles of World War II and Korea. STRICOM's mission, said Wheeler, would be to "provide a general reserve of combat ready forces to reinforce other unified commands, plan and conduct contingency operations as directed by the Joint Chiefs of Staff, and plan for and conduct *normal* operations in the Middle East/Southern Asia and Africa South of the Sahara (the MEAFSA role)."[53] Of interest is STRICOM's mission in the "hot spot" areas of budding or ongoing insurgencies, namely, the Middle East,

Southern Asia, and Africa. Both plans and operations were to be "normal." It was hoped that if standard Army units found themselves in an insurgency environment such as Vietnam, the combination of U.S. tactical advice, modern firepower, rapid communications, air support, and the growing mobility provided by armored personnel carriers and air transport would provide the needed margin of superiority.[54]

In fact, as late as 1963, instructors at the C&GSC had their students conduct hypothetical "counterinsurgency" operations involving some 15,000 armed insurgents backed by 100,000 civilian supporters in a fictitious country resembling the West African state of Ghana. The approved solution was the dispatch of two U.S. Army STRICOM divisions with standard combat service support to defeat the insurgents. Despite the vehement objections from British student officers who had had firsthand experience in the Malayan insurgency, the C&GSC faculty would not abandon its belief that this scenario represented the role of the Army in future insurgencies.[55] This strong focus on the development of an optimal force structure for conducting operations according to the Concept would serve to retard the development of airmobility and would nearly eliminate it.

Activation of the Airmobile Division

Despite the Army leadership's lack of enthusiasm for airmobility, its proponents continued pushing for its acceptance. The thrust of their arguments fell along two lines: the first, and most important, contended that airmobile combat forces enhanced the Army's ability to wage conventional war in Europe; the second offered the helicopter as a technological "fix" for the ARVN's lack of success in countering the Communist insurgency.

The Stilwell Report was an early reflection of the second argument. Citing the RVN's need for air support to facilitate counterinsurgency operations, the report called for CONARC "to determine, as a matter of priority, the role and responsibilities of Army aviation in support of paramilitary and psychological operations, offensive and defensive, in war and short thereof."[56]

Responding to criticism leveled against its efforts on the counterinsurgency front, the Army Staff decided to adopt the report's recommendation. On 7 December 1961, CONARC was directed to submit a plan that would include a detailed operational concept for the conduct of operations against irregular forces with primary emphasis on airmobile operations and a training program and test suitable for use by a ROAD infantry division in developing detailed doctrine to support the operational concept provided.[57] Further impetus was given to the airmobility concept by the Howze Board, whose report reflected the strong interest of its chairman in the potential utility of helicopters in the Army's force structure. Following Secretary McNamara, the board recommended that "DA increase materially the procurement of HU-I helicopters."

These events notwithstanding, the Army continued dragging its feet on airmobility. The leadership's attitude regarding the creation of airmobile forces was similar to its perspective on Special Forces, the feeling being that they threatened projects (such as ROAD) that were in consonance with the Concept by siphoning off funds and personnel.[58] The Army leadership, Gen. Harry W. O. Kinnard recalled, held that it was "better to take these 'Fancy Dan' type elements and disperse them throughout the Army so you have a [widespread] leavening of quality . . . instead of draining off the quality by putting [them] in special units."[59]

Fortunately for the airmobility advocates, one of their members, Gen. Robert R. Williams, was working in OSD at the time. Williams helped persuade the systems analysis civilians close to McNamara "that the Army had not thought out what its real requirement was for Army Aviation."[60]

Having gained the ear of the secretary of defense through his assistants, General Williams, along with one of his aides, Col. Edwin L. Powell, wrote a draft directive to the Army Staff instructing it to set up an airmobility board with General Howze as chairman and to fill out the board with other airmobility enthusiasts. At the same time, to prevent any watering down of the board's findings by the Army Staff, they drafted a letter to the secretary of the Army directing him to forward the board's findings directly to OSD.[61] To the surprise of Williams and Powell and the anger of the Army brass, McNamara approved both letters on 19 April. General Kinnard recalled that General Decker "was quite upset about this obvious attempt to tell the Army how to do its work."[62] Yet, the feeling was that had General Williams not made his secret end run around the Army Staff, the Army would have continued soft-pedaling airmobility indefinitely.

Within a week after receiving McNamara's directives, the Army appointed General Howze, commander of STRAC and the XVIIIth Airborne Corps, as president of the ad hoc U.S. Army Tactical Mobility Requirements Board, with instructions to reexamine the Army's role in aviation and the corresponding aircraft requirements. The Howze Board on Army Airmobility, as it became known, worked the better part of the summer to complete its task. Evidently, board members saw it as an opportunity to sell the Army on how well airmobility could conduct conventional operations. As General Williams put it, "Vietnam was pretty much on the back burner at that time." Kinnard, who would command both the test organization of the airmobility concept (the 11th Air Assault Division) and the Army's airmobile division (the 1st Air Cavalry), recalled that Howze felt that if the airmobile concept "only worked in the lowest intensity the Army would never make a major commitment to it. It had to be valid in the mid- and high-[intensity conflicts]." "We felt," said Kinnard, "that if we could make it applicable to mid-intensity and high-intensity . . . it would be effective at a lower level."[63]

The board submitted its final report on 20 August. It called for the addition of an air assault division to the Army's force structure comprising 459 aircraft (nearly all helicopters), as opposed to roughly 100 aircraft in ROAD divisions. The board also recommended the organization of an air cavalry brigade comprising 316 aircraft, 144 of which would be attack helicopters. The cost of the divisional structure was projected to be 50 percent greater than that of an infantry division, although its firepower would be significantly less.

The board presented five program options, with the preferred option deleting five ROAD divisions from the proposed sixteen-division Army force, replacing them with an equal number of air assault divisions. Also included in the new force structure were three air cavalry brigades and five air transport brigades. General Howze saw the primary advantages of the airmobile forces as mobility, utility in delay operations, the ability to "ambush" conventional forces, and the ability to provide direct firepower. The general made no direct reference to their usefulness against insurgents.[64]

Meanwhile, fifteen armed HU-1 "Huey" helicopters were deployed to Vietnam in September. They were to be evaluated as to their suitability in counterinsurgency operations by the Army Concept Team in Vietnam (ACTIV), headed by Brig. Gen. Edward Rowny, a member of the Howze Board. ACTIV, established as an Army test team by approval of the secretary of defense on 11 September, was directed to conduct tests for the purpose of "evaluating new or improved operational and organizational concepts, doctrine, tactics, techniques and procedures, and to gain further information on materiel."[65] According to Rowny, the team sought better ways to "find and fix" guerrillas.[66] To this end, his concern focused almost exclusively on armored vehicle performance, communications, and air-mobility; indeed, nearly half of the team's effort was in the helicopter field. Reflecting the Army's tendency to fit the insurgency within the familiar parameters of the Concept, the team scored its greatest successes in these areas. ACTIV's work helped ensure that when large numbers of helicopters were introduced into the RVN, they would facilitate traditional Army operations, not counterinsurgency. The Army's willingness to accept the airmobility provided by helicopters in lieu of the foot mobility required for counterinsurgency operations is another example of the Army's failure to adapt its forces and doctrine to the requirements of a new conflict environment. As one of General Harkins's corps advisers stated, "Mobility means vehicles and aircraft. You have seen the way our Vietnamese units are armed—fifty radios, thirty or forty vehicles, rockets and mortars and airplanes. The Viet Cong have no vehicles and no airplanes. How can they be mobile?"[67]

While the Army utilized helicopters in Vietnam as a means of increasing its ability to engage in traditional military operations, it was not accepting the Howze Board's call for a massive revision in its force structure. As Howze recalled, the recommendation "did not sell." Yet the Army, faced with pressure from OSD, needed to do something. Lieutenant General Hamlett, then the DCSOPS, told General Decker that he felt "we had to try at least a division structure of this type of thing, and I recommended to him that we approve the formation of an airmobile division."[68]

Also heavily influencing the Army was its ongoing feud with the Air Force over the provision of close air support to Army units. The Air Force, quick to realize the threat posed by a vast increase in Army aviation, formed its own study group, the Disosway Board, whose findings, not surprisingly, refuted the Howze Board's report.[69] In October the JCS, instructed by McNamara to review both reports, were drawn directly into the conflict. The result was a JCS request to test the airmobility concept against the Air Force's idea of a joint service combat team structure.[70] At the time, relations between the services had deteriorated in Vietnam to the point where armed helicopters were limited to providing supporting fires for ARVN troops beginning one minute before an airmobile assault and lasting until no longer than one minute after the last helicopters had departed the landing zone. Helicopters were to use their guns only in defensive fire, and Air Force officers quickly pointed out any instances where helicopters appeared to be furnishing close air support to ground forces in the RVN. Following approval by McNamara in early January, the Army directed the formation and testing of an air assault division and an air transport brigade. As directed by General Wheeler, "the over-all purpose of the tests is to determine the extent to which light aircraft can augment the soldier's mobility [which] is now based upon his own leg power and upon ground vehicles. The aim is to improve significantly our ability to find, out-maneuver and destroy the enemy in ground combat."[71] The airmobility concept would be evaluated under the supervision of STRICOM. The Army moved quickly, activating the 11th Air Assault "Division" around a few battalions and commencing its own evaluations.

During the testing phase, in 1963–64, the Army viewed the airmobile concept in terms of conventional warfare. The use of helicopters in a counterinsurgency environment focused on seeking out and destroying main-force guerrilla units, with success being a function of the number of helicopters employed. The tests were conducted in a mid- and high-intensity environment. The concept of the division was not focused on the counterinsurgency type of warfare that it was sent to fight. General Williams recalled that "by the time we started the tests and were in the middle of running the tests, we really hadn't given too much thought to how we would fight it [counterinsurgency] or what changes [there] would be or how it would fit as an airmobile division in a counterinsurgency, or say a Vietnam-type operation."[72]

Doctrine also reflected the absence of emphasis on counterinsurgency, or the distortion of counterinsurgency principles in favor of the Concept. The Pentagon and CDC wanted airmobility counterinsurgency operations "directed toward the destruction of guerrilla forces through offensive tactics."[73] As late as August 1964, CDC issued manuals, such as one on aerial rocket artillery, with no reference to their operation in an insurgency environment. One searches in vain for the designation of airmobile forces as a reaction force in pacification operations. Firepower was to be spent freely regardless of the conflict environment. As stated in CDC's "Concept of Operations" for airmobile forces, "Firepower and mobility are employed to fix enemy forces, reduce enemy firepower, limit enemy maneuver capabilities, and support friendly maneuver forces in the seizure of terrain and the destruction of the enemy. Airmobile operations are characterized by *rapid execution* and *timely withdrawal*."[74] Unfortunately, these operations contribute little toward securing a population. As one airmobile commander ruefully stated after the war, "We should have done less flittin' and more sittin'."[75]

The test program quickly gained momentum, and in September the Army conducted its Air Assault I exercise, testing an airmobile battalion at Fort Stewart, Georgia. The results were promising enough for DOD to authorize further Army and Air Force testing, and by January 1964 the Army Staff was actively contemplating the inclusion of an airmobile division in its force structure. During this period the Army also received input regarding airmobile units from an NSC staffer, Robert W. Komer, who would later head the U.S. pacification effort in South Vietnam.

In his "Critique of the Army Force Posture," Komer offered an outsider's perspective on the airmobility test program and the use of such forces for counterinsurgency. Komer presented a picture of an Army that was tasked with preparing for a variety of contingencies, from nuclear war to counterinsurgency, but was moving very slowly, if at all, in adapting its forces for efficient operations at the lower end of the conflict spectrum. Komer said that the Army "does not yet seem to have made a clear decision as to which missions (capabilities) should receive priority. In other words, the Army is still preparing more for the worst case [war in Europe] than the most likely case [counterinsurgency]." Komer argued that the Army's force structuring for counterinsurgency "betokens a lack of genuine forward planning."[76] The Army, however, continued viewing the airmobile test program primarily in relation to its competition with the Air Force over the roles and missions of close air support. Airmobility as it related to counterinsurgency was, at best, on the fringe of the service's consciousness.

On 11 February 1964 the 11th Air Assault Division was activated at Fort Benning, Georgia, for the purpose of expanding the test program. Then Brig. Gen. Harry Kinnard was designated its commander, and the division underwent brigade-level tests named HAWK STAR from May through August in preparation for an exercise of the entire division that fall. The Air Force also remained busy, conducting the Indian River tests, which paralleled the Air Assault I exercises, from June through September.

The culmination of the interservice competition came in October/ November with the joint brigade-level test of the Air Force's concept under STRICOM supervision at Fort Leonard Wood, Missouri (GOLDFIRE I), and the Army's unilateral test of the airmobility concept under STRICOM evaluation at Forts Benning and Stewart in Georgia (Air Assault II). It quickly became evident that the Air Force was not offering anything new or innovative in the close air support of ground forces; GOLDFIRE I merely streamlined existing procedures and demonstrated that with the dedication of large amounts of tactical air support, an Army division had increased firepower. The Air Assault II tests, however, did demonstrate that the "advantages of increased mobility and maneuverability inherent to the air assault division offers a potential combat effectiveness differential that can be decisive in tactical operations."[77]

The success of Air Assault II, coupled with the uninspiring results of

GOLDFIRE I, led to a JCS recommendation (with the Air Force Chief dissenting) in January 1965 that GOLDFIRE II be canceled.[78] McNamara's approval opened the door for the Chiefs (again, with the Air Force dissenting) to recommend approval of the Army's request to add an airmobile division to its force structure, deleting one infantry division.[79] On 15 June 1965 McNamara authorized the organization of the 1st Cavalry Division (Airmobile), eight days after General Westmoreland's famous 44-battalion request.

Ironically, in winning its battle with the Air Force over the airmobility concept, the Army lost the "war" in developing airmobile forces for counterinsurgency operations. The service placed minimal emphasis on counterguerrilla operations during the test period. Air Assault II, the culmination of the airmobility test program, provides a good case in point. The exercise ran for five weeks. In the first phase, the division "exercised its unique capability to operate as a covering force for a larger force on the advance to contact." The second phase, involving the 11th Air Assault Division's protecting the flank of a corps, offered a preview of search-and-destroy operations. As the evaluation report stated:

An example of large air mobile forces in the attack began on the evening of 4 November, when the 1st Brigade received a warning against targets of opportunity in the 5th Mechanized Division (simulated) zone. Reconnaissance in the zone that evening gave indications that aggressor forces were assembling in the vicinity of Mount Vernon Church. . . .

In the above action, two infantry battalions, supported by two artillery battalions, were moved a distance of 41 miles to attack an objective deep in the enemy's rear. This unprecedented move, which involved the coordination of Air Force close support and organic aerial fire support, was effectively accomplished in a few hours.[80]

Counterinsurgency operations were limited to the participation of one battalion over a five-day period. The operations centered on the "find 'em, fix 'em, fight 'em, finish 'em" philosophy, with no emphasis on the use of airmobile forces in a reaction force role as part of an overall population control program. Significantly, the battalion admitted having had a hard time locating "small groups of well-disciplined guerrillas" and noted that ground reconnaissance and search action was normally required before contact could be made.[81] Once air assault units were in Vietnam, the problem of locating well-disciplined guerrillas would be ignored in favor of the more conventional mission of searching for main-force insurgent units.

Regarding Air Assault I and II, Kinnard, the division commander, felt that it was "perfectly fair to say that it [counterinsurgency] was a minor portion as compared to the others. That may be because the people writing the scenarios, from their background . . . understood more about divisions and corps than they did guerrillas."[82] Analyzing the exercises, a CDC report concluded that air assault forces were particularly well suited for many traditional Army operations, such as economy-of-force, link-up, exploitation, mobile-defense, and retrograde operations. As for the usefulness of airmobile forces in a counterinsurgency environment, Major General Yorck, whose 82d Airborne Division provided the "aggressor" force for the exercise, remarked that the air assault unit commanders "placed unwarranted confidence in the ability of firepower to neutralize/destroy the enemy."[83]

Nevertheless, the report concluded that "no further large scale tests of the concepts are required." It recommended that an air assault division be included in the Army's force structure and that an air transport brigade be formed as well. Thus the brass involved in the airmobility test program supported the modification in the service's force structure, not in response to the growing insurgency in Vietnam, but as an enhancement to the main forces designed for conventional war.

The bankruptcy of the Army's airmobility concept for insurgency warfare was noted by Major General Kinnard. Referring to Yorck's critique of the division in Air Assault II, Kinnard declared it "a fair statement, and I think it was borne out in Vietnam. If the guerrilla chooses to lie low in the jungle . . . it would probably be very difficult to locate him."[84]

Yet while the airmobile forces were busy "flittin' "—searching for main-force guerrilla units—they allowed the guerrilla to achieve his purpose: infiltration into the villages and subversion of the rural population. This, Kinnard admitted, was a problem for airmobile forces operating in the manner developed during exercises like Air Assault II, because "if he [the insurgent] can be a so-called fish swimming in a sea of people [and] he loses his identity as a soldier, airmobility isn't going to solve that problem for you." General Williams, co-author of the McNamara directive on airmobility, provided perhaps the best summary of the Army's indifference concerning the relationship between airmobile forces and counterinsurgency:

I remember one night at Fort Jackson when General Johnson, then the Chief of Staff of the Army, came down and we were sitting in one of the little white houses.

And there was General Rich, who was the test director; and General Kinnard, who was commanding the division; General Knowles, the assistant division commander; and General Wright and myself. And General Johnson said, "How well do you think an airmobile division would do in conflicts such as in Vietnam?" And actually we had to stop and think and debate a little while. We hadn't even really thought about [an] airmobile division like the 11th Air Assault Division fighting in Vietnam. . . . Our whole attention, our whole thought was the air assault division in mid-intensity conflict.[85]

Maj. Gen. Delk Oden, who served as director of Army aviation during the early period of airmobility testing, recalled thinking upon hearing that an airmobile division would be sent to Vietnam, "Here they [airmobile forces] come, all indoctrinated and set to fight the mid-intensity war, and here is this damned brushfire war."[86]

Despite its admitted orientation on the conventional operations favored by the Army, the Air Assault Division (AAD) was not quickly accepted into the Army force structure. Before the Chief of Staff would request implementation of the Air Assault II report's recommendations, CDC was directed to conduct wargame tests of the division. These were completed in December 1964. Of the eight games conducted, five focused on conventional operations, two on nuclear war, and only one on low-intensity conflict.[87]

The sole war game dealing with counterinsurgency operations uncovered many of the same problems experienced in Air Assault II. Predictably, the AAD was not given a true counterinsurgency mission but was tasked instead to "seek out and destroy Red Forces located in the division zone [of operations]." In accomplishing this mission, the division experienced considerable difficulty. It was quickly realized that in an insurgency environment "base vulnerability is a weakness." Thus, the AAD needed to employ "approximately one-third of the combat power of each brigade to provide adequate base security." This problem was remedied by assigning an ARVN brigade to secure the division's base. There was little appreciation of the fact that in placing the ARVN in static security roles U.S. forces would be assuming the combat burden of the war, while RVNAF combat skills would not be developed; on the contrary, they would be prone to atrophy.

Another problem for the AAD was finding the insurgent forces. The results of the war game indicated that the AAD had difficulty in collecting sufficiently accurate and timely intelligence to capitalize fully on its mobility. Efforts at correcting the problem centered on the use of firepower. Patrolling was carried out only to a distance of ten kilometers from the division base and utilized well-traveled existing trails. Not a single sighting was produced. The AAD did inflict 1,131 casualties through its prodigious use of firepower. The large ratio of rounds expended to casualties produced was explained away as the result of the terrain, insurgent tactics, and minimal target information. The lack of discretion in the application of firepower ran counter to one of the basic tenets of counterinsurgency doctrine: protecting the population and securing their support has priority over killing guerrillas. Yet it conformed with the Concept's prescription for the lavish application of firepower. As for pacification, it was "recognized and considered as an important function, but game play did not address this problem." Despite the problems of base security, target identification and discrimination, and excessive reliance on firepower, CDC concluded that the AAD was "capable of effective combat operations in . . . stability operations."[88]

Not Combat-Ready

In the period leading up to direct U.S intervention in the Vietnam War, the Army failed to structure its forces for counterinsurgency contingencies. Fearful of diverting its limited resources away from the ROAD system designed for conventional conflict, the service localized its counterinsurgency force structure around the Green Berets. The major innovation in the Army's force structure, airmobile forces, developed primarily from the efforts of an influential minority to apply technology to the nuclear battlefield in Europe, abetted by the Army's long-term interservice rivalry with the Air Force over close air support. Oddly enough, airmobile forces were dispatched to Vietnam in large numbers as the situation progressively worsened. They were sent, not because they had been developed for the counterinsurgency contingency, but because the Army had failed to organize forces for such a contingency. With its perspective on counterinsurgency distorted by its Concept, the Army convinced itself that airmobile forces provided the ability to conduct counterinsurgency operations using traditional operational doctrine. In the final analysis, airmobile forces served, not to enhance counterinsurgency operations, but as a technological doctrinal "fix" that helped the Army avoid them.

Two

YEARS OF INTERVENTION
1965–1968

5

Forty-four Battalions across the Rubicon

From 1954 to 1965 the Army failed to generate forces in the RVNAF capable of efficiently combating insurgencies. Although South Vietnamese troops fared poorly against the insurgents, their failure was not attributed to either doctrine or force structure. Rather, it was written off as the result of poor soldiering on the part of the ARVN, corruption within the Vietnamese government, and infiltration of forces and supplies from outside the RVN. That the Army supported the use of U.S. combat forces similar in structure to the ARVN and following the same operational methods is indicative of the service's belief that its approach to counterinsurgency warfare was correct and that what was needed was increased application of its Concept through the augmentation of unit firepower and mobility.

The Army remained convinced that the essence of the conflict was military, not political. Politics would take a back seat while the Army inflicted sufficient damage on the insurgents to force them to the peace table. Once it became clear that U.S. ground combat forces were necessary to prevent the fall of South Vietnam to the Communists, the Army's primary concern was the deployment of forces to execute the same strategy that the ARVN had been failing at for years, only with greater resources and increased intensity.

Although the Army would be presented with alternatives regarding its approach to counterinsurgency, they were given short shrift by the service's hierarchy. The Army was interested in waging the war it had prepared for, and while there would be great frustration over the limits imposed on horizontal (geographical) escalation of the war, the civilian leadership gave the commander in the field his traditional freedom to escalate vertically, that is, to escalate the level of violence within the RVN, as long as that level remained beneath the nuclear threshold.

Plans and Wargaming for Intervention

During 1964 the focus of Army plans and war games remained on traditional operations. OPLAN 32-64 was the basic plan to be implemented in the event of a commitment of U.S. forces to Southeast Asia.[1] The plan, which took eighteen months to formulate, was an update of CINCPAC OPLAN 32-59. Both plans focused on a mid-intensity conflict between, on the one hand, North Vietnam and possibly Communist China, and, on the other hand, SEATO forces led by the United States. While the plan provided a framework for the logistical buildup to support U.S. intervention, it was wholly inappropriate for the insurgency-style conflict environment facing the Army in 1965. As Maxwell Taylor noted, both plans were "hardly more than outline plans."[2] The Army did have a plan, USARPAC OPLAN 37-64, which had as its goal ensuring the stability of South Vietnam. The Army's assumptions for implementing the plan were: ARVN progress in defeating the insurgency; the active cooperation of Thailand and Laos; the lifting of restrictions on U.S. operations in implementing the plan; and a mobilization of the Army's reserves.[3] Yet the Army would commit its combat forces to Southeast Asia without realizing any of these conditions.

Throughout 1964 there were signs that the conditions the Army had set in OPLAN 37-64 for even a minimal infusion of ground combat forces would not be met. As early as June, McNamara directed the Army to determine whether it could implement the Southeast Asia contingency plans without mobilizing the reserves.[4] Thus, over a year before Westmoreland's 44-battalion request, the administration was back-pedaling on a condition that the Army considered essential to its participation in the conflict.[5] Nor was the administration about to widen the war by authorizing a military campaign in North Vietnam. No one in the president's inner circle was seriously discussing anything like the large-scale bombing campaign the Chiefs were proposing in the fall of 1964, much less the overt invasion of the DRV by American/SEATO forces.

Finally, the ARVN was losing ground in its struggle against the insurgents. The newest pacification plan, Hop Tac, was not progressing well. As one colonel reported over a back channel to the Chief of Staff in the fall of 1964: "Hop Tac was launched last week. That's too optimistic a word. In a launching a ship slides quickly down the ways and is ready to roll. Our launching was more a miscarriage. We hope Hop Tac will flush out the VC and we can kill them. But they may recede before it and later shift back in. . . . [But] it is a conventional war as our side fights it." While the colonel felt that pacification was faltering, his solution was to get "a spark of some sort. We've got to get kills. We've got to get a box score."[6]

General Johnson and the JCS were not at all sanguine concerning the ARVN's chances. In the JCS review of the situation following the attack on the airfield at Bien Hoa in November the Army Chief of Staff felt that "all of Southeast Asia and the area around it was sort of going to hell in a handbasket."[7] Johnson's visit to South Vietnam in December only re-inforced this judgment. He noted that "the insensitive conduct of some GVN forces towards the civilian populace in a number of provinces creates disaffection and resentment, and undermines popular support for the government."[8] Nevertheless, the general contended that even though the political and societal dimensions of the conflict were being lost, the "military aspects of this conflict can be won."[9] Thus, "the positive factors, on balance, appear to outweigh the negative ones."[10]

Even if the conditions set forth in OPLAN 37-64 had obtained (and it is revealing that the political and societal aspects of insurgency warfare were not addressed in it), the results of war games conducted during this period ought to have given the Army pause. One war game, code-named SIGMA I, was played in the late autumn of 1963. Among the players were many key figures of the Johnson administration. For example, Maxwell Taylor, George Ball, and William Sullivan headed up the red (VC/NVA) team, while Alexis Johnson and John McCone headed up the blue (US/RVN) team. The results of SIGMA I were disturbing. Bombing the North achieved little —the DRV rapidly increased its infiltration rate into South Vietnam to match the infusion of American troops. After five days (equivalent to ten years in actuality), the VC had increased the territory under their control despite the presence of some 600,000 U.S. troops. Furthermore, there was a public uproar at home against a strategy that was both costly and ineffective. General Curtis LeMay, the Air Force's Chief of Staff, claimed that the game had been rigged against the Air Force and de-manded that another game be conducted, one that would be more "real-istic."[11]

The failure of traditional American military operations to achieve U.S. policy objectives could have produced one of two results: the military could have realized that its strategy was ineffective and altered it, with all the attendant changes in doctrine and forces that that implied; or it could have changed the characteristics of the threat to fit the original strategy, as General LeMay attempted to do. A second set of war games, SIGMA II, was conducted in September 1964. This round saw the DRV less willing to

General Harold K. Johnson and General Cao Van Vien, South Vietnamese Army, discuss the tactical situation in III Corps during General Johnson's visit to South Vietnam in December 1964.   *courtesy U.S. Army*

commit forces to the South, the U.S. committing more forces more quickly, and a better outcome for the generals' preferred strategy.

The problem of whether or not to commit Army ground forces, however, was not faced during the U.S. election campaign in 1964. As General Westmoreland stated, "In the summer and fall of 1964 the presidential campaign was in full swing. The election wasn't until November and everything was stopped during that period. Any further commitment was unthinkable."[12]

Crisis in Vietnam

With the dawning of a new year, the situation in South Vietnam continued to deteriorate. There was some evidence that the VC were moving into phase 3 of the insurgency. For the first time VC units were operating in coordinated units of regimental size. In a series of major engagements around Binh Gia between 28 December and 4 January, the VC attacked and occupied the village, located about forty miles east of Saigon. In their efforts to dislodge the insurgents, government forces suffered 201 men killed in action; VC losses were pegged at 132, although only 32 could be confirmed by body count.[13] The engagements caused a considerable degree of anxiety in the White House, and General Wheeler was directed to forward a report of the battle to McGeorge Bundy.

As reports of the ARVN's latest debacle at Binh Gia began to filter in to the White House, President Johnson, his popular mandate assured through his landslide victory at the polls in November, decided that the time was right for the introduction of U.S. ground forces into Vietnam. In a cable dispatched to Ambassador Taylor on 30 December, Johnson bluntly stated that instead of bombing, "what is much more needed and would be more effective is a larger and stronger use of rangers and special forces and marines. . . . I am ready to look with great favor on that kind of increased American military effort, directed at the guerrillas and aimed to stiffen the aggressiveness of Vietnamese military units up and down the line."[14]

On 5 January Ambassador Taylor replied to the president. Citing an analysis by COMUSMACV and his staff, Taylor contended that with 15,100 advisers in country, "we have gone about as far down the advisory route as it is practical to go without passing the point of clearly diminishing returns." Having said this, Taylor offered the following courses of action: (a) introduction of between 8–25 U.S. combat battalions to provide reserve striking forces (20,000–60,000 troops); (b) integration of U.S. combat battalions into ARVN regiments, requiring 31 infantry battalions and associated support units (roughly 60,000 troops); (c) establishment of 3 coastal enclaves to secure ports, airfields, and major population centers, requiring 3 divisions, or a total of 75,000 troops; and (d) increased U.S. combat support for the RVNAF.

The ambassador contended that MACV found none of these alternatives desirable. Deploying U.S. ground troops in strike force battalions (option a), Taylor noted, would drive up U.S. and VC casualties, while the VC would blame noncombatant losses on the United States. Integrating U.S. battalions into ARVN regiments (option b) would place Americans under Vietnamese officers, an unacceptable alternative for obvious reasons. The enclave idea (option c) offered an "indefinite direct confrontation with Asiatic communists" with uncertain prospects for success and unknown costs in U.S. resources. Increasing current support activities (option d) was viewed as "more of the same" and therefore unlikely to make a difference in the war effort. Taylor concluded: "The Vietnamese have the manpower and the basic skills to win this war. What they lack is motivation. The entire advisory effort has been devoted to giving them skill and motivation. If that effort has not succeeded there is less reason to think that U.S. combat forces would have the desired effect."[15]

U. Alexis Johnson, Taylor's deputy in Saigon, recalled that the pressure from the president was intense: "Washington was asking Saigon, 'Can't you use some troops?' LBJ was pushing for it—'Do something!' "[16]

The cable laid out many of the problems that the Army would face if ground forces were committed. It is curious that Army doctrine and force structure were not viewed as problems. At this point, however, Taylor supported bombing the North, the perceived source of insurgent strength, as opposed to emphasis in the South.

Taylor's cable dampened the White House's interest in deploying ground combat forces, but only briefly. In a memo dated 27 January, McGeorge Bundy offered President Johnson two basic alternatives on the war: negotiate or use military force to bring a change in Communist policy. Speaking for McNamara, Bundy stated, "We both agree that every effort should still be made to improve our operations on the ground and to prop up the authorities in South Vietnam as best we can. But we are both convinced that none of this is enough, and that the time has come for harder choices."[17] William P. Bundy ("Mac" Bundy's brother), then at State, also wrote a memo to Dean Rusk concerning the situation in South Vietnam. Rusk had been reluctant to join the emerging majority within the president's brain trust who were willing to actively consider the commitment of American ground forces to the war. Speaking for his colleagues, Bundy wrote that the "introduction of limited U.S. ground forces into the northern area of South Vietnam still has great appeal to many of us, concurrently with the first air attacks into the DRV. It would have a real stiffening effect in Saigon, and a strong signal effect to Hanoi."[18]

The sense of urgency over the deteriorating situation in South Vietnam was heightened when the VC struck the American barracks at Pleiku in the Central Highlands on 7 February. Eight Americans died and over sixty were wounded. McGeorge Bundy, in Vietnam during the attack, agreed with Taylor and Westmoreland that retaliatory air strikes were in order and so notified Washington. On 11 February the JCS forwarded their proposal for military action, recommending air strikes supplemented by the deployment of an Army brigade to Thailand and a Marine Expeditionary Brigade (MEB) to Da Nang. The deployments were not for counterinsurgency purposes but were intended to deter overt Chinese/DRV intervention. The focus remained on conventional war and on activity outside South Vietnam. For example, when Robert Kleiman of the *New York Times* interviewed generals in February 1965 about what Hanoi would do, he was told by a member of the Joint Chiefs that if the NVA were committed, it would take eight American divisions, "just like in Korea," to stop them.[19]

The Army was aware that while forces might be dispatched for "deterrence" purposes, many more would be required if the United States were to involve itself in ground combat. Taylor recalled that "to keep all Vietcong mortars out of range of one airfield like Bien Hoa would require about six American battalions of infantry, and we estimated that similar protection for all our facilities would demand over 75,000 troops."[20]

Looking at these numbers, the civilian leadership must have found a bit of deterrence coming from a show of force and some punitive bombing to be attractive alternatives. Taylor, long a bombing proponent, was having his way at last, or so it seemed. The ambassador felt that "the inhibitions which had restrained the use of our air power against the enemy homeland were finally broken, and a new phase of the war had begun."[21] Taylor notified Washington that "we have no choice now but to clear the decks and remove any possible vestige of doubt about our determination to back South Vietnam in its fight for its freedom."[22]

The bombing attacks on the North (code-named FLAMING DART) commenced on 11 February, and the military began pushing for the deployment of ground troops to safeguard American bases. Discussion on the deployment of an MEB was effected as early as 16 February between COMUSMACV and Adm. U.S.G. Sharp, the CINCPAC. Justification was no longer presented in terms of deterring an overt attack by the People's Republic of China (PRC) or North Vietnam; rather, the force was intended to protect Da Nang from an attack by the VC and/or PAVN forces, which MACV saw the ARVN as incapable of handling.[23] On 18 February, Admiral Sharp forwarded Westmoreland's request to the JCS, with CINCPAC's concurrence. The force's deterrent value focused on preventing insurgent attacks on U.S. bases. Gone was the rationale around which OPLAN 32-64 was devised, that of an overt invasion of the RVN. Nevertheless, the OPLAN would still form the basis for the deployment of forces despite the fact that both the military and the civilian leadership generally conceded that the Chinese would not intervene unless their border were threatened.[24] The fact that such forces were configured and trained for execution of the OPLAN in conventional operations and not for counterinsurgency operations was absent from the deliberations of COMUSMACV and CINCPAC. One might argue that their intended role was static security; however, the relatively short interval between their deployment and involvement in combat operations would indicate otherwise.

Westmoreland obtained Taylor's approval for the troop request when a member of his staff, Brig. Gen. William E. Depuy, returned from a trip to I Corps with accounts of the ARVN's poor showing during recent operations. Thus, the final rationale for deploying the Marines centered on providing base security, freeing Regional Forces (RF) companies for action elsewhere (only two were transferred), sending a "signal" to Hanoi, and bolstering Vietnamese morale.

While Ambassador Taylor accepted the deployment of the Marine battalions, he was uneasy about committing large numbers of ground troops to Vietnam. Taylor recalled feeling that "if you brought that first battalion of Marines ashore at Da Nang, you're starting something that God only knows where it's going to stop."[25] Taylor's anxieties were reflected in a cable dispatched to Washington on 22 February in which he again expressed "grave reservations" about "the use of Marines in mobile counter-VC operations." Taylor concluded that the American soldier, "armed, equipped, and trained as he is, [is] not suitable as [a] guerrilla fighter for Asian forests and jungles."[26]

Ambassador Taylor's cable outlined many problems that U.S. ground forces would face should they be committed to the conflict, but they went unappreciated by General Westmoreland and the JCS. The most probable explanation for this divergence rests in Taylor's faith in a U.S. bombing campaign against North Vietnam, coupled with the greater breadth of experience that his being ambassador had given him. A bombing campaign would play to the United States' suit of attrition by relying on superior U.S. resources and technology. It promised to go straight to the source of aggression—Hanoi—rather than continue the inconclusive struggle in the South. It would avoid another Korea—American ground troops would not be bogged down in a land war in Asia; U.S. casualties could be averted, while the enemy's resources would be destroyed from the air; and there would be no sanctuaries. Taylor's rationale fit the Army's "never again" mentality. But his thoughts were strongly affected by his position as ambassador, where he was exposed to events from a perspective that was no longer purely military. As Taylor himself recalled, Wheeler, Johnson, and Westmoreland were "military men," while he, Taylor, had the advantage of also seeing the political and international aspects of the war, which the generals were too busy to concentrate on.[27]

Thus Taylor's position as ambassador provided an educational effect. Forced to consider aspects of the insurgency other than the purely military, the ambassador acquired a sense of uneasiness concerning the Army's ability to fight a well-organized insurgent movement and win. Better to avoid it and follow the Concept by going "up on top" and bombing the North.

As it turned out, CINCPAC openly disagreed with Taylor's professed anxieties, noting that "the Marines have a distinguished record in counterguerrilla warfare."[28] On 26 February, Washington approved the two-battalion proposal. While the decision to bring U.S. ground combat troops into Da Nang was being made, there were new indications that the GVN was rapidly losing its ability to combat the insurgents and that the South Vietnamese regime was facing political and social crises, as well as a military collapse. A USIA study prepared for the president and presented on 27 February noted that "the principal problems facing us in obtaining the support of the Vietnamese population are inadequate security and ineffective Government." The USIA researchers concluded, "The population is largely apathetic and is primarily interested in ending the twenty years of war; they care less as to which side will win, although there appears to be a substantial degree of approval of the Viet Cong."[29] But MACV and the Army were not focusing on the political or social dimensions of the conflict. The "conditions" that the Army had set for intervention in OPLAN 37-64 were forgotten as the service geared up for war in Southeast Asia.

On 1 March, DOD, which had hinted at the president's desire to deploy combat troops in Vietnam, began to actively promote it. In a memorandum to all departments within DOD, McNamara stated, "I want it clearly understood that there is an unlimited appropriation available for the financing of aid to Vietnam. Under no circumstances is lack of money to stand in the way of aid to that nation." When General Johnson sought clarification on how the Army would be expected to contribute, McNamara replied that the "policy is: anything that will strengthen the position of the GVN will be sent."[30]

The Army, far from questioning the wisdom of such an approach, quickly jumped on board. There were no General Ridgways willing to step forward and make a case against intervention; to the contrary, the military leadership acted quickly to position U.S. forces for the conflict. On 4 March the JCS recommended the following deployments to the secretary of defense: nine tactical fighter squadrons to the Western Pacific (WESTPAC); thirty B-52 bombers from CONUS to Guam; an MEB to Da Nang; an Army brigade to Thailand; one carrier task force to WESTPAC; an MEB from Hawaii to WESTPAC; and alerting the 173d Airborne Brigade, and the remainder of the 25th Infantry Division in Hawaii.[31] The perception, or perhaps the hope, was that if U.S. forces were introduced, the conflict would develop along conventional lines. This was evident to Depuy, who watched as MACV quickly changed "from a staff that originally was very much concerned with counterinsurgency . . . to a staff concerned with [large-scale] operations."[32]

Given the president's determination to succeed in Vietnam, and in Westmoreland's words, the "VC's demonstration . . . that he was willing to move into Mao Zedong's Phase Three, the big unit war," the perception among the Army leadership was that the big-unit war so conducive to conventional operations was now at hand. Thus the Army could commit its ground forces comforted by the fact that it would be fighting a war it knew how to win. Or so it seemed. Little consideration was given to the prospective utility of Army forces in the event of an insurgent reversion to phase 2 operations. There was little appreciation of the fact that denying the insurgents victory in phase 3 was not the same as victory; rather, it would signal a return to phase 2, where the political and social elements of insurgency strategy, as well as the protracted nature of the conflict, would prove to be as important as pure military power, if not more important. It was a situation the Army was not equipped to handle.

On 5 March, General Johnson departed for Vietnam to consult with his Army colleagues Taylor and Westmoreland. Prior to Johnson's departure, the president cornered him in the White House elevator and emphasized his desire for a greater U.S. role in the war. Thumping the Chief of Staff on the chest with his finger, he told him to "get things happening. I want some solutions. I want some answers."

It quickly became obvious to the Army brass in Saigon that the Chief of Staff had come with the intention of getting Taylor and Westmoreland to recommend increased U.S. ground force deployments as per the president's wishes. Major General Oden, then on the MACV staff, recalled: "We gave him [the Chief of Staff] a regular briefing for about two hours and then he asked everyone to leave the room but the generals. Then he said, 'Gentlemen, as you know, I don't come as the Army Chief of Staff. I am here as a representative of the President of the United States. Mr. Johnson asked me to come and tell you that I came with a blank check. What do you need to win the war?' "[33]

Westmoreland dutifully proposed that Army brigades be deployed to Bien Hoa and Vung Tau and that an Army division be sent to the Central Highlands. An additional battalion of Marines for Da Nang was also requested. The proposal, coupled with the already-scheduled arrival of Marines at Da Nang, would have provided COMUSMACV with seventeen maneuver battalions, roughly two divisions. Inherent in Westmoreland's proposal was the use of American troops in offensive operations.

Taylor, on the other hand, was not willing to acquiesce to the introduction of U.S. combat troops. In an effort to "hold the line," Taylor concurred in the dispatch of the third battalion of the 9th MEB (to Phu Bai, as it turned out); however, he rejected the idea of sending an Army division to Vietnam. Furthermore, he was against the use of American forces in offensive operations, contending that they should remain in enclaves along the coast.[34] The ambassador presented his views in a meeting with General Johnson on 7 March and in an estimate of the situation cabled to the Department of State four days later. In discussing the course of events in the RVN, Taylor expanded on his position regarding the introduction of ground forces, presenting a picture of a South Vietnam rapidly losing the political and social cohesiveness necessary to continue the struggle.[35] While painting a bleak picture in the South, Taylor pushed his preferred option of striking directly at the source of the problem—North Vietnam. Taylor argued, "The current program of retaliatory bombing of the North does not yet seem to have affected Hanoi's will to continue support of the VC. North Vietnamese support appears unlikely to be curtailed without continued, vigorous and mounting countermeasures which would convince Hanoi that the price it must pay is too costly to bear."[36]

Westmoreland, viewing the action from his role as the commander of U.S. forces in South Vietnam (CINCPAC would be responsible for the bombing campaign in the North), saw enclaves as going entirely against the grain of the Army Concept. The MACV Staff felt, and Westmoreland had concurred, that enclaves represented "an inglorious, static use of U.S. forces. . . . that would leave the decision of where and when to strike to the enemy," thereby leaving allied forces open to defeat in detail and moving combat into the densely populated areas.[37] Westmoreland wanted the opportunity to seek out and destroy the enemy's main force units, the VC/PAVN battalions and regiments. He felt, quite correctly, that Army units, with their firepower and airmobility, would be ideal instruments for breaking up the insurgents' emerging large-scale operations. His error was in not anticipating what lay beyond the initial big battles.

On 8 March the first Marine BLT (battalion landing team) splashed ashore at Da Nang. Taylor, on hand to watch the marine deployment, was appalled by the amount of heavy equipment, such as tanks and self-propelled artillery, that the leathernecks were bringing into Da Nang. Taylor, Westmoreland recalled, was "visibly piqued" and reminded COMUSMACV that he, Taylor, was still in charge.[38] The ambassador viewed the deployment of Marines with their heavy equipment as part of the push by Generals Westmoreland, Johnson, and Wheeler to get U.S. troops into South Vietnam. Nor was Taylor's concern allayed when General Johnson returned to Washington on 12 March supporting Westmoreland's call for more troops. In a report circulated to McNamara and the JCS, Johnson laid out his views in support of Westmoreland's request, a request that he had been sent to Saigon to engineer:

With the continuance of present trends, and provided that no new power elements are brought into play, six months from now the configuration of the RVNAF will essentially be a series of islands of strength clustered around district and province capitals clogged with large numbers of refugees in a generally subverted country-side; and the GVN itself will be beset by "end the war" groups openly advocating a negotiated settlement.[39]

To arrest the deterioration, Johnson called for implementation of a twenty-one-point assistance program designed to "strengthen the over-taxed GVN military forces, to increase interference with and force discontinuation of [North Vietnamese] support of infiltration, to improve hamlet and village security, and to improve the appeal of the pacification program."[40] (When Taylor heard about General Johnson's program, he observed sarcastically that the Army Chief of Staff "must feel we can win this war on points.")

Johnson then discussed the proposed combat troop deployments that he and COMUSMACV had agreed upon. Couching his request in terms of "measures to free some ARVN forces for offensive operations," Johnson advanced two alternative deployments:

1. Deploy U.S. combat units to assume responsibility for the security of the Bien Hoa–Tan Son Nhut airbase complex, Nha Trang, Qui Nhon, and Pleiku. . . . This proposal, which is logical under a policy of slow escalation, is made *not because it is militarily sufficient but because it may be the maximum action which is politically feasible within the U.S. at this time.*

2. Deploy U.S. combat units to assume responsibility for defense of the provinces of Kontum, Pleiku and Darlac in the II Corps Tactical Zone. . . . Of these two alternatives, the assumption of responsibility for the highland provinces is preferred because it gives a clearer area of responsibility to U.S. forces, affords an opportunity to interdict the infiltration routes leading into the highland area from Laos, and provides a buffer between the Laos staging area and ARVN units engaged in the coastal area.[41]

Having advanced Taylor's enclave approach as the "politically feasible" option for the time being, along with Westmoreland's expanded option, General Johnson added a third alternative, one that reflected the Army's belief that "the measures listed in the two foregoing categories will alleviate but may not remedy the military situation." Johnson added that accordingly, the following military measures might be required:

Invoke the SEATO Treaty and provide an International Force south of the 17th Parallel deployed across northern Quang Tri Province and the panhandle of Laos to the Mekong. Alternatively, deploy a United States ground force in the same geographical area. The force required is estimated to be about four division forces. This action is designed to stop land infiltration, to pose a threat to North Vietnam in the event other threatening measures fail, and to establish a significant presence for exploitation in any negotiations that might occur in the future.[42]

It is evident from his proposal that General Johnson viewed the introduction of Army ground forces in traditional, conventional terms. A military solution could be achieved, contended Johnson, if the Army restored the border along the DMZ as it had in Korea, with main-force Army divisions conducting conventional operations. As Johnson later recalled, the trip laid out the groundwork for the major combat troop commitments announced in July. Indeed, as Johnson saw it, "the announcement in July was simply a confirmation of the report I had made back in March . . . simply a confirmation of decisions made months before."[43] Thus, far from resisting deployment of U.S. forces, the Army brass actively promoted it, primarily at the prompting of the president himself. The only impediment to American entry in the ground war, as General Johnson noted in his report, was the president's concern over the timing of the commitment.

Taylor's ire would certainly have been raised had he been aware of these developments promoting the introduction of ground troops. The ambassador, however, was being phased out of the action by the president and the Army, both of whom wanted U.S. troops deployed quickly, or at least as quickly as "politically feasible." U. Alexis Johnson, Taylor's deputy, observed that "the thrust for bringing U.S. combat forces into Vietnam came from Washington, not from Vietnam (the country team)."[44]

While the Chiefs examined Johnson's proposal, a Joint CIA-Defense Intelligence Agency (DIA)-State memorandum was issued on 17 March outlining VC strength in South Vietnam. The memo presented some chilling data: while the RVNAF strength stood at 567,000 (including 245,000 regulars), VC strength had risen to between 50,000 and 60,000 regulars and roughly 100,000 irregular, or militia, forces.[45] Given the traditional ratio necessary for the counterinsurgent forces to prevail of 10–20 government troops to 1 insurgent, this implied that even given Army advantages in firepower and technology, the United States and/or the GVN would have to increase force levels by roughly 1 million men to quell the insurgency. And this calculus omitted any consideration of North Vietnamese participation in the conflict.

The Army brass might have asked themselves whether the insertion of several divisions (or even the seven General Johnson talked about) would redress this situation. In a conventional war, where firepower and technology served as "force multipliers" driving down the numerical ratios, the problem might have been manageable; in the conflict environment of insurgency, however, they were not applicable, save in the latter (phase 3) stages of the war. The Army leadership ignored this fact and in succeeding months utilized the "force multipliers" of mid-intensity conflict in arriving at the force ratios necessary for success.

In accordance with this viewpoint, on 20 March the JCS officially requested that a three-division force (including one Republic of Korea [ROK] division) be sent to South Vietnam for offensive action against the VC. The Chiefs contended that "the requirement is not simply to withstand the Viet Cong, however, but to gain effective operational superiority and assume the offensive. To turn the tide of the war requires an objective of destroying the Viet Cong, not merely to keep pace with them, or slow down their rate of advance."[46]

The JCS recommended that one U.S. Marine division conduct, on order, offensive operations to kill VC with or without a centralized GVN/U.S. command structure. The Marines should expand their existing Technical Area of Responsibility (TAOR) as the force grew in size. The U.S. Army division would be deployed to Pleiku. While the JCS pursued General Johnson's proposal, the Army Chief of Staff and COMUSMACV worked to introduce additional forces. On 17 March, General Westmoreland requested the deployment of yet another BLT, this one slated for Phu Bai; this prompted another telegram from Taylor, who, while concurring with Westmoreland's request, noted that the proposal "is a reminder of the strong likelihood of additional requests for increases in U.S. ground combat forces in SVN."[47] At the same time, Taylor lobbied hard against the request. In a cable to Washington the following day, the ambassador repeated the concerns he had expressed in previous communications.

While Westmoreland was requesting additional battalions, the Chief of Staff was contemplating the deployment of an entire corps. Even as the JCS went forward with their recommendation of 20 March, General Johnson was commissioning an Army study that would involve three Army divisions, an airborne brigade, and an MEB to "seal off" South Vietnam. The force would deploy along the DMZ through Laos to the Mekong River at Savannakhet. The Chief of Staff was quickly apprised of the enormity of the task by the Corps of Engineers. Nearly 18,000 engineer troops, plus large numbers of indigenous laborers, would be needed to support such an undertaking. Work could not begin until 1 November, the start of the dry season. Of course there was no guarantee that the infiltrators would not conduct an end run around such a barrier by going through Thailand.[48] The question of how to handle the insurgency in Vietnam was left unanswered. Simply stated, having failed over the past decade to produce forces and doctrine capable of executing a counterinsurgency strategy, the Army was trying to fit a strategy to its force structure and doctrine.

This flurry of activity concluded when, on 26 March, COMUSMACV sent the JCS his "Commander's Estimate of the Situation in South Vietnam." In it, Westmoreland interpreted the mission of U.S. forces to be to force the DRV to stop supporting the insurgency in South Vietnam.[49] Westmoreland viewed U.S. strategy as focused on North Vietnam, basing his analysis on the assumption that the "basic strategy of retaliatory and punitive air strikes against NVN will, in time, bring about desired results, that is, supply and support of the insurgency will be terminated by DRV and hopefully DRV/VC High Command will direct the cessation of offensive operations." The general submitted the three options worked up between Johnson and himself during the Chief's visit in early March for implementing the strategy. Option 1 focused on General Johnson's twenty-one-point program; option 2 focused on the 20 March JCS request; and option 3 added the Chief of Staff's anti-infiltration force.

While on the surface Westmoreland appeared to agree with Taylor's basic strategy of bombing, he noted that the bombing might not be successful or would take effect only slowly. Thus, he recommended placing one division in the Central Highlands and the commitment of ground forces to offensive operations. COMUSMACV supported his position by noting that this "would frustrate VC efforts to cut South Vietnam in two by attacking through the Central Highlands." This, Westmoreland stated, "together with basic bombing strategy, establishes [the] basis for ultimate victory."

Taylor, having read Westmoreland's estimate and having received no reply to his cable of 18 March, dispatched yet another message to Washington in an effort to keep his concerns before the eyes of the decision makers. The cable was a rebuttal of COMUSMACV's estimate and reflected Taylor's growing awareness that events were passing him by. Even as his cable was being digested by the president's aides, Taylor was returning to Washington for a meeting of the NSC scheduled for 1 April. The battle lines, already drawn, were firmed up in a meeting between McNamara, Taylor, and the JCS on 29 March. Generals Wheeler, Johnson, and Westmoreland reiterated their call for the introduction of a three-division force, including the ROK division. Taylor demurred. He indicated that three divisions seemed high; that South Vietnamese Prime Minister Quat was not persuaded that more troops were necessary; and that anti-American sentiment lay just under the surface.[50] McNamara waffled. He stated his concern over the adverse force ratios facing the RVNAF but favored deployment of U.S. forces conditioned by Taylor's political, logistical, and operational constraints. It was agreed by all, however, that the bombing campaign (ROLLING THUNDER) should be stepped up.

The NSC meetings on 1–2 April were a partial victory for Taylor, or at least they appeared to be. The president authorized only two BLTs for Vietnam—one each to Da Nang and Phu Bai. U.S. troops would be used more actively, but the level of activity would be worked out between McNamara and Rusk. On the other hand, ROLLING THUNDER would increase in intensity, but only at a "slowly ascending tempo."[51] The president appeared to be won over by Taylor's arguments and his contention that currently there was no crisis in Saigon. Furthermore, CIA Director McCone warned against the deployment of large numbers of troops, stating that the United States would get mired down in a war it could not win.[52]

The JCS took exception to the president's apparent willingness to "take it slow." They were not interested in defensive enclaves, limitations on bombing, or the restrictions imposed on what they perceived as necessary operations. On 2 April they sent McNamara a bold memorandum in which they recommended clearing the decks of all "administrative and procedural impediments that hamper us in the prosecution of this war." The Chiefs went on to list a whole panoply of problems that they felt were causing unnecessary headaches in providing support to General Westmoreland. The JCS memorandum was a direct appeal that the military staff be allowed to run the show. McNamara quickly told General Wheeler that the JCS could continue planning for the introduction of a two- or three-division force into Vietnam, with the logistical troops being sent to the RVN serving as an advance party. McNamara's problem, however, rested not with the JCS but with Ambassador Taylor.

Encouraged by McNamara's response, CINCPAC set up a planning conference in Honolulu for 9 April. The two-day session ended with JCS and PACOM representatives recommending the deployment of the 173d Airborne Brigade to Bien Hoa–Vung Tau for security purposes and another Army brigade to Qui Nhon–Nha Trang to prepare for the introduction of a full division. As U. Alexis Johnson later recalled, "Westy was now getting enthusiastic" concerning the deployment of troops.[53] In his message to Admiral Sharp, Westmoreland looked beyond the decisions made at the NSC meetings of 1–2 April and focused on McNamara's reassurances to the JCS in arguing for the deployment of a brigade to the Bien Hoa–Vung Tau area.[54] Westmoreland also contended that the time was ripe for forming a small, single combined staff headed by a U.S. general officer. Discussions with Vietnamese officials, said Westmoreland, had suggested that such an arrangement would be palatable.

These requests went forward without the knowledge of Taylor, as evidenced in his cable of 12 April, in which he discussed the logistical buildup (which he supported) but reiterated his stand against the deployment of additional combat forces, stating that "it was my understanding in Washington that, if the Marines demonstrate effectiveness in operating out of Da Nang in an offensive counterinsurgency role, other offensive enclaves may be established along the coast and garrisoned with brigade-size contingents for employment similar to the marines."[55] The ambassador continued operating under the impression that the decisions made by the president in early April were still operative, that is, that the enclave strategy was in effect, with no further troop commitments allowed until the strategy was tested and the bombing campaign given time to work. It would therefore be an understatement to say that Taylor was shocked to discover only two days later, as he read the cable traffic from the JCS to CINCPAC, news of the 173d's impending deployment to South Vietnam.[56] The ambassador immediately fired off a stinging cable to Washington:

I have just learned by the reference JCS message to CINCPAC that the immediate deployment of the 173rd airborne brigade to Bien Hoa–Vung Tau has apparently been approved. This comes as a complete surprise in view of the understanding reached in Washington that we would experiment with the Marines in a counterinsurgency role before bringing in other U.S. contingents. . . . I recommend that this deployment be held up until we can sort out all matters relating to it.

Recent actions relating to the introduction of U.S. ground forces have tended to create an impression of eagerness in some quarters to deploy forces into SVN which I find difficult to understand.[57]

Taylor's confusion was quickly remedied, and it provided yet another surprise for the general turned ambassador. Far from reaffirming the go-slow approach that Taylor thought he had won in Washington, the president's men sought to bring him on board for the deployment of the 173d. They were, nevertheless, well aware that a person of Taylor's position and stature could cause problems if he went public with his dissatisfaction. The same day Taylor's cable arrived in Washington, the president received a memo from his national security adviser, McGeorge Bundy, informing him that McNamara would be delivering to the president for his approval that evening a cable to Taylor outlining additional steps for expanding the U.S. role in the war. "My own judgement," said Bundy, "is that direct orders of this sort to Taylor would be very explosive right now. . . . He heard about the airborne brigade by a premature JCS message of yesterday and has already come in questioning it." Bundy recommended that things be slowed down a bit, arguing that "I am sure we can turn him around if we give him just a little time to come aboard."[58] Taylor evidently saw the handwriting on the wall: it would be bombing plus troops, although as it turned out, neither Taylor nor the Army would get enough to suit them. Taylor felt that his position was being undercut by the president, who he now realized had been egging on the JCS all along for a major introduction of U.S. ground forces. "He [Lyndon Johnson] was the fellow with the black snake whip behind them saying, 'Let's get going—now!' " recalled Taylor. "He did all this behind my back. . . . Once he made his decision, he couldn't get going fast enough."[59] U. Alexis Johnson concurred that it was "salami tactics by the president." The consequences were never thought out, either by LBJ and his advisers or by the JCS.[60]

Taylor's protest elicited the telegram from McNamara referred to in Bundy's memo. McNamara informed Taylor that the "highest authority" (that is, the president) believed that "something new must be added in the South to achieve victory."[61] The implication was that since the president's mind was made up, Taylor's duty was to support the introduction of ground combat forces.

Clearly, the president was moving beyond the agreement that Taylor thought they had reached in the recent NSC meetings. The ambassador, realizing President Johnson's true position on the issue, scaled down his objections and, waging a rear-guard action, requested a period of careful experimentation with the four Marine battalions on hand, noting that recent "hasty and ill-conceived proposals" for the introduction of troops were not warranted in light of the current situation in Vietnam.

It was now evident that Taylor was the only major figure in the government opposed to introducing large numbers of American combat forces into Vietnam. For this reason, the military had left the ambassador in the dark shortly after the request for the 173d had gone in. Cable traffic during this period confirms that the JCS were going ahead with planning for the introduction of a three-division force and the partial execution of OPLAN 32–64.[62] The combat forces were to engage in search-and-destroy operations. For instance, General Johnson, in his memorandum to the JCS prior to their meeting with the president on 13 April, contended that the basic requirements involved in providing security were to find the enemy, fix him in place so that he could be engaged successfully, and fight and finish him off.[63] General Johnson noted that actions were under way to double the number of helicopters in Vietnam, equip the ARVN with weapons of increased firepower, introduce anti-intrusion devices, and give U.S. combat elements responsibility for additional areas in South Vietnam. It was more of the same, but now the Army would involve its forces directly against the insurgents.

Further supporting the military's move to take the offensive were the instructions given on deploying the 173d Airborne Brigade. Westmoreland was informed that the brigade's mission was "to provide initial security of U.S. installations and facilities, to be expanded to include engagement in counterinsurgency [i.e., search-and-destroy] combat operations."[64] As Taylor later recalled, the Army leadership expressed no reservations over these commitments; all in all, the president's push "was welcomed by military people."[65]

The ambassador was finally brought on board at a one-day conference in Honolulu on 20 April. Present were McNamara, McNaughton, William Bundy, Taylor, Wheeler, Sharp, and Westmoreland. As recorded in his memorandum for the president the following day, McNamara was able to achieve unanimous support for the plan to increase the U.S. commitment to the RVN. Representative of the group's misunderstanding concerning the dynamics of insurgency warfare, on which the Army men present— Taylor, Wheeler, and Westmoreland—were presumably the experts, was the report's conclusion that "it would take more than six months, perhaps a year or two, to demonstrate VC failure in the South." The strategy for "victory" was to "break the will of the DRV/VC by denying them victory."[66]

In his memorandum to the president, McNamara reported that Taylor "stated what appeared to be a shared view, that it is important not to 'kill the hostage' by destroying the North Vietnamese assets inside the 'Hanoi do-nut.' They all believe that the strike program is essential to our campaign—both psychologically and physically—but that it cannot be expected to do the job alone."[67] Thus, Taylor continued his support for the bombing campaign against the North. It was agreed that the air strikes would be focused away from the North Vietnamese industrial infrastructure and toward the interdiction of men and supplies moving south.

Taylor's "conversion" was evidenced by his support for increases in U.S. ground force levels. In all, the group recommended two Army brigades (six battalions) for the Bien Hoa–Vung Tau and Qui Nhon–Nha Trang areas, along with a Marine brigade for Chu Lai. This would more than triple the number of U.S. ground force maneuver battalions in the RVN, from four to thirteen.[68] In explaining his shift in position, Taylor stated that "by that time I knew what the president wanted. He was going to get all the ground forces in [South Vietnam] the field commander wanted, and get them there as fast as he could. It was as simple as that."[69]

Thus, Taylor reluctantly joined his former comrades-in-arms— Westmoreland, Harold Johnson, and Wheeler—in supporting the introduction of American combat forces. While they were not sanguine regarding the prospects of the RVNAF, there was a belief that once U.S. ground forces took the offensive, the insurgency would be brought under control. McNamara reported to the president the Chiefs' opinion that in order to keep the ground war from dragging on indefinitely, it was "necessary to reinforce GVN ground forces with about 20 or more battalion equivalents in addition to the forces now being recruited in SVN. Since these reinforcements cannot be raised by the GVN, they must inevitably come from U.S. and third country sources."[70]

With Taylor back in the fold, the Army moved forward on the three-division deployment it had sought since March. Spurred on by the CIA-DIA memo confirming the presence of one regiment of the 325th PAVN Division in northern South Vietnam, the Army pressed for quick acceptance of its proposal. On 30 April the JCS forwarded JCS memorandum 321-65 to OSD. The document presented a detailed program for introducing the forces discussed at Honolulu. It is significant that it referred to the proposed deployments as a step toward the introduction of a three-division force. Absent was any reference to the enclave strategy; forces deployed would initially secure their bases and then engage in counterinsurgency operations with the RVNAF.

The military's rush to introduce ground forces contrasted sharply with the information available on the situation in Vietnam and the Army's own criteria for intervention. On the same date that JCS memorandum 321-65 was finalized, the CIA issued a special memorandum on Vietnam emphasizing the bleakness of the U.S. position. Noting that VC strength currently stood at roughly 150,000 men, the CIA argued that if the United States committed large numbers of ground combat forces to the war, "there will be constant danger that the war weary people of South Vietnam will let the U.S. assume an even greater share of the fighting."[71] Unfortunately, Washington no longer had much interest in such analyses. The efforts of the Army Staff were now focused on deploying forces to South Vietnam with as few restrictions as possible on their employment.

On 8 May, three days after the first elements of the 173d Airborne Brigade began arriving at Vung Tau, COMUSMACV, with Taylor's concurrence, forwarded his concept of operations for U.S. and allied ground forces in support of the RVNAF. Westmoreland advocated a three-stage operation: "In Stage One the units were to secure enclaves, which I preferred to call base areas, and in defending them could operate out to the range of light artillery. In Stage Two the units were to engage in offensive operations and deep patrolling in co-operation with the ARVN. In Stage Three they were to provide a reserve when ARVN units needed help and also conduct long-range offensive operations."[72] The operational focus of MACV's proposal was in line with the Concept: the Army would search out and destroy as many insurgents as possible as quickly as possible, convincing the VC that they could not win. It was a thoroughly conventional approach to the problem, one that ignored the realities of insurgency warfare. General William B. Rosson, arriving in Saigon for a tour of duty in Vietnam, found Westmoreland and the MACV Staff less interested in the first three phases than in a fourth. Already, in fact, the Army was focusing on the use of inland bases to conduct search-and-destroy operations, while consigning ARVN units to local operations in support of pacification.[73]

In his message Westmoreland deviated from the Army position calling for deployment of the airmobile division in the Central Highlands. Instead, he called for stationing the division on the coast, at Qui Nhon and Nha Trang. This was likely the result of Westmoreland's desire to get the division in-country rather than a change in philosophy, particularly since Taylor and Admiral Sharp had expressed reservations over a Central Highlands deployment. Less than one week later, in a message to the Army Staff, Westmoreland reversed his deployment position and requested that airmobility experts (*not* counterinsurgency experts) be sent to MACV to assist in determining the concept of operations for the airmobile division.

One possible reason for Westmoreland's quick change of heart may have been the increased leverage that accrued to him as a consequence of main-force VC attacks on ARVN forces in Phouc Long Province, where they briefly seized the capital at Song Be, and in Quang Ngai Province, where they ambushed and destroyed an entire ARVN battalion and the relief force sent to rescue it. According to one report, in the latter incident ARVN commanders displayed "tactical stupidity and cowardice" in the face of the VC. Westmoreland recalled thinking at the time that Mao Zedong's phase 3 was coming up. From their recent abysmal performance, it appeared that the ARVN could not handle the VC, either in phase 2 or in phase 3. It appeared that a crisis was fast approaching.

Prescriptions for action varied. President Johnson suggested the encadrement of U.S. troops in Vietnamese units. He felt that other U.S. ground forces should experiment in a counterinsurgency role; if successful, such operations "should be followed promptly by requests for additional U.S. forces."[74] Meanwhile, the JCS doggedly pursued the deployment of the three divisions initially proposed in March.

Clark Clifford, an influential Washington attorney who had served as an adviser to a number of presidents and who was counted among Lyndon Johnson's friends, observed the events in Vietnam with great concern. Despite his well-deserved reputation as a hawk on the war, Clifford was uneasy concerning all the talk of committing U.S. ground forces to South Vietnam. Writing the president on 17 May regarding U.S. ground force commitments, he expressed his belief that U.S. ground forces in South Vietnam should be kept to a minimum, consistent with the protection of U.S. installations and property in that country. "My concern," he said, "is that a substantial buildup of U.S. ground troops would be construed by the Communists, and by the world, as a determination on our part to win the war on the ground. This could be a quagmire. It could turn into an open end commitment on our part that would take more and more ground troops, without a realistic hope of ultimate victory."[75] Clifford's letter, however, failed to have an impact.

By June COMUSMACV was convinced that the thirteen U.S. maneuver battalions already approved for deployment to South Vietnam could not stem the rising VC tide. In a cable to Washington on 5 June, Taylor and Westmoreland laid out the politico-military situation. The cable noted the chaotic political situation in Saigon and the absence of leadership within the government and among the potential successors to the Quat regime. The report began by citing the increased tempo of VC activity in May and marveling at the insurgent's remarkable ability to replace his losses. It concluded that "to meet the shortage of ARVN reserves, it will probably be necessary to commit U.S. ground forces to action."[76]

This message was followed two days later by Westmoreland's 44-battalion request, calling for major infusions of U.S. ground forces into South Vietnam. In stating the rationale for his request, Westmoreland detailed the increased threat of intervention from NVA forces, particularly elements of the 325th and 304th PAVN divisions, which were believed to have units in the Central Highlands and the Laotian panhandle, respectively. ARVN forces, Westmoreland noted, "are already experiencing difficulty in coping with this increased VC capability." He concluded, "The GVN cannot stand up successfully to this kind of pressure without reinforcement."[77]

Having outlined the problem, Westmoreland called for deployment of an Army corps headquarters, the final two BLTs of the 3d Marine Division, the Army's airmobile division, the remainder of the ROK division, and retention of the 173d Airborne Brigade and its replacement brigade. The JCS were advised that further reinforcements might be necessary. Westmoreland also pointed out that an enclave strategy was "no answer." If South Vietnam was to survive, he argued, MACV had to have "a substantial and hard-hitting offensive capability on the ground to convince the VC that they cannot win." "No more niceties about defensive posture and reaction"; the Army "had to forget enclaves and take the war to the enemy."[78] Thus the appeal for moving out of the enclaves despite the fact that the populated areas would remain uncovered if the ineffective ARVN were relied upon for protection.

The magnitude of the 44-battalion request brought a flurry of activity in Washington and Saigon. Some questioned the need for such sizeable forces when there was strong evidence indicating that neither the PRC nor North Vietnam intended to initiate *overt* military action against South Vietnam.[79] The JCS were in turmoil as well, initially favoring the deployment of the airmobile division to the Highlands, then changing their minds and opting for a coastal deployment, as preferred by Ambassador Taylor and Admiral Sharp. Taylor was waging a rear-guard action against the generals, advocating an experimental period before full-scale operations began. Sharp was not a proponent of enclaves, but he was concerned over PACOM's ability to resupply the division if it were located inland. Thus, his interests regarding the division's placement coincided with Taylor's.[80]

Despite the weakness of the Saigon regime (Quat would be replaced by General Ky in a matter of days) and the absence of any immediate threat to either U.S. forces or the survival of the RVN, Westmoreland's request found considerable support at the NSC meeting of 11 June, attended by General Wheeler and Ambassador Taylor. In advancing the "Army" position, these two distinguished soldiers exhibited a strong misunderstanding of insurgency and an equally strong proclivity for viewing the situation through the lens of the Concept. In examining VC strength levels, for example, Taylor chose to include only VC regulars, fixing the level at 42,000–50,000, while discounting the 100,000 or so local VC militia who subverted and controlled the population. Both lauded the bombing campaign, Taylor contending that "the increase in the Viet Cong forces came before our bombing" and Wheeler of the opinion that "our bombing has slowed down the entire North Vietnamese transportation system."

The president concluded the meeting by indicating that Westmoreland's request would be granted but that U.S. actions should be guided by a need to obtain "the maximum protection at the least cost." President Johnson did not question the Army's emerging strategy for Vietnam except to note that the war must be conducted "without going all-out." The Army would be given its head in the prosecution of the war so long as it confined itself within the borders of South Vietnam.[81]

Meanwhile, in Saigon Westmoreland continued pushing his request, spurred by his conviction that South Vietnam's crisis was approaching the critical stage. Given this perception on Westmoreland's part, one finds it difficult to question his desire for more U.S. forces in South Vietnam. Other steps proposed by MACV, however, are more susceptible to criticism. For example, the need for quick commitment of U.S. forces to battle appears questionable, particularly in the absence of any coherent counterinsurgency strategy. Utilizing the Army's firepower and mobility as a means of attriting enemy forces coincided with the Army Concept but served as an end in itself, not as part of a comprehensive strategy for defeating the insurgents. Nevertheless, the need for U.S. ground forces in Vietnam in a combat role was uppermost in COMUSMACV's perspective of what was necessary to save South Vietnam. On 12 June, Westmoreland recommended that the U.S. forces' area of responsibility be extended from their base areas to include "all adjacent VC concentrations or base areas which threaten the installation in question." The general concluded that "we have reached a point in Vietnam where we cannot avoid the commitment to combat of U.S. ground troops."

In a cable dispatched the following day, Westmoreland detailed his concept of employment for incoming U.S. forces. It was a faithful representation of the Army's attitude on counterinsurgency warfare: give lip service to the classical doctrine while focusing primary attention on standard operations. COMUSMACV observed that

there is no doubt whatsoever that the insurgency in South Vietnam must eventually be defeated among the people in the hamlets and towns; however, in order to defeat the insurgency among the people, they must be provided security of two kinds:

(1) Security of the country as a whole from large well organized and equipped forces including those which may come from outside their country.
(2) Security from the guerrilla, the assassin, the terrorist and the informer.
MACV is convinced that U.S. troops can contribute heavily in the first category of security. . . . Therefore, the MACV concept is basically to employ U.S. forces . . . against the hardcore DRV/VC forces in reaction and search and destroy operations and thus permit the concentration of Vietnamese troops in the heavily populated areas along the coast, around Saigon and in the Delta."[82]

Westmoreland found support coming his way. On 15 June, McNamara authorized the Army to begin planning for the deployment of the airmobile division by 1 September, and instructions were given to formally organize the 1st Cavalry Division (Airmobile). Two days later Taylor confirmed to the State Department that the situation in South Vietnam was, in fact, as serious as MACV had contended. Thus, Westmoreland had all but cleared one of his most difficult hurdles, the State Department, in pushing for an American combat role in Vietnam.

Yet the Department of State was not willing to give in entirely, at least not yet. With Taylor behind Westmoreland's program, the momentum for deployment of U.S. ground forces would now be irresistible; nevertheless, there were still a few who were not yet willing to concede control of things to the Army. Under Secretary of State George W. Ball was such an individual. Ball had an appreciation for the unique political and social dimensions of insurgency warfare, and he introduced these factors, with the military elements, into the development of an alternative American counterinsurgency strategy. In a memo to the president on 18 June, Ball wrote: "Ever since 1961—the beginning of our deep involvement in South Viet-Nam—we have met successive disappointments. We have tended to underestimate the strength and staying power of the enemy. We have tended to overestimate the effectiveness of our sophisticated weapons under jungle conditions. We have watched the progressive loss of territory to Viet Cong control. We have been unable to bring about the creation of a stable political base in Saigon. This is no one's fault. It is in the nature of the struggle."[83] Ball voiced concerns that might have reasonably been advanced by the Army concerning the prospective deployment of large numbers of ground troops to South Vietnam. That the Army did not raise these issues is a tribute to the confidence the brass placed in their doctrine and forces for combating the insurgency.

Ball's warnings had little impact on what had become an inexorable movement toward intervention in the ground war. Indeed, it has often been said that Ball played the role of the president's in-house devil's advocate, providing "opposition" to the "real" policymaking discussions of Bundy, McNamara, and Rostow. On 23 June, McNamara authorized two more BLTs for Qui Nhon and Da Nang. The only holdup on notification of the Air Cavalry Division was the president's desire to ease into the conflict with a minimum amount of fanfare. Taylor was notified by William Bundy on 26 June that COMUSMACV now had the authority to commit U.S. forces to combat in any situation he deemed necessary to strengthen the RVNAF. The enclave strategy was officially dead.[84]

Westmoreland wasted no time getting his troops into action. The following day the 173d Airborne Brigade participated in search-and-destroy operations in War Zone D, a VC stronghold northwest of Saigon. Meanwhile, Ball, unwilling to sit and watch as momentum built up for a presidential announcement of the 44-battalion request, circulated a memo on the subject to State and Defense; the President received a copy on 1 July.

Ball's memo was striking in its grasp of the problems that the Army would encounter in trying to defeat the insurgents, as well as in its recognition of the futility in applying the Army Concept writ large. Ball contended that "without a clear demonstration that American ground forces will be able (*a*) to locate and make contact with the enemy; and (*b*) to fight effectively under the guerrilla conditions of South Viet-nam; we would be highly imprudent to commit substantially increased American forces to a ground war."

Ball also questioned the Army's fixation with the third phase of insurgency warfare, which was relatively conducive to conventional operations, stating that the Army's approach ignored the possibility that the VC, following the doctrine of protracted warfare, might merely retire to phase 2 operations: "Implicit in arguments for greatly augmented United States combat forces in South Viet-Nam is the assumption that the Viet Cong have entered—or are about to enter—their so-called 'third phase' of warfare, having progressed from relatively small-scale hit-and-run operations to large unit, fixed position conventional warfare. Yet we have no basis for assuming that the Viet Cong will fight a war on our terms when they can continue to fight the kind of war they fought so well against both the French and the GVN."

Even assuming that the Army could punish the DRV and the VC enough to make North Vietnam cease its support of insurgent operations, Ball observed, it would not result in victory, since the conditions for success would not have been achieved: "Even if we should succeed in forcing

Hanoi to cease its activities after protracted fighting, we might well win only a Pyrrhic victory. The fanaticism of the Viet Cong makes it almost certain that the insurgents would go underground rather than give up."[85] Ball recommended that U.S. force levels be held at fifteen battalions, that their mission be restricted to base security, and that the United States seek as graceful an exit as possible from the conflict. The memo created a brief flurry. NSC staff member Chester L. Cooper, in a memo to his boss, McGeorge Bundy, characterized Ball's position as "a pessimistic and, God help us, perhaps realistic account of what we confront in Vietnam."[86]

At State, William Bundy tried briefly, and unsuccessfully, to promote a course of action midway between Westmoreland's forty-four battalions and Ball's quick exit from the conflict. In essence, it was the old Taylor approach all over again: continue bombing while avoiding the Hanoi/ Haiphong "donuts"; deploy only eighteen of the thirty-four U.S. battalions requested; and go slow on the ground while testing U.S. troop effectiveness.[87] Taylor, who might have supported Bundy a month earlier, was now silent. He knew which way the wind was blowing. The president and the military were going to get the troops into Vietnam, and nothing would deter them from their purpose.

If Ball's memo made a dent at the Defense Department, it did not show in a Memorandum for the President dispatched to the White House on 1 July in which McNamara recommended that combined U.S./RVNAF ground strength be increased to effectively counter likely VC strength. The obstacle to achieving U.S. objectives was seen to lie in the achievement of a favorable counterinsurgent-to-insurgent force ratio. COMUSMACV contended that the forty-four battalions requested would stabilize the situation, but he could not state "what additional forces may be required in 1966 to gain and maintain the military initiative."[88]

The inability of the military to provide the president with an idea of what forces might be required must have been disconcerting to Johnson, who still had time to back away from a massive commitment of U.S. ground forces. Thus, McNamara was sent to Saigon by the president to find out what forces would be required to achieve victory.

How Much Is Enough?

COMUSMACV had directed that a study on force requirements be initiated in late June in response to a query from Washington on force levels required for 1966. The MACV Staff quickly realized that with the current force ratio at 1.7:1, traditional force ratios of 10:1 or 15:1 posited for counterinsurgency were out of reach. However, rather than question the Army's approach to the war, the staff fit the insurgency to suit the desired American strategy and the resources at hand for executing it.

First, it was decided that the forces of the opposing sides would be measured in maneuver battalions. While certainly appropriate in that it partially discounted the soldiers comprising the large logistical "tail" of U.S. units, the criterion omitted nearly 100,000 VC irregulars. Compounding the distortion, ARVN battalions were rated as equal to VC battalions, while U.S. Army and Free World Forces battalions were rated as equivalent to two VC battalions, and U.S. Marines as equivalent to three. By and large, ARVN battalions were inferior to their VC counterparts in both morale and leadership. They were also, on average, *smaller* than VC battalions, averaging around 350 effectives, compared with 450 for the VC.[89] Of course, the ARVN had more firepower, and that was what counted in evaluating them in terms of the Concept.

Further compromising their evaluation, the MACV Staff concluded that the conflict had passed into phase 3, the equivalent of conventional war for the Army (although not for the insurgents). Thus, a force ratio of 3:1 or 4:1 was acceptable—just as in other wars where it had proven its effectiveness.[90] This last step required a considerable leap of logic on the part of the staffers and the brass, who had to ignore not only insurgency warfare doctrine but CIA and DIA intelligence reports as well. For example, one CIA report submitted on 29 June noted:

The Communists continue to emphasize classic tactics of ambush and envelopment. . . . [relying] primarily on erosive tactics, including widespread terrorism, harassment, and sabotage. Combined with political subversion, these tactics are serving to undermine and discredit government authority in the countryside. . . .
   Their main force capability has by no means been fully committed as yet, and it is by no means certain that the Viet Cong are prepared to go all-out.[91]

Finally, the MACV staff added 10 percent to the number of friendly-battalion equivalents to account for their superiority in firepower and the airmobility factor.[92]

In spite of the "fudge factors" introduced into the study, the staff could only generate a 2.4:1 ratio in friendly-battalion equivalents to VC battalions (see table 3). With anticipated increases in VC/PAVN forces accounted for, the allied forces provided for in the 44-battalion request would only move the force ratio to 3.2:1. Nevertheless, it satisfied the 3:1 requirement, and that, not an analysis of the conflict, was the study's purpose. As for 1966, it was projected that 117 enemy battalions would be in the field. By adding on eighteen Army and six Marine battalions (plus twenty-nine new RF and ARVN battalions)—the "Twenty-four Battalion Add-On"—the 3:1 ratio could be maintained.[93] All this was presented to McNamara and Wheeler during their visit to Saigon. On 17 July, the day after their arrival, McNamara was informed by Washington that the president had decided to deploy the forces requested by Westmoreland.

Upon his return to Washington on 20 July, McNamara submitted a Memorandum for the President in which he noted that despite the weakness of the Ky government (General Ky had assumed control of the GVN in mid-June as head of a clique of generals) and the unfavorable force ratios then existing, he was recommending that the president comply with Westmoreland's request.[94] Furthermore, McNamara advised the president to authorize the call-up of 235,000 reservists for a two-year period and to increase the size of the armed forces by 375,000 men. The former action would provide 36 additional maneuver battalions by the end of 1965, while the latter would provide 27.[95] The 63 additional battalions would make up for the drain of the 58–61 battalions likely to be in the RVN during 1966.

Reflecting the absence of a coherent strategy, McNamara declared,

the forces will be used however they can be brought to bear most effectively. The strategy for winning this stage of the war will be to take the offensive—to take and hold the initiative. . . . The operations should combine to compel the VC/DRV to fight at a higher and more sustained intensity with resulting higher logistical consumption and, at the same time, to limit his capability to resupply forces in combat at that scale by attacking his LOC. The concept assumes . . . use of air in-country, including B-52s, night and day to harass VC in their havens.

Echoing the Army's rationale for the 3:1 conventional war ratio, McNamara stated: "The number of US troops is too small to make a significant difference in the traditional 10–1 government-guerrilla formula, but it is not too small to make a significant difference in the kind of war which seems to be evolving in Vietnam—a 'Third Stage' or conventional war in which is is easier to identify, locate and attack the enemy." Problems associated with the insurgents' reverting to phase 2 operations were noted but appeared "manageable": "It should be recognized, however, that success against the larger, more conventional, VC/PAVN forces could merely drive the VC back into the trees and back to their 1960–64 pattern—a pattern against which US troops and aircraft would be of limited value but with which the GVN, with our help, could cope."[96]

When the president asked whether there were any alternatives to this course of action, there was yet another flurry of warnings from the civilians at State. Robert Johnson, head of State's Policy Planning

TABLE 3. Allied-Enemy Force Ratios

	GVN/U.S./FW Battalions	Enemy Battalions
GVN (ARVN/VNMC/RF)	133	72
USMC (9 × 3)	27	
U.S. Army (5 × 2)	10	
Australia/New Zealand (1 × 2)	2	
Total	172	72
		172/72 = 2:4 to 1

Source: General William B. Rosson, "Four Periods of American Involvement in Vietnam: Development and Implementation of Policy, Strategy, and Programs, Described and Analyzed on the Basis of Service Experience at Progressively Senior Levels" (Ph.D. dissertation, University of Oxford, 1978), p. 204.

Council, wrote Walt Rostow on 22 July. Johnson shared his feelings of "helplessness and futility" with Rostow over the progress of events and outlined a proposal that closely approximated the demographic-frontier strategy advanced by civilians at DOD less than three years later. He wrote:

• The role of U.S. ground forces in SVN should be limited to maintaining indefinite control of coastal areas; under no circumstances should we become committed to major participation in the pacification effort within SVN.
• We should announce, in connection with the introduction of new ground forces, the indefinite suspension of air action against North Viet-Nam. . . .
• That we not expand further the use of air power in SVN in situations where we cannot do so without reasonable discrimination between VC and non-VC targets. . . .

Such a posture would provide us a territorial and an international political base which we could hold indefinitely—provided the GVN did not ask us to leave. It would provide, in other words, the basis for a less costly stalemate than would major U.S. direct involvement in counter-guerrilla operations.[97]

In addition to the Johnson memo, William Bundy had Thomas L. Hughes, director of Intelligence and Research at State, draw up an analysis for Rusk that strongly contested MACV's assertion that the war was moving into phase 3 operations. The analysis, submitted to the secretary of state on 23 July, observed:

We do not believe that the criteria established by Giap for the third stage—size of unit, scale of operation, and nature of attack—have been or are about to be met in South Vietnam. Our examination of Viet Cong capabilities . . . persuades us rather that the VC will continue to employ guerrilla tactics with only intermittent recourse to spectacular, multibattalion attacks against major ARVN targets. . . .

Moreover, during the earlier period of the war against the French, the Viet Minh had developed elaborate logistic lines and extensive supplies which permitted them to conduct protracted large-scale attack operations even though their tactical concepts remained oriented basically toward guerrilla rather than conventional or positional warfare. Communist forces in South Vietnam today do not have comparable logistic lines or supply; they are still essentially covert, partly because of the harassing capability of GVN and U.S. forces. Even though the introduction of material from North Vietnam has increased, it is not open or massive, and the Communists still rely heavily on locally captured weapons. In short, we do not believe that the Viet Cong, even with recent PAVN reinforcement, are now capable of initiating a drastically different phase of warfare.[98]

The analysis implicitly rejected COMUSMACV's force request, as well as his strategy. If anything, said Hughes, with U.S. forces present, the insurgents would be moving back to phase 2 operations. The need, as always, was to provide security to the population from VC terror and acts of coercion.

Moreover, although battalion-sized attacks have been more conspicuous in the first six months of 1965 than they were in the first six months of 1964 (28 as against 14), this is not a recent phenomenon. Rather the increase in battalion-sized attacks began in July 1964, when there were 12 (a number not yet exceeded), with the total for the second six months of 1964 mounting to 32.

The statistical record to date clearly fails to support the hypothesis that the Communists have abandoned the pattern of a relatively low but periodically peaking level of attacks, accompanied by a high and generally rising level of terrorism, harassment, and sabotage.

The analysis concluded by stating that the Communists were not about to play the game the way Westmoreland wanted them to: "*Under these circumstances, we cannot see them resorting to a strategy that would substantially increase their vulnerability to US power,* except as an act of desperation in which they might take major risks in the hope of bettering their position for immediate negotiating purposes. We believe that they are still far from such a point of desperation."[99] The VC would not wage war according to the Concept. In effect, Hughes was opting for Robert Johnson's strategy.

Henry Cabot Lodge, ambassador-designate to South Vietnam, attended the meetings in Saigon and wrote the president that the "oil spot" principle was still the key to victory: "If the opportunity offers, U.S. troops can fight the pitched battle with large units of the Viet Cong—as they attack our strong points, and possibly, in other places where they can be identified and where the circumstances are such that the outlook for destroying them is propitious. . . . But U.S. troops should not be committed to prolonged "search sweeps" in the jungle or to being permanently stationed in the jungle."[100]

Finally, the strategic problem for Westmoreland and the scores of maneuver battalions he was calling for were summed up succinctly by Chester Cooper. In a memo to McGeorge Bundy on 21 July, Cooper commented that that morning's discussion noted two possible military outcomes resulting from a substantial increase in U.S. forces: either the VC main forces would be forced to revert to guerrilla warfare or they would choose not to confront U.S. units head-on and would voluntarily revert to guerrilla actions. *"Either way, it would appear that we and the GVN will be faced with the problem of guerrilla rather than positional warfare.* The fact that this may mean that the VC cannot achieve a military victory offers small comfort; neither we nor the GVN have as yet demonstrated that we can win this kind of war."[101]

But the president's mind was made up. He would not deviate from the course he had set in December 1964. The United States would fight to save South Vietnam, and the commander in the field would be supported. On 27 July the NSC conducted an early evening session at the White House in which the president reviewed the bidding and approved the 44-battalion request to "give the commanders the men they say they need." Fearful of a congressional backlash that might endanger his Great Society programs should he put the nation on a war footing, Johnson decided not to call up the reserves but to wait until January and observe how the situation developed. Besides, noted LBJ, if the United States went all-out in this fashion, the Chinese and the Soviets would only increase their aid to the DRV (rather flawed logic given that if the president had really believed it, the introduction of several hundred thousand U.S. troops could have been, and indeed was, offset by the North Vietnamese themselves).[102]

Ambassador Lodge was present, and he asked whether the ratio of government forces to guerrilla forces had to be 10:1, noting that he had been grilled by the Senate Foreign Relations Committee on the matter, implying as it did astronomical U.S. force commitments. General Wheeler told Lodge not to worry—the mobility and firepower of U.S. forces had drastically cut the ratio, 4:1 being about right.

The NSC meeting was more of a formality than anything else. Johnson's decision of 17 July in favor of the commitment of large American ground forces remained unchanged. The following day, 28 July, the president called a press conference and informed the nation that the 1st Cavalry Division was being ordered to Vietnam along with other units, which would raise U.S. strength in that country to 125,000 men. Within twenty-four hours the first brigade of the Army's 101st Airborne Division was arriving in Vietnam. At the same time, a JCS memorandum showed nearly two hundred thousand men and thirty-four maneuver battalions slated for deployment. Its efforts to win the war through training and advising the Vietnamese a failure, the Army would now show them by example. The "first team" had at long last arrived.

6
A Strategy of Tactics

The Strategy of Attrition

With the deployment of American combat troops to South Vietnam in large numbers, the Army applied the doctrine and force structure it had developed for conventional contingencies in Europe and Korea against insurgent forces practicing a form of revolutionary warfare. The lack of progress in defeating the insurgents during the period 1965–68 can be attributed, in part, to an Army strategy reflecting traditional methods of operation in a conflict that was dramatically different from its wars over the previous half-century. Deeply embedded in the service's psyche, conventional operations held sway over the Army even as its civilian superiors lost faith in their effectiveness for counterinsurgency operations.

In a sense, simple attrition of insurgent forces and support systems was a natural strategy for MACV to pursue. It emphasized the Army's strong suits in firepower and strategic mobility and offered the prospect of minimizing U.S. casualties. The Army, being denied the opportunity to win a decisive battle of annihilation by invading North Vietnam, found the attrition strategy best fit the kind of war it had prepared to fight.

Basically, a strategy of attrition offered the Army the prospect of winning the war quickly, or at least more quickly than with traditional counterinsurgency operations, which promised to be long and drawn out. Attrition is a product of the American way of war: spend lavishly on munitions, materiel, and technology to save lives. How many citizens or governmental and military leaders would (or could) choose the other side of the coin? U.S. military leaders believed in the morale-raising and life-saving value of massive firepower whose success they had witnessed in World War II and Korea.[1]

An attrition strategy was a natural outgrowth of the force structure and doctrine developed by the Army. Units deployed to Vietnam in the summer of 1965 were not the Special Warfare task forces that the Army purportedly had formed for counterinsurgency contingencies but heavy units trained and equipped for mid-intensity warfare. As one general put it, "The infantry divisions of the Army were very, very heavy and difficult to deploy and . . . had limited mobility if they weren't in an area where there were roads."[2] The Army, said General Taylor, felt compelled to adopt a strategy of attrition because of the political ground rules that confined the Army's operations within the RVN. If the Army was denied a battle of annihilation through an invasion of North Vietnam, then attrition was the closest approximation available.[3]

Some have stated that the strategy of attrition was not a strategy at all but actually reflected the absence of one. The sheer weight of American materiel and resources seemed sufficient to the military leadership to wear down the North Vietnamese and their VC allies; thus, strategy was not necessary. All that was needed was efficient application of firepower.[4] It had worked against the Japanese and the Germans in World War II and against the Chinese in Korea. It would be tried again in Vietnam.

Attrition as Strategy

Initially, the Army had an open field in deciding how the war in South Vietnam would be fought. The president, concerned primarily with keeping the war contained, focused his attention on the bombing campaign against the North. So long as MACV restricted its operations to South Vietnam proper, interference would be minimal. McNamara, feeling that his expertise did not measure up to that of the Joint Chiefs, was similarly reluctant to get involved.[5]

Westmoreland's proposed strategy envisioned a three-phase process culminating in the destruction of all insurgent forces and base areas by the end of 1967. Phase 1 would see the stabilization of the situation by the end of 1965 using the 44-battalion commitment; phase 2 involved the 24-battalion add-on projected for 1966 and called for "the resumption of the offensive"; phase 3 was viewed as a mop-up period in which remaining insurgent forces would be eliminated.[6] Westmoreland recalled that he "came up with the concept of leveling off our buildup to achieve a well-balanced, hard-hitting force designed to fight in sustained combat and just grind away against the enemy on a sustained basis—something [the enemy] was not capable of doing, since he didn't have the logistics."[7]

Westmoreland explicitly rejected the alternative of paying less attention to the enemy's big units and breaking down U.S. units into smaller groups to concentrate on pacification. His position was rooted in the military operations conducted by the VC in November 1964, when they mounted a limited offensive in Binh Dinh Province. In their attacks, two VC regiments defeated a number of smaller ARVN units engaged in pacification operations. Speaking of this defeat in detail, Westmoreland maintained that "it was a lesson long to be remembered." He cited it as an example, saying that if he broke any U.S. forces down to engage in pacification, they would suffer the same fate.[8] Yet the incident was more a rationalization for the big-unit operations favored by MACV than an objective lesson against the perils of maintaining insufficient quick-reaction reserves, the real cause of the ARVN's November debacle. That MACV possessed these quick-reaction units in the form of its airmobile forces and thus could afford to concentrate heavily on pacification was a point that was lost on the MACV Staff and their superiors.

Westmoreland's approach was seconded by the chairman of the Joint Chiefs, Gen. Earle Wheeler. As Wheeler saw it, "the ground operations in the South would increase the communists' consumption and the bombing would reduce [their] supply."[9] MACV simply developed a strategy to suit the Army's preferred *modus operandi,* force structure, and doctrine. According to Westmoreland, "Superior American firepower would be most advantageously employed against the big units, and using it in remote regions would mean fewer civilian casualties and less damage to built-up areas."[10] Again General Wheeler agreed, contending that U.S. combat power and mobility "will enable us to find the enemy more often, fix him more firmly when we find him, and defeat him when we fight him . . . our objective will be to keep the combat tempo at such a rate that the Viet Cong will be unable to take the time to recuperate or regain their balance." It was Harkins's old Plan Explosion all over again. This approach, Wheeler concluded, "provides a strategy which, in my opinion, gives the best assurance of military victory in South Vietnam."[11]

Westmoreland, like Taylor, argued that given the geographical limitations involved, there was no alternative to attrition. He claimed that population security could not be provided if the enemy's big units were at large. When it was pointed out that 90 percent of the country's population lived along the narrow coastal plain and in the Delta and that VC battalions in the remote, sparsely populated Highlands would be isolated from the people, Westmoreland demurred, contending that "it was not enough merely to contain the big units. They had to be pounded with artillery and bombs and eventually brought to battle on the ground if they were not forever to remain a threat."[12]

This was essential if the Army's strategy of attrition was to succeed. Yet Westmoreland himself revealed the fatal flaw in this strategy. What if the enemy's big units refused to fight? What if they continued to wage an insurgency in the traditional sense, with the people, instead of the opponent's military forces being the objective? The general conceded that "unlike the guerrillas, if we avoided battle, we could never succeed. We could never destroy the big units by leaving them alone." Yet *the guerrillas avoided battle* and drew the Americans away from the population. As Westmoreland later admitted, "From the first the primary emphasis of the North Vietnamese focused on the Central Highlands and the central coastal provinces, with the basic end of drawing American units into remote areas and thereby facilitating control of the population in the lowlands."[13] By focusing on population control, Westmoreland might have forced the guerrillas to come to him. As things turned out, the Army would neither secure the population nor get its decisive battles with the insurgents.

Furthermore, either out of organizational hubris or slavishness to the Concept (or both), COMUSMACV ignored the lack of success of previous search-and-destroy operations. Even in the recent quasi–phase 3 period of the insurgency they had proved largely ineffective, as found in a MACV staff report submitted in March 1965 which found that ARVN search-and-destroy operations frequently "failed to establish any contact with major VC units." Despite the ARVN's shortcomings, the report concluded, "the ability of the VC to break contact and 'disappear' from view does not depend upon luck or some special technique" but on the inherent advantages that accrued to skilled insurgent forces.[14]

For Westmoreland, this process of fitting the war to the Concept led to his perception of the insurgency as somewhat akin to a previous war in which standard Army operations had prevailed. As he saw it: "Vietnam was a war of movement, an area war. It was somewhat analogous to the [American] Civil War. There were certain troops in static positions, around base areas and airfields, but other than that it was a war of movement. Instead of having a horse, as was the case in the Civil War, we had the helicopter. It was a war of fluid situations. It was impossible for us to seize and hold terrain after seizing it because we didn't have the troops. . . . You 'homed' on the enemy as in the Civil War and tried to bring the enemy to combat. Once you've done that, then you regroup, move, and continue to try and find the enemy and force him to combat."[15]

The result of viewing the war through the perceptual lens of the Concept was the perpetuation of search-and-destroy operations from the advisory era into the period of intervention. While men like Sir Robert Thompson argued for concentrating on the local guerrilla forces, which provided sustenance to the VC's main-force units, MACV claimed that it was the other way around—the big units were supporting the local guerrillas.[16] Not only did the Army's assertion turn insurgency doctrine on its head but it was untrue. A Pentagon study conducted in 1966, when VC forces were even larger than in the previous year, estimated that VC support requirements from outside South Vietnam totaled *only twelve tons per day!* Obviously, the bulk of insurgent support was provided from *within* the RVN. The Army leadership, however, refused to acknowledge this. There was no questioning of Westmoreland's approach by the Army brass back in Washington; both Wheeler and Harold Johnson were in agreement with the commander in the field. The JCS also supported the Army's approach. In JCS Memorandum 652–65, dated 27 August, the Chiefs called for increased pressure on the North and seizing the initiative as posited by COMUSMACV in the South. This was followed by JCS Memorandum 811–65, dated 10 November, in which the Chiefs visualized the use of U.S. ground forces as providing "heavy assault strength against VC forces and bases" in search-and-destroy operations. The ARVN was to be consigned to the unglamorous duty of population security, a role in which they had demonstrated considerable ineptitude in the past. Thus the Army left counterinsurgency to the RVNAF, while U.S. commanders went out in search of the big battles.[17]

The Chiefs appeared to have cause for satisfaction over their endorsement of MACV's strategy when, shortly after the forwarding of their memo, Army forces defeated the Communists in a major battle in the Ia Drang Valley.

The Ia Drang Valley and Validation of the Concept

While the attrition strategy was formulated in the summer of 1965, U.S. ground forces continued arriving in South Vietnam: two Army brigades in July, followed by a corps headquarters. A Marine regiment landed in August, and by the end of September the entire 1st Air Cavalry Division had been deployed to the Central Highlands. The remainder of the 1st Infantry Division was deployed by 7 October, and, finally, an entire ROK division was in-country on 8 November. U.S. strength at that time stood at 184,314 men. The pride of the U.S. forces, however, was the Army's 1st

Cavalry Division. It was deployed as the Army had wanted, to the Central Highlands, where insurgent strength was most formidable.

On 14 November elements of the 1st Cavalry encountered regimental-size formations of North Vietnamese in the Ia Drang Valley. The ensuing battle was both bloody and savage, with the Communists suffering over 1,200 killed, while U.S. losses exceeded 200. To General Westmoreland and the MACV Staff (particularly his G-3, Gen. William Depuy) the Ia Drang Valley campaign represented the successful application of the attrition strategy. Here were large enemy formations willing to go toe to toe with the Americans, and their big units were being smashed by the Army's firepower and high-tech mobility. Standard operations were working; therefore, no alternative strategies need be explored. No more feedback was required for MACV save the body counts that measured the attrition strategy's progress. For Westmoreland, "the ability of the Americans to meet and defeat the best troops the enemy could put on the field of battle was once more demonstrated beyond any possible doubt, as was the validity of the Army's airmobile concept."[18] General Johnson felt that "the worst was behind us."[19]

Indeed, from this point on, the Army began to discard any reluctance that it had concerning the deployment of heavy forces, such as armor. Whereas Westmoreland had originally questioned the utility of deploying armored formations in a low-intensity conflict environment, this soon gave way to a feeling of enthusiasm toward the use of tanks against insurgents. As early as the beginning of 1966 the Army Staff in Washington was pressing MACV to accept the new Sheridan tank for use in the RVN.[20] By then the M48 Patton tank had already been deployed with the 1st Infantry Division to test the effectiveness of armor against insurgents. Westmoreland's initial resistance to armor was overcome primarily by its ability to provide the firepower that he felt was needed for his strategy of attrition.[21] Armor had the additional advantage, from the Army's point of view, of allowing mechanized infantry to fight mounted, employing their armored personnel carriers (APCs) or tanks as assault vehicles in closing with and destroying the enemy.[22] Of course, it was not very difficult for the VC to determine when an armored unit was trying to close with them; thus, the American tanks were easily avoided. Often, APCs and tanks were employed in "jungle busting," plodding noisily ahead of the infantry, clearing a path through the jungle and setting off mines and booby traps. One disillusioned colonel remarked, "I saw personally only one example of jungle-busting: four kilometers progress in 16 hours by a troop and attached rifle company. The costs in maintenance (then and later) certainly outweighed the knowledge that a serpentine jungle path a few feet wide might have been temporarily freed of vc."[23]

The use of armored formations went against many principles of classical counterinsurgency doctrine. Armored units rarely operated at night, when the guerrillas were most active; they allowed for easy evasion of U.S. forces by the guerrillas; they encouraged the infantry to operate "buttoned up" inside their vehicles instead of out on patrol; they were "maintenance-intensive" pieces of equipment, requiring large numbers of support troops, who did not actively participate in operations; and finally, compared with the infantry, they were grossly indiscriminate in the application of firepower. In short, they were a blunt instrument for combating insurgency—save in its most advanced stages—but quite appropriate to the Army's notion of how wars should be fought.

A further addition to the Army's arsenal of firepower was the air support provided by tactical fighters and helicopters. The rationale for the lavish application of such firepower (and, in the case of the helicopter, additional mobility) was not for counterinsurgency operations but to support the Army's strategy of attrition. All this firepower and mobility, claimed General Wheeler, made traditional concerns relating to counter-insurgency inoperative: "These two air weapons—helicopters and fighter bombers—provide to South Vietnamese and to US forces an advantage in mobility and firepower—the fundamentals of combat—greatly exceeding that available to counterinsurgency forces in any other guerrilla war. Frankly, I do not know what is the required ratio of government to guerrilla forces in order for the government to prevail. I do know that it is not eight or ten-to-one in South Vietnam because we can achieve the preponderance of force required with less than that ratio."[24]

Despite the general's confidence in the Army's attrition strategy, students of insurgency warfare were uneasy over this radical departure from classical counterinsurgency strategy. Sir Robert Thompson, in evaluating the Army's approach to the insurgency, stated, "The major criticism I had tactically in Vietnam was that the one element in which you [the Army] were never mobile was on your feet. You got landed from helicopters and the battle took place, but when the battle was over and you had won the battle, you even went out by helicopter. No one ever walked out. Now the enemy, who was mobile on his feet, could actually decide whether he was going to have a battle with you in the first place, and he could break it off whenever he wanted to."[25] Thompson felt that victory could be achieved only through a long process involving the denial of enemy access to the people through intensive ambushing and patrolling in and around the populated areas and by the use of long-range patrols to harass the guerrillas in more remote areas. Sooner or later the VC, denied access to their primary source of supply, the population, would have to come out in the open and contest the government's control of the people. At that point the insurgent main forces could be defeated. Barring a gross error in judgment on the part of the insurgents, however, annihilation of the VC's main units would not happen before these conditions occurred. By adopting a strategy of attrition, the Army placed the VC in the position of merely having to survive in order to prevail.

Strategic approaches such as Thompson's did not gain a receptive ear within the Army, even as it became apparent to many civilian observers that the Army Concept was inappropriate for insurgency conflict. General Williams, author of the McNamara directive that gave birth to Army airmobility, recalled a discussion with an American correspondent while in Vietnam:

Sitting and talking to him, he made the charge. He said, "You are doing more in your helicopters to prevent our side from winning this war than anyone else." I said, "How's that?" He said, "Well, let me illustrate it this way. Everybody agrees that this is a war for the hearts and minds of the people. How do you expect our forces to win the hearts and minds of the people when all they do is take off from one Army base and fly overhead at 1500 feet while Charlie is sitting down there and he's got 'em by the testicles jerking, and every time he jerks their hearts and minds follow. Now, until the Americans are willing to get down there with Charlie, he's got their hearts and minds."

Reflecting upon this, General Williams agreed that "if you really want to be cost-effective, you have to fight the war the way the VC fought it. You have to fight it down in the muck and in the mud and at night, and on a day-to-day basis." Yet, the general told the correspondent, "that's not the American way, and you are not going to get the American soldier to fight that way."[26]

Although Williams felt that a true counterinsurgency strategy was not possible, junior officers in Vietnam, less indoctrinated in the ways of the Concept, were more inclined to support it. On a trip to Vietnam in December 1965, after supper one night General Johnson engaged in a gab session with lieutenants and captains of the 1st Infantry Division. The discussion quickly turned to strategy and tactics. The young platoon leaders and company commanders told the Chief of Staff that they could not engage the enemy if they were moving around in big outfits. What was needed, they said, was to operate in many small units, constantly moving and patrolling. Although Johnson "agreed with their philosophy," he rejected their ideas, since "we [the Army] were not going to be able to respond to the public outcry in the United States about [the] casualties" that might result.[27]

There was, however, one segment of the American ground forces in South Vietnam that opted for a close approximation of traditional counter-insurgency strategy. These combat units did not belong to the Army but were U.S. Marine units deployed in I Corps. As Sir Robert Thompson pointed out, "Of all the United States forces the Marine Corps alone made a serious attempt to achieve permanent and lasting results in their tactical area of responsibility by seeking to protect the rural population."[28]

Combined Action Platoons (CAPs): A Marine Challenge to the Concept

The Marine approach to counterinsurgency in Vietnam had its roots in the heritage of the service. A history of Marine participation in small wars had given them a background in the type of conflict environment they faced in South Vietnam. As early as 1940 the Marines had put out a manual on small wars which stated:

In regular warfare, the responsible officers simply strive to attain a method of producing the maximum physical effect with the force at their disposal. In small wars, the goal is to gain decisive results with the least application of force and the consequent minimum loss of life. The end aim is the social, economic, and political development of the people subsequent to the military defeat of the enemy insurgent. In small wars, tolerance, sympathy, and kindness should be the keynote of our relationship with the mass of the population.[29]

Once the Marines arrived in South Vietnam, they put their doctrine into practice. Gen. Lewis Walt, commander of the Marine forces under COMUSMACV, issued orders for all Marine combat units to conduct vigorous patrols and ambushes from sundown to sunup, when insurgent activity was greatest. Walt issued stringent orders regarding the application of firepower, keeping it to an absolute minimum. Reflective of the manner in which the Marines viewed the conflict was a story told by General Walt of some Marines who came upon an old woman mining a road used by U.S. forces. They discovered that the woman harbored no particular hatred toward Americans. She planted the mines because the VC threatened to kill her granddaughter, the only surviving member of her family, if she refused. Since neither the Marines nor the Saigon regime protected her from this form of revolutionary "justice," observed Walt, he could hardly condemn her actions.[30]

Although it would have been easy for the Marines to vent their frustration against the victims of insurgent coercion, Walt realized that that would only be playing into the enemy's hands. If the Marines were going to succeed, they would have to get close to the people and provide them with security from communist intimidation. Therefore, rather than hopping around in airmobile search-and-destroy operations or use helicopters for movement and logistical support, the Marines relied on the same roads used by the population. Walt observed that the Marines "could have depended almost entirely on sealift and airlift between major points on the north-south road through our area, but like many other things in Vietnam, the purely military consideration was never fully adequate. It was important that the roads be kept open for the people as well as for ourselves."[31]

The Marine approach to counterinsurgency was further refined through the efforts of Capt. Jim Cooper, commander of a Marine company operating near the Vietnamese town of Chulai. After a period in which his unit conducted repeated sweeps, patrols, and attempted ambushes, Cooper became frustrated at his inability to separate the guerrillas from the population in the hamlet of Thanh My Trung. He decided to deploy his Marines inside the hamlet and announced that henceforth the people would be protected from the VC, for he had come to stay. Cooper increased the number of night patrols and ambushes and brought the villages' paramilitary Popular Forces (PF) unit under his wing, gradually making the local force assume a greater share of responsibility for village security. Before long the PFs, along with the Marines, were engaged in continuous night patrols in the area immediately surrounding the village, stalking the VC, setting ambushes, disrupting the insurgents' plans and activities. The result was the VC's abandonment of the village.[32]

It did not take long for CAPs to catch on with the Marines. By 1966 there were fifty-seven such units in I Corps, and the number expanded to seventy-nine in 1967.[33] As it worked out, each CAP consisted of fifteen marines and 34 PFs living in one particular village or hamlet. Their mission called for giving high priority to the traditional elements of counterinsurgency strategy: destruction of the insurgent infrastructure, protection of the people and the government infrastructure, organization of local intelligence nets, and training of the PFs.[34] If CAPs suffered from problems, they centered on the language barrier between the Americans and their Vietnamese counterparts and the failure of the Marine Corps leadership to arrange the CAPs to provide for an interlocking network of units that would conform to the "oil spot" principle.[35]

The CAPs produced results, but like all successful counterinsurgency programs, it took time. By the summer of 1967 a DOD report noted that the Hamlet Evaluation System (HES) security score gave CAP-protected villages a score of 2.95 out of a possible 5.0 maximum, as compared with an average of 1.6 for all 1 Corps villages. Furthermore, there was a direct correlation between the time a CAP stayed in a village and the degree of security achieved, with CAP-protected villages progressing twice as fast as those occupied by the PFs alone.[36]

All this was achieved at a casualty rate *lower* than that found in units operating in search-and-destroy missions. Gen. Richard Clutterbuck, a British counterinsurgency expert, noted that "although [Marine] casualties are high, they are only 50% of the casualties of the normal infantry or marine battalions being flown around by helicopters on large scale operations."[37] Thus, the actual data on casualties belied Army concerns that such operations produced intolerably high American losses.

The Marines also initiated a program called GOLDEN FLEECE, which was rooted in traditional counterinsurgency doctrine. It involved saturating coastal farming areas with Marine guards and patrols during the harvest season so that the farmers could harvest, store, and eventually sell their crop free from VC taxation. Although the VC fought the system, they were no longer the fish swimming in a sea of cooperative people. They instructed the farmers to let the food rot in the fields or risk reprisals. When the farmers, emboldened by the long-term presence of the Marines and their assurance that they had come to stay, went ahead with the harvest, the VC tried to make good their threat, first attacking in small patrols but eventually moving up to battalion-size assaults. Each time, the Marines, assisted by local paramilitary units, beat them back. "Each catty of rice," wrote General Walt, "not going into Viet Cong bins meant that another catty had to be grown in North Vietnam and brought over the hundreds of miles of mountain trail by human bearers."[38]

Even though only a small percentage of the total Marine force in South Vietnam was utilized in these operations (a mere ten companies were involved in the CAP program during 1967), the results were impressive. Sir Robert Thompson noted that "the use of CAPs is quite the best idea I have seen in Vietnam, and it worked superbly."[39] At the same time, DOD survey teams observing the operations of CAPs went away concluding that then current Army training simulations (the "Vietnam villages") were "not by any means representative of real situations."[40]

The Army's reaction to the CAP program was ill-disguised disappointment, if not outright disapproval, from the top down. Gen. Harry

Kinnard was "absolutely disgusted" with the Marines. "I did everything I could to drag them out," he said, "and get them to fight. . . . They just wouldn't play. They just *would not play*. They don't know how to fight on land, particularly against guerrillas."[41] Major General Depuy observed sarcastically that "the Marines came in and just sat down and didn't do anything. They were involved in counterinsurgency of the deliberate, mild sort."[42]

Brigadier General Hunt of Great Britain, an expert on insurgency warfare, recounted his experience with the Army on one of his trips to I Corps: "The Marines had never been able to sell the idea of CAPS to the rest of the Americans [i.e., the Army]. It was only in the north where the CAPS were operating, and when I went down to MACV and referred to this [limitation of the program], they said that I had been fixed by the Marines—brainwashed! They did not agree and in any case said it would be too expensive. [They did not realize that] when you get an RF or PF man out in the village he is like the chicken's neck; he is in an extremely dangerous position. You have to make it clear to him that he is going to be supported if there is need."[43]

General Westmoreland was particularly upset over the Marines' use of CAPS, challenging as they did the concept of operations that he had drawn up. He stated in his memoirs that "they were assiduously [*sic*] combing the countryside within the beachheads, trying to establish firm control in hamlets and villages, and planning to expand the beachhead gradually up and down the coast. . . . Yet the practice left the enemy free to come and go as he pleased throughout the bulk of the region and, when and where he chose, to attack the periphery of the beachheads."[44] Westmoreland did not realize that the Marines were operating in the densely populated areas, leaving the VC little to recruit or exploit in the remote, largely uninhabited region they controlled. Furthermore, through long-range STINGRAY patrols, the Marines gained intelligence on the movements of large insurgent forces close to the populated areas. The efficacy of the Marine approach is borne out by the results: throughout the history of the program only *one* CAP was ever overrun.[45]

Westmoreland later conceded that the Marines achieved some "noteworthy results," but he continued to defend the Army approach, claiming that he "simply had not enough numbers to put a squad of Americans in every village and hamlet."[46] This was not supported by the facts. First, it was not necessary to place army squads in *every* village simultaneously; indeed, the "oil spot" principle called for gradual expansion outward from selected areas. Westmoreland's argument is more reflective of the Army's impatience for quick results in a conflict environment that would not produce them.

Second, even if encadrement of every village and hamlet had been the requirement, a 1967 DOD report found that it could be met by utilizing 167,000 U.S. troops, far fewer than the 550,000 eventually assigned to South Vietnam.[47] Some argue that of the 550,000 only about 80,000 represented the "foxhole strength" of American forces, that is, those men actually involved in the fighting. The counterargument, of course, is that the force mix was grossly overweighted in favor of support personnel necessary to maintain the firepower-intensive U.S. forces deployed in South Vietnam. Tanks, APCs and helicopters require considerable numbers of maintenance support personnel, along with a large logistical tail of soldiers to keep the flow of spare parts and munitions moving. Light infantry units, on the other hand, require far fewer support troops, enabling a greater percentage of soldiers to participate in the actual fighting. Such light infantry units, however, were few and far between in the heavy, firepower-oriented force structure of the Army. To strip down the ROAD divisions to fight a light infantry war would have required the Army to go against everything it had worked for during the lean years of the Eisenhower administration.

Given a 550,000-man ceiling, a force mix providing for CAP operations could have been effected, with several airmobile or ROAD divisions held in reserve to counter any large-scale VC/NVA incursions into areas undergoing pacification. Casualties would have been minimized, and population security enhanced.

While Westmoreland was just as disgusted as Depuy with the Marines' approach to the war, he realized that the carrot would work better than the stick in moving them toward MACV's strategic approach to the conflict. The marines, after all, were not a part of the Army; furthermore, if they wanted, they could drag their feet in complying with MACV directives or seek support from the Navy in resisting the Army's intrusion into their operations. Therefore, Westmoreland, with Depuy's help, wrote General Walt a note in an effort to persuade the Marines to conform to the Army strategy. In it, Westmoreland told Walt that he was "impressed with the professional competence of all echelons and with the grasp which your officers and men display regarding the problems of long term security and pacification." He was concerned, however, "about the situation throughout the part of I Corps which lies beyond the three Marine enclaves. Outside your enclaves the VC are largely able to move at will and they are rapidly consolidating very large areas. . . . The longer the VC have a free hand in the rest of the Corps, the more area they will consolidate, and the more difficult it will be for us in the long run. . . . Therefore, I believe very strongly that we must . . . seek out and destroy large VC forces."[48] The discussion focused on consolidation of terrain, not the population. In any event, the purpose of search-and-destroy operations was not to occupy territory but to engage in battle.

MACV did initiate an Army version of CAP involving mobile training teams (MTTs). This approach involved four-man Army teams and an ARVN officer working with village paramilitary forces for about a month and then moving on. The program reflected the Army's quick-fix approach to counterinsurgency and its desire for quick results. Four men providing hamlet security for one month was hardly the same as thirteen men involved over a prolonged period of time. The Army would not accept the fact that getting people to believe you were going to protect them required an effective government security force that was always going to be there, as well as a lot of time and resources. Counterinsurgency on the cheap would not work.

It must be said, however, that the Army succeeded in meeting the challenge to its preferred strategy that CAPs represented. In the end, the Marine CAP program remained limited, despite its demonstrated effectiveness. The bulk of Marine forces in I Corps remained involved in border surveillance and interdiction operations, one example being the Marine base at Khe Sanh.

How Much Is Enough? (Revisited)

For its chosen strategy to work, the Army gambled that it could attrite insurgent forces faster than the enemy could replace them, either by infiltration from the North or by recruitment within the South. In opting for this approach, the Army wagered that a strategy playing to its strong suits instead of the insurgents' weak points would be enough to provide victory.

The key to success in this strategic approach was forcing the VC and the NVA to fight. Having eschewed the traditional approach of having the insurgents fight to maintain access to the population, the Army relied on its technological and logistical strong suits—it would use sensors, infrared photography, helicopters, and a host of technological wonders to find the enemy, and firepower and mobility to destroy him. The Communists, however, had been and would continue to be successful in dictating the tempo of operations and, therefore, their level of casualties as well. The Army, faced with the potential bankruptcy of its strategy, responded, not by abandoning it, but by insisting, as it had during the advisory years, that the only necessary change was an increase in the scope and intensity of operations.

It became evident quite early on that the insurgents would stick to their strategy of protracted conflict: drawing U.S. units away from the populated areas to allow continued access to their logistical base (the population); generating U.S. casualties to attrite the will of the United States to continue the war; keeping U.S. forces in remote, static positions when possible (Khe Sanh, for example) to inhibit their operational effectiveness; and deploying sufficient NVA forces to entice the Army away from populated areas.

Evidence of the insurgents' strategic continuity was present early in the Army's intervention phase in Vietnam. It will be recalled that COMUSMACV authorized the 173d Airborne Brigade to participate in search-and-destroy operations in the Iron Triangle, a Communist redoubt northwest of Saigon, in late June, before the final decision was made on the 44-battalion request. During the three-day operation the brigade failed to make any significant contact with the enemy, although the unit was sweeping through an area long recognized as a VC stronghold.[49]

A little over three months later the 173d was again involved in search-and-destroy operations in the Iron Triangle, this time from 8 to 14 October. The after-action report submitted by the brigade indicated that the VC were avoiding U.S. forces and were retreating into phase 2 guerrilla warfare rather than slugging it out with the Americans in phase 3– type operations.[50] Nevertheless, Brigadier General Williamson, the 173d's commander, wrote that his unit had "torn apart" the Iron Triangle and destroyed "all enemy troops." The unit claimed forty-four enemy killed. Yet within a year the Army was again trying to clear the area of VC. Ignoring the implications of operations such as these, MACV chose to rest its estimate of enemy intentions on the victory of the 1st Cavalry in the Ia Drang Valley.

By late November MACV realized that the force ratios that the Army had creatively arrived at earlier did not reflect the true situation. On 23 November, Westmoreland notified the JCS that "the VC/PAVN buildup rate is predicted to be double that of US Phase II forces [now the 28-battalion add-on]."[51] The increase in enemy forces would leave the allied forces with a ratio of only 2.1:1 in "battalion equivalents" by the end of 1966. Rather than reevaluate the strategy of attrition, MACV forwarded a request for an additional 41,500 troops, raising Army phase 2 deployments to 154,000 men, for a total of nearly 375,000 by mid-1967. Meanwhile, the myth that the insurgents' main-force units were the principal source of support for local guerrilla forces persisted.[52]

Despite the victory in the battle of the Ia Drang Valley, Westmoreland quickly realized that his attrition strategy would take time and the infusion of large numbers of U.S. troops to reach the *crossover point*, the point where the enemy's losses in battle would exceed his capability to replace them. At a high-level conference in Honolulu from 7 to 9 February, William Bundy and John McNaughton drafted a program for increased U.S. forces for South Vietnam. While President Johnson and Prime Minister Ky were involved in their meetings the program was ironed out at Camp Smith by Westmoreland, Wheeler, Admiral Sharp, the CINCPAC, Bundy, and McNaughton.

Reacting to the president's exhortation to "nail the coonskin to the wall" in South Vietnam, the plan called for U.S. troop levels to be increased from 184,300 at the close of 1965 to some 429,000 by the end of 1966. The number of U.S. maneuver battalions would jump from 35 to 79. The intent was to more than double the rate of U.S. offensive operations, and primary emphasis was placed on achieving that objective, as opposed to pacification. The goal was to reach the crossover point by year's end.[53]

In March McNamara authorized JCS planning for deployment of the additional forces, with their deployment stretched out through mid-1967 to avoid a callup of the reserves. On 11 April McNamara approved, with minor exceptions, the deployment plan proposed; there would be seventy U.S. maneuver battalions in the RVN by year's end, and the remaining nine would be deployed by June 1967.[54] Thus, between July 1965 and the Honolulu Conference, Westmoreland upped the number of maneuver battalions required to do this job from fifty-eight (the number called for in the 24-battalion add-on) to seventy-nine.

In fact, the Army was pushing for an increase not only in the intensity of the war but in its scope as well. The JCS felt that the president "was not doing enough" and advocated carrying the war into the insurgent sanctuaries in Laos and Cambodia, if not North Vietnam itself.[55] General Johnson supported an operation into Laos to cut the Ho Chi Minh Trail, as did General Westmoreland, and in early 1966 MACV developed plans for such a maneuver. The desire to expand the war was largely the result of impatience and frustration on the part of many senior officers at their inability to force the enemy to stand and fight. Lieutenant General Kinnard, commander of the 1st Cavalry Division, expressed the views of most of his contemporaries when he said, "We were fighting their kind of

war, and I wanted to make them fight our kind of war. I wanted to turn it
into a conventional war—boundaries—and here we go, and what are you
going to do to stop us?"[56]

The initial plan, EL PASO I, saw the 1st Cavalry Division establishing
an airhead on the Bolovens Plateau in the Laotian panhandle, supported by
one incursion by the 3d Marine Division pushing west from Quang Tri
Province and another by the 4th Infantry Division driving up from the
Central Highlands. Here again the Army was fallng back on old, familiar
plans and ideas. General Johnson had commissioned a study in March
1965 to determine the feasibility of such an operation. As it turned out, it
was not feasible. Westmoreland's airhead was basically something that
had been advanced during the Laotian crisis in 1961–62.[57] MACV, however, was continually frustrated in its efforts to win presidential approval
for the operation.

Rejection of the plan notwithstanding, the attrition strategy persisted;
during the last five months of 1966, MACV invested 95 percent of its
combat battalion resources in search-and-destroy operations.[58] Westmoreland recalled one typical operation: "I called on the 1st Brigade,
101st Airborne Division, under Brigadier General Willard Pearson to join
the search and later the entire 1st Cavalry Division, commanded by Major
General Jack Norton. Patrolling relentlessly through the trackless jungle,
catapulting from one hastily built hilltop firepower support base to
another, those units through the summer killed close to 2,000 of the
enemy; when the cavalry division returned for another sweep in October, a
thousand more of the enemy would never make it into the populated
region."[59] Unfortunately, the enemy *already was* in the populated regions.
While the Army chased its elusive quarry through the country's interior
the insurgents continued operating along the densely populated Coastal
Plains. Over half of all significant contact with Communist forces in the
first half of 1966 took place, not in the interior regions, but along the
Coastal Plains.[60] The inference was clear: the insurgents would fight to
maintain access to the population while leading the Army on a wild-goose
chase inland, drawing MACV's maneuver battalions away from the people
they were purportedly protecting.

One year after the commitment of U.S. ground forces the Army had
made little headway against the enemy. VC forces, numbering 160,000 the
year before, now stood at some 220,000, not including some 38,000 NVA
troops. It was estimated that the enemy could recruit internally or infiltrate
into the RVN the equivalent of fifteen battalions a month.[61] During this
period, in March 1966, a study commissioned by General Johnson in July

Members of the 1st Cavalry Division (Airmobile) climb ladders to a hovering CH47A (Chinook) helicopter during an operation near Pleiku in January 1966.

courtesy U.S. Army

1965 was completed by the Army Staff. Entitled "Program for the Pacification and Long-Term Development of South Vietnam" (PROVN), it was the product of an eight-month effort of some of the brightest minds on the Army Staff, charged by the Chief of Staff with "developing new sources of action to be taken in South Vietnam by the United States and its allies which will lead in due time to successful accomplishment of US aims and objectives."[62]

The study was not received favorably by the Army leadership, and its conclusions and recommendations make the reasons clear. The authors of the report contended that there was "no unified effective pattern" to the Army's war effort, that the situation in Vietnam had "seriously deteriorated," and that 1966 might be the final opportunity to modify MACV's strategy before victory became impossible. The PROVN group recommended that pacification be given top priority in the war effort. Nevertheless, it stated that "the bulk of US and FWMA [Free World Military Assistance] Forces and designated RVNAF units should be directed against enemy base areas and against their lines of communication in SVN, Laos and Cambodia, as required; the remainder of Allied force assets must assure adequate momentum to activity in priority Rural Construction areas."[63] While PROVN was less than a ringing endorsement for a traditional counterinsurgency strategy, it at least acknowledged the need for direct Army participation in population security programs. PROVN also called for greater efforts to achieve some sort of unity of command and for development of a single, integrated plan for the counterinsurgency forces.

The study was briefed to COMUSMACV on 17 May in Honolulu. Westmoreland contended that most of PROVN's recommendations had been acted on and that the United States could not foist unity of command on the Vietnamese or force adherence to U.S. plan without risking the Saigon regime's being tagged as U.S. puppets. Thus, even though the study allowed for the continuance of current Army operations while the ARVN bore the brunt of pacification, the very notion that the Army had a major obligation to Revolutionary Development, as it was called, made the Army leadership uneasy. Nor was the Army brass thrilled with the idea that the U.S. ambassador (particularly one such as Lodge, with his apparent preference for traditional counterinsurgency doctrine) would set priorities and objectives for the Army.

The upshot of all this furor over PROVN and its recommendations was its suppression by the Army. The document was downgraded from a study to a "conceptual document," in no way binding on MACV or the Army; furthermore, for a period after its completion Army officers were forbidden to discuss the study, or even acknowledge its existence, outside DOD.[64] Despite Westmoreland's claims that MACV had responded to the PROVN study, the second half of 1966 saw MACV utilize its maneuver battalions almost exclusively in search-and-destroy operations.

Evidence of PROVN's negligible impact is found in another Army study completed in May 1967, entitled "Review and Analysis of the Evaluation of the US Army Mechanized and Armor Combat Operations in Vietnam"

(MACOV). Prepared by CDC, the evaluation found that "approximately 25% of all operations are security or minor pacification missions, and approximately 75% are search and destroy." Furthermore, "of 170 battalion task force size US initiated offensive operations by armor-mech units examined in the study, only one (0.59%) took place at night. . . . Of 509 company team size similar operations, fourteen took place at night (2.75%)."[65]

While the Army might have been successful in side-stepping the implications of the PROVN study, it had less luck with the civilians at OSD, where doubt and concern over the Army strategy for winning the war began manifesting themselves. On 18 June CINCPAC forwarded MACV's force request for calendar year 1967. Citing the proposed increases as "rounding out forces," the request called for U.S. strength in the RVN to increase to 90 maneuver battalions and 542,588 personnel. It was received by McNamara on 5 August with the Chiefs' stamp of approval. The secretary of defense balked at approving yet another increase, requesting "a detailed line by line analysis for these requirements to determine that each is truly essential to the carrying out of our war plan."[66] McNamara included in his memo to the JCS issue papers prepared by the Whiz Kids at Systems Analysis (OSA) questioning the need for additional troops.

On 10 August Westmoreland bluntly notified his superiors, "I cannot justify a reduction in requirements submitted." Given the strategy he had adopted, COMUSMACV was correct. The JCS labored over the objections presented by Alain Enthoven and the people at Systems Analysis and forwarded their defense on 24 September. Enthoven remained unpersuaded. The JCS had cut over half of the 70,000 slots to which OSA had objected, but this still left projected U.S. force levels at some 20,000 over the limits in OSA's Program 4. Before presenting this contentious issue to the president for a decision, McNamara decided on a trip to South Vietnam for a first hand evaluation of the situation, in the hope of avoiding an open clash between the generals and OSD's civilian brain trust.

McNamara was accompanied on his trip by General Wheeler, Robert Komer (the president's special assistant for pacification), and Assistant Secretary of Defense John McNaughton, among others. The mission arrived in Saigon on 10 October and departed on the 13th. The visit had a sobering effect on McNamara, confirming many of his doubts about the progress of the war. In a pessimistic memorandum to the president the day after his return, McNamara surveyed the situation in South Vietnam. He saw "no reasonable way to bring the war to an end soon [as the enemy] has adopted a strategy of keeping us busy and waiting us out (a strategy of attriting our national will)." Pacification was "a bad disappointment" that had, "if anything, gone backward"; the ROLLING THUNDER bombing campaign had produced insignificant benefits, if any. As for the strategy of attrition, McNamara stated that

the one thing demonstrably going for us in Vietnam over the past year has been the large number of enemy killed-in-action resulting from the big military operations. Allowing for possible exaggeration in reports, the enemy must be taking losses— death in and after battle—at the rate of more than 60,000 a year. The infiltration routes would seem to be one-way trails to death for the North Vietnamese. *Yet there is no sign of an impending break in enemy morale and it appears that he can more than replace his losses by infiltration from North Vietnam and recruitment in South Vietnam.*[67]

Since the war effort appeared to be going nowhere, McNamara offered some recommendations for improvement. He suggested leveling off U.S. forces at 470,000 and a vigorous pacification effort. McNamara strongly challenged Westmoreland's rationale for search-and-destroy operations in lieu of an emphasis on pacification, contending that "the large-unit operations war, which we know best how to fight and where we have had our successes, is largely irrelevant to pacification as long as we do not lose it."[68]

Finally, McNamara proposed constructing a barrier across the 17th-parallel DMZ dividing the two Vietnams. Some scientists, along with Harvard Law School professor Roger Fisher and John McNaughton, had sold McNamara on the idea of an electronic barrier that could be manned by some 10,000–15,000 troops. The barrier proposal was in some respects a scaled-down version of the Army proposal for eliminating infiltration by moving a four-division blocking force into northern South Vietnam and Laos. The military's reaction to McNamara's idea can best be summed up by the words of former marine officer William Carson, who wrote that "the only way to describe the barrier is to recognize it as just one more 'happening' in the Defense Department's Alice in Wonderland approach to insurgency."[69]

The barrier proved an expensive error in terms of both money and manpower expended. It tied down U.S. troops along the DMZ, subjecting them to harassing fire from VC and NVA forces. The Marines estimated that eighteen engineer battalions would be required on a sustained basis just to build and maintain the necessary access roads if the barrier were to run the entire length of the DMZ.[70] The most interesting aspect about the McNamara Line, however, was that while the military dismissed it as an idiotic civilian fantasy, MASV could still seriously plan for the establishment of an anti-infiltration barrier across the 17th parallel *and* the Laotian panhandle!

While McNamara staked out his position for stabilized force levels, a strong commitment to pacification, and a barrier across the DMZ, the Joint Chiefs responded rapidly and angrily to his proposals. In a JCS memorandum sent to the president on the same day as McNamara's report, the Chiefs objected to the 470,000-man force level advanced by McNamara, as well as the planned diversion of ARVN forces away from offensive operations into pacification activities, citing the increased burden on U.S. forces that would result.[71]

Despite their disagreement with the McNamara proposals, the Chiefs were prepared to yield to pressure from above—but only a little. They maintained that the military situation had "improved substantially over the past year." Thus, they would agree to the use of a "substantial fraction" of the ARVN for pacification purposes, and they recommended that COMUSMACV be placed at the head of the pacification program "to achieve early optimum effectiveness." Several weeks later, after the Manila Conference, the Chiefs recommended that they be allowed to begin "mining ports, [a] naval quarantine, spoiling attacks and raids against the enemy in Cambodia and Laos, and certain special operations [to] support intensified and accelerated revolutionary development and nation building programs."[72] The Chiefs, it seems, just could not get the hang of counterinsurgency warfare.

By early November the military's willingness to accommodate McNamara had filtered down to COMUSMACV's Combined Campaign Plan (CCP) for 1967, issued on 7 November. The plan called for the RVNAF to support pacification with the majority of its forces; however, the ARVN formed only one component of the RVNAF, with the PFs and RFs making up the remainder. The primary mission of the U.S. and FWMA force contingencies would remain the destruction of VC/NVA main forces and base areas through a series of offensives. The emphasis on attrition continued. As General Taylor explained, the CCP "had language in it that seemed to indicate Westy's responsibility for clearing the enemy out of every square foot of soil in all [of] South Vietnam and probably accounted for his willingness to engage the enemy in places where terrain and distance to base areas was very favorable to him [the VC]; that is, they were right up against the border. The defense of Khe Sanh seemed to confirm the impression that he felt he had to control those worthless valleys way over there toward Laos."[73]

On 11 November, Program 4, as it was called, was published by OSD.

The program provided the military with authorization to increase U.S. force levels in Vietnam to the 470,000 troops Enthoven had recommended to McNamara the previous month.[74] This represented a shortfall of 7 Army maneuver battalions and roughly 53,000 troops requested in the JCS package. Six days later McNamara laid out the reasons for his decision in a Draft Presidential Memorandum (DPM). The significance of the memorandum lies in the concerns voiced by McNamara over the strategy the military was pursuing in Southeast Asia. McNamara felt that the United States had two choices: (1) to continue pouring combat forces into South Vietnam in an effort to reach the elusive crossover point through search-and-destroy operations; or (2) to level off U.S. forces at a point where they could keep the enemy's big units "neutralized," that is, away from the populated regions. McNamara advocated the latter course, arguing that "if MACV estimates of enemy strength are correct, we have not been able to attrite the enemy forces fast enough to break their morale and more US forces are unlikely to do so in the foreseeable future."[75] The secretary of defense supported his decision by citing the inability of MACV to reach the crossover point. The Army, McNamara said, had reached the point of diminishing marginal returns, where the commitment of additional troops had only a negligible impact on the enemy casualty rate.

Thus did the civilians in OSD conclude that the Army's attrition strategy was not working and that its prospects for producing an eventual victory were exceedingly dim. The nonprofessionals, the Whiz Kid analysts whom the Army brass detested so much, were actually out in front on the "learning curve" of what was really transpiring in Vietnam. The Army leadership, burdened by its rigid conceptual approach to the conflict, echoed the familiar refrain: "more of the same." The Chiefs filed a JCS memorandum disputing the force levels set and the secretary of defense's priorities the day following his DPM, but to no avail. In the coming months the Army Concept would come under increasing criticism from civilians in the Defense community, with the Army, as always, promising results if given more resources to grind the enemy down.

As the war moved into 1967, Westmoreland's need for additional forces remained acute. The general believed more than ever that with enemy strength continually on the increase, U.S. forces had to fight in the remote border regions to prevent the Communists from interfering with the pacification program. On 18 March, Westmoreland forwarded a request to the JCS for an increase in U.S. forces of at least 2⅓ divisions, with 4⅔ divisions considered an optimal addition to MACV's order of battle. The request saw U.S. troop strength in South Vietnam reaching at least 559,000 (108 maneuver battalions) by mid-1968, with 676,000 men (130 maneuver battalions) included in the "optimum" package. Westmoreland stated that unless the 2⅓ divisions were forthcoming, he would have to divert ARVN forces engaged in pacification operations to help take up the shortfall in offensive operations.[76]

MACV's list of troop requirements was formally reported to McNamara on 20 April. Five days later Westmoreland arrived in Washington to discuss the situation in Vietnam with President Johnson. In their meeting the general pressed for the introduction of ARVN forces into the Laotian panhandle and the eventual development of southern Laos into a major battlefield to take pressure off the South. When Westmoreland brought up the 2⅓-division request, Johnson replied, "When we add divisions can't the enemy add divisions?" Westmoreland contended that the attrition strategy was working and observed, "It appears last month we reached the crossover point in areas excluding the two northern provinces."[77] Westmoreland maintained that MACV had forced that enemy's main-force units into remote areas just as planned; however, extra forces were needed to protect the northern provinces against a possible incursion by North Vietnamese units.[78]

President Johnson, as evidenced by his discussion with Westmoreland, doubted that the Army could reach the crossover point. These doubts were fed by a number of key civilians and civilian organizations—OSD, the CIA, and Robert Komer (the designated head of Civil Operations and Revolutionary Development Support [CORDS]) among them—who were increasingly skeptical of MACV's ability to achieve victory using the current strategy.

Komer had penned a memo to the president prior to departing for South Vietnam on 24 April. Never known to mince words (a characteristic that earned him the sobriquet "Blowtorch"), Komer called for a redirection of U.S. strategic emphasis toward pacification, upgrading the paramilitary forces, jacking up the ARVN and letting them take on the bulk of the fighting, and placing all forces in a unified command under the Americans.[79] Thus Komer, who had been the president's special assistant for pacification since March 1966, implicitly rejected the call for more U.S. forces and the strategy that mandated their request.

Meanwhile, the CIA had published a study that concluded that no decisive advantage could be gained from U.S. incursions of the sort Westmoreland was advocating. The CIA maintained that the vast majority of VC/NVA supplies continued to be generated from *within* South Vietnam. MACV was incensed over the CIA's contention, particularly with respect to

Cambodia, where, the Army claimed, over a thousand metric tons of military supplies from the PRC had arrived in the port of Sihanoukville in 1966. Yet, even if *all* the supplies had been destined for South Vietnam, it would have amounted to *less than three tons per day* for a force of over 285,000 guerrillas, hardly a make-or-break operation.[80]

Perhaps the most damning evidence against the Army Concept came from the Systems Analysis people at OSD. In their efforts to measure progress in a war with no fronts, Alain Enthoven and his Whiz Kids applied their form of analysis to the struggle in Southeast Asia. Having no independent means of acquiring information on the war, they based their studies on data supplied by MACV itself. Using that statistical base, in January 1967 OSA began issuing a series of monthly Southeast Asia Analysis Reports that, to the annoyance of the Army, elaborated on the failure of the attrition strategy. In two memos to the secretary of defense on 1 and 4 May, OSA challenged MACV's force request and Westmoreland's contention that progress was being made in South Vietnam. Using the Army's Armored Combat Operations in Vietnam (ARCOV) study and MACV after-action reports, OSA showed that if the Army's strategy remained the same, force increases would have very little impact on the war.

The ARCOV reports showed that 88 percent of all engagements were initiated by the enemy.[81] Thus the VC had the initiative. They could either refuse or accept battle on their terms and, in doing so, could control their casualty level. Hence, the attrition strategy was unfeasible, since MACV could not force the enemy to do battle. The OSA report went on to say that while MACV was still prosecuting the war as though phase 3 insurgency operations were being conducted, the numbers of VC/NVA attacks of battalion size had been decreasing since the arrival of U.S. ground forces in the latter part of 1965. Indeed, the monthly average of such attacks had decreased from 9.7 per month in the final quarter of 1965 to 1.3 per month in the final quarter of 1966. Meanwhile, the number of small-scale enemy attacks had increased by 150 percent over the same period. The implication was obvious to OSA: the Communists had reverted to phase 2 operations.[82]

While MACV had been out in the border regions chasing the enemy in fruitless attempts to drive up insurgent casualties, it had not provided a shield for pacification, as Westmoreland contended, but had actually left the population exposed to the guerrillas. Indeed, OSA noted that *fully 90 percent of all incidents in any given quarter were occurring in the 10 percent of the country that held over 80 percent of the population.*[83] What was even more distressing, the 1967 incident rate was roughly the same as in 1966 and 1965. Search-and-destroy operations had not succeeded in assisting the government to effect better control of the people. As one OSA report noted, the big-unit war was irrelevant to the pacification effort as long as the enemy could not initiate big battles and win them. As for the Army's contention that if units were broken down to assist in pacification, they risked being defeated in detail, OSA observed that "our forces routinely defeat enemy forces outnumbering them two or three to one. In no instance has a dug-in US company been overrun, regardless of the size of the attacking force, and nothing larger than a company has come close to annihilation when caught moving."[84] Thus, shifting the bulk of U.S. and ARVN forces into pacification efforts hardly constituted the threat that the Army claimed it did. Beginning in November 1966, OSA maintained that a change in tactics was needed if the attrition strategy was to succeed. MACV needed to focus on an effective population security program to deny the VC their sources of recruitment rather than attempt to obliterate enemy forces on the battlefield.

Turning to the MACV request, Enthoven expressed amazement at the absence of any coherent rationale to support the additional deployments, observing that the MACV requirement was based on "unselective and unquantified goals. . . . What is surprising to me is that MACV has ignored this . . . information in discussing force levels." The OSA report concluded by recommending rejection of Westmoreland's request and calling for the Army to commence serious efforts to upgrade the RVNAF before they assumed a greater role of the defense burden.[85]

Enthoven's analysis carried the day with McNamara. On 19 May a DPM was drawn up recommending that no additional forces be dispatched to South Vietnam other than those already called for in Program 4.[86] The Chiefs, however, persisted. The Army rejected the OSA evaluation out of hand. Furthermore, it sought to exclude other individuals and organizations from having access to the SEA Reports. On at least two occasions General Wheeler strongly recommended to McNamara that the reports "be limited for internal OSD use only" in order to "reduce the dissemination of incorrect and/or misleading information to senior officials of other government agencies, as well as commanders in the field."[87] The day after the DPM was drafted, the Chiefs, in their "Worldwide Posture Paper," reaffirmed their support of Westmoreland's request, claiming that such forces would help "regain the Southeast Asia initiative and exploit our military advantage."[88]

The wrangling over what additional forces should be sent to MACV continued over the next two months. During this period the State Department also became involved in the debate, in the form of a series of options presented by Under Secretary of State Nicholas Katzenbach. Katzenbach initially offered two alternatives, one supporting the JCS position, the other the stand taken by OSA. Predictably, a stalemate quickly ensued. Additional alternatives followed, representing the all-too-familiar practice of finding the middle ground acceptable to all. On 12 June, McNaughton sent a DPM to the president outlining three courses of action.[89] Before a decision was made, however, McNamara visited Saigon on 7 July armed with data from Enthoven showing that 3⅔-division equivalents could be provided Westmoreland by 31 December 1968 without callng up the reserves.

McNamara arrived in a war zone that had experienced the attrition strategy for nearly two years without any appreciable results. The prototypical military operation since the 173d Airborne Brigade had conducted its first assault on the Iron Triangle back in June of 1965 remained search and destroy. In June 1967, fully 86 percent of MACV's battalion operations time was dedicated to such operations.[90]

Large search-and-destroy operations such as ATTLEBORO (September–November 1966), CEDAR FALLS (January 1967) and JUNCTION CITY (February–May 1967) attempted to bring the enemy to battle so that his forces could be attrited by U.S. firepower. To MACV, attacking enemy strongpoints or base areas was the best way to bring the elusive guerrillas out into the open. For example, ATTLEBORO saw 22,000 U.S. and ARVN troops, complete with B-52 bomber air support and massive artillery fire, conduct a drive into War Zone C, the VC stronghold northwest of Saigon. The seventy-two-day operation was declared a success, since the enemy suffered an estimated 1,100 dead and lost a considerable amount of supplies. Yet, before long the VC reoccupied the area and were operating as before. Major General Depuy, then commander of the 1st Infantry Division, a participant in the operation, recalled the difficulties involved in locating the enemy: "They metered out their casualties, and when the casualties were getting too high . . . they just backed off and waited. I really thought that the kind of pressure they were under would have caused them to perhaps knock off the war for awhile, as a minimum, or even give up and go back north. But I was completely wrong on that. I was surprised a little bit, too, after I took over the division [at] the difficulty we had in trying to find the VC. We hit more dry holes than I thought we were going to hit. They were more elusive. They controlled the battle better. They were the ones who decided whether there would be a fight."[91]

ATTLEBORO was followed by CEDAR FALLS, an incursion into the Iron Triangle. Two infantry divisions participated in the nineteen-day operation that saw U.S. forces kill over 700 VC and capture 613 weapons.[92] The Army's "success" in generating enemy casualties and capturing enemy supplies in these operations led to another large-scale assault into War Zone C, JUNCTION CITY. The operation utilized the Army's 1st Infantry Division, the 173d Airborne Brigade, the 11th Armored Cavalry Regiment (ACR), and a brigade of the 9th Infantry Division. Their mission was to destroy VC/NVA forces and installations in the northern and eastern portions of the War Zone. As General Westmoreland noted, JUNCTION CITY completed the Army's transition of the insurgency into a mid-intensity conflict: "The operation employed for the first time all our different types of combat forces, including paratroopers and large armored and mechanized units."[93]

JUNCTION CITY lasted for nearly two months, from 22 February to 15 April. U.S. forces killed 1,776 VC while capturing vast amounts of ammunition, medical supplies, and more than 800 tons of rice. The Army claimed that CEDAR FALLS and JUNCTION CITY "confirmed the ATTLEBORO experience that such multi-division operations have a place in modern counterinsurgency warfare."[94] Yet the operation was anything but a success. The target, the 9th VC Division, was not rendered ineffective, and with one exception, the only significant engagements were those initiated by the VC. One general stated that "it was a sheer physical impossibility to keep the enemy from slipping away whenever he wished if he were in terrain with which he was familiar—generally the case."[95] The Army utilized massive amounts of firepower: 3,235 tons of bombs and over 366,000 rounds of artillery.[96] Thus, several tons of ordnance were required to kill one VC.

Although Westmoreland claimed that operations like JUNCTION CITY convinced the enemy that basing units near populated areas was "foolhardy," such was not the case. As one Army general conceded, "In neither instance were we able to stay around, and it was not long before there was evidence of the enemy's return."[97] Captured enemy documents and statements issued by the North Vietnamese leadership indicated that not only had the Army failed to seize the initiative but there was every indication that MACV was playing into the hands of the Communist strategy of protracted warfare. For example, VC documents captured during CEDAR FALLS revealed that the enemy strategy was based on concentrating North Vietnamese Army and VC main forces in numerous remote areas to prevent concentration of American forces in the populated Coastal Plain.

The objective, as Giap stated at the time, was to draw American forces away from pacification and engage them in inconclusive battles along the frontiers, inflicting U.S. casualties in the process and sapping U.S. will to continue the war.[98] Yet MACV continued to claim that search-and-destroy operations were a success, that they forced the enemy away from the populated areas so that the pacification program could be carried out.

Again, the information available did not bear this out. An analysis of enemy activity in III Corps Tactical Zone (CTZ) during the period 1965–67 showed a dramatic increase in engagements in the four border provinces, from 38 in 1966 to 273 in 1967. While MACV claimed that this proved the validity of search-and-destroy operations, OSA concluded otherwise, noting that "if allied forces had pushed the enemy to the border provinces, we would expect the attack rates elsewhere in III CTZ to have diminished. They doubled."[99] Even worse, the big battles the Army was seeking were not occurring, despite the purported success of operations such as JUNCTION CITY. The enemy was moving away from direct assaults on U.S. positions in favor of hit-and-run mortar attacks which were more effective in inflicting U.S. casualties. Although MACV refused to admit it, the Army was in a small-unit war: by 1967 over 96 percent of all engagements with enemy forces occurred at company strength or less.[100]

Although this information was available to MACV and the Army Staff, it was never systematically evaluated. The only information or feedback that the Army required concerned how well the service was implementing its strategy of attrition, that is, factors such as the body count, weapons captured, enemy supplies destroyed, and so on. The Army, having convinced itself of the validity of its Concept for insurgency warfare in the battle of the Ia Drang Valley, was concerned only with the need to apply it with greater intensity.

This, then, was the operational environment and the organizational attitude McNamara found upon his arrival in Saigon. During his visit Westmoreland reluctantly agreed to a force level of 525,000 troops, an increase that would provide MACV with an additional 19 maneuver battalion equivalents. In the end, the 3⅔ division equivalents outlined by Enthoven as the maximum available were whittled down by only some 14,400 spaces. On 14 August a memo from OSD initiated Program 5, directing the chiefs to bring U.S. troop strength in South Vietnam to 525,000 as expeditiously as possible.

As the conflict moved into 1968, Westmoreland forwarded MACV's year-end assessment of the situation in Vietnam. The tone of the report was optimistic. The general held that the arrival of the Program 5 forces would allow for increased offensive operations.[101] The VC, said West-moreland, had lost control "over large areas and population" in 1967. So confident was Westmoreland that in January he dispatched two brigades belonging to the 1st Cavalry Division to the I CTZ border region around Khe Sanh, drawing them away from the populated region only days before the enemy's biggest offensive to date, the nationwide assault on the populated areas during Tet, the Vietnamese New Year's celebration. The stage was now set for the enemy to deliver a shock that would see the civilian leadership openly challenge the Army's strategy for the war.

7
Counterinsurgency American-Style

The Go-It-Alone Approach

The Army brass exhibited such faith in the Army Concept that they perceived the RVNAF's failure as a failure of implementation rather than a failure induced, at least in part by misapplication of doctrine and improper force structuring. Once in Vietnam, the Army shunted the ARVN aside so that the "first team" could bring the full brunt of U.S. firepower and mobility to bear upon the enemy. The Army's attitude in this instance went against yet another maxim of traditional counterinsurgency doctrine, unity of command.

When it became evident in the late winter of 1965 that U.S. ground forces were going to Vietnam, the initial concerns of the American military were not international but intramural; having viewed U.S. intervention as part of a larger SEATO operation, CINCPAC and the Chiefs were concerned over where CINCPAC's authority would end and where that of the Commander, United States, Southeast Asia (COMUSSEASIA), would begin.[1] Although Westmoreland had given some consideration to the eventual necessity for a combined U.S.-RVNAF joint command in 1964, nothing in the way of serious discussions occurred until after the Marines landed at Da Nang in March 1965. At that time Brigadier General Depuy, then G-3 of MACV, discussed the possibility of such an arrangement with his counterpart, General Thang, who was unenthusiastic over the prospect.[2] However, when General Johnson broached the idea to Prime Minister Quat during his visit to Saigon that March, Quat responded favorably.[3]

The model of joint command for the United States was the relationship that had existed between U.S. and South Korean forces in the Korean War. U.S. commanders, including Generals Ridgway and Taylor, had commanded the Eighth U.S. Army and the South Korean army, firing incompetent Korean commanders freely and replacing them with the best men available.[4] In this manner they had created a strong officer corps capable of providing the necessary leadership for the ROK army. In Saigon and in Washington the Army brass contended that circumstances in South Vietnam would not permit the same sort of command arrangements. A joint command under U.S. auspices raised the colonialism issue, Westmoreland pointed out, and besides, the South Vietnamese military was against it, and for good reason. Most promotions in the RVNAF came as a result of political relationships, not battlefield experience. Promotions from the grade of major on up were decided on in Saigon by a small coterie of officials and officers serving the president. One can only imagine the thorough housecleaning the U.S. commanders would have conducted had there been a joint command.

Thus, when McNamara gave MACV his approval for the establishment of a "small combined coordinating staff," both Westmoreland and Taylor argued against it, stating that pressing the issue would make the GVN reluctant to accept increases in U.S. ground forces.[5] The solution finally arrived at provided for Brig. Gen. James Lawton Collins, Jr., to serve as COMUSMACV's special representative to the Vietnamese JGS. There were some efforts to provide window dressing; for example, CCP was published yearly (it proved to be a document more in form than in substance), and TAORS were established for U.S., FWMA, and RVNA forces. TAORS, however, often provided the VC with room to operate in the "seams" between areas, complicating the territorial missions of province and district chiefs.[6]

The arrangement committed the Army to fighting without the benefit of a unified military effort, much less the centralized direction of all military, political, law enforcement, economic, social, and intelligence activities necessary for successful counterinsurgency operations. Westmoreland's justification for this fractured command arrangement centered on the colonialism problem and the South Vietnamese military's resistance to the idea. For his part, Westmoreland contended that he "never encountered serious disagreement with senior South Vietnamese officers . . . that could not be solved by frank discussion." In the final analysis, Westmoreland believed that he "had the leverage to influence the South Vietnamese, and they knew it."[7] Indeed, Westmoreland once boasted to Maxwell Taylor, "I can get them to do anything I tell them to do."[8] In reality, the dual-command arrangement was not satisfactory; nor were the reasons for not pressing for a joint command conclusive.

Some of the drawbacks of the compromise agreement (the ineffectual

CCP, TAORS) have already been mentioned. Others include West-moreland's inability to deal with the continual shortcomings of the ARVN officer corps. Furthermore, the ARVN was quickly pushed aside upon the arrival of U.S. ground forces; the roles of executing the strategy of attrition fell to U.S. units. The "other" war, pacification and population security, was reserved for the RVNAF. As Maxwell Taylor reflected, "We never really paid attention to the ARVN Army. We didn't give a damn about them."[9] Gen. Matthew B. Ridgway, commander of the combined American and Korean forces during the Korean War, contended that he "never could understand why they had a dual command in South Vietnam. Why in hell didn't they put the ARVN under Westmoreland?"[10]

As for the argument that a joint command would smack of colonialism, the precedent of the United States and South Korea demonstrated that U.S. command over the forces of a newly independent state was not an insurmountable problem. Perhaps the best response given Westmoreland on the colonialism argument was that of Robert Komer, who, in charac-teristically blunt fashion, replied, "Hell, with half a million men in Vietnam, we are spending twenty-one billion dollars a year, and we're fighting the whole war with the Vietnamese watching us; how can you talk about national sovereignty?"[11]

A more plausible reason for the Army's pooh-poohing the necessity for unity of command lies in the Army Concept, specifically in the Army's confidence in it and the strategy of attrition. If the Army felt that its Concept would produce victory by sheer force of application, there was little need for assistance from South Vietnamese units, which "couldn't get it right" during the advisory years and which, in any event, were lacking in the necessary attributes for executing the Concept in Vietnam— a lot of mobility and firepower. Better to allow such forces to conduct the "other" war, while the Army went in search of the "real" war. Viewed from this perspective, the absence of U.S. control over all military operations must have seemed far less odious than it would have been had the Army been truly interested in conducting counterinsurgency operations.

Firepower and Body Counts

The Army's attrition strategy was nothing more than the natural outgrowth of its organizational recipe for success—playing to America's strong suits, material abundance and technological superiority, and the nation's profound abhorrence of U.S. casualties. In searching for the elusive crossover point, the number of enemy killed in action (KIA) served as the measure of how well the strategy was working. Mass application of firepower, as in Korea and World War II, was felt to be the most efficient method of generating an enemy body count while minimizing U.S. casualties. Large search-and-destroy sweeps were carried out in an attempt to find the enemy. When guerrillas were located, the infantry took cover while massive firepower support attempted to destroy the insurgents. As General Depuy noted, if "you just wanted to analyze what happened in Vietnam you'd say the infantry found the enemy and the artillery and the air killed the enemy."[12] When General Westmoreland was asked at a press conference what the answer to insurgency was, his reply was one word: "Firepower."[13]

Yet in roaming the countryside in search of targets for its unparalleled firepower, the Army ignored the basic requirement of counterinsurgency: a secure population committed to the government. In adopting a strategy that measured success by the body count, the Army gave its combat leaders no incentive to stay put and gradually gain control over an area. Thus, while the Army killed many VC, it never denied the enemy his source of strength—access to the people. The result was a seemingly perpetual rejuvenation of the insurgent forces. As Lieutenant General Tolson, then commander of the 1st Cavalry Division, later admitted, his highly mobile force occupied only "small dots," not vast areas. Although airmobility greatly extended the division's combat power, he found that "it was often necessary to go back into an area time and time again to defeat not the same enemy but perhaps the same numbered unit that had regrouped from local recruits and replacements from the north."[14] Referring to the Army's preoccupation with minimizing casualties, Sir Robert Thompson pointed out that "the argument that anything which saves the life of one American boy is permissible will in the long run waste the deaths of many more. When lives are at stake it takes a very tough commander . . . who is prepared to risk increased casualties to achieve the right effect rather than hold down casualties (by using massive firepower) to get a statistical result but the wrong effect. That these fewer casualties may have been entirely wasted does not occur to many."[15]

In waging its kind of war, the Army missed the opportunity to apply its formidable resources in areas that would have produced long-term results by gaining support for the government and denying the VC badly needed manpower and supplies. MACV often complained that it could not participate in pacification programs (such as CAPs) because of the nonavailability of troops. Yet, of the 543,000 men that the United States had in Vietnam in 1968 only 80,000 were actually combat troops. The rest were engaged in supply and service tasks, involving primarily the provision of firepower and creature comforts to Army personnel stationed in Vietnam. One can only guess at the number of effectives the Army could have put in the field had it emphasized the light infantry war in lieu of its big-unit war.

The Army, growing increasingly concerned over reaching the crossover point amid the emerging civilian disenchantment in Washington, embraced firepower more, not less, as the enemy retreated into phase 2 operations. For example, in mid-1967 Col. Sidney B. Berry, Jr., one of the Army's topnotch young brigade commanders, authored a popular pamphlet advocating new tactics based on the technique of maneuver and fire. The prescribed method saw the commander locating the enemy through sweeps and destroying him with supporting firepower. "He [the commander] spends firepower as if he is a millionaire and husbands his men's lives as if he is a pauper. . . . During search and destroy operations, commanders should look upon infantry as the principal combat reconnaissance force and supporting fires the principal destructive force."[16] Berry's approach was endorsed by General Wheeler, who observed that "despite inevitable casualties, I am sure you know the high degree of care and concern of the Army Forces for the young men entrusted to us. The United States policy is to expend money and firepower, not manpower, in accomplishing the purpose of the nation. The firepower support being given to our fighting men in Vietnam, three times the rate expended in Korea, exceeds the amount of support available to any other force in history. None of us would have it any other way."[17] On another occasion Wheeler stated that "these two weapons, helicopters and offensive airpower, provide friendly forces with advantages in mobility and firepower greatly exceeding those available to counterinsurgency forces in any other anti-guerrilla war in history. And . . . mobility and firepower are the fundamental keys to success in combat."[18]

Had the Army's reliance on firepower only caused it to focus its efforts away from counterinsurgency operations, the damage would have been bad enough. Unfortunately, however, the use of massed firepower as a crutch in lieu of an innovative counterinsurgency strategy alienated the population and provided the enemy with an excellent source of propaganda. Officially, the Army maintained that it closely observed very restrictive rules of engagement (ROE) throughout the war, thereby minimizing the chances that civilians might somehow become the inadvertent targets of American firepower. Yet, by placing the body count above population security in its list of priorities, the Army provided the incentive for its commanders to shoot first and worry about the hearts and minds later. General Johnson admitted as much when he said that too much firepower was applied "on a relatively random basis." The United States, concluded Johnson, "just sort of devastated the countryside."[19] British Brig. W. F. K. Thompson agreed and added that it was to be expected. "We saw it in Korea with their firepower. They used that ghastly word, prophylactic firepower, which means if you do not know where the enemy is, make a big enough bang and you may bring something down."[20]

General Westmoreland's efforts to ensure compliance with the ROE proved unsatisfactory in the face of the strong incentives that his strategy provided for commanders to generate a high body count. For example, every six months the ROE were republished and issued out to units, but distribution to lower units was often inadequate. A survey of Army generals who served in Vietnam found that only 29 percent felt that the ROE were well understood prior to the My Lai massacre, and only 19 percent claimed that they were carefully adhered to.[21]

All in all, the ROE were generally misunderstood or suffered from "creative application," while enforcement against violators was effectively nonexistent."[22] Thus, there was a strong incentive to circumvent the ROE. As the enemy broke into smaller units and the Army grew increas ingly desperate in its efforts to reach the crossover point, civilians often became the targets of American firepower, a circumstance aided and abetted by the guerrillas. General Khuyen of the ARVN observed that "hatred was our enemy's major instrument to turn the people against us. . . . Communist guerrillas usually drew retaliatory fire from our gunships and artillery by sniping at our aircraft, convoys or outposts. More often than not, it was the local people who were exposed to our fire because by the time it came, the guerrillas had fled or taken shelter underground."[23] This enemy tactic proved quite useful in disrupting the pacification program in various districts. One pacification official wrote, "With increasing frequency VC and NVA forces enter a hamlet, raise their flag and announce that they are staying. In order to get them out, we often have to destroy the hamlet."[24]

In another instance, pacification officials found units of the 25th Infantry Division using heavy weapons in response to VC fire coming from hamlets. When pacification officials complained, a division spokesman stated that if the population wanted to avoid such destruction, they should come forward and warn the Army of the VC presence in their hamlets.[25] It was in the Mekong Delta, however, in the 9th Infantry Division's area of operation, that perhaps the most flagrant ROE abuses occurred. There Army units, particularly helicopter gunships, played so fast and loose with the ROE that civilians scrambled for cover whenever they heard them approach. The helicopter pilots often interpreted this action on the civilians' part as "evidence" that they were VC trying to flee and sprayed the area with ordnance.

The most imposing means of fire support available to the Army were the B-52 bomber raids, code-named ARC LIGHT. As early as 14 May 1965, COMUSMACV had recommended that the aircraft be made available, and that year 1,320 sorties were flown against targets in South Vietnam.[26] Although the enemy operated primarily in small units in 1966 and 1967, the number of B-52 sorties increased fivefold. While there is evidence that ARC LIGHT operations were useful as a "terror" weapon against the insurgents, this hardly justified their use against small, elusive targets.[27] There is also evidence that the VC developed an early-warning system against ARC LIGHT attacks. Furthermore, ARC LIGHT strikes often presaged the initiation of a major Army sweep through the target area; thus, the VC frequently departed before the arrival of U.S. forces, leaving MACV's search-and-destroy operations swiping at thin air. A CINCPAC study issued on 1 February 1969 found that ARC LIGHT strikes were effective when initiated in June 1965. As time passed, however, the average number of casualties per effective strike dropped from 151 in 1965 to 32 in 1968. Yet even these body counts are highly suspect, as only 13.5 percent of ARC LIGHT strikes were followed by on-the-ground evaluation of the results.[28]

Despite the high cost of ARC LIGHT operations and their diminishing returns over time, they remained very popular with the Army brass. Douglas Kinnard's survey of generals found tht 47 percent felt that the strikes were "very valuable," while only 15 percent felt that they were "not worth the effort."[29] Major General Julian J. Ewell, commander of the 9th Division, spoke for most Army commanders when he said that the ARC LIGHT strikes were a "good thing" for which there was always excess demand.[30] However, in a war where control of the population provided the key to victory, the resources devoted to ARC LIGHT could have been put to far better use in training and equipping the paramilitary RF and PF units, for instance, or in strengthening the capabilities of the national police against the VCI.

If B-52 support proved hard to get at times, the same could not be said of the close air support provided by fighter and fighter-bomber aircraft. In fact, only 10 percent of the fixed-wing air strikes in South Vietnam were flown in support of allied forces *actually in contact* with the enemy. Most air support did not involve assisting U.S. forces in combat but concentrated instead on interdicting enemy supplies and, occasionally, personnel movements. MACV concentrated air support on where the enemy might have been rather than on where he was.[31] The story was the same with the Army's artillery fire support. With the exception of the Tet Offensive, 70 percent of U.S. artillery rounds in Vietnam were fired in situations of light or inactive combat.[32] Artillery was employed not so much out of necessity as out of sheer availability, its use fed by the Army's need to generate enemy casualties while minimizing its own.

The greatest portion of artillery fire was expended as Harassment and Interdiction (H&I) fire. Supposedly based on intelligence concerning the movement of enemy troops and supplies, H&I missions were often fired routinely, with no particular purpose in mind other than to keep the enemy on edge. Lt. Gen. Frank T. Mildren, deputy commanding general of USARV (U.S. Army, Vietnam), contended that "purely H&I fires in [a] Vietnam environment have little, if any, value while doing practically no damage to the enemy."[33] Furthermore, a study by Brig. Gen. S. L. A. Marshall found that artillery support was rarely effective, even in a situation where U.S. forces were in contact with the enemy, because of the VC tactic of "hugging," or staying as close as possible to, U.S. troops, thereby exposing them to risk as well in the event that artillery fire support was called in.[34] Studies done by the Systems Analysis people at OSD concluded that "our unobserved fire alienates the local peasants in most cases, thus harming our efforts to break down their loyalty to and support for the Viet Cong."[35]

Ironically, the extensive use of firepower was a *significant cause of U.S. casualties*. This condition obtained as a result of two circumstances. First, the dud rate of artillery ordnance was roughly 2 percent of all shells fired; that of bombs dropped by B-52s, 5 percent. Second, the enemy undertook prodigious efforts to utilize booby traps and mines against American servicemen.[36] The result was that in 1966 alone, some 27,000 tons of dud bombs were available for use in VC mines and booby traps. Over 1,000 U.S. soldiers died that year as a result of wounds inflicted from such devices.[37] During the first six months of 1967, 17 percent of all U.S. casualties were caused by mines and booby traps—539 killed and 5,532 wounded.[38] Given the small returns accrued from the liberal use of heavy firepower systems, the extremely high costs incurred in terms of U.S. casualties, the loss of the population's goodwill, and the monetary expense ($2–3 billion per year), one wonders why its use persisted throughout the period of U.S. involvement.

In the case of artillery support (and sortie rates as well), the Army (and the Air Force) had built-in incentives for their use. Not only were artillery officers evaluated on their body count but, as Robert Komer observed, "in the absence of sufficient hard intelligence on the results of their activities, artillery and air unit commanders tended to be evaluated largely on the ammo expenditures or sortie rates of their units."[39] These incentives were reflected in the statement of one battery commander: "We had a real trucking problem in hauling that ammo to our firing batteries. But the ammo kept coming whether or not we had targets for it, so the batteries fired their allotments every opportunity they had, whether there was actually anything to shoot at or not."[40] After the war, General Johnson summed up the situation when he observed that U.S. forces were "trained for the kind of war that we conducted, which was a firepower war, [and] I expect we'll continue to rely heavily on firepower, simply because we can produce ammunition and we've got very splendid delivery systems for it."[41]

Thus, massive firepower was the primary means utilized by the Army to achieve the desired end of the attrition strategy—a body count. During the years of intervention the Army's preoccupation with reaching the crossover point made the body count the enemy of traditional counter-insurgency doctrine, which dictates that protection of the people must come before destruction of the enemy. By giving top priority to the body count, the Army gave its officers the incentive to bend the ROE in favor of killing "potential" insurgents, although in many instances they might have been innocent civilians. The availability of firepower and technology (in the form of sensors, radar, and so on) made it easier to "send a bullet" instead of a soldier, who could have made the distinction between friend and foe.

The body count quickly became the criterion for measuring success in Vietnam. As Maxwell Taylor put it, the press and the people in Congress had to be told how the war was going.[42] Success in counterinsurgency was made a function of the rate at which U.S. forces killed VC. The task of each Army unit commander became to bring the enemy to battle and destroy his forces in combat; if this was not possible, estimates of kills could be generated through H&I fires or reconnoiter fire on areas of "suspected" enemy concentration. If the commander before you had killed x number of VC, you had best kill $x + 1$. Under these circumstances, the incentive for inflation of body counts by commanders was strong indeed. Upping the count often provided a graceful explanation for why a particular U.S. unit suffered heavy casualties in an engagement; it also provided MACV with welcome data in its struggle to reach the crossover point.[43]

As in the advisory years, when the ARVN inflated body counts and pacification statistics, MACV accepted information that reinforced its strategic approach while overlooking data that suggested a lower level of enemy casualties. When compared with other estimates of enemy casualties, MACV estimates always proved more optimistic. For instance, a MACV study of seventy captured VC/NVA documents concluded that the true body count in 1966 was probably 4.5 percent above the number officially reported. When analysts in Washington examined the same documents, they concluded that 20 percent *fewer* KIAs than the number officially reported had been achieved. A study of eighty-four documents in Washington found that the VC/NVA suffered 30 percent *fewer* casualties between 1965 and 1968 than claimed by MACV. Kinnard's survey of general officers found that 61 percent of the respondents were in agreement with the contention that the body count was "often inflated." A final Washington study, of 136 enemy documents, concluded that enemy losses were probably *half* the number officially estimated by MACV.[44]

A report filed by Douglas Robinson of the *New York Times* after MACV had completed a particularly "successful" operation told how U.S. headquarters had issued a body count of ninety-two enemy dead in a sharp clash ending at 7:00 P.M. MACV's announcement was ready at 8:30 A.M. the next day, which seemed to indicate that U.S. soldiers had stayed up all night counting enemy bodies by flashlight in an area probably within sniper range and certainly exposed to possible mortar or rocket fire. "It does sound incredible, doesn't it?" was the MACV spokesman's reply.[45]

Perhaps the acme of the body-count mentality was found in the Army's 9th Infantry Division in 1968–69. The division, commanded by Major General Ewell, referred to by some as the "Delta Butcher," operated in the relatively open country of IV Corps in the rice paddies of the Mekong Delta. Ewell's approach was direct and single-minded: do everything possible to achieve high enemy-to-friendly kill ratios. To accomplish this he applied the principles of the Concept: firepower supplemented by technology, or as Ewell put it, "Once one decided to apply maximum force, the problem became a technical one of doing it with the resources available. In many areas this required real skill and iron determination."[46]

Ewell had his staff conduct studies of unit combat effectiveness in which the "most relevant statistical index of combat effectiveness was the average number of Viet Cong losses inflicted daily by the unit in question."[47] The division developed terms such as the *exchange* (kill) *ratio* to determine the "professional skill" of a unit and, no doubt, of its company or battalion commander as well. Units were also graded on what was called *contact/success ratio*, the number of times a contact with the enemy produced a body count.[48]

The division utilized many technical innovations in its operations. Ground radars and sensors were emplaced to detect enemy movement, whereupon troops were inserted to corner and destroy them. However, since the targets detected were often "moving and highly perishable," artillery fire support or air cavalry gunship support was often substituted for troops.[49] Of course it was not always possible to verify whether the movement detected was that of the VC or of civilians. The division made prodigious use of its helicopters, often flying night (hunter-killer) missions using gunships with searchlights mounted on them. On occasion, the gunships mistook civilians for the enemy. One officer who served on Ewell's staff recounted that some brigade commanders felt so pressured to get their quota of kills that they resorted to flying helicopters under unsafe conditions. One commander was observed "literally flying the blades off the helicopters and killing Americans to increase the body count."[50]

The measurement of unit effectiveness through body counts could not help but affect the manner in which the division's units operated. Commanders were threatened with relief if they did not meet their quotas. Indeed, Ewell once remarked to his assistant division commander, "They're [VC kills] getting harder to get." Whereupon the ADC replied, "Brigade commanders aren't."[51] While General Ewell admitted that "you couldn't expect a guy to pump water out of a dry well" (that is, that units in areas of light activity would not run up as high a body count), he also noted that "if a battalion saw that some other battalion was getting four hundred or six hundred kills a month, and they were getting fifty, they'd immediately think, I'd better get off my ass and do something."[52]

Despite the push by units to meet their quota, the division staff appeared perplexed that, as one report noted, "units have been unsuccessful in their efforts to capture or destroy weapons in percentages commensurate with the number of enemy killed or captured."[53] It was Ewell, however, who gave the best explanation for the division's abnormally low ratios of weapons captured to people killed: "The Riverine Force [one element of the 9th Division] had really good success for a year or more. Well, the Viet Cong weren't stupid and . . . they began to move elsewhere. Then, some of these operations would just fall on thin air. I mean, there wasn't anybody there even though you thought there was. It tended to be a little expensive in terms of friendly casualties."[54] One officer in the division summed up the situation quite succinctly when he said, "We really blew a lot of civilians away."[55]

Reflective of the Army's priorities in South Vietnam is that Ewell was rewarded for his contribution toward reaching the crossover point. After his tour of command with the 9th Division, he was promoted to lieutenant general and placed in charge of an Army corps in Vietnam. After the war, Ewell was asked by the Army to write down his methods for waging counterinsurgency as part of the Vietnam Studies series, in effect giving his methods official sanction and perpetuating them for use in future insurgency conflicts.

Personnel Actions

Soldiers familiar with the people, culture, and geography of the region in which they operate are indispensable to a successful counterinsurgency program. The experience gained by government forces operating in one area for an extended period of time provides them with a knowledge of the terrain and people as intimate as that of the guerrilla, allowing for effective patrolling, particularly at night, better selection of ambush locations, improved population control, and good relations with the people, among other things. And, of course, military units perform better the longer they work together. As Napoleon once said, "Soldiers have to eat soup together for a long time before they are ready to fight."

Yet the Army in Vietnam instituted a personnel policy about as detrimental to the conduct of counterinsurgency operations as if it had set out with the worst intentions in mind. The Army gave priority to those personnel actions concerning tour lengths and duty assignments that promoted traditional service goals rather than successful counter-insurgency operations. As the deployment of U.S. ground forces became a reality in early 1965, General Westmoreland sent a message to the JCS requesting that the twelve-month standard tour length be increased to nineteen months; but this applied only to general officers and a select number of key personnel.[56] While the request was approved by the secretary of defense, the Army moved no further toward extending combat tours, even when large numbers of ground forces were deployed that summer. The standard tour remained twelve months in length; furthermore, officers in command positions could serve only six months before being transferred.

Why the insistence on such short tours in a war that demanded a protracted commitment of individuals to a given area? Generals Johnson and Westmoreland offered several explanations. Regarding the twelve-month tour, Westmoreland held that it was "politically impossible" to do anything else and that it was "good for morale" because it "gave a man a goal."[57] Johnson contended that "the one-year tour was adopted primarily so that the hazards of combat might be shared by more than just a limited number of people, who would stay there until they were either wounded or killed." As for the six-month command tour, Johnson contended that "a man began to wear out after about five months, and he just got to a point of exhaustion."[58] Westmoreland gave a different rationale. It was incumbent upon the Army, he said, "to look after its long-term interests"; the more officers with command experience, the better off the organization would be for future wars.[59]

These justifications lack credibility for a number of reasons. First, the shortness of the tours invariably retarded the service's ability to learn how to cope effectively with the insurgency. As John Paul Vann noted, "The United States has not been in Vietnam for nine years, but for one year nine times." Second, General Johnson's burnout theory had no basis in reality; officers engaged in combat in World War II served "for the duration," and there were not many burnout victims. In a 1976 survey of officers conducted at the Army's Command and General Staff College, only 8 percent of the Vietnam veterans stated that burnout was a factor at the end of their six months' command; the majority felt that frequent changes in command were *detrimental* to morale and discipline.[60] An analysis of unit performance in Vietnam further discredits the burnout theory: those battalion commanders who managed to command longer than six months suffered battle deaths at a rate of only two-thirds that of their less experienced contemporaries.[61] Third, his assertions to the contrary, *Westmoreland did not believe that it was going to be a long war.* If he had, there would have been no reason to rotate command so frequently.[62] It will be recalled that in his concept of operations issued in the summer of 1965 Westmoreland projected that U.S. forces would destroy all significant insurgent forces and base camps by the end of 1967. Thus, there was a need to provide officers with command experience in a hurry.

If the Army brass was not giving an adequate explanation for why it adopted what one senior officer later called "the worst personnel policy in history," what were the reasons behind its actions? They certainly were not directed toward enhancing the Army's counterinsurgency capability. Short command tours contributed to the commander's incentive to get a good "box score" by generating a large body count; long-term commitments to pacification, the results of which would not show up for months or even years, were hardly conducive to winning the commander a "max" efficiency report. The concern for officer morale and burnout cited by the generals was more reflective of a fear that if only a small percentage of officers had combat command experience, they would preempt the "fast" track for future promotions. Believing that the war would be relatively short and that its Concept would work, the Army was willing to short-change counterinsurgency in order to give its officers the sprinkling of command and staff experience that would be needed if the Army ever found itself in a fight with the Russians. Finally, the six-month tour helped provide the commander with the incentive to get a good body count and make his contribution toward reaching the crossover point.

If the war effort was handicapped by the Army's personnel policies regarding tour lengths, it suffered even more from its advisory effort. Although the Army was charged with helping the RVNAF become a self-sustaining force capable of handling the insurgency on its own, Army personnel policies often frustrated the accomplishment of the mission. The advisor's tour of duty was initially set at one year, with those in ARVN battalions rotated every six months if the situation permitted. Furthermore, while the advisory program was theoretically important to the Army's mission of helping the Vietnamese help themselves, once the main-force units arrived in 1965, advisers were considered to be out of the mainstream.[63] The Army training program for advisers suffered problems from its inception in 1962, the result of a shortage of instructors, time, and service motivation. This led to the dispatch to South Vietnam of advisers, who, as one of them put it, "learned more about Vietnam and insurgency around the pool of the Rex Hotel in Saigon than we ever learned in the states."

As early as September 1963 the Army was aware of a problem with its advisers. That month a DCSOPS summary concluded that "officers assigned to these activities are becoming increasingly concerned that such duty is detrimental to their careers [and] will adversely affect their chances for selection to schools and for promotion."[64] Two studies point out the low esteem in which advisory duty was held by Army officers and NCOs. One, by Brig. Gen. Peter Dawkins, surveyed 509 officers who served as province or district advisers during the war; the other, by HumRRO, examined responses from 607 officers and NCOs who served as advisers in 1969 and 1970.[65] Dawkins divided his survey into three time segments: war 1, covering the period from January 1962 to September 1965, when the big units arrived; war 2, from October 1965 until June 1967, when the Army began actively promoting advisory duty; and war 3, from July 1967

TABLE 4. Officer Perceptions of Adviser Duty

War	Period	Career Advantage	Career Detriment
1	January 1962–September 1965	54.4%	26.5%
2	October 1965–June 1967	36.0	49.5
3	July 1967–January 1970	36.1	48.3

Source: Peter M. Dawkins, "The United States Army and the 'Other War' in Vietnam: A Study of the Complexity of Implementing Organizational Change" (Ph.D. dissertation, Princeton University, 1979), p. 79.

to January 1970. Dawkins found that once the Army introduced its main-force units, the perceived career impact of province/district advisory duty changed dramatically (see table 4).[66] The Army officer and NCO corps realized that main-force units were where the action was; furthermore, efforts made by the Army beginning in 1967 to make advisory duty more attractive did not convince these men, who remained skeptical (and rightly so as it turned out) of the benefits.

The upgrading of advisory duty received some support from the Office of the Secretary of the Army. Shortly before the Chief of Staff began to actively promote advisory duty in 1967, he received a memo from Under Secretary of the Army David E. McGiffert, who had been in South Vietnam for a look at the pacification program. McGiffert wanted the Army to respond to the problems that he saw in the advisory effort: Advisers, he said, "believe a command assignment to a unit in a combat zone is far and away the best 'ticket' to promotion. . . . Furthermore, because our best people tend to be assigned or picked off by the tactical units or headquarters in Saigon, we are probably not on the average putting our most competent people into the advisory positions."[67] The under secretary's views coincided with those submitted in a MACV report noting that "concern has been expressed that officers assigned as division or sector/province advisors consider the slot as a temporary one until they can find a position in a US unit [and] that they do not view advisory duty with a sufficient degree of importance. It is almost axiomatic that a competent and ambitious officer considers a command position in a US unit as preferable to any other position, including advisory positions."[68]

Although MACV and the Army Staff supported measures to make advisory duty more attractive, the men in the field refused to believe that service outside main-force units (battalions, brigades, and so on) could enhance their career. For example, a strong majority of officers felt that promotion and senior service school boards gave advisory work less weight than command time (see table 5).[69] In the HumRRO survey 47 percent felt that combat experience as an adviser did not help their career

TABLE 5. Officer Perceptions of Impact of Advisory Duty on Promotions and Service School Selection

		PERCENTAGE WHO SAID MORE WEIGHT GIVEN BY:	
War	Period	Promotion Board	Senior Service School Board
1	January 1962–September 1965	58.0%	54.8%
2	October 1965–June 1967	66.7	67.5
3	July 1967–January 1970	64.6	68.3

Source: Peter M. Dawkins, "The United States Army and the 'Other War' in Vietnam: A Study of the Complexity of Implementing Organizational Change" (Ph.D. dissertation, Princeton University, 1979), p. 79.

as much as combat service with a U.S. unit and 63 percent agreed that command time as an adviser helped them less than command of a U.S. unit. The survey also found that even after the Army incentive program had been initiated, only 24 percent of those serving as advisers had requested the assignment.[70] Oddly enough, early promotion to lieutenant colonel and colonel among those surveyed by General Dawkins ran *slightly better* than the Army-wide average. Nevertheless, many advisers viewed this as a short-run phenomenon; they believed that once the war wound down and the shortage of advisers ended (no one expected counterinsurgency to remain a significant part of the Army's mission), they would be on the outside looking in as the Army rededicated itself to traditional operations.[71]

The perception of many officers and NCOs that advisory duty was undesirable served to lower the quality of personnel involved in the program. The tour length of twelve months (later extended to eighteen) also reduced the effectiveness of the advisory effort. According to Lt. Gen. Cao Van Vien, head of the JGS,

The good performance of a tactical adviser, however, seemed to depend on a certain continuity and stability of effort devoted to a unit. This would require him to stay at least 18 months with a unit, but two years would have been better. The one-year tour . . . did not maintain enough continuity to make the advisory effort as effective as desired. . . .

Time was also required for the adviser to demonstrate his abilities, obtain confidence and to establish his influence within a unit. He needed opportunities to prove himself and to show the ARVN troops what he could do for them. Only then would his advice be welcomed and his recommendations heartily accepted.[72]

In addition to the inadequate tour length, a lack of training in both language and counterinsurgency operations handicapped advisers. The HumRRO survey discovered that only 194 out of 605 individuals surveyed had been to the MATA course, only 55 had taken the Military Assistance Programmer Course, and a mere 37 had completed the Special Warfare Counterinsurgency course.[73] And these were individuals serving in the RVN in 1969-70, long after the Army supposedly had committed itself to developing an adviser-training apparatus. As for the language problem, over 57 percent of the advisers queried said that their lack of language training detracted "seriously" or "moderately" from their duty performance.

Thus, by means of both its tour-length and policy and the perceived rewards of the officers and men involved in competing for regular unit and advisory slots, the Army promoted traditional operations and career needs over the requirements of the "other" war. Where Army personnel policies failed directly to promote them (such as in the adviser incentives program), the risks involved in the individuals' bucking past trends were not commensurate with the anticipated rewards, which offered, at best, treatment equivalent to that received by those in the "mainstream."[74]

Defoliation

MACV's defoliation campaign in South Vietnam from 1962 to 1970 represented another Army attempt to wage counterinsurgency on the cheap by applying a technological fix in lieu of seriously dealing with the problem of the enemy's access to the nation's food supply and his use of foliage for cover and concealment. Defoliants were the product of ARPA, the Advanced Research Projects Agency, which in the early 1960s developed chemicals capable of defoliating jungle grass and trees. Although originally they were aimed at eliminating the enemy's cover, soon they were used to deny him access to food as well.[75]

While limited testing of defoliants in the Saigon area was first authorized by President Kennedy in January 1962, their use was expanded at the prompting of MACV and the South Vietnamese. By March 1963 authority for conducting defoliation operations was delegated to COMUSMACV, the ambassador in Saigon, in cooperation with the RVNAF Joint General Staff. Despite the reservations of the State Department, defoliant operations by the U.S. Air Force under the code name RANCH HAND increased dramatically, from 5,681 acres destroyed in 1962 to 1,570,114 acres destroyed in 1967. Destroyed acreage dipped by about 15 percent in 1968-69, to about 1,360,000, and then dropped sharply in 1970 to approximately 300,000 acres.[76]

Early reports on the use of herbicides/defoliants by MACV were encouraging. One submitted to the U.S. ambassador in September 1963 claimed that "use of herbicides forces VC to adopt alternatives which complicate and make his operations more difficult. Herbicide operations have a favorable impact on morale of RVNAF. . . . Chemical crop destruction has assisted in the reduction of VC food resources and caused some VC dislocation."[77] The favorable reports issued by MACV were challenged by the senior Australian military adviser in Saigon, Colonel Serong, who contended that crop destruction, even in remote areas occupied by the Montagnards, forced people to leave their homes and alienated them from the very government that was trying to win their support. Serong observed that MACV's defoliation operation would not reduce ambushes unless at least several hundred yards of vegetation were removed on either side of the road; otherwise, the VC would have a clear field of fire, and the ambushed force would have that much further to move before it could establish contact.[78]

The use of defoliants soured relations between the Americans and the Vietnamese even in supposedly secure areas. When the II Field Force began deploying to South Vietnam in the summer of 1965, for example, defoliants were used to clear the Long Binh area, which would serve as its headquarters. Unfortunately, the defoliants sprayed on the brushlands drifted over the farmland of neighboring Bien Hoa and Lai Thieu, resulting in heavy damage to the rich crops. It happened overnight. Fruit fell from trees, and the rubber trees on nearby plantations turned brown and lost their leaves. Once the people discovered the cause of this calamity, they became worried that the spraying was dangerous to animal and human life. In successive years, the birth of a defective baby was invariably blamed on the Americans and their defoliants.[79]

These problems notwithstanding, MACV's use of defoliants increased. The response from Army field commanders remained positive. One Field Force commander stated that the crop destruction program was important "because it supports the objective of denying the enemy local supplies of food." One joint report to COMUSMACV from the commanders of the 4th Infantry Division and the 173d Airborne Brigade held that "defoliation and crop destruction operations have been effective in enhancing the success of allied combat operations. The effectiveness of this program is indicated by the large numbers of Montagnards who have come down from the mountains with reports that their crops have been poisoned. The same Montagnard ralliers indicate that they have been supplying food to the VC/NVA."[80] Another unit in the same area reported that "following extensive crop destruction in Dak Payan Valley in October 1967, a significant increase in VC/NVA raids on Montagnard villages to the West of the valley was noted. The main purpose of these raids was procurement of food stuffs."[81]

A MACV report at the time noted that all major commanders considered herbicide use to be beneficial for military operations and wanted herbicides used much more extensively. While the Army felt that herbicide use was beneficial in the conduct of military operations, a number of civilian studies concluded that their use was detrimental to the conduct of the war as a whole. A RAND Corporation evaluation of defoliation noted "no significant relationship . . . between [VC] rice rations and the percentage of regional rice lands sprayed." On the other hand, "the civilian population seems to carry very nearly the full burden of the results of the crop destruction program; it is estimated that over 500 civilians experience crop loss for every ton of rice denied the VC." In effect, the VC were confiscating crops from the people (as in the case of the raids on the Montagnards mentioned above) to make up for any shortfalls caused through defoliation. The report contended that "the basic reason for the low effectiveness of the program is that the VC are a very small percentage of the population, yet they control or have access to almost the entire rural economy in one fashion or another."[82]

Thus, the inability of the U.S., allied, and GVN forces to effect a workable population security program resulted in the people's shouldering the burden of the herbicide program. The RAND study concluded that its results strongly implied "that the relationship between the VC and the rice economy is so intimate and pervasive that significant or crippling effects on VC rice consumption would result only if a major proportion (perhaps 50 percent or more) of the rural economy were destroyed."[83] A study done by the U.S. embassy in Saigon concluded that "the VC/NVA grow somewhat less than 10% of their requirements. On the average, therefore, *we destroyed more than ten times as much rice as the VC/NVA grew.*"[84]

Interrogation of captured VC supported the conclusions of these studies. Concerning rations for VC soldiers, "whenever soldiers report that the population was short for rice, the soldiers still ate, and . . . if they ran short of food on rare occasions due to battle dislocations, the matter was invariably immediately remedied. This would indicate that crop destruction, while depriving the villagers, continues to fail in denying food to the enemy."[85]

As one former South Vietnamese official recalled, the defoliation program was not executed with an eye toward winning the heart and minds of the population.

Because there were no absolute bars against crop destruction there, local officials ignored the vulnerability of the Montagnard farms to defoliants used in the jungles. . . . This exacerbated the general ill-feeling of the Montagnards toward the government and was exploited by the Communists to good effect. . . .

The attitude of some of our local officials was not calculated to win the hearts and minds of the people. Some of them would tell their people that if they wanted to be spared the effects of defoliation, they either had to rid themselves of the enemy, or had to leave their homes to settle in government controlled areas. This "take it or leave it" line was not only unfair but counterproductive. How could the people chase the enemy from their areas?[86]

These were the same Montagnards whose crop destruction from de-foliation was viewed by Army field commanders as a great success. Compensation for crops destroyed by defoliants was planned for; how-ever, the bureaucratic apparatus set up to process the claims of the peasants was grossly inefficient. It usually took at least eight months to process a claim; even then, the proportion of the compensation to the actual loss was very low.[87]

The Army's approach to the use of herbicides and defoliants fit neatly into its Concept. It represented an attempt at effecting a technological fix to a problem that was not amenable to such a solution. The only sure way to deny the insurgents logistical support from the people was to deny them access to those people. When the Army adopted a big-unit war of attrition, it abandoned any idea of pursuing the counterinsurgent's traditional role. The Army looked at defoliation in military terms and ignored the broader political and social damage. The people, not the VC, suffered the resulting food shortages. Alienation of the population followed, fueled to some extent by VC propaganda, which, true or not, was often effective.

Conclusion

Army operations in South Vietnam were oriented overwhelmingly toward the Army Concept, with its bias toward mid-intensity conflict, big-unit operations, and minimization of U.S. casualties through heavy firepower. The attrition strategy developed by MACV provided for the scaling of priorities, incentives, and rewards according to how well units operated according to traditional Army principles. The result was that any changes that might have come about through the service's experience in Vietnam were effectively short-circuited by Army goals and policies: tours were kept short, field commanders' missions were kept simple (kill VC), firepower was readily available to accomplish the attrition strategy, and inflated body counts were acceptable, if not officially promoted. By the same token, these goals and policies frustrated attempts to conduct counterinsurgency operations. Pacification was the "other" war, the ARVN's war. It took too long to produce results. Besides, the Army was never around long enough to really grasp the feel for the area, the people, and the culture necessary for waging that kind of war. It was far easier to fall back on the logistical and technological elements of strategy— sensors, ground radars, firepower on call, helicopter gunships, herbicides and defoliants—all of which gave the Army the opportunity to wage counterinsurgency American-style.

8
The "Other" War

CORDS and Pacification

Despite the Army's emphasis on the strategy of attrition, it did funnel a portion of its enormous resources into traditional counterinsurgency operations. In fact, MACV was the primary U.S. agent for the pacification program, the development of local security forces (the RFS and the PFS), and intelligence activities. Unfortunately for MACV, its focus was so overwhelmingly on the big-unit war that the resources devoted to these counterinsurgency operations—the "other" war—were insufficient for the task at hand. Thus, to a great extent, the problem of U.S. strategy in Vietnam was a problem of resource allocation.

While the Army engaged in these kinds of operations, however, it rarely allowed them to interfere with its top priority, namely, winning the war through the destruction of enemy forces on the battlefield. Furthermore, Army attempts to adjust to insurgency warfare were often counterproductive in that they actually hampered the war against the insurgents. As Sir Robert Thompson observed, pacification is "an offensive campaign designed to restore the government's authority by a sustained advance in accordance with national priority areas and, at the same time, to protect the individual against a selective reprisal attack so that he can safely play his part within the community, in co-operation with the government, against the Viet Cong."[1] While the GVN had many shortcomings that severely compromised its ability to carry out a successful pacification program, the Army, through its predominant role in the war, could not help but have a major impact on the success or failure of pacification in South Vietnam.

To be successful, pacification must combine security from insurgent coercion for the villager with a rationale for his support of the existing regime. Providing the latter, referred to as "winning the hearts," is often accomplished through civic action programs, land reform, and a measure of political participation. Efforts at winning the hearts of the people will come to naught, however, if the insurgent is able to control the population by "winning their minds" through terror, assassination, and reprisals for pro-government activities. In short, physical security is the *sine qua non* in any strategy aimed at defeating an insurgent movement.

Prior to the introduction of U.S. combat troops in 1965, a series of poorly conceived and executed pacification programs (Agrovilles, Strategic Hamlets, Hop Tac) made the population wary of Saigon's willingness and ability to defend and assist them. Irrespective of the increasing tempo of U.S. assistance programs, the people had to be convinced that they were secure from Communist reprisals and that the government forces were on the road to victory before they would risk supporting the Saigon regime. Basically, the programs foundered owing to the GVN's reliance on form over substance in pacification operations and the relative indifference of the Vietnamese and U.S. armed forces to the "other" war. The ARVN, for their part, would typically sweep through an area and then depart in short order, allowing the guerrillas to quickly reassert their control. The VC were fond of telling the villagers that "the government forces will soon leave, but we will be here forever."[2] There was also a strong element of naiveté on the part of the Americans. One military man, S. L. A. Marshall, wrote, "The one most effective way to win the confidence and friendly cooperation of the people in a strange hamlet is to go in with a Polaroid camera and start photographing the children. That will convert the adults within a couple of hours."[3] Unfortunately, the Polaroid approach to winning the hearts and minds proved insufficient.

As the ground war dragged on through 1966 and into 1967 with little progress made in either the war of attrition or pacification of the countryside, Secretary of Defense McNamara became increasingly committed to placing a ceiling on U.S. ground force deployments and a stronger emphasis on pacification operations. A major step was taken at the Manila Conference, in October 1966, when South Vietnamese leaders indicated a willingness to commit up to 60 percent of the ARVN's infantry battalions in support of Revolutionary Development (RD) operations, as they were called. The United States, for its part, reorganized its pacification support structure into the Office of Civil Operations (OCO); however, few U.S. ground forces were committed to support the pacification effort.[4] As it turned out, the creation of OCO was merely an interim move by the president in his efforts to get the "other" war into the mainstream of the overall war effort. The final solution, adopted in May 1967, at the direction of the president himself, placed pacification under the aegis of the military. The rationale, according to Robert Komer, was "a very simple one: if you are going to get a program going, you are only going to be able to do it by stealing from the military. They have all the trucks, they have all the planes, they have all the people, they have all the money."[5] The JCS and General Westmoreland were strongly behind the move and helped confirm the president's opinion that to be successful, any centralized program required access to military pesonnel and equipment. Thus, the programs of OCO were mated with the MACV organizational structure, producing the office for CORDS. To emphasize his interest in CORDS, Johnson appointed Komer, his special assistant for pacification, as deputy to COMUSMACV for CORDS with the rank of ambassador. In this position Komer had coequal status with all members of Westmoreland's primary staff. This arrangement existed throughout the organizational chain of command, so that, for instance, the CORDS chief at corps level was a deputy to the corps commander. At the province and district level the entire military advisory staff was placed under CORDS, with the chief being either a soldier or a civilian. Thus, CORDS represented not so much a military takeover of pacification as the formation of an ad hoc civil-military hybrid.

While the U.S. military had taken over the pacification effort structurally, the U.S. civilians managed both to preserve their own identity and to control the program through aggressive leadership, bureaucratic skill, real and perceived Presidential interest, and a degree of cooperation and tolerance that was remarkable among disparate U.S. foreign policy agencies.[6]

Although the civilians could not get the Army to modify its approach to the war, they could at least divert some Army resources to pacification and pull some Army officers along in their wake.

To his credit, Westmoreland offered Komer considerable support in getting CORDS off the ground, particularly in the ambassador's dealings with the MACV Staff. Such support appears to have been motivated, in large part, not only by MACV's assumption of the pacification mission (and responsibility for its success) but also by the growing belief among the civilian leadership that more was needed in the area of pacification. Even though the administration was making a "big push" for pacification, the Army nevertheless succeeded in limiting the potentially large damage such a change in priorities could have had on big-unit operations. McNamara did not push too hard at Manila for direct Army troop involvement in pacification, and Komer, for his part, did not interfere with the large search-and-destroy operations MACV was drawing up for 1967 and beyond. And the Army could now point to its new-found commitment to pacification to deflect some of the emerging heat from OSD over its war of attrition; and it would not hurt when requests for increased deployments were submitted.

CORDS had responsibility for the establishment and implementation of all plans and operations in support of pacification, including advising and training the RFs and PFs. Although at peak strength the military component of CORDS would outnumber the civilian element by roughly 6 to 1 (about 6,500 to 1,100), civilians held most of the top positions and exercised a measure of control greatly disproportionate to their numbers.[7] One cannot, therefore, evaluate the activities of CORDS without taking into account the existence of this civilian dilution of service "purity" with respect to pacification from mid-1967 on.

Komer realized that pacification had made very little progress since the infusion of U.S. troops. An example that best reflects the "progress" being made involves several trips made to South Vietnam by Henry Kissinger, then a Harvard academic and adviser to New York governor Nelson Rockefeller. Upon visiting the province of Vinh Long in October 1965, Kissinger was told that 80 percent of the area had been pacified. When he returned to Vietnam the following July, Kissinger went again to Vinh Long and looked up the same official to check on how pacification was progressing. The man told Kissinger that "enormous progress had been made" since his earlier visit: the province was now 70 percent pacified![8] From a military standpoint, the pacification problem centered on the fact that while the regular forces (MACV's big units and the ARVN) could push back any Communist main-force units, the predators—the VCI and the guerrillas—remained obstacles to success. Providing long-term security for the people required upgrading of the paramilitary forces directly charged with the responsibility for protecting them (the RFs and the PFs). This quickly became a top priority for CORDS.

Ruff-Puffs

For CORDS to be successful in its pacification efforts, the paramilitary RF and PF units (or "Ruff-Puffs," as they were often called) had to provide the local security necessary to screen the guerrillas from the population while allowing the police the opportunity to eliminate the VCI. These territorial units consisted of locally recruited men, most of them volunteers (motivated, in part, by a desire to avoid the draft). RFs served only in their own province, and PFs in their own village area. RFs typically operated in company-size units, whereas PFs comprised thirty-man platoons. One particularly desirable characteristic of the PFs (who served part-time and held regular jobs in the community) was their ability to maintain close ties with the local population far more readily than the ARVN or even the RFs. The idea was to have these forces engaged in counterinsurgency operations in and around the populated areas, conducting patrols and setting ambushes (particularly at night), making movement by the guerrillas a risky proposition. They would protect the hamlets and villages from attack, radioing for support from quick-reaction regular units when necessary. This had *always* been the plan for the paramilitary forces, but it had never been properly executed, primarily owing to a lack of support from the regular forces and the misuse of paramilitary forces to support main-force missions (such as the diversion of the CIDGs to a border patrol mission in Operation SWITCHBACK).

In the advisory years, 1961–65, the RF and PF commanders rarely had operational control over their units; actual control resided in the hands of the ARVN corps and division commanders. This led to their frequent use on search-and-destroy operations in support of ARVN units. This mal-employment, coupled with their maldeployment, led to high desertion rates among many paramilitary units.[9]

Nor did the RFs and PFs get their fair share of training, equipment, and personnel. The Army's Special Forces abandoned much of their pacification training mission after Operation SWITCHBACK. Weapons provided the RFs and PFs consisted primarily of World War II leftovers or worse. Finally, the ARVN was given priority in the competition for manpower, both in quantity and quality (so much so that in 1965 and 1966 the paramilitary forces actually *declined* in strength). There was a deep-rooted feeling on the regular forces' part that the Ruff-Puffs were inferior and should be treated accordingly. Yet the paramilitary had to perform some of the most onerous and dangerous tasks, as the casualty figures bear out.[10]

MACV finally pushed for the creation of more RFs at the expense of the regular forces during the period of intervention, arguing that per unit the RFs were considerably cheaper to field than were similar ARVN forces. Thus, creation of RFs did not threaten the Concept—on the contrary, since RF units were less expensive than ARVN units, fewer ARVN units would be diverted for pacification. At the same time, the GVN resisted MACV's attempts to give priority to the creation of RF units, no doubt feeling that the more heavily armed units the Americans formed, the better off the RVNAF would be after the U.S. pulled out.

As things turned out, MACV was successful in increasing RF billets in the RVNAF from 137,187 in 1966 to 155,322 in 1967. With the formation of CORDS, more emphasis was placed on the paramilitary forces. For example, most additional advisory billets were used to create some 353 Mobile Advisory Teams (MATS) to train the Ruff-Puffs. While not as effective as CAPS, the MATS did provide advice on small-unit tactics and pacification support. CORDS was also successful in getting an increase in RF/PF strength, seeing it rise from roughly 300,000 in 1967 to some 532,000 by 1971. Commensurate with the increase in numbers was an increase in the quality of the RF/PF equipment, with M16s and other light weaponry replacing the World War II–vintage equipment.[11]

CORDS also worked at changing the command arrangements to make the Ruff-Puffs more effective. Unfortunately, they were placed under the control of the sector and subsector commanders and their staffs, officers of low quality—the black sheep of the ARVN officer corps. In the ARVN, as in the U.S. Army, the big-unit war was where the action was, particularly in terms of career enhancement. Thus, the subsector commander frequently had little or no experience in the conduct of pacification operations. Command arrangements during this period, as in the advisory years, allowed VC exploitation of the "seams" between administrative areas, where the authority of one commander began and another left off.

In addition to the Ruff-Puffs' problems owing to the shortfall of U.S. and GVN support, they were also a prime target for VC attacks. The burden shouldered by the Ruff-Puffs vis-à-vis the support they were accorded was most perplexing to the civilians at Systems Analysis. They wondered why, "in view of the critical role the RF and PF should play in maintaining security for pacification," they continued to be given so low a priority for weapons, supplies, and training.[12] It was evident that the Ruff-Puffs in general, and the PFs in particular, were often subjected to a higher rate of attacks by the VC than were their counterparts in the ARVN.[13] Indeed, with the exception of the Tet Offensive, *the territorial forces consistently suffered casualties at a higher rate than did the ARVN* (see table 6).[14] Except in 1968, it was more dangerous to serve in the RF and PF units than in the ARVN. Furthermore, as time went on, the disparity in casualty rates between the forces actually grew wider. Thus, the paramilitary forces, manned by the dregs of the manpower pool and shabbily equipped compared with their counterparts in the ARVN, bore the brunt of the war.

Territorial forces also suffered from a lack of timely support from the so-called ARVN quick-reaction forces, purportedly designated to come to their assistance in the event of a VC assault on their village or hamlet. For

TABLE 6. RF/PF Casualties

RF/PF Casualties	1967	1968	1969	1970	1971
As percentage of the RVNAF	47%	48%	49%	51%	51%
As percentage of RVNAF KIAS	52	47	54	59	60

Source: Thomas C. Thayer, "How to Analyze a War without Fronts: Vietnam, 1965–1972," *Journal of Defense Research,* ser. B, *Tactical Warfare Analysis of Vietnam Data,* vol. 7B, no. 3 (1975), p. 887.

example, between October 1966 and March 1967, RF/PF units under attack in III Corps received support only 45 percent of the time, and ground reinforcements in only 11 percent of the attack situations. As late as 1969, the Ruff-Puffs realized only 30 percent of the Vietnamese-fired artillery support, half of which was H&I fire.[15]

Despite the numerous handicaps under which they operated, the territorial forces performed well. When the RF and PF units worked together, they had the greatest impact on the level of population security in a given area, and the PF operating alone had the next greatest impact.[16] As expected, population security increased when paramilitary forces, utilized together to provide both mobile and static defense, operated in an area over a prolonged period of time. That the Ruff-Puffs succeeded in boosting pacification was evidenced by the increased attention the VC gave to disrupting pacification activities, as reflected in captured insurgent documents.[17] Other indications of success were the disengagement of ARVN units from pacification operations in 1970 and the successful use of RF units during the Cambodian incursion that same year.[18]

Incredible as it may seem, the Ruff-Puffs actually contributed *more effectively* to MACV's attrition strategy than did the U.S. and South Vietnamese main-force units. The figures available demonstrate that although they received less than 20 percent of the total RVNAF budget and lacked the heavy organic firepower espoused by the Concept, the territorials accounted for roughly 30 percent of the VC/NVA combat deaths inflicted by the RVNAF. What is even more startling, the *RFs and PFs accounted for 12–30 percent of all VC/NVA combat deaths* (depending on the year), *yet they consumed only 2–4 percent of the total annual cost of the war.*[19] Unfortunately, paramilitary forces did not fit the Army's perception of the war and its propensity for seeking solutions through conventional operations. Thus, another traditional principle of counterinsurgency was ignored: the only certain way of forcing the insurgents out into the open is to deny them access to their source of sustenance—the population—through an effective pacification program of which paramilitary forces are an integral part.

The Army and Pacification

While about 6,000 MACV officers and men worked with the civilians in CORDS to develop a population security program, the bulk of the Army remained only peripherally concerned with pacification. Most Army units continued to engage in traditional operations. Thus, the dent made in the Army Concept by Komer and the civilians at CORDS remained limited. The Army's general view of the role of pacification was characterized by Lieutenant General Ewell, who said, "I had two rules. One is that you would try to get a very close meshing of pacification . . . and military operations. The other rule is the *military operations would be given first priority in every case*. That doesn't mean you wouldn't do pacification, but this gets at what you might call winning the hearts and minds of the people. I'm all for that. It's a nice concept, but in fighting the Viet Cong and the NVA, if you don't break their military machine you might as well forget winning the hearts and minds of the people."[20]

Using data from the HES established by CORDS, as well as data on unit operations provided by MACV, OSA showed how maneuver battalion days of operation in a given area contributed little to population security. On the other hand, VC activity in an area was closely associated with a decline in security.[21] The lesson, once again, was that big-unit sweeps did not promote pacification—you had to stay in an area; otherwise the VC would come in right behind you and undo any pacification gains you had made. The Army's misperception of what was required for successful pacification of an area, combined with an organizational philosophy reflective of Ewell's, on a number of occasions led to military operations that worked against pacification rather than in support of it.

One such operation occurred shortly after the 1st Cavalry Division's victory in the Ia Drang Valley. Code-named MASHER (later WHITE WING), it involved a sweep through the northern portion of Binh Dinh Province in II Corps. The division spent nearly a month and a half, from 24 January until 6 March 1966, attempting to make contact with the VC. In its combat after-action report, submitted on 28 April, the division reported 1,342 killed. Tremendous amounts of firepower were utilized—over 132,000 rounds of artillery alone. Thus the Army spent, on average, 1,000 rounds of artillery to kill 1 VC, in addition to the fire support received from helicopters and tactical air units.

While a satisfactory body count was achieved, the impact on the "other" war was far from beneficial. The lavish use of firepower by the Army contributed toward increasing the refugee population in the town of

Bong Son from 7,806 to 27,652. In Hoai An District the total rose from 7,514 to 17,622. According to the Army, operations in Hoai An "freed over 10,000 war victims most of whom occupied vacant buildings or moved into homes of friends." The division did construct a well and a latrine at the new Bong Son refugee camp, a meager gesture considering that by year's end Binh Dinh Province contained 85 refugee camps holding some 129,202 people.[22] These hardships imposed on the population of Binh Dinh might have been accepted more easily had Operation MASHER/WHITE WING been the prelude to the introduction of a comprehensive pacification program. It was not. The division quickly moved on to other operations, having improved pacification not a whit while alienating thousands of homeless victims, who, as refugees, had to start their lives over again from scratch.

Not quite a year later, on 1 February 1967, the 1st Cavalry Divison, reinforced with a brigade of the 25th Infantry division, returned to Binh Dinh Province. This time the mission was to "fully pacify" the province—in three months. The plan, code-named THAYER II (1–11 February), then PERSHING (12 February–30 April), opened with "extensive" search-and-destroy operations that "failed to locate" the fleeing enemy units once contact was lost (which it invariably was, typically in short order). These operations continued until 19 March. Shortly thereafter, the Army began forceably to evacuate civilians from several locations, including the inhabitants of the valleys of Kim Son and Soui Ca. Some 12,000 people sought refuge "voluntarily" because of the destruction wrought by the search-and-destroy operations. To accommodate this mass of humanity, USAID could offer only some 560 family units in the Tam Quan and Bong Son areas. Later, two Vietnamese marine battalions drove another 5,200 people out of An Lao Valley; unfortunately, only 1,886 could be resettled. It was hoped that the others would be "absorbed" into the Bong Son population. The division's civic action activities through all of this consisted of daily sick calls at refugee camps and several band concerts, characterized by the division as assistance of the "short-duration, high-impact" type. Once the refugee populaton had been moved out of the aforementioned locations, the Vietnamese air force began crop-destruction operations to deny the VC food.[23]

The operation itself was termed a success by the Army, even though the division would have preferred a "realignment" of the rules of engagement to permit unit commanders to authorize reconnaissance by fire on suspected areas of enemy activity.[24] Nevertheless, the problem with the ROE appears to have been circumvented by many anxious commanders during

General William C. Westmoreland addressing men of the 1st Cavalry Division (Airmobile) during Operation Thayer II, approximately 30 km north of Qui Nhon.

courtesy U.S. Army

the operation.[25] Again, the division got its body count: 1,757 enemy killed. By way of achieving this total, the division expended over 136,000 rounds of artillery and over 5,000 rounds of naval gunfire support. There were 171 B-52 sorties flown, as well as 2,622 fighter-bomber missions; and 500,000 pounds of napalm and over 35,000 pounds of CS (tear) gas were dropped. All this in an area that the Army had characterized as "densely populated."[26] As in the previous year, when the operation was completed, the big units quickly moved on. Thus pacification served, at best, as an adjunct to the Army's operational plan for U.S. units. Given its view of the Army's role in pacification as one of driving off the enemy's big units and getting the population behind barbed wire, MACV could give its units the objective of pacifying the Binh Dinh Province within three months and see it as a reasonable mission. In trying the achieve quick results, the Army waged counterinsurgency on the cheap. Since the Army viewed the conflict through the lens of its Concept, it saw the participation of its units in pacification as of little enduring consequence.

Refugees

In light of all this, it is appropriate to look at the Army's role in the refugee problem that plagued South Vietnam throughout the period of U.S. intervention. The reader will recall that forced resettlement of the population for the purpose of denying the enemy access to it represents an extreme step on the government's part, taken only with great care and as a last resort. The Army generally accorded low priority to the refugee problem. For MACV, people living in rural areas represented barriers to the creation of free-fire zones. It required a greater effort to protect them than it did to protect citizens in densely populated regions, and their crops might sustain the VC. Finally, they might serve as sources of intelligence for the VC concerning the activities of allied forces. To the Army with its perception of the nature of insurgency warfare distorted by the conceptual lens through which it viewed the conflict, it appeared that a great blow could be struck against the enemy in the big-unit war, and in the "other" war as well, by relocating people to areas of greater safety.

Plans for relocating segments of the population were initiated by MACV in 1966, although as operations such as MASHER/WHITE WING bore out, large numbers of refugees were already being created. During this period the Army viewed the large refugee population as an indicator of its success in the "other" war. General Wheeler, when asked how the war was progressing in April 1966, replied: "[An] indicator is the number of refugees. As has occurred everywhere communists have tried to take over territories, people have fled in great numbers *from* communist regimes. I think it speaks for itself that people have never fled *toward* communist regimes. Not anywhere, at any time. South Vietnam holds some 860,000 refugees, most of whom have fled from the Viet Cong. 460,000 of them are still in temporary shelters. 100,000 of them have returned to their original villages, now made safe. And 300,000 have been resettled in new, safe areas."[27]

While the Army may have convinced itself that 860,000 people in South Vietnam were willingly and gratefully moving to the protection of refugee camps out of fear of the VC, this was not the case. First, most refugees moved neither voluntarily nor to flee communist oppression. The Army's own PROVN study, issued in mid-1966, concluded that "US-

RVNAF bombing and artillery fire, in conjunction with ground operations are the immediate and prime causes of refugee movement into GVN-controlled urban and coastal areas."[28] The PROVN analysis was supported by several other studies carried out in 1966 and 1967.[29] Second, if people were not fleeing the rural villages and hamlets out of fear of the VC, they were often *remaining* there specifically because the communists had threatened to redistribute the land of those who departed. This threat was frequently successful and no doubt contributed to the high percentage of refugees who were forced to flee by the GVN and MACV relative to that of those who fled out of fear of the communists.[30] Third, as General Wheeler's figures indicated, the ability of MACV and/or the GVN to handle those refugees generated by the vicissitudes of war, let alone those created by intent, was notoriously deficient. As early as 1965 COMUSMACV was well aware of the GVN's corruption, inefficiency, and, in many cases, outright indifference to the refugee problem.[31] Refugees streaming into urban areas more often than not had to fend for themselves, since government resettlement assistance was minimal. The VC quickly took advantage of the situation by reminding the people that they had been forced from the place of their ancestors, their homes destroyed by ARVN or U.S. bombs and their crops poisoned by herbicides.

VC infiltration and indoctrination of refugees proved extremely successful in some areas. Troops regularly accompanied government officials on visits to the Cua Viet Camp in Quang Tri Province to protect them from some 3,000 of their countrymen who had supposedly fled communism. In Binh Dinh Province, where the 1st Cavalry Division had conducted its search-and-destroy operations, the camp at Berin Sac was considered unsafe for government visitors. In many camps in Kieh Tuong Province—Hoa Cu, Kinh Cha, and Tan Lap among them—a large percentage of the refugees were considered either VC or VC sympathizers.[32]

The Army was slow to learn that merely forcing people into "safe" areas did not constitute winning the "other" war. While creation of refugees may have facilitated search-and-destroy operations by creating more free-fire zones, it served neither to gain control of the people nor to win their support. Between 1964 and 1969 over 3 million South Vietnamese, 20 percent of the population, were refugees at one time or another as a result of the attrition strategy and the policy of population relocation. This does not include those people "temporarily displaced by acts of war," such as the nearly a million people who had their homes destroyed during the Tet and post-Tet offensives in 1968.

With the formation of CORDS in May 1967, MACV began moving away from the deliberate creation of refugees. When Westmoreland's CCP for 1968 was published in December 1967, it called for an end to the policy. Nevertheless, the damage had been done. A report on the refugee situation filed in January 1968 stated that "while some of the refugees left their home at government order, the majority of those responding to the surveys say they moved only when military operations, usually friendly bombing and shelling made it impossible for them to continue living and working in their homes."[33] In Vietnam the Army was not the guardian of great numbers of South Vietnamese refugees fleeing Communist oppression but, rather, a primary cause of this calamity. MACV's handling of population relocation ended with the majority of refugees' blaming the United States and the GVN for their plight. Economic production in the areas cleared was reduced to zero, while the GVN was faced with the task of trying to relocate and support a significant portion of its population. Refugees often brought VC or VC sympathizers with them and were themselves frequently receptive to insurgent propaganda. Relocation did not make the population more secure, since the big units left the area shortly after their brief attempt at "pacification." The GVN appeared incapable, in the eyes of its people, of providing for their protection, further undermining its legitimacy. Finally, the military lost a potential source of intelligence in those areas cleared of people.

The War against the VCI

In counterinsurgency, priority in intelligence gathering is focused on the insurgents' infrastructure, since only by eliminating the roots of the insurgency can local security forces truly protect the people from a resurgence of enemy activity from within. Traditional counterinsurgency doctrine accords the role of attacking the insurgent infrastructure to the national police. It is their work in the towns and villages that, ideally, leads to the elimination of insurgent cells among the people. Once this is accomplished, guerrillas in the area are denied information, and the people can cooperate with the government without fear of insurgent reprisals.

The national police of the RVN suffered from numerous shortcomings, many of their own making and most unrelated to Army operations. However, to the extent that the Army was involved in counterinsurgency operations, it failed to appreciate that no matter how many casualties were inflicted on the enemy, the VCI would continue recruiting (or impressing) personnel, collecting taxes, and otherwise organizing the VC manpower and logistical base in the villages and hamlets of South Vietnam. With their attention focused on conventional operations, both the Army and the ARVN believed that the national police had primary responsibility for the VCI, while they, the military, had little or no responsibility to assist them. As one high-ranking ARVN officer stated, "military unit commanders felt little enthusiasm to launch operations against an enemy that was not an armed unit but lived, from outward appearances, like all law-abiding citizens. They felt that this unarmed enemy was not their proper adversary; he was the responsibility of the National Police."[34]

Since the successful breakdown of the insurgent infrastructure is predicated on protecting the police from guerrilla attack by units of the regular military, the reluctance of Army and ARVN units to engage in these operations severely compromised the effectiveness of the national police. The police were further hampered by the low priority accorded them for men and materiel. The RVN mobilization law gave the ARVN the cream of the nation's manpower, leaving recruits of marginal ability available for recruitment by the police. Pay was low compared with that received by members of the ARVN performing in comparable positions of responsibility. The effect of these personnel policies was a police force of marginal quality at best. The impact was evident in the GVN's pacification record: the police, while often impressive in numbers (increasing from some 66,000 men in 1966 to over 120,000 in 1972), lacked the leadership and teamwork with regular military units necessary in implementing an effective assault against the VCI. This, coupled with the pervasive corruption of the police force, resulted in the GVN's failure to root out the insurgent's infrastructure. While Sir Robert Thompson succeeded in persuading the GVN to effect reforms in the national police in the early 1970s, they proved to be too little too late.

Once established, CORDS attempted to provide some measure of assistance to the police in their war against the Communist infrastructure, primarily through the controversial Phoenix program. Phoenix (or Phung Hoang, as it was referred to by the South Vietnamese) was intended to oversee the efforts of district and provincial intelligence operations coordinating committees (DIOCCs and PIOCCs) in locating, identifying, and eliminating VCI cadres.[35] The U.S. role was intended to be purely advisory in nature. While the program scored some successes, a combination of police corruption and ineffectual leadership prevented Phoenix from materially decreasing the strength of the VCI. Indeed, at the end of his tour in 1970 Robert Komer concluded that "to date, Phung Hoang has been a small, poorly managed, and largely ineffective effort."[36] In 1970–71, for example, only 3 percent of the VCI killed, captured, or rallied were full or probationary Party members above the district level. Furthermore, the majority of those individuals killed or captured were not even Party members. The final irony is that only about 20 percent of the VCI killed, captured, or rallied were accounted for by forces assigned to Phung Hoang; correspondingly, the Ruff-Puffs' share ran between 39 percent and 50 percent annually.[37]

As for the Army's main-force units, their intelligence effort focused on the enemy's big units. Lieutenant General Yarborough observed that the weight of the intelligence effort was aimed at discovering how many divisions they had, not how many were placed at the village level or the hamlet level.[38] Robert Komer best described Army intelligence's preoccupation with finding the enemy's big units when he observed that it focused on what was familiar—the enemy order of battle—"the identification and location of the main enemy units so that we can target them and clobber them." They did this, said Komer, "to the total neglect of the guerrillas and the so-called Viet Cong infrastructure, the political-military apparatus that was really running the war."[39] The South Vietnamese found U.S. officers trying to combat the insurgency by following the principles they had been taught in FM 30-5 (*Combat Intelligence*), a manual geared to mid- or high-intensity conflict against an adversary such as the Soviet Union in the European environment. Consequently, the ARVN leadership judged the professional expertise of Army intelligence officers to be "minimal" for what the war required, and their knowledge "primarily technical or procedural."[40]

The shortcomings of Army Intelligence officers in waging the "other" war were further compounded by the one-year-tour-of-duty policy established by the Army. Brief tour lengths contributed to the attitude prevalent among many intelligence officers that familiarity with the culture, language, and society of Vietnam was not essential in the performance of their duty. In failing to appreciate the necessity of destroying the insurgents' political infrastructure as a precondition for victory, the Army failed to render counterinsurgency intelligence operations the priority they deserved. While the efforts of CORDS foundered on the relatively low priority given these operations by MACV and the national police, the Army's intelligence personnel suffered from the service's preoccupation with its traditional approach to war.

The Special Forces units that the Army structured for counterinsurgency fared no better. Even in the early days before Operation

SWITCHBACK, Special Forces intelligence operations were hampered by a lack of familiarity with the language and culture of the people with whom they were working as well as by the absence of any Army procedures for the procurement of such intelligence. Once the Green Berets came under the control of MACV in 1962–63, Special Forces intelligence efforts were redirected toward supporting Army main-force units. The results were predictable. The emphasis on producing reliable intelligence for use by conventional forces led to the decline of "local" intelligence. Under the early CIDG program, emphasis had been placed on intelligence covering the local VC underground organization. When priority was given to intelligence for conventional forces, local intelligence efforts deteriorated, and there was a corresponding decrease in the effectiveness of local area development. Finding and destroying the VC countrywide by conventional military methods took precedence over the more subtle tactic of systematically rooting out the VCI. Thus, the talents of the Special Forces in pacification were subordinated to the big-unit war. The blame for failing to crush the VCI cannot, however, be laid principally at the Army's doorstep. Such operations are primarily the province of the police and local security forces. Nevertheless, the Army could have done a lot more in this area than it did.

Special Operations

While traditional counterinsurgency doctrine places primary emphasis on population security and control, it also posits the desirability of having some small units penetrate into guerrilla territory ("sanctuaries," or remote base areas) for the purpose of setting ambushes along routes of guerrilla movement, raiding guerrilla base areas, gathering intelligence (particularly on guerrilla movements that would indicate that an attack on an area under pacification was imminent), and exerting psychological pressure on the guerrilla, making him realize that there are, for him, no true sanctuaries from government attack. During both the advisory era and the period of intervention the Army formed a number of these special units with the intention of accomplishing these missions.

One of the early special units was organized by the U.S. Mission in May 1964 under the name Leaping Lena. It called for Special Forces troops to train Vietnamese Special Forces and CIDG troops to conduct long-range reconnaissance patrols (LRPs or LRRPs, pronounced *lerps*). Not long after its inception, Leaping Lena was transferred to MACV as part of Operation SWITCHBACK and renamed Project Delta. The program was the first of a number established by MACV's Studies and Observation Group (sog), a "joint *unconventional* [*not* counterinsurgency] warfare task force" whose mission involved operations throughout Indochina.[41] The LRPs' primary mission quickly became gathering tactical intelligence through reconnaissance and surveillance operations in support of main-force search-and-destroy operations. These Delta forces, as they were called, consisted of twelve ten-man hunter-killer teams (two Special Forces soldiers and eight Vietnamese Special Forces soldiers per team) and four ARVN ranger companies with Special Forces advisers. The advantage of Delta forces derived from their ability to direct firepower, such as air strike, against enemy troop concentrations on short notice.

With the arrival of U.S. ground forces in 1965, the Apache Force concept was born. Apache Forces consisted of small reconnaissance/ pathfinder teams of indigenous personnel commanded by a Special Forces officer. These teams were employed by the Army in much the same manner as were Indian scouts during the Indian Wars. They operated under the control of a U.S. main-force commander, who used them in locating and monitoring guerrilla forces until the big units could arrive on the scene. Unfortunately, unit commanders often misjudged or misunderstood the mission and capabilities of Apache Force teams and frequently employed them as line infantry.[42]

In August 1966, MACV began creating mobile guerrilla forces to increase its conventional warfare capability. These forces were commanded by Special Forces personnel and were assigned to support I Field Force (Project Omega) in II Corps and II Field Force (Project Sigma) in III Corps. The units were utilized on forays into remote areas of the country considered to be VC/NVA safe havens. As with Apache Forces, the Omega and Sigma programs witnessed the diversion of Special Forces and CIDG units from their original mission of pacification.[43]

These units, along with two Marine reconnaissance battalions in I Corps and a few U.S. Navy SEAL (Sea-Air-Land commando) platoons in III and IV Corps, made up the bulk of what were generally referred to as strike teams. While their operations primarily reflected an unconventional warfare mission, they also fit within the parameters of counterinsurgency. Through their unconventional warfare operations, strike teams performed a useful economy-of-force role that, had MACV been focusing on counterinsurgency operations, would have freed many of the big units for population security missions.

Besides serving in an economy-of-force role, strike teams could furnish a screen for government pacification efforts. By saturating the "demographic frontier" (a band of territory just outside the densely populated coastal region in South Vietnam), strike teams could give advance warning of major enemy forces massing for attacks against the populated areas undergoing pacification. Teams operating further inland could call in air and/or artillery strikes on targets of opportunity or conduct ambushes and raids in lieu of search-and-destroy operations, allowing regular units the opportunity to participate in pacification activities and to serve as a formidable reaction force should the insurgents mass for a large-scale attack.

Contrary to conventional Army wisdom, the rate of contact for strike teams was *higher* than that for larger, conventional units engaged in search-and-destroy operations. Furthermore, attrition of enemy forces per soldier was *higher* for strike teams than for the big battalions. Like the Marine CAPS, strike teams suffered proportionally *lower* casualties than Regular Army maneuver battalions.[44]

Although a sufficient number of strike teams operating within a traditional counterinsurgency strategy would have sharply curtailed the need for search-and-destroy operations, the requirement for significant numbers of conventional forces to act as mobile reserves would have remained. They would have had the mission of driving off any enemy force that had somehow pinned down a strike team and did, in fact, conduct such operations during the war. Naturally, the big units would also have had the responsibility (along with fire support units) of blunting any emerging VC/NVA main-force incursions into the populated areas. Unfortunately, MACV viewed small-unit actions as an adjunct or an aid to a big-unit strategy, not an alternative. The strike teams never possessed the numbers or the support necessary for carrying out a broad-based counter-insurgency program.[45]

Conclusion

To the extent that Army efforts at pacification, intelligence gathering, destruction of the insurgent infrastructure, and employment of strike teams reflected counterinsurgency doctrine, they did so primarily because of the efforts of small sub-organizations, such as the Special Forces and the civilian-run CORDS, that were out of the service's "mainstream." While their activities occurred along the fringes of the Army's domain, the overwhelming majority of its forces in South Vietnam continued to practice counterinsurgency American-style. To the extent that Regular Army units participated in counterinsurgency operations, they either looked for quick, cheap solutions that did not exist, as in the case of

THAYER II/PERSHING, or misused the forces that had been designed to provide some effectiveness in combating insurgents.

Whenever the Army had to choose between priorities—whether it was manpower and training for the Ruff-Puffs versus the ARVN, creation of refugees versus restrictions on the application of firepower, identifying the VCI versus locating a VC battalion, or unconventional warfare operations in support of counterinsurgency operations versus in support of conventional operations—it unstintingly devoted a disproportionate amount of its resources to those activities that conformed most closely to its preferred method of waging war.

While Army participation in pacification, given the chronic corruption and absence of leadership displayed by the GVN and RVNAF, would not have provided a cure-all for the problems involved in achieving population control and security, it is clear that MACV could have eased those problems considerably had it adopted a more flexible approach to the conflict. If the Army had followed a counterinsurgency strategy, both the human and financial costs of the war would have been significantly lower. This, in turn, would have assisted to some extent in maintaining popular support in the United States for U.S. participation in the war. It would have placed the Army in a position to sustain its efforts in a conflict environment certain to produce a protracted war. True to its Concept, the Army focused on the technological and logistical dimensions of strategy while ignoring the political and social dimensions that formed the foundation of counterinsurgency warfare. The result was a high-cost, low-payoff strategy.

Three

YEARS OF WITHDRAWAL
1968–1973

9
Tet: Defeat in Victory

At the beginning of 1968, despite the absence of appreciable progress, the Army's faith in its attrition strategy remained unshaken. Nothing was wrong with the way the Army was fighting the war, the brass maintained. The Army would prevail—eventually. If speedier results were desired, said the generals, it would be necessary to increase the intensity of operations—more bombing of the North with no restrictions on targets; okaying MACV's Laotian incursion (with, perhaps, an amphibious hook into North Vietnam's panhandle region); and finally, a drive into Cambodia to clean out the enemy sanctuaries.

While the Army had not achieved victory, it had not suffered any significant defeats on the battlefield either. Given the failure of Kennedy's attempted revolution from above and the Army advisers' revolt from below, it appeared that the only prospect for changing the attrition strategy at this late date would be the shock of a dramatic defeat for MACV, or the approval of the military's plans for a wider war as part of a strategy of annihilation. For the American people and the Johnson administration, the Tet Offensive provided the shock that led to their loss of faith in the Army's strategy. For the Army, however, the Communist offensive proved insufficient to overcome the Concept's hold over its approach to the war. The military's response to the implications of the Tet Offensive was the same as it had been throughout the war: apply the Concept, but at a higher level of intensity.

The Tet Offensive

Beginning in October 1967, VC/NVA forces engaged U.S. and South Vietnamese forces in a series of battles in the remote border regions of South Vietnam. Initially centering their assaults in the northern three military regions, the Communists gradually extended their activity into the Mekong Delta by year's end. In January the NVA positioned two of its divisions, the 304th and 325th, so as to threaten the Marine forces located at Khe Sanh, an outpost situated near the junction of the Laotian–North Vietnamese borders with South Vietnam. Allied forces in Khe Sanh totaled five battalions—four Marine and one ARVN. Khe Sanh had been occupied to defend against infiltration and to provide a jump-off point for possible operations into Laos. Responding to this threat, MACV quickly diverted the 1st Cavalry Division and a brigade of the 101st Airborne Division to Thua Thien Province. Indeed, beginning in the late fall and continuing until Tet, Khe Sanh drew most of the U.S. command's attention and concern.[1] This diversion of American units to the remote border regions of the country may have been what the Communists were hoping for. Even though the border clashes caused heavy casualties among the VC/NVA forces, they persisted in their attacks. Communist losses, while substantial, served their overall strategic purpose. As General Giap noted, "Every minute, hundreds of thousands of people die all over the world. The life or death of a hundred, a thousand, or tens of thousands of human beings, even if they are our own compatriots, represents really very little."

Practically speaking, the defense of these remote areas made little sense, particularly given the great number of troops that were diverted away from the populated coastal areas. Even General Taylor admitted his confusion, observing that "Khe Sanh just looked like the last place you would want to have a large garrison." "When you observed how the Marines really dug themselves into the place," said Taylor, "it reminded you of the old French idea of digging in right up to their ears but never patrolling beyond the next ridgeline just beyond the range of their light weapons. So how the troops in Khe Sanh were influencing infiltration was, again, awfully hard to understand."[2]

According to General Westmoreland, captured enemy documents provided MACV with advance warning of the Communist general offensive. Despite this information, however, Westmoreland risked uncovering the populated areas in an effort to take the war to the enemy, asserting that he had "no intention of sitting back to wait the enemy's move."[3] A series of search-and-destroy operations was planned. U.S. forces began deploying to the border regions, preparing for sweeps into War Zones C and D, as well as along the Laotian border in the four northern provinces. It was hoped that the latter operations, directed at reestablishing control over the A Shau Valley in Thua Thien Province, would be used as a springboard for an eventual assault into Laos.

Fortunately, these operations were short-circuited in mid-January when Lt. Gen. Fred C. Weyand, commander of Army forces in III Corps, prevailed upon Westmoreland to cancel the forays into the war zones. Shortly thereafter, the northern operations were similarly postponed. Thus, while U.S. forces were not in the best possible position to blunt the attack, they were not entirely out of position. Nevertheless, when the enemy offensive hit in full force the night of 30–31 January, it sent the allied forces reeling. Employing 100,000 troops, the VC/NVA launched assaults on Saigon as well as 36 of the 43 provincial capitals, 5 of the 6 autonomous cities, and 64 of the 242 district capitals. The Communists succeeded in penetrating into Saigon, Quang Tri, Hue, Da Nang, Nha Trang, Qui Nhon, Kontum City, Ban Me Thout, Dalat, Phan Thiet, My Tho, Can Tho, and Ben Tre. In most instances allied forces quickly regained the upper hand and succeeded in driving the VC/NVA forces out within a few days. In Saigon the process took somewhat longer, and in Hue, where the enemy committed eight battalions of regulars, the fighting was both protracted and bloody. The situation in Hue notwithstanding (it would take nearly four weeks to recapture the city), the Communist offensive sputtered to an end on 11 February, two weeks after the initial assaults.

According to MACV's criterion, the Tet Offensive represented a disastrous failure for the Communists. The body count at the end of February was estimated at 37,000, with another 6,000 captured. The VCI bore the brunt of the losses. Instructed to come out into the open and instigate mass uprisings against the Saigon regime, these cadres, the heart of the insurgency, suffered enormous casualties, with some estimates running as high as 30 percent. For the Army, then, Tet provided a long-awaited opportunity to destroy large numbers of enemy forces. From the perspective of the American generals in Saigon and at the Pentagon, the battles of January and February provided the Army with its greatest success to date. General Westmoreland went so far as to compare Tet with the Battle of the Bulge—the last-gasp effort of an enemy on his last legs. The only aspect of the entire operation that puzzled the Army leadership was the apparent irrationality of the enemy attack. The Army's surprise at the extent of the assault was genuine, emanating from a belief that the insurgents were crazy to challenge the formidable military machine the U.S. had put in the field in South Vietnam.

The Concept Discredited

Even as VC and North Vietnamese forces fell in droves, the price of their overt onslaught into the populated areas, the perception of Tet as a major victory for the allied forces was coming into question by both the Johnson administration and the American people. Having been informed by Westmoreland that 1968 was to be the year when the allies would finally turn the corner in Vietnam, the civilian leadership was taken aback by the enemy's strong attacks. Many were perplexed that the insurgents could penetrate with such apparent ease into the nation's populated areas, particularly since MACV's search-and-destroy operations supposedly had been providing the shield behind which the people would be secure. This concern, coupled with yet another request by MACV for more troops, led to a full-blown review of U.S. strategy in Vietnam, ending in the explicit rejection of the Army strategy by the civilian leadership.

On 12 February, with the enemy offensive on the wane, General Westmoreland submitted a formal request to Washington for reinforcements. Encouraged by McNamara's rapid and positive response to items requested for the defense of Khe Sanh and by General Wheeler's indication that the president would be receptive to the dispatch of reinforcements, COMUSMACV petitioned for the deployment of a Marine regiment and a brigade of the Army's 82d Airborne Division.[4] No sooner had Westmoreland submitted his request, however, than the JCS recommended *against* meeting it. The reason was that the consequences of the Tet Offensive were now causing the military to bump up against the limits within which it could fight the war in Vietnam and still maintain a minimal level of readiness to meet other contingencies. No additional forces should be deployed, held the Chiefs, unless the president was prepared to take the necessary steps to "reconstitute the strategic reserve."[5] This implied a call-up of the reserves, an action the president had been loathe to direct. With the crisis atmosphere in Washington surrounding the enemy offensive and the siege of Khe Sanh, Wheeler felt that he finally had the set of circumstances for which he had been looking in order to force Johnson's hand on the issue. Thus his encouragement of Westmoreland to request forces, which he then rejected in the hope of forcing the president to call up the reserves.

In spite of the Chiefs' concern over the strategic reserve, McNamara quickly approved Westmoreland's request, directing the deployment of 10,500 troops to South Vietnam. The Chiefs reacted forcefully. While General Wheeler admitted that MACV had no significant operational reserve in the event of an ARVN collapse (an unlikely prospect in mid-

February, when the offensive had pretty much run its course) and that Westmoreland was still "owed" some 25,000 troops to reach his current ceiling of 525,000, he nevertheless felt that he could not possibly acquiesce in this deployment.[6] On 13 February the Chiefs recommended that a call-up of the reserves be directed.

Thus it was that the president, faced with a call-up of the reserves and stunned by the strength of the Tet assault, sent General Wheeler to Saigon to assess the situation and determine, along with Westmoreland, what forces would be required. Wheeler arrived in Vietnam on the twenty-third and quickly informed Westmoreland that the "strategic reserve here in the United States was completely depleted." Other than the 82d Airborne Division (one brigade of which was already detailed to MACV) the only unit close to being ready was the 5th Mechanized Division, and it could not deploy even with one brigade for six to ten weeks.[7]

This problem notwithstanding, the two generals worked up an ambitious deployment plan. Westmoreland wanted one division sent to Vietnam in May. Wheeler recalled that he and COMUSMACV agreed that "we should prepare ourselves for future eventualities by having another division which would be deployable sometime in early September. And as a matter of prudence, we would have a third division, which possibly could have been deployed in . . . December of 1968."[8]

Wheeler returned to Washington on the twenty-sixth and briefed President Johnson the following day. The general conceded that while the enemy's losses had been heavy, "the judgment is that he has the will and the capability to continue." Wheeler admitted that "there is no doubt that the RD program had suffered a severe setback. The enemy is operating with relative freedom in the countryside, probably recruiting heavily and no doubt infiltrating NVA units and personnel."[9]

Wheeler's report reflected the bankruptcy of the Army's strategy. Although in the Tet Offensive the Army had destroyed enemy forces in far greater numbers than in any other period in the war, it had had a negligible impact on the United States' prospects for victory. In essence, what Wheeler said was that for all his losses, the enemy had both the capability and the will to continue the struggle indefinitely. Despite this admission, Wheeler told the president that he and Westmoreland felt that once the enemy offensive had been blunted, MACV should "regain the initiative through offensive operations" similar to those search-and-destroy operations being planned prior to Tet.[10]

More specifically, Wheeler informed the president that COMUSMACV was currently deploying 50 percent of his maneuver battalions along the

DMZ and in the border regions, leaving insufficient forces available for the resumption of offensive operations in the remainder of the country. More troops would be needed to carry out the operations outlined by MACV. The chairman presented the president with five deployment options (see table 7).[11] The options presented the president with some hard choices. Although Westmoreland contended that he could get by with the 535,000 or so troops now either in the pipeline or in Vietnam, he clearly wanted more forces and, if possible, a horizontal escalation of the war into Laos and Cambodia.[12] For the president, compliance with the request of his field commander would necessitate a major call-up of reserve forces, a cost that Johnson had heretofore been unwilling to impose on the American people.

Before making a decision, Johnson decided to have DOD take a look at Westmoreland's request and seek the counsel of the "Wise Men," a group of senior statesmen, military officers, and security policy experts both in and out of government.

The civilians at OSA and ISA quickly produced memoranda highly critical of the military's request for more forces. OSA's, entitled "Alternative Strategies," characterized the Army's strategy in Vietnam as a failure. The memorandum observed that the military had staked everything on the big-unit war while ignoring the need to get the RVNAF squared away so it might stand on its own. The ISA memo proved prescriptive in nature, as well as critical. It was the product of the new assistant secretary of defense, Paul Warnke. Warnke sought to focus the discussion over additional forces on what the military could accomplish with them. He concluded that even with an additional 200,000 troops, Westmoreland could not drive the enemy from South Vietnam or destroy the Communist forces.[13] Despite the grievous losses incurred by the Communists in the Tet Offensive, Warnke noted, the enemy had decided when and where to fight—a situation that would continue to exist for the foreseeable future. Furthermore, in the past, as additional battalions had been deployed into the theater of operations, their body count totals had exhibited decreasing returns to scale. This meant that the attainment of the crossover point was becoming an increasingly expensive, and elusive, proposition. Echoing OSA's critique, ISA stated that 700,000 U.S. troops in South Vietnam meant nothing less than the total Americanization of the ground war, while the RVNAF, whose effectiveness showed no signs of improvement, would have even less incentive to whip themselves into fighting trim. Why, Warnke wondered, was more pressure not placed on the ARVN to assume a greater portion of the burden? Underlying ISA's military analysis

TABLE 7. Post-Tet Deployment Options

Option	Total U.S. Personnel	U.S. Maneuver Battalions	U.S. Artillery Battalions	Annual Cost ($ billions)	Reserve Recall
A. Cut 50,000	485,000	103	68	23	0
B. Current plan	535,000	112	72	25	0
C. Add 50,000	585,000	118	77	28	65,000
D. Add 100,000	635,000	124	83	30	200,000
E. Add 200,000	735,000	133	92	35	250,000

Source: Mike Gravel, ed., *The Senator Gravel Edition: The Pentagon Papers* (Boston: Beacon Press, 1971), vol. 4, pp. 548–50.

was a strong belief that the political ineptitude of the GVN made discussion of military victory spurious.

The memorandum concluded with a recommendation that went beyond the normal discussion of troop strengths, actually proposing an *alternative strategy* for MACV, one that focused on traditional counterinsurgency operations and abandoned the strategy of attrition. The basic elements of the alternative strategy held that

those forces currently in or near the heavily populated areas along the coast should remain in place. Those forces currently bordering on the demographic frontier should continue to operate from those positions, not on long search-and-destroy missions, but in support of the frontier. . . .

Based just beyond the populated areas, the forces on the demographic frontiers would conduct spoiling raids, long-range reconnaissance patrols and, when appropriate targets are located, search-and-destroy operations into the enemy's zone of movement in the unpopulated areas between the demographic and political frontiers. They would be available as a quick reaction force to support the RVNAF when it [*sic*] was attacked within the populated areas.[14]

In effect, Warnke was arguing for priority to be given to denying the Communists access to the great majority of the nation's population which resided along the coast, around Saigon, and in the Delta.

ISA listed eight advantages of this new strategy, the most prominent being that VC/NVA lines of communication would be lengthened; more forces would be available for patrolling and securing the populated areas; allied units actively operating just outside the demographic frontier would be able, with their mobility and firepower, to blunt future Tets before the enemy could mass against the populated areas; the Americans would now be fighting on ground of their own choosing; and U.S. casualties would be reduced.

Warnke's hopes of having his memorandum adopted as policy centered on his ability to win over the new secretary of defense, Clark Clifford, a reputed hawk on Vietnam who had replaced the disenchanted McNamara on 1 March 1968. While Clifford had had reservations concerning the introduction of U.S. troops into South Vietnam in 1965, he nevertheless firmly supported U.S. military operations once they were committed.

While Clifford was a staunch supporter of the "hard line" in Vietnam (even going so far as to oppose the bombing halts), he did not assume the position of secretary of defense with a closed mind. Thus, when he read Warnke's paper, it had a "tremendous impact" on him.[15] On the morning of 1 March, his first day on the job, Clifford called a meeting in his office to discuss the profound implications of the ISA memorandum. Among those present were Warnke, General Wheeler, and Deputy Secretary of Defense Paul Nitze. Warnke recalled that he was ready to go to the mat over the memo—it he could not convince Clifford that MACV's strategy was bankrupt, he would resign.

Warnke's presentation shocked General Wheeler, who wasted no time informing the group that he was appalled at this attempt to dictate strategy to MACV. The general then went on to cite two "fatal flaws" in ISA's alternative strategy: First, the proposed strategy would mean increased fighting in or close to population centers, resulting in increased civilian casualties; second, by adopting a posture of static defense, the United States would be allowing the enemy an increased capability of massing near population centers, especially north of Saigon.[16]

Warnke responded to Wheeler's critique in a meeting the following day. He began by noting that the current military strategy had not prevented the enormous civilian losses suffered in the Tet Offensive. If U.S. forces were pulled back from the remote regions of the country, Warnke contended, the population would be better, not less, protected; furthermore, abandonment of offensive operations in remote areas of the country did not signal a switch to static defense. Allied units would continue to conduct mobile sweeps in the demographic frontier separating the populated areas from the insurgent "badlands."[17]

During the course of the debate, General Wheeler marshaled some additional ammunition of his own, in the form of two documents. The first was a back-channel message from COMUSMACV, dated 2 March, which addressed how additional forces would be employed (in reality, Westmoreland was replying to an urgent back-channel message from Wheeler sent the previous day). It stated that MACV's top priority would be to clear enemy main forces out of the populated regions pursuant to the resumption of offensive operations postponed because of the Tet Offensive. Additional forces would help forestall another Tet, Westmoreland argued, and over the coming year would make it possible to "move progressively from north to south with a continuing series of hard hitting offensive campaigns to invade base areas, interdict and disrupt infiltration routes, and eliminate or evict VC/NVA forces from SVN." Westmoreland also urged anew that he be permitted to drive into Laos to cut the Ho Chi Minh Trail. He further suggested that consideration be given to the placement of U.S. forces in Thailand to assist in the operation. Support was also mustered from Admiral Sharp, the CINCPAC, for an invasion of the North using carrier task groups and Marines.[18] In short, COMUSMACV intended to continue his strategy for fighting the war.

The second document that Wheeler presented was an informal analysis drawn up by the Joint Staff. It held that "the basic strategy which must be followed by MACV *in any circumstances* is to defeat the current enemy offensive. . . . *Allied forces are not conducting offensive operations of any great magnitude or frequency and therefore they are not wresting control of the countryside from the enemy.*[19] The Joint Staff advocated the addition of 206,500 troops to MACV's order of battle and petitioned for the "relaxation of restrictions on operations in Cambodia, Laos, and North Vietnam." In other words, there was nothing wrong with the current strategy that a more forceful application would not cure.

Secretary Clifford was troubled by the military's judgment that more of the same would do the trick. A key exchange between Clifford and the brass convinced him that the current strategy had failed. Clifford asked whether sending the 200,000 troops would do the job. They could not say. "Well, then," said Clifford, "can anyone give me an idea when we could bring the war to a conclusion?" The Chiefs replied that they did not know when but that if the United States continued grinding down the enemy, the attrition would eventually become unbearable for him. Clifford recalled, "I got down to the point of asking the Joint Chiefs, 'What is our plan for military victory in Vietnam? The fact is we do not have a plan for military victory.' All we had was the advice from the military that if we continued to pour troops in at some unknown rate and possibly in an unlimited number for an unknown period of time that ultimately it was their opinion the enemy would have suffered that degree of attrition that would force the enemy to sue for some kind of peace."[20] Wheeler and Westmoreland still wanted more of the same, or better yet, more of the same on a broader scale. Theirs was not an innovative approach, only a rigid conformity to a deeply entrenched and dearly held Army perception of how wars ought to be fought.

The meeting of the secretary of defense's working group failed to reach a consensus. Aware of his position as a newcomer to the administration and of the problems involved in getting a new strategy adopted, let alone executed, by a hostile Army, Clifford directed Warnke and Phil G. Goulding, assistant secretary of defense for public affairs, to draft a far less controversial memorandum for the president than the one ISA had originally put forth.[21] The memorandum, presented to President Johnson on the evening of 4 March, omitted any direct challenge to the Army's ground strategy. It recommended meeting Westmoreland's initial request for some 22,000 troops and calling up the reserves to cover the balance of the request, if approved, to restore the strategic reserve. Finally, it advocated an immediate, in-depth study to examine "possible new strategic guidance for the conduct of US military operations in South Vietnam." The memorandum counseled to hold the balance of the additional forces contained in Westmoreland's request in abeyance pending completion of the study. Thus, while Clifford did not challenge the Army's strategy directly, he expressed serious reservations concerning both the deployment of additional troops to Vietnam and their employment. Nowhere is this lack of confidence in the military's ground strategy expressed more clearly than in the following passage, concerning policy and strategic guidance:

There can be no assurance that this very substantial additional deployment would leave us a year from today in any more favorable military position. All that can be said is that the additional troops would enable us to kill more of the enemy and would provide more security if the enemy does not offset them by lesser [sic] reinforcements of his own. There is no indication that they would bring about a quick solution in Vietnam and, in the absence of better performance by the GVN and the ARVN, the increased destruction and increased Americanization of the war could, in fact, be counterproductive.[22]

At a White House meeting on 13 March, President Johnson decided to deploy to Vietnam two Army brigades and other associated support forces, in addition to the 10,500-man emergency augmentation already approved. In effect, this new package of 30,000 men would meet Westmoreland's request, as recommended in Clifford's memorandum. Army Secretary Resor quickly informed Secretary Clifford that 45,000 reservists would have to be called up and over 13,000 additional support troops would have to be deployed if the 3d Brigade of the 82d Airborne Division, part of the emergency deployment of forces from the United States to South Vietnam during the Tet Offensive, were to remain in South Vietnam indefinitely. OSA estimated that if this were approved, the new deployment ceiling would have to be placed at 579,000, with 50,058 reservists required in March, followed by an additional call-up of some 48,393 shortly thereafter.[23] The call-up of nearly 100,000 reservists was bound to cause political problems for Johnson, who from the beginning had steadfastly refused to exercise this option.

Meanwhile, other events were narrowing the president's base of support for his Vietnam policy. The following day, Johnson barely squeaked by a relatively unknown, "antiwar" candidate, Senator Eugene McCarthy, in the New Hampshire presidential primary. Shortly thereafter, Senator Robert Kennedy announced that he, too, would challenge Johnson for his party's nomination. Finally, on 18 March, 139 members of the Congress joined in sponsoring a resolution calling for an immediate congressional review of Johnson's policy in Southeast Asia.

Even as this political challenge to his policy was being launched, the president was calling together a group of distinguished friends and associates to advise him on the future of U.S. involvement in Vietnam. The group, dubbed the Wise Men, arrived in Washington on 18 March and immediately began receiving briefings on the war. Among those in attendance were Dean Acheson, George Ball, Cyrus Vance, General of the Army Omar Bradley, Generals Taylor and Ridgway, McGeorge Bundy, Henry Cabot Lodge, Arthur Goldberg (U.S. ambassador to the United Nations), Robert Murphy (an ambassador during the Truman-Eisenhower years), and Abe Fortas (a sitting associate justice of the Supreme Court). The group met over dinner with Rusk, W. Averell Harriman, Clifford, Wheeler, Rostow, Nitze, CIA Director Richard Helms, William Bundy, and Nicholas Katzenbach. The discussion centered on pacification, military operations, and the GVN itself. After dinner the group received briefings from Major General Depuy (special assistant to the JCS for counterinsurgency), Philip Habib (deputy to William Bundy at State), and George Carver, a CIA analyst.[24]

The following morning, the group met at the White House. General Taylor, supported by Justice Fortas and Ambassador Murphy, endorsed the military's position. The remainder of the group coalesced around the position articulated by Warnke at ISA, namely, that the present strategy for prosecuting the war had failed to establish its effectiveness and had lost the support of the American public. After lunch with the president, they gave him their verdict: continued escalation of the war—intensified bombing of North Vietnam and increased American troop strength in the South—would be fruitless; it would be better to concentrate on improving the RVNAF and phasing out U.S. forces while seeking a negotiated settlement.[25]

Johnson was stunned by the group's recommendations.[26] He was profoundly impressed as well. On 22 March the president announced that General Westmoreland would be recalled from Vietnam to become the Army Chief of Staff. The conclusion reached by many was that Westmoreland was being kicked upstairs in a face-saving move by the administration. Four days later Westmoreland's deputy, Gen. Creighton Abrams (soon to be designated Westmoreland's successor), arrived in Washington for discussions with President Johnson and his senior advisers.

On 28 March General Johnson was notified by Lt. Gen. H. J. Lemley, the DCSOPS, that the Joint Staff had informed him that the new troop ceiling for Vietnam would be frozen at 549,500. Three days later President Johnson went on national television to announce his decisions to the American people. He detailed the recent troop increases and dramatically announced a partial suspension of the bombing campaign against North Vietnam. He saved his biggest surprise for last, however: in Shermanesque style he stated, "I shall not seek, and I will not accept, the nomination of my party for another term as your president."

On 4 April Clark Clifford formally informed the JCS of the 549,500-man ceiling in Deployment Program 6—none of the 200,000 additional troops requested were to be deployed.[27] The Army approach to the war in Vietnam had lost its credibility with the political leadership of the United States. The nation had needed either a quick victory in Vietnam or a low-cost strategy that could be maintained almost indefinitely. The former option was impossible in a conflict that was by nature protracted. It was now clear that the military was incapable of providing the latter. Thus, a plan for the withdrawal of U.S. forces became both a military and a political necessity.

Tet—Who Really Won?

Which side won the Tet Offensive remains a hotly debated question even today. For the Army, Tet has represented a victory for U.S. and allied forces and a disastrous defeat for the Communists. For General Westmoreland, Tet was a battle the VC and NVA forces "could not win," an offensive "foredoomed to failure."[28] Certainly the enemy suffered enormous casualties in his assault—over 40,000 by MACV's somewhat inflated estimates. The VCI, so important to the maintenance of insurgent access to the population, was badly mauled when its members came out into the open to support the attack. As General Westmoreland pointed out, the enemy had been driven back, and the road appeared to be open for the assumption of the initiative by MACV, particularly if more troops were forthcoming. Thus, Tet was a victory in the eyes of the Army leadership because it advanced the accomplishment of its goals. The destruction of large numbers of enemy forces was just what the doctor had ordered for the strategy of attrition. If the insurgents wanted to come out into the open, where American firepower could be brought to bear with maximum efficiency, so much the better. From MACV's perspective, they were playing right into the Army's hands.

By projecting the Army approach to the war onto the enemy, Westmoreland could rightly claim that the Communists had utterly failed in their attacks. The VC/NVA forces had failed to take and hold terrain and had not won anything approaching a military victory; therefore, they had been beaten. Unfortunately for the Army, its approach to the war did not reflect the strategic imperatives of the insurgency-style conflict the Communists were waging, focusing as they did on the war's political and social dimensions. While COMUSMACV evaluated the Tet Offensive within the conceptual framework of mid-intensity conventional war (the Battle of the Bulge and the Korean War), the Communists maintained their perspective of the war as a protracted conflict and were therefore able to look at the outcome of their offensive from within a different strategic framework.

Thus, even though from a traditional military viewpoint the Communists lost the Tet Offensive, they achieved victory in the most important strategic dimensions of insurgency warfare. This is readily apparent when the Communists' objectives are evaluated. They included, first, as a best-case outcome, a mass uprising against the GVN, combined with the collapse of the RVNAF. This would have left MACV with nothing left to fight for and would almost certainly have precipitated a ceasefire followed by an American withdrawal. Secondary objectives included the derailment of the fledgling pacification effort; running up U.S. casualties, an attrition strategy that focused on whittling away America's will to continue the war; demonstrating even to those South Vietnamese who lived in the urban areas that they were not safe from insurgent retribution, as the atrocities in Hue and countless other cities, towns, and hamlets illustrated; and increasing the refugee population, and by extension the economic burden on the GVN, which was responsible for caring for them.

If we examine Hanoi's objectives in this light, all of them, save the best-case outcome of a popular uprising, were achieved. The pacification program was dealt, in the words of COMUSMACV, a "substantial setback."

The creation of 800,000 refugees no doubt exacerbated the problem. As Westmoreland acknowledged, "If imposing hardship on the civilian population was an objective of the enemy's Tet attacks, he was eminently successful."[29] The Communists were particularly active in applying the insurgent's weapon of terror. In Hue, anyone who had an affiliation with the regime in Saigon, no matter how tenuous (priests, for example), was either executed, often in gruesome fashion, or simply buried alive. The message to the people was brutally clear: even in the supposedly safe cities, they were not safe from revolutionary "justice."

At enormous cost to themselves, the VC/NVA forces succeeded in killing 1,001 American servicemen. While the exchange ratio was overwhelmingly in favor of the United States, Giap did not have to concern himself as did Westmoreland, with a public highly vocal over the casualty rolls.[30] In fact, to the extent that a strategy of attrition was operative in Vietnam, the Americans, with their strong aversion to casualties, were at a disadvantage. For the American public, MACV's casualties were measured, not against those inflicted upon the insurgent forces by U.S. troops, but against previous American casualty rates. The jump in U.S. KIAs during Tet led Americans to question just what the United States had to show for all the national treasure it had poured into Vietnam. When Secretary of Defense Clifford and the Wise Men failed to elicit a satisfactory response from the military, the resulting policy changes demonstrated that the Communists, aided by an ineffective approach to insurgency warfare on the part of the U.S. military, had worn down the will of the American people more quickly than MACV could wear down the insurgent forces. Indeed, as was brought out in Warnke's ISA paper and later by Clifford and some of the Wise Men, the large body count rung up by MACV during Tet was in itself meaningless. Giap had gambled on a big offensive before—in 1951 against the French—and lost. Viet Minh casualties that year had been in excess of 20,000. Then, as in 1968, the insurgent forces had merely dropped back into a lower phase of protracted warfare, rebuilt their strength, and returned to fight another day.

In the final analysis, then, Tet was a victory for Hanoi. It resulted in the civilian Defense establishment's loss of faith in the Army's strategy. A ceiling was set on the level of U.S. troop deployments to the RVN, and the search began for a way to cut U.S. losses and turn the war over to the South Vietnamese. Yet the Tet Offensive brought about no reevaluation of the Concept within the Army itself. The Army had convinced itself that it had won the Tet Offensive; therefore, no soul-searching was necessary. The enormous number of enemy casualties proved it: the Army was winning.

End Game

Following the Tet Offensive and the decisions of late March 1968, the primary focus of U.S. policy in Vietnam centered not so much on defeating the Communists as on transferring responsibility for the war effort to the GVN and withdrawing American troops—Vietnamization, as it came to be called. Even as the debate on U.S. troop reinforcements raged during Tet, President Johnson was approving Secretary Clifford's proposals for large augmentations in RVNAF force levels and equipment. Once this latest buildup of RVN forces began in earnest, it proceeded rather quickly, as did the withdrawal of American ground troops.

Vietnamization looked impressive on paper. The RVNAF would be increased from the current force level of 685,000 to 801,215 (including some 335,135 ARVN, 218,687 RFS, and 179,015 PFS) by FY 1970. Unfortunately, throughout the war the problem with the RVNAF was not so much a shortage of men as a lack of leaders—the officers and NCOs who could make effective use of these forces.[31] The lack of any unity of command had all but eliminated the ability of the Army to affect the ARVN's highly political (that is, corrupt) promotion practices.

In April 1968 Secretary Clifford ordered the development of a program to gradually shift the burden of the war to the South Vietnamese. The result was a two-phase approach: phase 1, approved on 23 October, called for upgrading the ARVN with the tools of American firepower and mobility—tanks, guns, and helicopters; phase 2, approved on 18 December, provided for the creation of a self-sufficient RVNAF capable of defeating the insurgents.

With the election of Richard Nixon to the presidency and his inauguration in January 1969, the Vietnamization process was accelerated. Under the Nixon Doctrine, as it became known, the U.S. role in Third World conflicts would be transformed from one of direct participation to one of serving as trainer and supplier to indigenous forces. Nixon judged, quite correctly, that the American people wanted "No More Vietnams."

Post-Tet Army Operations

Not surprisingly, given the Army's claim of victory in the battles of the Tet Offensive and in the absence of any critical self-evaluation on the service's part, MACV operations after Tet continued to reflect the Army's bias toward traditional, conventional tactics. To the extent that the Army modified its *modus operandi*, it was a function of two circumstances: the enemy's reversion to a "deep" phase 2 level of insurgency and a return to small-unit operations; and the withdrawal of U.S. ground forces from MACV, leaving fewer forces available for large operations.

An example of the Army's post-Tet attitude is found in a letter from John Paul Vann (now a civilian and the senior American adviser in II CTZ) to the deputy director of AID in South Vietnam. In it Vann recounted how General Westmoreland had arrived at I Field Force headquarters on 4 March for a briefing from the corps staff. The general, said Vann, was all set to "kick ass" and energize the Army units in the area to engage in offensive operations. Westmoreland, reported Vann, had "all the wind . . . taken out of his sails" by the Army briefers, despite the fact that "not one mention was made of the fact that the VC guerrillas were being given more freedom to intimidate the rural population than ever before in the past two-and-a-half-years."[32] What the briefing did center on, as usual, was the impressive body counts the Army had scored, and that was sufficient to cool off Westmoreland.

Meanwhile, the siege of Khe Sanh dragged on until mid-March, when the Communists began pulling their units back into Laos. On I April the 1st Cavalry Division launched Operation PEGASUS to reestablish overland communications with the Marines inside the base. A linkup was effected on 6 April (the enemy offered only minimal resistance), and the siege was officially over. The siege at Khe Sanh was declared a victory by MACV. By the Army's standards, U.S. forces had prevailed. Estimates of enemy casualties ran between 3,000 and 15,000. Only 205 Americans were killed, certainly an acceptable exchange under the strategy of attrition.

As with Tet, however, the enemy could also claim a victory. The Marine forces inside the remote base represented over 5 percent of MACV's operational strength, with another 15–20 percent of MACV's maneuver battalions tied down in reserve positions, to come to the relief of the base should the Communists attack. With U.S. forces deployed in this way, the job of getting insurgent forces into the populated areas to launch the attacks during Tet was made all the easier. As usual, the Americans were oriented on infiltration and body counts, the insurgents on controlling the population.

On I July, Gen. Creighton Abrams replaced General Westmoreland as COMUSMACV. Abrams had been associated with the 1966 PROVN study, which had called for a reorientation of the war effort toward pacification and population security. With the insurgents moving back into phase 2 and, in some cases, phase I operations, and given the heavy blows dealt the VCI during Tet, Abrams had a unique opportunity to redirect MACV operations and score substantial gains against the enemy.

General Creighton W. Abrams, General Westmoreland's replacement as COMUSMACV in July 1968. General Abrams presided over the beginning of Vietnamization and the withdrawal of U.S. forces from South Vietnam.   *courtesy U.S. Army*

General Abrams did, in fact, attempt to alter Army operations away from their conventional orientation. The MACV Staff drew up a new, "one war" plan (pacification was no longer to be considered the "other" war) in which population security, not the body count, would be the criterion of success. It stated that "the key strategic thrust is to provide meaningful, continuing security for the Vietnamese people in expanding areas of increasingly effective civil authority."[33] Nevertheless, it took Abrams nearly a year to fabricate this new approach. During that period the Concept was as much in vogue as ever. The reader will recall that Abrams's command marked the heyday of such commanders as Major General Ewell of the 9th Infantry Division (and later II Field Force). Ewell saw a problem in the enemy's reversion to low-level insurgency; the solution, as he said, was to "bring the enemy to battle on *our* terms rather than *his* terms."[34] The means arrived at was to operate in smaller units to seek out and destroy the enemy, and it resulted in the proliferation of smaller American operations backed up by prompt and massive firepower support. It was here that the night-hunter and night-search operations made their debut.

Meanwhile, on 31 August 1968, MACV's Long Range Planning Task Group was instructed by Abrams to report on the current situation in Vietnam and to recommend a change of strategy, if appropriate. When the group briefed Abrams on 20 November, it called for a major change in MACV's operational approach to the war:

All of our US combat accomplishments have made no significant, positive difference to the rural Vietnamese—for there is still no real security in the countryside. Our large-scale operations have attempted to enable the development of a protective shield, by driving the NVA and the Viet Cong main force units out of South Vietnam—or at least into the remote mountain and jungle areas where they would not pose a threat to the population. In pressing this objective, however, we have tended to lose sight of *why* we were driving the enemy back and destroying his combat capability. Destruction of NVA and VC units and individuals—that is, the "kill VC" syndrome—has become an end in itself—an end that at times has become self-defeating. To accomplish the most difficult task of the war—*and, really the functional reason for the US to be here*—that of providing security to the Vietnamese people—we have relied on the numerous, but only marginally effective, ill-equipped and indifferently led Vietnamese paramilitary and police units.

The Viet Cong thrive in an environment of insecurity. It is essential for them to demonstrate that the GVN is *not* capable of providing security to its citizens. And, *they have succeeded.*[35]

Even though General Abrams okayed the adoption of the task group's "one war" approach, the effect on the units in the field was minimal. In late 1968 and into 1969 the "kill VC" syndrome reached new heights, particularly in the 9th Division. It remained *the* primary method of evaluating commanders, particularly those under Ewell. As the general reported: "In the last half of 1968, under Colonel George E. Bland, the Brigade began to tighten up; in Jan. and Feb. 1969 it hit its stride; and in the months of March, April, and May under Colonel Rodman C. Rainville, the Brigade reached a plateau of skill and effectiveness which was really amazing. In these three months, the brigade averaged over 1000 enemy per month eliminated. Its exchange ratios were astronomical, peaking at 158 to 1, an elimination ratio which is possibly amongst the highest achieved in Vietnam. (By contrast, its elimination ratio in a somewhat comparable period in 1968 was 4.3 to 1.)"[36]

Night-hunter and night-search operations were frequently incapable of distinguishing the VC from noncombatants. The command emphasis on high kill ratios led to the practice of shooting first and asking questions later, as exemplified in Operation SPEEDY EXPRESS, which lasted from 1 December 1968 until 1 June 1969. The operation placed elements of the

9th Division in the densely populated provinces of the Delta region. As Guenther Lewy observed after looking at the division's reports:

During the six months of combat the division reported to have killed 10,883 of the enemy at a cost of only 267 Americans killed, a ratio of 40.8:1. Most engagements were small-scale and about half of the enemy kills were reportedly made by helicopter-borne air cavalry units and helicopter gunships; 40 percent were achieved in night operations.

And yet there were indications that the amazing results of Operation SPEEDY EXPRESS could not be accepted at face value. The most unusual feature was the small number of weapons captured—748 in all, resulting in a ratio of enemy killed to weapons seized of 14.6:1. The normal ratio was 3:1, in other IV CTZ operations in 1969 it was 3.5:1 and in III CTZ 4.1:1. The division's after-action report attributed the low weapons count to such factors as the high percentage of kills made at night and by air cavalry and Army aviation units and to the fact that "many individuals in the VC and guerrilla units are not armed with weapons." This was another way of acknowledging that many of those killed were not really combatants.[37]

It is revealing that despite the prodigious kill ratios purportedly achieved by the 9th Division during the operation, population security in the area remained basically *unaffected*.[38]

When Ewell assumed command of II Field Force in mid-1969, he quickly drove up the exchange ratio in III Corps through application of the same operational approach that had proven "successful" in the Delta with the 9th Division.[39] Since command of a field force (corps) was considered a plum, second only to the position of COMUSMACV, it was evident that despite Abrams's "new" strategy, the rewards continued to flow to those who practiced the art of war as prescribed by the Concept.

Even within the MACV Staff the Long Range Planning Task Group's "new" strategy failed to convert the headquarters to a "one war" approach. In October the staff was still firing off rebuttals to OSA's Southeast Asia Reports, contending that U.S. forces held the all-important initiative in the war. MACV charged that contrary to OSA's conclusions, "there is serious doubt that control of casualties is a 'good measure of military initiative'; for example, efforts to conserve casualties may do little to extend control over the combat situation. Said another way, a side which uses its 'military initiative' principally to avoid combat is not trying to dominate the battlefield but only to maintain a presence there; this is not military initiative." OSA responded:

We suspect that the ability to control casualties is an integral part of the overall enemy strategy in Vietnam. His attacks and other activities are designed to have the maximum psychological impact by inflicting heavy allied casualties, projecting an aura of countrywide strength and continual presence, and gradually reducing the US will to continue. This in turn implies that the enemy must expend his resources at a rate low enough for him to hold out longer than the allies. It must be clear to him after his spring offensive that he cannot win by engaging us in short, decisive combat and that he must frame his strategy within the rules of protracted conflict. In such a conflict, control of the casualty rates is critical.

The fact that the VC/NVA can nearly always find us and we usually can't find him unless he wants us to or our intelligence is exceptionally good, is at the heart of the military initiative in Vietnam. *The implicit assumption in the comments is that both sides are operating under identical objectives, strategy, and tactics as in a conventional war.*[40]

Thus, despite all the talk and staff action over redirecting Army efforts toward the "other" war, the Army remained focused on its traditional mission of closing with and destroying enemy main-force units.

Ewell was not the only commander to engage in standard Army operations to the detriment of the "one war" approach. For example, operations conducted by the Army's American Division in early 1969 demonstrated little deviation from the supposedly defunct strategy of attrition. In January, elements of the division launched an assault on the village of Chau Nai, in Quang Ngai Province, utilizing over 648,000 pounds of bombs in the form of air support and 2,000 rounds of artillery to kill 47 guerrillas. The division continued operations through February and March, with results reminiscent of those achieved by the 1st Cavalry Division during 1966–67 in Binh Dinh, Quang Ngai's sister province to the south. During that period the division attempted to root out elements of what appeared to be an NVA regiment supplemented by local VC forces that had seized hamlets during the 1969 Tet Offensive. As under the strategy of attrition, firepower was liberally applied. While the operation was a military success, it was a political disaster: over 300 civilians were killed, nearly 400 were wounded, and over 3,000 homes were severely damaged.[41] As in the case of the 1st Cavalry, the American Division remained in the area for several weeks and then moved on, leaving only some Ruff-Puffs to await the next enemy assault.[42]

Another example of nonapplication of the "one war" strategy was the May 1969 assault on "Hamburger" Hill in the A Shau Valley, near the Cambodian border, by elements of the 101st Airborne Division. The division, on a sweep through the valley, came upon an NVA force occupying Apbia Mountain. Maj. Gen. Melvin Zais, the division commander, promptly ordered an attack. At the cost of 50 American dead, the division inflicted 597 enemy casualties and took the hill. The Army claimed that the battle represented a victory, citing as justification the

Members of the 5th Bn, 10th Regional Forces, run toward UH-1D (Huey) helicopters following a search and clear operation in 1970.   *courtesy U.S. Army*

favorable exchange ratio, as was done during the war of attrition. Of course, under the "one war" strategy, it was the insurgents who had won, as they had before, by drawing Army units out into remote areas to fight on their terms, all the while leaving the population open to exploitation by the Communists.

To the extent that gains were realized in population security during the post-Tet era (and there was substantial progress), they were primarily a function of factors unrealized to MACV military operations, such as the self-inflicted decimation of the VCI during the Tet Offensive, the pacification efforts directed by the civilians at CORDS, and the augmentation of RF/PF forces. "I was there when General Abrams took over," Robert Komer stated, "and remained as his deputy. *There was no change in strategy whatsoever. . . .* The myth of a change in strategy is a figment of media imagination; it didn't really change until we began withdrawing."[43]

In the two years following the Tet Offensive, Army main-force units continued to operate much as they always had. While there were cases of units breaking down into smaller elements and providing population security over an extended period of time, they were the exception. Following one last great search-and-destroy operation into Cambodia in April–May 1970, the withdrawal of U.S. ground forces proceeded apace, and questions of strategy became academic. The Army was going home.

10

Paths Untaken, Paths Forsaken

When U.S. ground forces were introduced into South Vietnam in substantial numbers in 1962 and, later, when combat forces were sent in 1965, the official rationale for their deployment was to buy time so that the GVN could take steps and enact reforms to preserve its independence in the face of Communist aggression. The implication was that South Vietnam would have to be built up to the status of a Korea—capable of defending itself against the problem of insurgency while relying on U.S./SEATO forces in the event of overt aggression from North Vietnam and/or the PRC. Viewed in this manner, the effectiveness of U.S. ground operations in South Vietnam can be measured, first, in terms of their ability to buy time for the GVN—with minimal expenditure of U.S. resources, both human and material—to establish its legitimacy and build its strength to the point where it could cope with the insurgency without U.S. combat forces. That the expenditure of U.S. human and material resources be minimal was necessary, given the nature of protracted warfare and the need to maintain popular support at home for a continued U.S. military presence after the immediate crisis passed, as in Korea.

A second measure of the effectiveness of U.S. ground operations was the extent to which they contributed to the defeat of the insurgent forces. When U.S. military operations weakened the insurgents, they increased the relative strength of the South Vietnamese government, thereby accelerating the GVN's resumption of responsibility for its own internal defense. Implicit in this criterion is the prospect of a trade-off in U.S. casualties for progress against the insurgent movement. Thus, U.S. withdrawal from the ground war against the insurgents could have been speeded up by accepting higher casualty rates, but this would have had to be weighed against the accelerated erosion in U.S. popular support for the war effort that such an increase would have implied. One can view General Westmoreland's strategy of attrition, then, as a willingness to endure a relatively high rate of casualties in the short term in the hope that his concept of operations—that the enemy would be so worn down by 1968 that a major U.S. ground combat role would no longer be necessary—would prove correct.

The Army failed on both counts. It expended human resources at a relatively high rate and material resources in a profligate manner as part of a strategy of attrition. Yet the Army achieved neither a quick victory nor the maintenance of support on the home front for a continued U.S. presence in Vietnam. Viewed from this perspective, the Army's conduct of the war was a failure, primarily because it never realized that insurgency warfare required basic changes in Army methods to meet the exigencies of this "new" conflict environment. MACV's strategy of attrition represented a comparatively expensive way of buying time for South Vietnam, in human and material resources. The strategy's great reliance on large amounts of firepower did not in the long run serve, as in previous wars, to reduce U.S. casualties and wear out the enemy. In effect, MACV attempted to adapt what had been the low-risk strategy of attrition in a mid-intensity conflict environment to a low-intensity conflict in the hope of achieving similar results. The nature of insurgency warfare, however, made such a strategic approach a high-cost, high-risk option for MACV by mandating a quick victory before the American public grew weary of bearing the burden of continuing the war.

In developing its Vietnam strategy to use operational methods successful in previous wars, the Army compromised its ability to successfully combat lower-phase insurgency operations at anything approaching an acceptable cost. In focusing on the attrition of enemy forces rather than on defeating the enemy through denial of his access to the population, MACV missed whatever opportunity it had to deal the insurgent forces a crippling blow at a low enough cost to permit a continued U.S. military presence in Vietnam in the event of external, overt aggression. Furthermore, in attempting to maximize Communist combat losses, the Army often alienated the most important element in any counterinsurgency strategy— the people. A strategy of attrition calling for the intentional creation of refugees, defoliation and crop-destruction programs, and a higher priority for body counts than for population security sabotaged progress in the campaign against the insurgents and failed to serve the objectives of U.S. policy.

Thus, three years after the deployment of U.S. combat troops and six years after the first large-scale commitment of U.S. advisers, the Johnson administration began planning for their withdrawal. This despite the U.S. military leadership's concession that the internal threat to South Vietnam's security had not abated, while the external threat had, if anything, increased. All the Communists had to do after the Tet Offensive was exhibit patience, and victory would be theirs. From that point on, questions of American "strategy" revolved around how best to extract U.S. troops from South Vietnam, not how they might be used to achieve some kind of victory.[1]

Nevertheless, throughout the war a learning process went on within the Army, trying to free the service from the Concept's perceptual straightjacket. The reader will recall the Special Forces operations in the Buon Enao program and the revolt from below of Army advisers against MACV's institutionalized optimism. Later, after the introduction of ground forces in 1965, with prompting from the civilian leadership, the Army gradually conceded the need for a more vigorous approach to pacification and contributed over 6,000 men to work within CORDS for the promotion of population security. During this period the Ruff-Puffs were upgraded, as was the national police. Thus, as time went on, the weight of resources devoted to the war effort did shift somewhat in the direction of counterinsurgency and away from conventional-style operations.

However, compared with the demands of the situation in Vietnam, these examples of change, which for the most part proved to be too little too late, and too brief, do not offer much solace. First, much of this learning occurred at the lower echelons of the service—junior MAAG staffers, advisers, officers assigned to CORDS—or among those considered out of the "mainstream" of Army operations. Second, counterinsurgency operations never assumed a priority anywhere near that given more conventional operations: the establishment of a low-level commitment to combating the insurgency was never expanded upon to include significant numbers of main-force Army units. Third, the Army made little effort to preserve the learning that had occurred during the war; rather, it expunged the experience from the service's consciousness. Fourth, those who saw their careers most enhanced were the officers who served in "mainstream" positions, as battalion commanders and main-force-unit staff officers, and whose experience in classical counterinsurgency operations was minimal. Thus, the changes that did occur were too little to make a significant impact on the Army or its approach to the war, implemented too late in the war to achieve results, and retained for too brief a period in the service to have an impact on preparations for future low-intensity wars.

Does It Matter?

Several alternative strategic approaches were offered during the course of the war, some by the Army, others by civilians. Would adoption of any of these have made a difference in the outcome of the conflict, or was the end result preordained, as in some Greek tragedy, irrespective of what strategic course the Army might have adopted? While hindsight is always twenty-twenty and *post hoc* analyses of "what if" options can never claim to provide a definitive answer for the alternative histories they imply, there is nevertheless some value in such an exercise if only to challenge some of the more egregious claims made for them by their authors. Four alternatives to the strategy of attrition developed over the course of the war: invasion of North Vietnam; incursion into Laos (to seal the border between North and South Vietnam); enclaves; and the demographic frontier.

The invasion of North Vietnam was called for in war plans prior to 1965 in the event of overt aggression against South Vietnam by the DRV and/or Communist China. The invasion strategy, never seriously considered by the Johnson administration, retained a strong measure of support in Army circles both during and after the war.[2] The notion implicit in this approach was that the United States lost in Vietnam, not because the Army failed to adapt its Concept to insurgency warfare, but because the Concept had not been fully applied. This notion is reflected in General Taylor's belief that the United States "should never have put a soldier into South Vietnam." Instead, it "should have gone directly to Hanoi by amphibious/airborne landing" as called for by the old OPLANS.[3]

The invasion approach presented several problems, not the least of which was war with Communist China, a proposition the American public had shown itself ill-inclined to support during the Korean War. Furthermore, in the spring of 1965 the RVNAF were being defeated *by the* VC, not the NVA. While several PAVN regiments were situated in the northern provinces of South Vietnam at the time, they had yet to join the fight. Thus, a U.S. invasion of the DRV would not have significantly altered the unfavorable circumstances that persisted in South Vietnam. Furthermore, there is no evidence to suggest that a U.S. occupation of North Vietnam would have produced results any different from those produced by the 1946 French reoccupation. The specter of PAVN forces retreating to their old sanctuaries in Laos and China for a continuation of the struggle against the United States was the nightmare of American strategists. Given this strategic approach, the Army would have been faced with the necessity of maintaining expeditionary forces in both Vietnams and assuming the primary burden of the war over an indefinite period while at the same time positioning a large reserve in the area should the Chinese intervene.

That this strategic war of annihilation against North Vietnam still evokes support in some Army quarters reinforces the notion that for some the learning process proceeds at a glacial pace, if at all. The alternative strategy of invasion focused not on combating the insurgency in South Vietnam but on trying to fit the war to the needs of the Army's *modus operandi*. By failing to materially assist the South Vietnamese against the VC, the invasion proponents would not have bought any significant respite for the GVN against the insurgents. Certainly Army casualties resulting from an invasion and prolonged occupation of the North would have been heavier than those suffered under the attrition strategy. Erosion of U.S. public support for the war effort would have proceeded at an accelerated pace, and prospects for a long-term U.S. military presence in the region would have diminished.

The second alternative strategy—the Laotian incursion—has achieved a great deal of notoriety within the Army, primarily owing to a book written by Col. Harry G. Summers, of the U.S. Army War College, entitled *On Strategy: The Vietnam War in Context*. The book has been widely promoted within the Army, particularly in the senior service schools. More important is the fact that "many officers regard it as the most incisive defense yet written on the role of the Army . . . in the war."[4] The incursion strategy popularized by Summers was essentially a revisionist's call for the execution of the EL PASO Plan drawn up for General Westmoreland by his MACV staff in 1966. It called for a joint U.S.-ARVN-ROK push across the Laotian panhandle from the DMZ to Savannakhet on the Thai-Laotian border. Once in place, the plan held, such a force could have blocked North Vietnamese access to South Vietnam, isolated the battlefield (and the VC), and allowed the RVNAF to destroy the insurgents in the South, a job in which, Summers contends, the Army should not have become involved. Indeed, Summers states that the Army's fatal mistake was its becoming *overly involved* in combating the insurgents, thereby missing the real threat—the North Vietnamese.

Summers's critique of MACV's strategy in Vietnam has gained acceptance largely owing to its appeal to traditional Army notions of war. He contends that the proper strategy for the war was denied the Army by the civilian leadership (Westmoreland's unconsummated EL PASO Plan). In Summers's eyes, the Army's problem was that it was untrue to its Concept. Advocates of the Laotian incursion argue that by executing the

EL PASO Plan the Army could have maneuvered in conventional fashion to cut off the Ho Chi Minh Trail and established a blocking force of eight divisions (five U.S., two ROK, and one ARVN) along the DMZ through Laos to Savannakhet. This purportedly would have set up a situation in which U.S. forces could assume the tactical and strategic defensive from well-prepared positions, thereby minimizing U.S. casualties. North Vietnam—the root of the problem according to Summers—would have been excluded from the RVN, leaving the VC to "wither on the vine" and disintegrate under pressure from the ARVN.[5]

Would it have worked? It seems unlikely. First of all, the plan had been considered by the Army Chief of Staff, General Johnson, in the spring of 1965 and shelved when the enormous support requirements for such an operation (over 18,000 engineer troops alone) became evident. Furthermore, until the Tet Offensive of 1968, the VC were by far the principal force in the field against the RVNAF, receiving the bulk of their logistical support from *within* South Vietnam. Placing U.S. forces along the DMZ and in Laos would have continued the disintegration of the RVNAF which U.S. forces purportedly were deploying to prevent. Summers offers no persuasive reason why North Vietnamese infiltrators could not have conducted an end run around the barrier force by going through Thailand. As for allied participation, given allied concern over casualties, there is reason to believe that the two ROK divisions assigned to the barrier force would have been withheld by the South Korean government, leaving the Americans to take up the slack. Finally, the barrier force, operating from fixed positions, would hardly have been different from U.S. forces operating behind the McNamara Line along the DMZ (indeed, they would have formed part of the barrier force). Yet the forces pulling such duty were constantly subjected to harassing fire, particularly from artillery and mortars, and required large numbers of support troops to maintain their positions. It is unlikely that casualty levels would have been any lower for similar forces in Laos, while support requirements would have been onerous.

Given these considerations, the incursion strategy appears to be a *post hoc* justification for an absence of Army analysis on the war and its continued faith in the methods that had proved successful in previous conventional wars rather than a true strategic alternative. Like the Army during the war, Summers seems intent not so much on understanding this "alien" conflict environment as on fitting it into a form that justifies the continued application of the Army's preferred methods of waging war. The execution of the EL PASO Plan would not have limited or reduced U.S.

casualties or defeated the insurgent movement in South Vietnam. To the extent that this strategy advocated the RVNAF's assuming the entire counterinsurgency mission, the duration of U.S. deployments could only have been prolonged, with all the attendant ill-effects on American casualties and U.S. public support for the war.

It is interesting to note that these first two alternative strategies involve a shifting of Army resources away from counterinsurgency operations and toward the conventional style of war prescribed by the Concept. That the Army failed to attempt some version of them was owing, not to self-imposed constraints, but to those imposed on the Army by the nation's political leadership. Both alternatives promised increased attrition of enemy forces or their exclusion from South Vietnam, but only provided the war could be projected into a mid-intensity type. The weight of evidence indicates that neither strategic alternative would have brought time any more cheaply—quite likely, it would have done so more dearly—than MACV's strategy of attrition, and either one would have contributed even less to the defeat of the VC in South Vietnam.

The remaining two alternative strategies both advocated shifting re- sources and emphasis away from the kind of warfare favored by the Concept and toward counterinsurgency operations. Thus, the four stra- tegic alternatives can be viewed as apportioning different mixes of Army assets toward internal (insurgent) and external (overt/conventional) threats to South Vietnam's security, with the Army leadership favoring a mix heavily weighted toward the latter consideration, while the nature of the conflict mandated an orientation primarily focused on the former.

The first of these two "southern" strategies was the enclave approach proposed by Ambassador Taylor during the months of crisis in early 1965 and supported, with variations, by George Ball, Robert Johnson, and Thomas Hughes in the State Department. The enclave strategy called for the military to recognize that the war had to be won by the South Vietnamese and that the most effective role for American troops would be to aid the RVNAF by controlling the densely populated coastal areas. The ARVN would combat the guerrilla forces inland while U.S. forces in their coastal enclaves protected American bases against enemy attack. On those occasions when the Communists deployed in major strength and offered the opportunity to fight a pitched battle, U.S. forces might be committed to destroy them. Advocates of the strategy at State pointed out that the United States had to realize that the enemy was unlikely to adopt a strategy that would substantially increase his vulnerability to U.S. firepower. They contended that given the nature of the conflict, U.S. forces could not win the war for the RVNAF, nor could the Army be driven out of Vietnam by Communist military action. The enclave strategy accepted the stalemate imposed at the lowest cost to the United States in casualties and resources. The intent, of course, was to allow the RVNAF to get back on their feet and wrest control of the countryside away from the Communists, secure in the knowledge that their rear areas were protected.

Critics of the enclave approach contend that it would have put U.S. forces in too close a contact with the South Vietnamese, risking alienation of the population owing to cultural dissimilarities. They add that U.S. troops would have developed a garrison mentality and lost their combat edge if forced to sit along the coast while the ARVN fought the guerrillas in the rural inland areas. The enclave strategy was also criticized as failing to take into account Army advantages in firepower and mobility that could have been put to good use against guerrilla forces. Finally, the critics observe that such a strategic posture would have left the initiative of where and when to attack to the enemy.

In responding to these alleged shortcomings, supporters of the enclave strategy point out that given the stalemated situation, enclaves would have bought time for South Vietnam at a relatively low price in American casualties and resources. They also argue that by securing the populated coastal areas, the Army would have contributed to the weakening of insurgent forces, thereby hastening the day when the South Vietnamese would be able to handle the insurgents on their own. As for the criticism of cultural contamination, one is hard put to find a more glaring case than what actually transpired during the years of intervention, when thousands of U.S. support troops were deployed in the populated areas to maintain the high level of combat intensity called for in the attrition strategy. To the extent that there is a direct relationship between numbers of troops and degrees of contamination, by positing fewer troops and a lower level of support requirements for combat operations, the enclave strategy would have reduced the degree of cultural contamination, not increased it.

Fears over the development of a garrison mentality among the troops and the lack of Army firepower and mobility utilization reflect more an impatience to carry out the traditional infantry mission of seeking out and destroying the enemy than an appreciation for the nature of insurgency conflict. The Marine CAP program, combined with the constant threat of sabotage and terrorist activities, clearly demonstrates that in this kind of war there were no rear areas. Following Ambassador Taylor's suggestion that U.S. troops operate out to a fifty-mile radius from their enclave base would have provided Army troops with a long-term challenge, not a garrison mentality. Indeed, the attrition strategy, positing rapid airmobile sweeps through enemy territory followed by a quick return to the unit firebase, created just such a garrison mentality; it was dubbed "firebase psychosis." As for U.S. firepower and mobility, they could have come into play in the event that the VC/NVA were foolish enough to mass for a major assault, as occurred, for example, in the 1972 Easter Offensive. In the interim, U.S. forces could have assisted ARVN units engaged in major battles with the Communists, arriving quickly and providing necessary fire support.

In hindsight, the enclave strategy offered the advantage of buying time for South Vietnam at costs substantially less than those borne through the strategy of attrition. Through the prospect of reduced U.S. casualties and a lower level of resource expenditure, enclaves also held out the possibility of maintaining U.S. public support for the war over a longer period. Finally, in promoting population security over big-unit operations, the enclave approach contributed more toward crippling the insurgent movement by reducing VC access to their primary base of support.

The final strategic alternative advanced during the war was the strategy of the demographic frontier proposed by ISA during the Tet Offensive of 1968. Coming as it did relatively late in the period of U.S. intervention, this strategic alternative benefits from the hindsight afforded its proponents after three years of U.S. ground combat involvement in the war. Perhaps the best way to view the strategy of the demographic frontier is as an expanded enclave approach. In basic terms, it called for denying the Communists access to the population; but instead of U.S. forces' being deployed in enclaves, they would have been situated along the entire narrow band of the populous Coastal Plain which runs from the DMZ to Saigon. The effect would have been to link the enclaves originally proposed into one continuous belt. The priority of missions for U.S. ground forces would have been, first, to secure and pacify the densely populated Coastal Plain and, second, to move forward to the demographic frontier, that area separating the Coastal Plain from the sparsely populated interior, for the purpose of isolating the insurgents from the people. Special Forces units would have been used as strike teams just beyond the frontier, detecting any attempts by the enemy to concentrate his forces for an attack upon the populated region. Sufficient main-force units would have been kept in reserve to blunt any enemy attempt to launch a major conventional assault against the pacification program.

Not surprisingly, criticism of the demographic-frontier approach fell along the same lines as did criticism of the enclave strategy, with similar points offered in rebuttal. Opposition also centered on Army concerns that this approach would force allied units to fight close to populated areas, that the initiative would pass to the enemy (resulting in future Tets), and that it left open the possibility that some of the more remote provincial capitals might be seized by the Communists. Proponents of the strategy held that if forces had been pulled back from the sparsely populated regions of South Vietnam, the population would have been better protected; furthermore, future Tets would have proved more difficult for the enemy to plan and execute owing to the allied forces' redeployment and the thick screen of strike teams patrolling along the demographic frontier. Had the Communists attempted to seize a few remote provincial capitals, they would likely have suffered heavy losses. As demonstrated at Khe Sanh, if necessary, such besieged strongpoints could have been relieved through the use of U.S. firepower and mobility. If VC and NVA forces had been willing to stand and fight over the control of an inland city, they would have been permitting the Army to conduct those operations that it was best equipped to carry out —hardly an advantage for the Communists. Finally, if for some reason an interior city had had to be abandoned to the enemy, it would have been better to cede it than to uncover the densely populated areas by transferring allied forces to recover it. As more of the populated areas came under allied control, the initiative, which heretofore had rested with the insurgents, would have begun to pass to the government. The criticism of lost initiative is only relevant if one assumes a conventional conflict.

For reasons similar to those associated with the enclave strategy, the demographic-frontier alternative offered advantages over the invasion and incursion alternatives—as well as the attrition strategy—primarily through buying time for the South Vietnamese at a reduced cost in U.S. casualties and resources. It placed greater emphasis on defeating the insurgent threat than even the enclave strategy. In doing so, if offered the best hope for strengthening the GVN and shortening the time needed before the South Vietnamese could handle the internal threat to their security without U.S. assistance.

One observes here, then, as with the enclave strategy, not the abolition of a role for the Army's main-force units but, rather, a reduced emphasis on their role relative to that of light units engaged in security operations. In this sense the strategies discussed represent, not diametrically opposed alternatives, but alternatives in defining the proper emphasis for allocating resources to combat the lower phases of insurgency activity versus those dedicated against the quasi-conventional threat lurking beyond the borders of South Vietnam. Viewed from this perspective, the essence of the strategic problem is that the Army placed a disproportionate emphasis on combating the external threat, one that was more manageable in terms of its Concept. The tragedy is that the nature of the war required that emphasis be placed, first and foremost, on the internal threat to the stability and legitimacy of the South Vietnamese government. Indeed, one could argue that the external, conventional threat was formidable because of the internal strife within South Vietnam and that without the insurgency threat, South Vietnam—with U.S./SEATO backing—would have been a redoubtable deterrent to North Vietnamese aggression.

In conclusion, the strategies of attrition, invasion, and incursion were all heavily weighted toward employing the Army's men and resources to win the mid-intensity war characterized in phase 3 insurgency operations. Given the Army Concept, it is not surprising that these strategies have found support within the service, both then and now. Yet, in combating an insurgency, winning the big battles is not decisive unless you can proceed to defeat the enemy at the lower levels of insurgency operations as well, destroying his infrastructure and guerrilla forces as well as his main-force units. By failing to promptly and adequately address this aspect of insurgency warfare and by adopting a strategic approach congruent with its emphasis on conventional war, the Army accelerated the dissipation of support for the war in the United States while failing to effectively advance the defeat of the internal threat to the survival of South Vietnam.

The ironic result of this misplaced strategic emphasis was that in 1972 and again in 1975, when the Communists shifted to those phase 3 operations most conducive to conventional operations, the administration and the Army lost the support of the American public necessary for further participation in the war. Thus the Army, in fighting the war it was not prepared to fight, lost the opportunity to fight the war it knew how to win.

Lessons Unlearned

The U.S. Army is presently enjoying a renaissance of sorts in generating forces and doctrine for special operations. The service is now at work revising doctrine for counterterror operations, unconventional warfare, and foreign internal defense (FID, formerly counterinsurgency) while increasing the forces available for special operations after a decade of neglect. Two of the four Special Forces groups disbanded following the Army's withdrawal from Vietnam have been re-formed, with another scheduled for activation by 1990. The service's three Ranger battalions have been organized into a Ranger regiment. For the first time, the Green

Berets and the Rangers have been grouped, along with their associated headquarters and some support elements, in the 1st Special Operations Command (SOCOM). Furthermore, Army Chief of Staff Gen. John A. Wickham has directed the formation of several light infantry divisions, in part to augment 1st SOCOM forces in low-intensity conflict contingencies. Once again, it seems, the Army is back in the counterguerrilla warfare business, just as in the early years of the Kennedy administration.

There is one important difference, however, say Army officials. The Army, they contend, has learned a lesson from its Vietnam experience and will resist being drawn into another low-intensity war unless certain conditions exist that allow for a successful outcome. These conditions, as formulated by people such as former Army Chief of Staff Gen. Edward C. "Shy" Meyer and Army War College strategist Col. Harry Summers and enunciated by Secretary of Defense Caspar W. Weinberger, hold that U.S. combat forces should not be committed overseas unless the interests involved are vital to U.S. security, the troops committed are sufficient in number to accomplish the mission, and the American political leadership has "the clear intention of winning." Finally, they contend, an atmosphere of popular and congressional support for the war must be present.[6]

These conditions are drawn, in Secretary Weinberger's words, from "lessons we have learned from the past." To a great extent, they represent the Army's lessons from Vietnam, and they signify the service's determination to ensure that for it there will be "No More Vietnams." And yet, if one examines closely the resurgence of Army interest in low-intensity warfare, there exist many disturbing parallels between what transpired before the Vietnam War and what has happened since the war. Indeed, the similarities drive the observer toward the ineluctable conclusion that if the Army has learned any lessons from Vietnam, it has learned many of the wrong ones.

The Army emerged from the Vietnam War far more disillusioned than it had after the Korean War. There existed considerable bitterness toward the political leadership that had committed the Army to the conflict and then, seemingly, abandoned it. There was also bitterness toward the American public for its lack of support or appreciation for the sacrifices made by the nation's men and women in uniform, who, after all, were only carrying out the policies of the country's leaders, elected by the people themselves. Finally, there was an inner-directed anger at having been pushed into fighting a war on the enemy's terms instead of its own.

A "No More Vietnams" club has emerged since the war's end, determined not to commit U.S. combat troops to combat unless, as stated by

Secretary Weinberger, the political leadership has "the clear intention of winning." This represents a built-in excuse for failure, should the military become frustrated in future low-intensity wars, to escalate into the more congenial environment of mid-intensity conventional conflict.[7] If you cannot cope with insurgents in El Salvador, confront the "main" adversary in Nicaragua or (if need be, one would assume) Cuba. Furthermore, the "support of the American people and their elected representatives in Congress" is mandated. This, it would seem, is intended to preclude the lack of popular and congressional support that plagued the Army during the Vietnam War. Yet, from the time President Kennedy dispatched large numbers of combat advisers to South Vietnam in December 1961 to the Tet Offensive over six years later, the Army did not lack for popular or political support. It is difficult to fault the American people or their elected representatives when, after that long a period of active engagement, the Joint Chiefs of Staff could only offer more of the same for an indefinite period with no assurance of eventual success.

Committing U.S. combat forces only to areas of "vital" interest is yet another vague prescription reflecting a lesson unlearned from the Army's Vietnam experience. Indeed, the only two areas that can claim a clear consensus as representing vital U.S. interests—Western Europe and Japan—are sites for future mid- or high-intensity conflict. If the service defines low-intensity conflict contingencies in this manner, it is essentially defining away the need to address this form of warfare. Yet, the military acquiesced in the invasion of Grenada, a traditional military operation. Does this imply a broad definition of "vital" U.S. interests in the Third World? Or is an approval of employing U.S military forces in familiar, conventional operations the key element for the services?

The problem, of course, is that pinning down just which countries represent vital interests to the United States is a very subjective exercise. South Korea, not a vital interest according to Dean Acheson's speech to the National Press Club in January 1950, became "vital" literally overnight that June when it was invaded by forces of the Communist North. Nicaragua, considered peripheral to U.S. interests under the Carter administration, is considered a threat to U.S. vital interests now that Ronald Reagan is president. In sum, it seems that the military is more concerned about the intestinal fortitude of the executive and congressional leadership and the will of the American people than it is about the tough questions of its own doctrine and force structure.

While it is easy to sympathize with the Army's desire to avoid becoming the victim of the strategic dilettantism—for example, the

McNamara Line—that often prevailed in the Kennedy, Johnson, and Nixon administrations, the sources of the Army's failure in Vietnam run far deeper than that. In any event, attempting to set conditions for the commitment of U.S. combat forces is likely to be as ineffective in the 1980s and 1990s as it was during the years prior to the Vietnam intervention, when the Army shortchanged itself on both the doctrine and the force structure needed to fight effectively in an unfamiliar conflict environment. Thus, in Vietnam the Army ended up trying to fight the kind of conventional war that it was trained, organized, and prepared (and that it *wanted*) to fight instead of the counterinsurgency war it was sent to fight. By focusing on perceived civilian shortcomings to the exclusion of a hard look at its own failures in the war, the Army is perpetuating the fiction that its Concept of war remains valid in all conflict environments and that the problem in future FID conflicts will come from a weak-kneed American public, a foppish Congress, and an indecisive chief executive. The blame for this perpetuation of the Concept cannot, however, be laid entirely at the doorstep of a myopic military leadership. For if the Army is still naively attempting to set the same kind of conditions for intervention that it did in the decade following the Korean War, it has received (when compared with the effort made during the Kennedy years) little incentive to change its organizational bias. Indeed, it seems that the civilian leadership has endorsed its viewpoint rather than challenged it.

Examining the Reagan administration's push to have the Army generate Special Operations Forces (SOF), as they are now called, gives one a strong sense of *déjà vu*. This time around, however, the revolution from above is being led without the strong presidential personal interest evinced by John Kennedy. Nor is there anything resembling the Special Group (Counterinsurgency), which, while flawed, at least provided a sense of high-level concern for low-intensity conflict and a mechanism for linking together the numerous departments and agencies that would have to work together in any future U.S. involvement in foreign internal defense. Today oversight of Army special operations is carried out by only a handful of civilians in the Pentagon with the verbal blessing, but not the direct involvement, of Secretary of Defense Weinberger.

The prospects for change through a revolt from below do not appear promising, either. There exists no cadre of high-visibility advisers, as in Vietnam, to lead the move toward change. The men running today's Army saw their careers boosted in Vietnam when they commanded battalions or served as staff officers in main-force units, not in advisory duty. Indeed, once the Army completed its pullout from South Vietnam, the service sought to expunge the memory of the counterinsurgency experience from its officer corps. The 1973 Arab-Israeli War was seen as a godsend by the Army War College and the Command and General Staff College, which used the war to focus attention away from low-intensity conflict and back to mid-intensity conventional conflict. The "Vietnam Syndrome," which engulfed the United States in the mid-1970s, found the Army right in step as instruction on foreign internal defense at its service schools literally disappeared.[8] For the Army, counterinsurgency became, as one general put it, a "fad," something that was "all the rage" in the days of the New Frontiersmen but now should be forgotten in favor of the long-neglected big-war contingency in Europe.

Since that time, some steps have been taken to reintroduce low-intensity operations into the curricula at the Army's various branch and service schools. Yet, the time devoted to such study remains small compared with that given "normal" (as opposed to "special") operations. Recent Army manuals, such as the Special Forces' *Command, Control and Support of Special Forces Operations* (FM31-22) and the capstone FM100-20, *Low Intensity Operations*, still emphasize the kinds of quasi-conventional operations carried out in Vietnam. Thus one finds FM31-22 stressing Special Forces in unconventional operations, which lend themselves more readily to the support of main-force operations, and making almost no mention of FID.[9] Furthermore, Special Forces units are evaluated and rated almost exclusively on their ability to carry out this traditional unconventional warfare mission.[10]

FM100-20 was most recently issued in January 1981. The manual is little more than a restatement of FM31-16, *Counterguerrilla Operations*, issued in 1967. A perusal of FM100-20 provides useful lessons on the contemporary Army's difficulty in setting aside conventional doctrine and force structures for low-intensity conflict and on the lessons the service took away from its Vietnam experience. For example, the manual declares that the "organization of counterguerrilla forces is designed around light infantry fighting elements," but it goes on to prescribe roles for armored and mechanized infantry units (owing to their enhanced firepower and mobility). While the use of firepower is guided by the principle of "minimal essential force," commanders are exhorted to search for main-force guerrilla units and bases and, once they have located them, to give top priority to their destruction. Thus the commander's dilemma that existed in Vietnam persists: What has priority—the traditional mission of closing with and destroyng the enemy or population safety and security? As in Vietnam, winning the hearts and minds of the people finishes a poor second to seeking out main enemy forces and bringing them to battle. Although pacification requires units to stay put until security and popular confidence in the government's ability to protect the people solidifies, the manual informs commanders that they will "not normally occupy the area for an extended time following a successful attack." Search-and-destroy operations experience a rebirth in the manual as "strike campaigns."[11]

Unfortunately, these manuals are quite reflective of the Army's operational concept for FID missions. For instance, in a recent article entitled "How to Win in El Salvador," the co-author, a former commander of U.S. military trainers in El Salvador, states that the Salvadoran soldier's first priority should be to "learn the subtle art of locating his enemy's base camps."[12] This approach is also consistent with the Army Staff's concept of operations for FID, which sees Special Forces involved in operations against insurgent base areas, infiltration routes, and in remote, isolated areas, in that order, precisely the role they played in Vietnam under MACV.[13] Nowhere is the term *population security* or its equivalent mentioned; rather, the document claims that "there is little functional difference between FID and UW [unconventional warfare]."[14]

Similarly, the Army's personnel policies do not encourage the development of expertise in low-intensity operations. Soldiers, by and large, are rotated in and out of their units every couple of years, creating considerable turmoil and retarding the development of the language and cultural expertise required of men who may have to interact closely, and over a prolonged period, with the populace of a particular Third World nation. For example, officers and NCOs who serve a tour or two in the Special Forces are likely to spend a considerable amount of time in heavy, divisional units over the course of their career. Those serving in the Army's new light infantry divisions (LIDs) face even greater problems, since LIDs have a number of mid-intensity conflict missions that overshadow low-intensity conflict contingencies. Adding to the problem, the political leadership is unlikely to make change any more attractive now in terms of additional resources than was the case under the Kennedy and Johnson administrations. The ends-means disconnect that existed during the days of the "two-and-a-half-war" strategy, in the early 1960s, exists today.

Since 1979 the Army has seen the Carter and Reagan administrations commit it to a major new contingency in the Persian Gulf and a spate of potential low-intensity contingencies in the Third World, in addition to the traditional NATO and Northeast Asia scenarios, yet the Army's size has remained essentially unchanged. This has forced some tough choices on the Army leadership. Working within manpower limitations that are only partially self-imposed, the service has made some units all things to all contingencies. This is not new. It occurred with the Army's "straight leg" infantry divisions of the Kennedy era, which were slotted for both European and Asian contingencies and as Special Action Forces backup brigades against low-intensity, brushfire war contingencies as well.[15] The Army's LIDs represent but the latest attempt to stretch limited resources over seemingly unlimited requirements. Designed to be highly transportable by strategic airlift, LIDs can be moved with relative speed to the Persian Gulf, Korea, or Central Europe, where they would operate primarily in mountains, forests, or urban areas against enemy forces in a mid-intensity conflict environment.[16] Concerns are already being voiced within the service that because of these requirements, LIDs may need to become heavier. For example, the armor branch has expressed its belief that LIDs would be better off with their own organic tank forces (light tanks, of course), while the artillery is lobbying for the introduction of heavy howitzers.[17] LID military intelligence assets appear to be oriented on conventional conflict intelligence requirements (such as determining the enemy order of battle) as opposed to the more demanding human intelligence functions that play a key role in FID operations.[18] As in the Kennedy years, these modifications are motivated by a shortage of manpower resources and a belief that it *really is* a relatively easy proposition to shift gears from conventional war to counterinsurgency. As Lieutenant General Yarborough sadly observed, "We didn't cope with irregular warfare in Asia . . . and, rather than recognizing that we didn't learn our lessons, we are turning back again in the hope that the next war will be a conventional war."[19]

Conclusions

Low-intensity warfare represents the most likely arena of future conflict for the Army, and counterinsurgency the most demanding contingency. Yet, if the service is to be spared another frustrating experience in counterinsurgency warfare, it will most likely be through the wisdom of U.S. Third World allies like Ramon Magsaysay or the incompetence of America's adversaries, as occurred, for example, with the Communists in Greece. As in the period following the end of the Korean War, the Army is erecting barriers to avoid fighting another Vietnam War, just as it sought to avoid another Korea. The result has been that instead of gaining a better understanding of how to wage counterinsurgency warfare within the unique social, economic, political, and military dimensions comprising that form of conflict, the Army is trying, through the six tests enunciated by Secretary Weinberger, to transform it into something it can handle. Unfortunately, as the Army ought to have learned in Vietnam, America's enemies are not going to play to its military strong suits; rather, they will exploit its weak points.

While this book is devoted to the Army and the effects of its Vietnam experience, I would be remiss in failing to point out that the Army's present situation is, at least in part, a result of the political leadership's corresponding lack of emphasis on low-intensity conflict. There exists today no persistent, direct, high-level emphasis for the development of an interdepartmental approach to the problem of foreign internal defense. As flawed as Kennedy's Special Group (Counterinsurgency) was, it at least recognized that a counterinsurgency capability requires the coordination of a nation's economic, social, and political assets, as well as its military power. Thus, it drew together representatives of the various departments and agencies (State, Defense, JCS, CIA, USIA, USAID, and NSC staff) who would have to work together if an American counterinsurgency strategy were to succeed. This kind of group, with power to oversee the development of an integrated capability to carry out U.S. policy in defense of Third World states threatened by insurgency, is not merely a desirable but a necessary element working to change the Army's perspective on FID. With a structural void such as that which exists today comes a scarcity of the resources and/or incentives necessary to motivate the Army to overcome its institutional bias and inertia and develop a true capability for FID contingencies.

In the absence of a national security structural framework that addresses the interdepartmental obligations associated with FID operations, and considering the lack of incentives for organizational change within the Army, it is presumptuous for the political leadership to believe that the Army (or the military) alone will develop the capability to successfully execute U.S. security policy in Third World countries threatened by insurgency. This being the case, America's Vietnam experience takes on a new, more tragic light. For in spite of its anguish in Vietnam, the Army has learned little of value. Yet the nation's policymakers have endorsed the service's misperceptions derived from the war while contemplating an increased U.S. role in Third World low-intensity conflicts. This represents a very dangerous mixture that in the end may see the Army again attempting to fight a conventional war against a very unconventional enemy.

Notes

Chapter 1. Brushfires on a Cold Dawn

1. See, for example, Graham T. Allison, *Essence of Decision* (Boston: Little, Brown & Co., 1971); Herbert Simon, *Models of Man* (New York: John Wiley & Sons, 1957); John D. Steinbruner, *The Cybernetic Theory of Decision* (Princeton: Princeton University Press, 1974); Morton H. Halperin, *Bureaucratic Politics and Foreign Policy* (Washington, D.C.: Brookings Institution, 1974); and Karl W. Deutsch, *The Nerves of Government* (New York: Free Press, 1966). See also Robert Jervis, "Hypothesis on Misperception," in *Readings in American Foreign Policy,* ed. Morton H. Halperin and Arnold Kanter (Boston: Little, Brown & Co., 1973).

2. An excellent overview of post–World War II wars of insurgency is Robert B. Asprey, *War in the Shadows,* vol. 2 (Garden City, N.Y.: Doubleday & Co., 1975). For more specific analyses see Col. Robert N. Ginsburgh, "Damn the Insurrectos," *Military Review* 44 (January 1964); Maj. Gerald H. Early, *The United States Army in the Philippine Insurrection, 1899–1902* (Fort Leavenworth, Kans.: U.S. Army Command & General Staff College, n.d.); and Alvin H. Scaff, *The Philippine Answer to Communism* (Stanford: Stanford University Press, 1955). See also Edward Wainhouse, "Guerrilla War in Greece, 1946–49: A Case Study," in *Modern Guerrilla Warfare,* ed. Frank Osanka (Glencoe, N.Y.: Free Press, 1962); and D. G. Kousoulas, "The War the Communists Lost," in *Guerrilla Warfare,* ed. Victor N. Krulak (Annapolis: U.S. Naval Institute, 1964), 248–54.

3. See John E. Mueller, *War, Presidents, and Public Opinion* (New York: John Wiley & Sons, 1973); and Andrew F. Krepinevich, Jr., "Public Opinion and the Vietnam War" (Harvard University, Department of Government, 1979).

4. Bernard Brodie, *War and Politics* (New York: Macmillan Co., 1973), 457–58.

5. For well-written analyses of counterinsurgency doctrine and theory see David Galula, *Counterinsurgency Warfare* (New York: Frederick A. Praeger, 1964); Osanka, *Guerrilla Warfare;* Robert G. K. Thompson, *No Exit from Vietnam* (New York: David McKay Co., 1969); Douglas S. Blaufarb, *The*

Counterinsurgency Era (New York: Free Press, 1977); and Nathan Leites and Charles Wolf, *Rebellion and Authority* (Chicago: Markham Publishers, 1970).

6. Gen. Vo-Nguyen Giap, *People's War, People's Army* (New York: Frederick A. Praeger, 1962), 46–47.

7. Osanka, *Guerrilla Warfare*, 136.

8. Mao Tse-tung, *Aspects of China's Anti-Japanese Struggle* (Bombay, 1948), 48.

9. T. E. Lawrence, "Guerrilla Warfare," *Encyclopaedia Britannica*, 1950 ed.

10. Giap, *People's War*, 29; Mao Tse-tung, *China's Struggle*, 106; Osanka, *Guerrilla Warfare*, 137 (see also the preface by Samuel P. Huntington, xv–xxii).

11. Galula, *Counterinsurgency Warfare*, 50; Thompson, *No Exit*, 32–33.

12. Roger Hilsman, *To Move a Nation* (New York: Doubleday & Co., 1967), 433–34.

13. Giap, *People's War*, 49, 106, 109.

14. While the need for reform may be obvious, it may not always be possible in that certain reforms may threaten the very foundation upon which the regime's power rests. One thinks here of the inability of a regime to effect land reform out of the fear that in doing so it would lose the support of the agrarian aristocracy upon which its power is based. The result is a "Catch-22" situation for the government which can be exploited by the insurgent movement to its advantage.

15. Charles Wolf, *United States Policy and the Third World* (Boston: Little, Brown & Co., 1967), 52–53.

16. John McCuen, *The Art of Counterrevolutionary Warfare* (Harrisburg, Pa.: Stackpole Books, 1966), 50–75; Galula, *Counterinsurgency Warfare*, 107–35; Robert G. K. Thompson, *Defeating Communist Insurgency* (New York: Frederick A. Praeger, 1966), 50–63; idem, *No Exit*, 163.

17. Thompson, *No Exit*, 166.

18. Albert L. Fisher, "To Beat the Guerrillas," *Military Review* 43 (December 1963): 84.

19. Brig. R. C. H. Miers, "Both Sides of the Guerrilla Hill," *Army* 12 (March 1962): 47.

20. William Manchester, *American Caesar* (New York: Dell Publishing Co., 1978), 685–88.

21. *Horizontal limitations* are limits on the spread of a conflict geographically, whereas *vertical limitations* are limits on the intensity of the war, e.g., refraining from escalating the conventional war to a nuclear war.

22. Cited in Joseph C. Goulden, *Korea: The Untold Story of the War* (New York: McGraw Hill, 1962).

23. Col. R. Ernest Dupuy, *The Compact History of the United States Army* (New York: Hawthorne Books, 1961), 284–85; Russell F. Weigley, *History of the United States Army* (New York: Macmillan Co., 1967), 516–18; Hilsman, *To Move a Nation*, 129.

24. John Foster Dulles, "The Doctrine of Massive Retaliation," in *American Defense Policy*, 4th ed., ed. John E. Endicott and Roy W. Stafford, Jr. (Baltimore: Johns Hopkins University Press, 1977), 65–67.

25. Maxwell D. Taylor, *The Uncertain Trumpet* (New York: Harper & Bros., 1959), 39–40.

26. Maj. Stephen L. Bowman, "The United States Army and Counter-insurgency Warfare: The Making of Doctrine, 1946–1964" (M.A. thesis, Duke University, 1980), 23.

27. Mike Gravel, ed., *The Senator Gravel Edition: The Pentagon Papers*, 5 vols. (Boston: Beacon Press, 1971), 2:56 (hereafter cited as *Papers*); Asprey, *War in the Shadows*, 2:874–76, 883–85; McCuen, *Counterrevolutionary Warfare*, 266–68.

28. *Papers*, 1:432–33.

29. Ibid., 509–10.

30. Ibid., 472.

31. Brig. Gen. James Lawton Collins, Jr., *The Development and Training of the South Vietnamese Army* (Washington, D.C.: GPO, 1975), 1–2; *Papers*, 1:215. The French were generally viewed by the American military as "losers" with nothing to offer in terms of their Indochina experience.

32. At the time, South Vietnam's armed forces numbered some 205,000.

33. *Papers*, 1:216–17

34. Lt. Gen. Dong Van Khuyen, *The RVNAF*, Indochina Monographs (Washington, D.C.: U.S. Army Center for Military History [CMH], 1980), 9; Col. Hoang Ngoc Lung, *Strategy and Tactics*, Indochina Monographs (Washington, D.C.: CMH, 1980), 63. SEATO was a collective security alliance whose members included the United States, France, Britain, the Philippines, Thailand, Australia, and New Zealand. Those countries formed out of French Indochina were barred from joining such alliances by the Geneva accords.

35. See Maj. Gen. David Ewing Ott, *Field Artillery: 1954–1973*, Vietnam Studies (Washington, D.C.: GPO, 1975), 22; and Collins, *South Vietnamese Army*, 2–4. Technically, the head of the French forces in South Vietnam, General Paul Ely, was head of TRIM. Ely, however, served as a figurehead and rarely sought to influence U.S.-directed operations during the phaseout of French forces

36. Lung, *Strategy and Tactics*, 64.

37. Collins, *South Vietnamese Army*, 8–9.

38. Interview with Gen. Maxwell D. Taylor, Washington, D.C., 17 June 1982.

39. Interview with Major General Ruggles by CMH, Washington, D.C., 27 February 1980.

40. Ibid.

41. Lt. Gen. Samuel Williams, "MAAG-TERM Activities Nov 55–Nov. 56," Military History Institute [MHI], November 1956, pp. 5–7, Carlisle Barracks, Pa.; Gen. Cao Van Vien et al., *The U.S. Advisor*, Indochina Monographs (Washington, D.C.: CMH, 1980), 27, 158; Hilsman, *To Move a Nation*, 417.

42. Vien et al., *The U.S. Advisor*, 31–32.

43. Khuyen, *The RVNAF*, 209.

44. Interview with Gen. Samuel L. Myers by CMH, Washington, D.C., 8 February 1980. TO&ES represent the force structure of a given unit, including the number of personnel, their rank, and the quantities and types of equipment in the unit.

45. Williams, "MAAG-TERM Activities," 34.

46. Khuyen, *The RVNAF*, 65.

47. Interview with Colonel Dannemiller by CMH, Washington, D.C., 26 March 1980; Gen. Donne A. Starry, *Mounted Combat in Vietnam*, Vietnam Studies (Washington, D.C.: GPO, 1978), 17–18.

48. *Papers*, 1:308–9.

49. HQ, MAAG-Vietnam (MAAG-V), "MAAG-Vietnam Narrative Statement," 8 November 1959, MHI, 35.

50. Col. Francis J. Kelly, *U.S. Army Special Forces, 1961–1971*, Vietnam Studies (Washington, D.C.: GPO, 1973), 4; Department of the Army (DA), *Special Warfare, U.S. Army* (Washington, D.C.: GPO, 1962), 8.

51. HQ MAAG-V, "Narrative Statement."

52. Hilsman, *To Move a Nation*, 419.

Chapter 2. The Revolution That Failed

1. Interview with Taylor, 17 June 1982.

2. Taylor, *Uncertain Trumpet*, 39–40; Hilsman, *To Move a Nation*, 414.

3. Hilsman, *To Move a Nation*, 414.

4. Interview with Taylor, 17 June 1982.

5. Interview with Gen. Maxwell D. Taylor, U.S. Army War College Senior Officer Debriefing Program (hereafter cited as Officer Debrief), by Col. Richard A. Manion, 16–17 February 1973, MHI.

6. Interview with Lt. Gen. William P. Yarborough, Officer Debrief, by Col. John R. Meese and Lt. Col. Houston P. Hauser III, 15 April 1975, MHI.

7. John F. Kennedy, *Public Papers of the President: John F. Kennedy, 1961* (Washington, D.C.: GPO, 1962), 236.

8. DA, "Additional Spaces to Increase the Counterinsurgency Capability of the U.S. Army in FY 1963," 25 January 1962, CMH, Hilsman, *To Move a Nation*, 415.

9. *Papers*, 2:10.

10. Interview with Elvis J. Stahr by Robert H. Farrell, CMH, 18 August 1964, 33.

11. Thomas W. Scoville, "United States Organization and Management for Pacification, Advice and Support in South Vietnam, 1954–1968: Bureaucratic Politics and Presidential Power" (Draft of Ph.D. diss., 1975), 50.

12. Lloyd Norman and John B. Spores, "Big Push on Guerrilla Warfare," *Army* 12 (March 1962): 33.

13. Walt W. Rostow, "Countering Guerrilla Attack," ibid. 11 (September 1961): 56; Asprey, *War in the Shadows*, 2:1082.

14. Asprey, *War in the Shadows*, 2:1082; Hilsman, *To Move a Nation*, 424–25.

15. Blaufarb, *Counterinsurgency Era*, 207.

16. William W. Kaufmann, *The McNamara Strategy* (New York: Harper & Row, 1964), 49.

17. Interview with Taylor, 17 June 1982.

18. Arthur Schlesinger, *A Thousand Days* (Boston: Houghton Mifflin Co., 1965), 439.

19. Interview with Taylor, 17 June 1982.

20. Lloyd Norman, "No More Koreas," *Army* 15 (May 1965): 22, 24.

21. Col. Robert C. Cassibry, "Development of Doctrine," *Military Review* 36 (May 1956): 22.

22. DA, *Field Service Regulations, Operations*, FM 100-5 (Washington, D.C.: GPO, February 1962).

23. Ibid., 139.

24. Bowman, "Making of Doctrine," 94.

25. DA, *Guerrilla Warfare and Special Forces Operations*, FM 31-21 (Washington, D.C.: GPO, February 1958).

26. DA, *Guerrilla Warfare and Special Forces Operations*, FM 31-21 (Washington, D.C.: GPO, September 1961: with change 1, September 1963).

27. DA, *U.S. Army Counterinsurgency Forces*, FM 31-22 (Washington, D.C.: GPO, November 1963).

28. Maj. Gen. William B. Rosson, "Accent on Cold War Capability," *Army Information Digest* 17 (May 1962): 6, quoted in Bowman, "Making of Doctrine," 111.

29. Interview with Gen. William E. Depuy, Officer Debrief, by Lt. Cols. Bill Mullen and Les Brownlee, 26 March 1979, V-2.

30. U.S. Army Combat Developments Command (CDC), "Doctrinal Literature for Special Warfare" (draft), January 1964, CMH, 2,

31. DA, Office of the Chief of Staff, "Current Army Views on Policy Matters," 1 December 1964, CMH.

32. CDC, "CDC Program for Analysis and Development of Counterinsurgency Doctrine," 26 February 1965, CMH.

33. H. Heymann, Jr., and W. W. Whitson, *Should the United States Preserve a Military Capability for Revolutionary Conflict?* (Santa Monica, Calif.: RAND Corporation, 1972), 37

34. Ibid., 38–39; DA, CDC, "USCONARC Comments of the Review and Analysis of the Evaluation of U.S. Army Mechanized and Armor Combat Operations in Vietnam (MACOV)," 15 May 1967, CMH.

35. DA, *Counterguerrilla Operations*, FM 31-16 (Washington, D.C.: GPO, 1967), 36, 38, 54, 57; Richard A. Hunt, "Strategies at War: Pacification and Attrition in Vietnam," in *Lessons from an Unconventional War*, ed. Richard A. Hunt and Richard H. Schultz, Jr. (New York: Pergamon Press, 1981), 26.

36. Lt. Col. Raymond R. Battreall, Jr., "Armor in Vietnam," *Armor* 75 (May–June 1966): 8.

37. Capt. Brian W. Brady, "The Future of Armor," ibid. 75 (November–December 1966): 47.

38. Lt. Thomas E. Noell III, "Redlegs in the Jungle," *Army* 13 (May 1963): 27, 30.

39. DA, CDC Special Warfare Group, "Annual Historical Report," 12 November 1964, 1–2, 5, quoted in Bowman, "Making of Doctrine," 77.

40. DA, Office of the Chief of Staff, Memo to Brig. Gen. William B. Rosson from Major General Throckmorton, "Terms of Reference," 29 January 1962, CMH.

41. Gen. William B. Rosson, "Four Periods of American Involvement in

Vietnam: Development and Implementation of Policy, Strategy and Programs, Described and Analyzed on the Basis of Service Experience at Progressively Senior Levels" (Ph.D. diss., University of Oxford, 1978), 101.

42. ODCSOPS, Memo for DCSOPS, "Special Warfare Activities," 26 October 1961; idem, Memo for DCSOPS, "Strength Increases for Special Warfare Division," 31 October 1961; DA, Office of the Secretary of the Army, Memo for the Secretary of the Army from Brig. Gen. Richard G. Stilwell, "Army Activities in Underdeveloped Areas Short of Declared War," 13 October 1961 (hereafter cited as "Stilwell Report") 27–28—all located at CMH. Interestingly enough, the Office of the Chief of Special Warfare had been abolished in June 1958 and incorporated into ODCSOPS. The "reorganization" was conducted ostensibly in recognition of "the importance of special warfare . . . and the necessity to retain emphasis in these matters," yet three months later, in September 1958, the directorate within DCSOPS was downgraded to a division and reduced in personnel and oriented almost exclusively toward the kind of unconventional warfare support required in conventional conflicts.

43. Rosson, "American Involvement in Vietnam," 101–2.

44. "Stilwell Report," 47, 102.

45. Ibid., vii, xvi, 3, 11–25, 31, 35, 48.

46. DA, Office of the Chief of Staff, Memo from Gen. George H. Decker to Secretary of the Army, "Army Activities in Undeveloped Areas Short of Declared War, Dated 13 October 1961," 8 December 1961, CMH.

47. CG CONARC to Lt. Gen. Hamilton H. Howze, "Directive for the Conduct of a Study to Inquire into All Aspects of Special Warfare Operations," 14 December 1961, CMH.

48. USCONARC, Historical Division, "Special Warfare Board Final Report" (hereafter cited as "Howze Board"), in Summary of Major Events and Problems, hq, USCONARC, FY 1962, vol. 1b, enclosure 5, sec. 7, pp. 4–5, 99.

49. Ibid., 51.

50. Board President to CG USCONARC, "A Study to Inquire into All Aspects of Special Warfare Operations," 28 January 1962, CMH.

51. HQ, USCONARC, "Counterinsurgency Conference Report," 23–24 March 1962, v, A-1-1, quoted in Bowman, "Making of Doctrine," 85.

52. HQ, USCONARC, Counterinsurgency, pamph. 515-2 (Fort Monroe, Va.: CMH, April 1962).

53. Interview with Yarborough, 15 April 1975.

54. ODCSOPS, "Status of Development of Counterinsurgent Forces," 28 July 1961, CMH, 5.

55. Ibid., annex C.

56. JCS, Memo from Gen. Lyman Lemnitzer to SGCI, "Military Training Related to Counter Insurgency Matters," 30 January 1962, quoted in Bowman, "Making of Doctrine," 96.

57. ODCSOPS, Memo from Major General Throckmorton to DCSOPS, "Counterguerrilla Training Program for Reserve Component Units on Active Duty," 24 January 1962, CMH; USCONARC, annex N to USCONARC Training Directive, "Counterinsurgency/Counterguerrilla Warfare Training," 30 March 1962, CMH See also Maj. Gen. William R. Peers, "Subversion's Continuing Challenge," Army 15 (November 1965): 71.

58. JCS, Memo from Gen. Lyman Lemnitzer to Special Assistant to the President for National Security Affairs, "Summary Report, Military Counterinsurgency Accomplishments since 1961," 21 July 1962, CMH.

59. JCS 1962/326, "Joint Counterinsurgency Concept and Doctrinal Guidance," 3 April 1962, CMH.

60. Interview with Yarborough, 15 April 1975, II-24. Oddly enough, one of the officers under consideration for the commandant's position during the expansion of the Special Warfare Center was one Maj. Gen. William C. Westmoreland, whose name was suggested by Walt Rostow (see NSC Staff, Memorandum, Walt W. Rostow to the President, "The Future of the Special Warfare School" [draft], 12 July 1961, CMH, 3).

61. Ibid., II-18; "Howze Board," Enclosure 10, secs. 7 and 5, p. 4. The board had recommended a two-week course for senior officers, but CONARC trimmed it to one week.

62. Interview with Dr. Ivan J. Birrer by Maj. Robert A. Doughty, "Service at the Command and General Staff College, Ft. Leavenworth, Kansas, 30 January 1948 to 30 June 1978," Fort Leavenworth, Kans., 76.

63. Richard A. Hunt, "Notes from BG Yarborough Papers," 16 September 1977, CMH.

64. Confidential interview 2.

65. Hunt, "BG Yarborough Papers."

66. USCONARC, "CONARC Contributions to U.S. Army Operations in Vietnam, July–December 1963," CMH.

67. JCS, Memo from Lieutenant Colonel Fairfield to Secretary, JCS, "Three-Year Program for U.S. Military Personnel and Material Support of South Vietnam (SVN) (SACSA-M703-62)," 7 February 1963, CMH.

68. U.S. Army Infantry School, *Program of Instruction for 7-A-C20 Infantry Officer Orientation Course* (Fort Benning, Ga., 1959–64); idem, *Program of Instruction for 2-7-C20 Officer Basic Course* (Fort Benning, Ga., 1965–69).

69. U.S. Army Infantry School, *Program of Instruction for 7-A-C22 Infantry Officer Career Course* (Fort Benning, Ga., 1959–64); idem, *Program of Instruction for 2-7-C22 Infantry Officer Advanced Course* (Fort Benning, Ga., 1965–69).

70. U.S. Army Armor School, *Program of Instruction for Armor Officer Basic Extension Course* (Fort Knox, Ky., 1959/60–67); idem, *Program of Instruction for Armor Officer Basic Course* (Fort Knox, Ky., 1968–69).

71. U.S. Army Armor School, *Program of Instruction for Armor Officer Advanced Extension Course* (Fort Knox, Ky., 1959/60–1967); idem, *Program of Instruction for Armor Officer Advanced Course* (Fort Knox, Ky., 1968/69).

72. Starry, *Mounted Combat in Vietnam*, 86.

73. Gen. Earle Wheeler, "From Marchiennes to Bien Hoa" (Speech delivered to the Annual Reunion of the 2d Armored Division, Washington, D.C., 7 August 1965), in *Addresses by General Earle C. Wheeler, Chairman, Joint Chiefs of Staff*, 2 vols. (N.p., n.d.), 2:57.

74. Capt. Robert D. Stachel, "Limited Warfare Requires Adaptable Training," *Armor* 74 (May–June 1965): 51.

75. Brady, "Future of Armor," 48.

76. Interview with Birrer, n.d.

77. U.S. Army Command and General Staff College (C&GSC), *Program of*

Instruction for 250-A-C2 *Command and General Staff College Officer Regular Course* (Fort Leavenworth, Kans., 1959/60–1961/62); idem, *Program of Instruction for Command and General Staff Officer Course* (Fort Leavenworth, Kans., 1963–67).

78. Dr. Ivan Birrer to Dr. Dastrup, 23 July 1982, West Point, N.Y. I am grateful to Lt. Col. Robert A. Doughty for allowing me access to this document.

79. U.S. Army War College, *Curriculum* (Carlisle Barracks, Pa.: MHI, 1964/65–1973).

80. Royal United Services Institution (R.U.S.I.), *Lessons of the Vietnam War* (Whitehall, U.K., 12 February 1969), 19.

81. Interview with Robert Amory by Joseph E. O'Connor, 9 February 1966, JFK Library Oral History Program, 99, quoted in Blaufarb, *Counterinsurgency Era*.

82. JCS, Memo from Fairfield to Secretary, JCS, "Three-Year Program," 7 February 1963.

83. ODCSOPS, Memo from Lieutenant Colonel Kidd to Director of Special Warfare, "Special Warfare Activities Field Report," 15 August 1962, CMH.

84. See Maj. Gen William B. Rosson and Brig. Gen. William P. Yarborough to Gen. George H. Decker, "Special Warfare Activities Field Inspection Visit to Okinawa, Thailand, Laos, Vietnam, and Malaya," 2 May 1962, CMH.

85. DA, Office of The Adjutant General, "Special Warfare Program, FY 1964 (U)" 13 February 1964, CMH.

86. JCS, Memo from Lemnitzer to Special Assistant to the President for National Security Affairs, "Summary Report," 21 July 1962.

87. Brig. Gen. Bruce Palmer, Jr., and Capt. Roy K. Flint, "Counterinsurgency Training," *Army* 12 (June 1962): 32. Ironically, one observes here the Special Forces, supposedly the Army's prime counterinsurgent force, conducting their training as a guerrilla force in their traditional role of unconventional warfare.

88. U.S. Strike Command (STRICOM), "Outline of Significant Exercise (SWIFT STRIKE III)," 24 April 1963, MHI.

89. Maj. Harry E. Trigg, "A New ATT," *Army* 13 (February 1963): 38.

90. Col. John K. Singlaub, "Special Warfare Training," *Military Review* 44 (March 1964): 57.

Chapter 3. Into the Quagmire

1. Interview with Ruggles, 27 February 1980, 6.

2. Ibid.; confidential interview 2.

3. Commander, MAAG-V, "Tactics and Techniques for Counterinsurgent Operations," 10 February 1962, 1, 3.

4. Ibid., 31.

5. See MAAG-V, Memo from Lt. Gen. Lionel C. McGarr to Senior Advisers, "Anti-Guerrilla Guerrilla," 10 December 1960, CMH.

6. BDM Corporation, *A Study of the Strategic Lessons Learned in Vietnam*, vol. 6, bk. 1; *Operational Analysis* (McLean, Va., 1980), 135.

7. *Papers,* 2:38–40.

8. Ibid., 48.

9. JCSM 320-61, 10 May 1961, quoted in ibid., 48–49.

10. MAAG-V, Staff Study, "Requisite RVNAF Force Structure." 18 May 1961, CMH.

11. Lt. Gen. Lionel C. McGarr to Gen. George H. Decker, 15 June 1961, CMH.

12. *Papers,* 2:70.

13. Ibid.

14. Ibid.; David Halberstam, *The Best and the Brightest* (New York: Random House, 1969), 150.

15. Walt W. Rostow to Dean Rusk, 13 July 1961, CMH.

16. ODCSOPS, Summary Sheet, "Requirements for Increase in Strength of US Army (U)," 27 January 1961, CMH.

17. ODCSOPS, "Limited War Capabilities Study—1961" (draft), 4 August 1961, CMH.

18. Ibid., 5; *Papers,* 273.

19. *Papers,* 2:73, 78.

20. Ibid., 76.

21. Ibid., 78.

22. Gen. Maxwell D. Taylor, *Swords and Plowshares* (New York: W. W. Norton, 1972), 233.

23. *Papers,* 2:85.

24. Interview with Taylor, 17 June 1982.

25. Saigon Message 536, General Maxwell D. Taylor to the President, 25 October 1961, and Baguio Messages 0005 and 0006, Taylor to the President, 1 November 1961, quoted in *Papers,* 2:86–87 and 88–91, respectively.

26. *Papers,* 2:91.

27. Ibid., 98.

28. DOD, Memo from Robert S. McNamara, Roswell Gilpatric, and the JCS to the President, 8 November 1961, quoted in ibid., 108–9; DA, Message, CINCUSARPAC to DCSOPS, 27 October 1961, CMH; DA, Message, DCSOPS to Commander, USARPAC, 27 October 1961, CMH; and Memo, Robert S. McNamara and Dean Rusk to the President, 11 November 1961, quoted in *Papers,* 2:112.

29. Taylor, *Swords and Plowshares,* 247; Memo, McNamara and Rusk to the President, 11 November 1961, *Papers,* 2:114.

30. Message, Ambassador Galbraith to the President, 21 November 1961, quoted in *Papers,* 2:122–23.

31. David Halberstam, *The Making of a Quagmire* (New York: Random House, 1964), 60; idem, *Best and Brightest,* 185.

32. Interview with Taylor, 17 June 1982.

33. Hilsman, *To Move a Nation,* 437.

34. H. H. Gardner, Memorandum for the Record, "Meeting of the Special Warfare Coordination Group (Focal Point) for May 1962," n.d., CMH.

35. *Papers,* 2:141.

36. Ibid., 142–43. McGarr also found the need to compromise, for Thompson had found an ally in Hilsman at State. McNamara indicated that he would

support a plan that called for the ARVN to "take *one* place, sweep it and hold it in a plan" (my emphasis).

37. USOM, Earl J. Young, Provincial Report, "Long An Province," 31 July 1964, CMH; U.S. Embassy, Saigon (hereafter referred to as U.S. Embassy), Frederick W. Flott to Gen. Paul D. Harkins, 2 October 1963, CMH.

38. Rosson and Yarborough to Decker, "Special Warfare Activities Field Inspection Visit," 2 May 1962, 6.

39. *Papers*, 2:150.

40. Thompson, *Defeating Communist Insurgency*, 141–42.

41. Lung, *Strategy and Tactics*, 38–39.

42. Milton E. Osborne, "Strategic Hamlets in South Vietnam: A Survey and a Comparison" (Data Paper No. 55, South East Asia Program, Cornell University, 1965, Xerox), 29.

43. MACV, Lt. Col. John Paul Vann, "Senior Advisor's Final Report," 1 April 1963, CMH, 4.

44. U.S. Embassy, Flott to Harkins, 2 October 1963, 3.

45. ODCSOPS, Talking Paper, "Special Forces in Vietnam," 4 June 1964, CMH, 1. A Special Forces Group consisted of a headquarters company, three or more Special Forces companies, a signal company, and an aviation detachment. Each Special Forces company (normally called a "C" detachment) was commanded by a lieutenant colonel. Each "C" detachment had three "B" detachments, each of which, in turn, had four twelve-man "A" detachments, the basic Special Forces unit.

46. Kelly, *Special Forces*, 20, 26; MACV, Briefing for Ambassador Lodge, "Current Military Assistance to the Republic of Vietnam," 25 July 1963, CMH. The popularity of the program was also owing to the Special Forces' ability to arm the villagers so that they could provide for their own defense, a concession made reluctantly by Saigon.

47. Kelly, *Special Forces*, 27–28. See also n. 38 above.

48. CIA Report, "The Civilian Irregular Defense Groups (CIDG) Political Action Program," 3 March 1965, CMH.

49. See n. 38 above.

50. Maj. Gen. William B. Rosson, Memorandum for the Record, "Discussion between the Military Assistant to the President and Major General William B. Rosson, 1600–1700, 28 May 1962," 31 May 1962, CMH.

51. Ibid.; ODCSOPS, Memo for DCSOPS, "CIA Operations in Vietnam (s)," 13 July 1962, CMH; Chief of Staff, Army, to Chairman, JCS, Talking Paper, n.d. CMH. Harkins was initially reluctant to take control of the Special Forces because of his uncertainty over whether MACV would be able to duplicate the CIA's unique logistical support system for them. The DCSOPS quickly developed a support package to accommodate MACV and keep the transfer of Special Forces on track.

52. ODCSOPS, Fact Sheet, "Status of Operation SWITCHBACK (U)," 22 April 1963, CMH.

53. Interview with Depuy, 26 March 1979, v-3.

54. ODCSOPS, Cable, Lt. Gen. Barksdale Hamlett to General Collins, 15 August 1962, CMH.

55. W. Scott Thompson and Donald D. Frizzell, eds., *The Lessons of Vietnam* (New York: Crane Russak & Co., 1977), 250.

56. Khuyen, *The RVNAF*, 336–37.

57. Col. Wilbur Wilson to COMUSMACV, "Integration of Montagnard Village Defenders and Strike Forces into GVN Forces," 12 March 1963, CMH.

58. ODCSOPS, Report of Col. William Depuy, "Special Warfare Visit to Vietnam and Okinawa, 13–30 January 1963," 19 February 1963, CMH, 5.

59. Kelly, *Special Forces*, 40–42; Col. Francis P. Serong, Report to COMUSMACV, "Situation in South Vietnam Following Change of Government," November 1963, CMH.

60. HQ, USASF, V, Colonel Leonard to Director, Special Warfare, DCSOPS, "Debriefing," 5 August 1964, CMH; Cable, COMUSMACV to Commander, USASF, V, "U.S. Support of Border Surveillance Program," 26 October 1963, CMH.

61. Interview with Gen. Harold K. Johnson, Senior Officer Debrief, by Lt. Col. Rupert F. Glover, 28 December 1972, 8 and 22 January and 23 April 1973, MHI, IX-27.

62. ODCSOPS, Memo for Director, Special Warfare, from Lt. Gen. Harold K. Johnson, "Special Warfare Doctrine," 14 April 1964, CMH.

63. USASF, V, Col. John H. Speers, "Commander's Debriefing Letter," CMH, 1.

64. DA, Office of the Chief of Staff, Memo from Col. Wilbur Wilson to Gen. Harold K. Johnson, "Problems of Vietnam," 8 April 1965, CMH.

65. HQ, USASF, V, Letter of Instructions Number 1, "The Special Forces Counterinsurgency Program," 1 January 1965, CMH; ODCSOPS, Information Brief, "Roles and Missions, U.S. Special Forces, Republic of Vietnam (RVN) (U)," 24 February 1965, CMH.

66. Army Concept Team in Vietnam (ACTIV), Final Report, "Employment of a Special Forces Group," 10 June 1966, CMH.

67. Taylor, *Swords and Plowshares*, 288; Adam Yarmolinsky, *The Military Establishment* (New York: Harper & Row, 1971), 20.

68. Marine Corps Operational Analysis Study Group 1, "Characteristics of U.S. Marine Corps Helicopter Operations in the Mekong Delta, 1962," April 1963, 11.

69. Halberstam, *Making of a Quagmire*, 86.

70. Rosson, "American Involvement in Vietnam" 123.

71. Ibid., 136; Rosson and Yarborough to Decker, "Special Warfare Activities Field Inspection Visit," 2 May 1962.

72. *Papers*, 2:176.

73. Vincent Demma, "Historian's Notes and Working Papers on CPSVN," CMH; MACV, COMUSMACV to CINCPAC, "Comprehensive Plan for South Vietnam," 19 January 1963, CMH, 4.

74. Hilsman, *To Move a Nation*, 449.

75. MACV, Cable, COMUSMACV to General Taylor, 10 January 1963, CMH.

76. Halberstam, *Making of a Quagmire*, 157.

77. Vann, "Senior Advisor's Final Report," 4; Guenther Lewy, *America in Vietnam* (New York: Oxford University Press, 1978), 168.

78. *Papers*, 2:180 (my emphasis).

79. The RVN was divided into four corps sectors. I ("eye") Corps ran from the DMZ to just north of the Central Highlands; II Corps consisted primarily of the Highlands region; III Corps, the area north and west of Saigon; and IV Corps, the Mekong Delta, southwest of the capital.

80. ODCSOPS, DCSOPS to USCONARC, "Special Orientation of U.S. Army Personnel Being Assigned to Vietnam," 16 May 1963, CMH, 1, 3.

81. HQ, IV Advisory Group, Col. Daniel B. Porter, Jr., to COMUSMACV, "Final Report," 13 February 1963, CMH, 11–12; Collins, *South Vietnamese Army*, 38.

82. HQ, IV Corps Advisory Group, Porter to COMUSMACV, "Final Report," 13.

83. MAAG-V, III Corps, Memo from Col. Wilbur Wilson to Generals Dinh and Phat, "Population and Resources Control," 18 November 1963, 2.

84. Col. Hal D. McCown to DCSOPS, Director of Special Warfare, "Debriefing of Officers Returning from Field Assignments (U)," 10 October 1963, 1, 3, 7.

85. Interview with Col. Rowland H. Renwanz by Charles von Littichau, Long Binh, South Vietnam, 21 October 1967, CMH.

86. Vann, "Senior Advisor's Final Report," 4.

87. Interview with Gen. William C. Westmoreland by Maj. Paul L. Miles, 6 March 1971, CMH, 5. According to Westmoreland, General Harkins fired Vann because Vann "was pessimistic about the way things were going down in Dinh Tuong Province, which was about 90 percent Viet Cong–controlled. Vann was very critical of the optimistic assessments. Harkins threw him out of the theater."

88. Interview with Gen. Barksdale Hamlett, Officer Debrief, by Col. Jack Ridgeway and Lt. Col. Paul Walter, 11 March 1976, 1.

89. Lt. Col. John Paul Vann, JCS Briefing, "Observations of the Senior Advisor to the South Vietnamese Seventh Infantry Division," 8 July 1963, 3–4.

90. Ibid., 8.

91. Michael V. Forrestal, "Memorandum for the President," February 1963, quoted in *Papers*, 2:717–25 (my emphasis).

92. USARPAC, "Analysis of Counterinsurgency Operations in South Vietnam," 14 January 1963, CMH, pt. 5, p. 6.

93. CINCPAC, Cable, CINCPAC to JCS, 14 February 1963, CMH.

94. CINCPAC, Cable, CINCPAC to JCS, 9 March 1963, CMH; William A. Nighswonger, *Rural Pacification in Vietnam* (New York: Praeger, 1966), 64; Thompson, *Defeating Communist Insurgency*, 141–42.

95. C. V. Sturdevant, *Pacification Requirements for South Vietnam* (Santa Monica, Calif.: RAND Corporation, March 1965), v.

96. State Department, Memorandum of Conversation, "Situation in Vietnam," 22 May 1963, CMH, 2–3; Hilsman, *To Move a Nation*, 506–7.

97. Yarmolinsky, *The Military Establishment*, 165; Halberstam, *Best and Brightest*, 270–71.

98. USIA, Memo for Mr. Murrow, "A Policy for Vietnam," 10 September 1963, CMH, 3; Hilsman, *To Move a Nation*, 504.

99. JCS, Office of the Special Assistant for Counterinsurgency and Special

Activities (SACSA), Memo for McGeorge Bundy, "Long An Province," 11 September 1963, CMH.

100. MAAG-V, "Report on Visits to the Delta by British Advisory Mission," 21 September 1963, CMH.

101. British Advisory Mission, Saigon, "Reports on Visits to Delta Provinces, April–May 1963," CMH.

102. *Papers*, 186; Taylor, *Swords and Plowshares*, 297.

103. *Papers*, 2:187.

104. JCS, SACSA, Talking Paper, "Department of State Research Memorandum, RFE-90, October 22, 1963 (Inclosure to Tab A) (U)," 4 November 1963, CMH.

105. Robert S. McNamara to Dean Rusk, 7 November 1963, CMH. The problem would later surface with OSD's *Southeast Asia Reports*. The reports, ironically, would be compiled within DOD, in the Systems Analysis section. In February 1964 the CIA issued four reports out of Saigon sharply critical of the war effort. Although it was generally agreed that the reports were accurate, MACV took issue with the findings and requested that all future evaluations be "coordinated" with the military before being dispatched.

106. ODCSOPS, Talking Papers, "Current Operations to Achieve U.S. Objectives in the Republic of Vietnam (RVN) (U)," 1 December 1963, and "Additional Actions Which Could Be Taken to Facilitate Attainment of U.S. Objectives in SVN," 30 November 1963, both CMH. The proposal would have seen COMUSMACV reporting directly to the JCS instead of through CINCPAC.

107. "Report on the Visit of the Secretary of Defense to South Vietnam, 19–20 December 1963," CMH, 3.

108. JCSM 46-64, "Vietnam and Southeast Asia," 22 January 1964, quoted in *Papers*, 3:496–99.

109. *Papers*, 2:194.

110. MACV, "Counterinsurgency Vitalization," 10 March 1964, CMH; Scoville, "Pacification, Advice and Support," 18–19. General Stilwell was the author of the Stilwell Report (see above, chap. 2, n. 42).

111. Lt. Gen. Harold K. Johnson, DCSOPS, "After Action Report, re: Trip to Vietnam 24 March–8 April 1964," Personal Papers of General Johnson, MHI.

112. NSC Staff, Memo, Michael Forrestal to McGeorge Bundy, "Vietnam," 18 March 1964, CMH (quoting General Anthis, General Krulak's successor as SACSA).

113. Ibid.

114. Cable, CINCPAC to JCS, "U.S. Redeployment Posture in Southeast Asia (S)," 21 March 1964, CMH.

115. Cable, JCS to CINCPAC, "Air Strike Target List for North Vietnam," 10 June 1964, CMH.

116. Gen. Earle Wheeler to CG CONARC, 9 April 1964, CMH; DA, Office of the Chief of Staff, Memo from Secretary, General Staff, to General Richardson, "Personnel Feasibility Study—CINCPAC Army Force Requirements," 30 June 1964, CMH.

117. Gen. William C. Westmoreland, *A Soldier Reports* (Garden City, N.Y.: Doubleday & Co., 1976), 67.

118. Interview with Hamlett, 11 March 1976, 3.

119. Westmoreland, *A Soldier Reports,* 101.

120. Interview with Taylor, 16–17 February 1973, V-5.

121. Taylor, *Swords and Plowshares,* 321.

122. DE SOTO patrols involved the use of U.S. destroyers to observe DRV naval activity in support of the VC (primarily related to the infiltration of supplies) and for intelligence-gathering purposes.

123. JCS, Cable to Adm. U. S. G. Sharp and Gen. William C. Westmoreland, "Improvement U.S. Posture SVN," 15 August 1964, CMH.

124. Memo, McGeorge Bundy to the President, 31 August 1964, CMH.

125. *Papers,* 3:208.

126. Ibid., 209; JCSM 955-64, 14 November 1964, quoted in ibid., 628; Vice Adm. Lloyd M. Mustin, Memo for the Chairman, NSC Working Group on Southeast Asia, "Comment on Draft for Part II of Project Outline on Courses of Action in Southeast Asia—'U.S. Objectives and Stakes in SVN and SEA,' " 10 November 1964, quoted in ibid., 621–28.

127. Ibid., 625.

128. Ibid., 223.

129. Ibid., 233–34. The use of *controlled program* and the mention of suspending operations as soon as U.S. objectives were achieved were designed to allay fears among the group's members that the military was proposing an uncontrollable escalation of the conflict.

130. Memo, Walt W. Rostow to Secretary McNamara, "Military Dispositions and Political Signals," 16 November 1964, quoted in ibid., 632–33.

131. Ambassador Maxwell D. Taylor, Briefing, "The Current Situation in South Vietnam—November 1964," 27 November 1964, quoted in ibid., 666–73.

Chapter 4. Gearing Up for Counterinsurgency

1. Corey Ford, *Donovan of the O.S.S.* (Boston: Little, Brown, & Co., 1970), 109, 129, 162; Stewart Alsop and Thomas Braden, *Sub Rosa: The O.S.S. and American Espionage* (New York: Reynal & Hitchcock, 1946), 15.

2. Col. Alfred H. Paddock, Jr., "Psychological and Unconventional Warfare, 1941–1952: Origins of a 'Special Warfare' Capability for the United States Army" (Carlisle Barracks, Pa.: U.S. Army War College, 1979), 36.

3. Ibid., 53.

4. DCSOPS, "Study on Guerrilla Warfare," 1 March 1949 (RG 319, Army Operations, 1949–52, Box No. 10, Hot Files, & 37064, National Archives), quoted in Paddock, "Psychological and Unconventional Warfare."

5. Paddock, "Psychological and Unconventional Warfare," 108.

6. DA, Office of the Chief of Psychological Warfare, "Special Forces Operations," 26 October 1951, National Archives.

7. DOD, *Department of Defense Semiannual Report of the Secretary of Defense and Semiannual Reports of the Secretary of the Army, Secretary of the Navy, Secretary of the Air Force, 1 January through 30 June 1952* (Washington, D.C.: GPO, 1952), 92. See also Paddock, "Psychological and Unconventional Warfare."

8. *Special warfare* was defined by the Army as encompassing psychological warfare, unconventional warfare, and counterinsurgency.

9. Paddock, "Psychological and Unconventional Warfare," 168–69.

10. Ibid.

11. In July 1959 the mission of the Special Forces was expanded to include assisting friendly governments against Communist-inspired insurgencies; however, this had a negligible impact on training and force structure.

12. ODCSOPS, Summary Sheet, "Increase in Special Forces Strength," 3 February 1961, CMH.

13. Gen. George H. Decker, Briefing for the President, "Army Capabilities for Guerrilla and Counterguerrilla Warfare," 23 February 1961, CMH; DCSOPS, Summary Sheet, "Additional Spaces to Increase the Counterinsurgency Capability of the U.S. Army in FY 1963 (U)," 29 January 1962, CMH.

14. Ibid.; ODCSOPS, Lt. Gen. Barksdale Hamlett to CG CONARC, "Requirements and Missions for Special Forces," 11 April 1961, CMH; ODCSOPS, "Grade and MOS Requirements for the Additional 3,000 Spaces for Counterinsurgency," June 1961, CMH.

15. ODCSOPS, "Increase of 500 Spaces for Special Forces and Psychological Warfare Units (U)," 18 May 1961, CMH; ODCSOPS, Summary of Actions, Lieutenant Colonel Brown to Secretary, General Staff, "Increase of 500 Spaces for Special Forces and Psychological Warfare Units," 17 May 1961, CMH; ODCSOPS, Hamlett to CG CONARC, "Requirements and Missions for Special Forces," 11 April 1961.

16. ODCSOPS, "Status of Development of Counterguerrilla Forces (U)," 7 November 1961, and "Concept for FLAG Element Relationship," app. A, both CMH.

17. Ibid.; ODCSOPS, "U.S. Free World Liaison and Assistance Group (US-FLAG) (U)," August 1961, CMH. The size of the FLAGs was projected to increase along with the growth of special warfare forces. The initial pilot FLAG was to comprise 600; by the end of FY 1962, FLAGs were to be at 1,840 men, reaching their full strength of 2,440 by the end of FY 1963.

18. Gen. George H. Decker to Brig. Gen. Theodore Clifton (draft), c. July–August 1961, CMH.

19. Ibid., tab A, pp. 1–2.

20. Ibid., tab A, p. 3. In the event that a STAF were committed, the FLAG size would increase to 9,943 men. Other schemes called for a FLAG "base" of 4,910 men, including the support units necessary to facilitate rapid introduction of the STAF.

21. See "Stilwell Report," vi, xviii, 3–4, 46–48.

22. DA, Office of the Chief of Staff, Decker to Secretary of the Army, "Army Activities in Underdeveloped Areas," 8 December 1961; Elvis J. Stahr, Memo for the Secretary of Defense, "Sub-limited Warfare Activities for Colombia," 16 December 1961, CMH.

23. ODCSOPS, Memo, Lt. Gen. Barksdale Hamlett to CG CONARC, "Improvement of U.S. Army Capability to Meet Limited and Cold War Requirements," 7 December 1961, CMH, 2, 8.

24. ODCSOPS, Staff Paper, Lt. Gen. Barksdale Hamlett to Gen. George H.

Decker, "Concept of Employment of U.S. Army Forces in Paramilitary Operations," 2 January 1962, CMH.

25. See n. 13 above.

26. "Howze Board," vol. 1a, chap. 5, pp. 13, 102.

27. Ibid., 31.

28. Ibid., 47.

29. Ibid., 49, 53.

30. Interview with Taylor, 17 June 1982. Referring to the development of Special Forces, Taylor said, "The Army never liked anything that seized a number of elite officers and men and put them in a single place."

31. "Howze Board," 2–7; ODCSOPS, Maj. Gen. William B. Rosson, "Revised Phasing of Counterinsurgency Buildup in FY 1963," 24 May 1962 CMH; ODCSOPS, Col. William H. Kinnard to CG USCONARC, CINCUSAEUR, and CINCUSARPAC, "Expansion of Counterinsurgency Forces in FY 1963," 26 February 1962, CMH.

32. "Howze Board," 9.

33. DA, Office of the Chief of Staff, "Special Warfare Study and Program, FY 1963–68," 21 June 1962, CMH, 69.

34. Ibid.

35. ODCSOPS, Memorandum for the Record, "Chief of Staff Briefing on Priority Application of Resources (Selective Modernization) Study (U)," 17 September 1962, CMH.

36. ODCSOPS, Generals Parker and William B. Rosson to CG USCONARC, "Implementation of the U.S. Army Special Warfare Program FY 1963–68 (U)," 25 October 1962, CMH.

37. ODCSOPS, Congressional Fact Papers, "Special Warfare and Special Forces," 1 April 1965, and "Special Warfare Program," 1 April 1965 both CMH.

38. HQ, USCONARC, Counterinsurgency Training, annex M to USCONARC training directive, CON Reg 350-1 (Fort Monroe, Va., 3 April 1967), 15, 18.

39. Interview with Hamlett, 11 March 1976, 62–63; Lt. Gen. James Gavin, "Cavalry—And I Don't Mean Horses," Harper's 208 (April 1954): 54–67.

40. Interview with Lt. Gen. John J. Tolson III, Officer Debrief, by Col. Glenn A. Smith and Lt. Col. August M. Cianciolo, 18–19 March 1977, MHI, IV-65.

41. Interview with Hamlett, 11 March 1976, 62–63.

42. Interview with Gen. Hamilton H. Howze, Officer Debrief, by Lt. Col. Robert Reed, 14 October 1972, MHI, IV-65.

43. Department of Combat Development (DCD), 1957 Estimate of the Situation (Fort Rucker, Ala.: U.S. Army Aviation School, n.d.) (my emphasis).

44. Interview with Tolson, 18–19 March 1977, 11.

45. Lt. Gen. John J. Tolson III, Airmobility, 1961–1971, Vietnam Studies (Washington, D.C.: GPO, 1973), 10.

46. Townsend Hoopes, The Limits of Intervention (New York: David McKay Co., 1969), 161–62.

47. U.S. Congress, House, Committee on Armed Services, Hearings on Military Posture (Washington, D.C.: GPO, 1962), 3162.

48. Tolson, Airmobility, 17.

49. Perry Poe, "How's Airmobility?" Army 13 (June 1963): 26.

50. Interview with Gen. George H. Decker, Officer Debrief, by Lt. Col. Dan

H. Ralls, MHI, III-65; OSD, Draft Presidential Memorandum (DPM), Robert S. McNamara to the President, "Recommended FY 1966–FY 1970 Army and Marine Corps General Purpose Forces (U)," 4 December 1964, CMH, 4.

51. Gen. Earle Wheeler, "A Course for the Future" (Address delivered to the Dallas Council on World Affairs and the West Point Society of North Texas), in *Addresses by General Wheeler*, 1:119.

52. HQ, CINARC (Combat Developments), "Briefing for General Eddleman," 10 January 1961, MHI; USCONARC, R&D, *War Game Evaluation of Road*, USCONARC PAM No. 70-9 (Fort Monroe, Va., April 1962), 1–4; DA, Gen. Clyde D. Eddleman to CG CONARC, "Reorganization of Infantry and Armored Divisions," 16 December 1960, MHI.

53. Gen. Earle Wheeler, "Why We Celebrate" (Address delivered to the Rotary Club, Martinsburg, W.Va., 25 May 1967), in *Addresses by General Wheeler*, 1:151 (my emphasis).

54. Kaufmann, *The McNamara Strategy*, 264.

55. Heymann and Whitson, *Revolutionary Conflict*, 29.

56. "Stilwell Report," xvi.

57. See ODCSOPS, Hamlett to CG CONARC, "Improvements," 7 December 1961, 2.

58. Interview with Gen. Robert R. Williams, Officer Debrief, by Col. Ralph J. Powell and Lt. Col. Phillip E. Courts, 29 March 1978, MHI, 57.

59. Interview with Lt. Gen. Harry W. O. Kinnard, Washington, D.C., 21 June 1982.

60. Interview with Williams, 29 March 1978, 54.

61. Ibid.; Interview with Howze, 14 October 1972, V-44, V-45.

62. Interview with Lt. Gen. W. O. Kinnard, Officer Debrief, by Col. Glenn A. Smith and Lt. Col. August M. Cianciolo, 31 March 1977, MHI, 2.

63. Interview with Kinnard, 21 June 1982.

64. Gen. Hamilton H. Howze, "Tactical Employment of the Air Assault Division," *Army* 13 (September 1963) 52–53.

65. ODCSOPS, Lieutenant General Parker to Gen. Earle Wheeler, "TD for Army Concept Team in Vietnam (U)," 6 November 1962, CMH; DA, Office of The Adjutant General, "Army Troop Test Program in Vietnam (U)," 6 November 1962, CMH, 1.

66. Interview with Major General Rowny by Charles van Luttihan, Stuttgart, Federal Republic of Germany, 20 February 1969, CMH; HQ, USARPAC, Memo, Lieutenant Colonel Harby to G-3, "SW & Tng Division Major Current Projects," 26 July 1963, CMH.

67. Halberstam, *Making of a Quagmire*, 192–93.

68. Interview with Hamlett, 11 March 1976, 62.

69. Department of the Air Force, "Report of the United States Air Force Tactical Air Support Evaluation Report" (the Disosway Board), 1 August 1962, quoted from Vincent Demma, Historian's Notes, CMH.

70. JCSM 936-62, JCS to Secretary of Defense, 26 November 1962, quoted from Vincent Demma, Historian's Notes, CMH; Tolson, *Airmobility*, 57.

71. Gen. Earle Wheeler, "Report from Washington" (Address to the Minuteman Chapter of the AUSA, Worcester, Mass., 21 March 1963), in *Addresses by General Wheeler*, 1:37.

72. Interview with Williams, 29 March 1978, 61.

73. DA, "The Army Air Mobility Concept," December 1963, MHI, II-4, II-5; DA, CDC, *The Division (Air Assault Supplement)*, St-61-100-1 (Fort Leavenworth, Kans., 1 July 1964), 4–11.

74. Ibid. (my emphasis).

75. Interview with Lt. Gen. John Norton, West Point, N.Y., May 1982.

76. Memo, Robert W. Komer to Brig. Gen. L. C. Shea, "Critique of Army Force Posture," 5 July 1963, CMH, I, 4, 10–11.

77. DA, CDC, *Army Airmobility Evaluation*, annex D (Fort Benning, Ga., 15 January 1965), 3.

78. JCSM 51-65, JCS to Secretary of Defense, 21 January 1965, quoted from Demma, Historian's Notes, CMH.

79. JCSM 205-65, JCS to Secretary of Defense, 20 March 1965, quoted from Demma, Historian's Notes, CMH.

80. DA, CDC, *Army Airmobility Evaluation*, 11–13, 18–19.

81. Ibid. The report noted that "Air Assault units do not offer the solution to the difficult job of finding a guerrilla force, but once it is found, they do have unique capabilities in fixing and fighting this kind of enemy."

82. Interview with Kinnard, 21 June 1982.

83. DA, CDC, *Army Airmobility Evaluation*, annex A, A-1-7, A-1-8.

84. Interview with Kinnard, 21 June 1982.

85. Interview with Williams, 29 March 1978, 61.

86. Interview with Maj. Gen. Delk Oden, Officer Debrief, by Col. Glenn A. Smith and Lt. Col. August M. Cianciolo, 27 May 1977, MHI, 18–19.

87. DA, CDC, *Army Airmobility Evaluation*, annex A, A-3.

88. Ibid., A2-1-2, A1-1-2, A2-1-7, A4-1-12, A-8.

Chapter 5. Forty-four Battalions across the Rubicon

1. Interview with Vincent Demma, 10 June 1982, CMH.

2. Interview with Taylor, 16–17 February 1973, V-11.

3. USARPAC, *OPLAN 37-64*, CMH.

4. DA, CSAM 64-316, *Basis for Active Army Force Structure*, 6 August 1964, CMH.

5. Interview with General William C. Westmoreland by author, New York, New York, 15 May 1982. Westmoreland recalled a discussion with McNamara in the spring of 1964 in which he recommended to the secretary of defense that President Johnson get "people-to-people" with the American public over the possibility of U.S. intervention. Westmoreland was told that the president wanted to keep everything "low-key" so as not to "rile up" the American people.

6. Col. John D. Austin, Deputy Senior Adviser, III Corps, to General Johnson, 8 September 1964, Personal Papers of General Johnson.

7. Interview with General Johnson, 28 December 1972, 8 and 22 January and 23 April 1973, VIII-53.

8. Memo, Gen. Harold K. Johnson to Secretary of Defense, 18 December 1964, MHI; the memo was not sent.

9. Memo, Gen. Harold K. Johnson to the JCS, 21 December 1964, Personal Papers of General Johnson.

10. See n. 8 above.

11. Ambassador William Sullivan, Lecture at the United States Military Academy, West Point, N.Y., 25 April 1984; Stanley Karnow, *Vietnam: A History* (New York: Viking Press, 1983), 399. I am grateful to Capt. William Bettson, Department of History, U.S. Military Academy, for his notes of Ambassador Sullivan's remarks.

12. Interview with Gen. William C. Westmoreland, 10 April 1971, CMH, 24.

13. JCS, Memo, Gen. Earle Wheeler to McGeorge Bundy, "Binh Gia Engagements, 28 December–4 January," 5 January 1965, CMH; Cable, COMUSMACV to CINCPAC, "Analysis of the Situation in Phouc Tuy, RVN," 8 January 1965, CMH.

14. Cable, President Lyndon B. Johnson to Ambassador Maxwell D. Taylor, 30 December 1964, National Security Files, LBJ Library. I am indebted to Col. Paul Miles, Department of History, U.S. Military Academy, for providing me a copy of this document.

15. Cable, Maxwell D. Taylor to the President, 5 January 1965, CMH.

16. Interview with U. Alexis Johnson by J. Angus McDonald, Tom Nadolski, and Tom Ware, 9 January 1979, CMH.

17. Memo, McGeorge Bundy to the President, "Re: Basic Policy in Vietnam," 27 January 1965, CMH, 2.

18. Memo, William P. Bundy to the Secretary of State, "Notes on the South Vietnamese Situation and Alternatives," 6 January 1965, CMH, 4.

19. Halberstam, *Best and Brightest,* 485–86.

20. Taylor, *Swords and Plowshares,* 334.

21. Ibid., 335.

22. Cable, U.S. Embassy to Secretary of State, 0721Z, 7 February 1965, CMH; Cable, Maxwell D. Taylor to Secretary of State, 0511Z, 9 February 1965, CMH.

23. Cable, COMUSMACV to CINCPAC, "Personal for Admiral Sharp from Westmoreland," 160139Z, February 1965, CMH, 2.

24. Cable, CINCPAC to AIG, "PACOM Watch Report No. 1-65," 050356Z, February 1965, CMH, 1; Westmoreland, *A Soldier Reports,* 124; Interview with Westmoreland, 10 April 1971, 14; Director of Intelligence, CIA, Intelligence Memo, "Threat of Foreign Volunteers to Aid the Viet Cong," 31 March 1965, CMH, 3; Interview with Westmoreland, 15 May 1982.

25. Interview with Gen. Maxwell D. Taylor, 11 July 1979, BDM Oral History, Washington, D.C.; Interview with Taylor, 17 June 1982.

26. Cables, Maxwell D. Taylor to JCS, 220620Z, 1–5, and 220545Z, 1–3, both February 1965, CMH.

27. Interview with Taylor, 17 June 1982.

28. *Papers,* 3:419–20.

29. USIA, Memo, Carl T. Rowan to the President, 27 February 1965, CMH.

30. *Papers,* 3:474.

31. Ibid., 421; Cable, JCS to CINCPAC, CINCSTRIKE, and CINCSAC, "Force Deployments to the Western Pacific Area (U)," 051507Z, March 1965, CMH. On 2 March, John McNaughton proposed that the 173d Airborne Brigade be substituted for the two Marine battalions slated for Da Nang. This was successfully resisted by CINCPAC, who wanted the 173d to remain its strategic reserve and because current OPLANs had the Marines positioned along the coast, with the Army projected for deployment in Laos and Thailand.

32. Interview with Depuy, 26 March 1979, V-7.

33. Interview with Oden, 27 May 1977, 20.

34. Cable, Ambassador Maxwell D. Taylor to Secretary of State, 180145Z, March 1965, CMH.

35. Cables, Ambassador Maxwell D. Taylor to Secretary of State, 070750Z, and Ambassador Taylor to Department of State, "Intelligence Estimate of the Situation in South Vietnam," 161357Z, both March 1965, CMH.

36. Ibid.

37. Westmoreland, *A Soldier Reports*, 130.

38. Ibid., 125; Interview with Westmoreland, 15 May 1982.

39. DA, Memo from General Johnson to Secretary of Defense and JCS, "Report on the Survey of the Military Situation in South Vietnam," tab B, 14 March 1965, CMH, 4; Interview with General Johnson, 23 April 1973, XII-18.

40. DA, "Report on the Survey of the Military Situation in South Vietnam," 6.

41. Ibid., 11–12 (my emphasis).

42. Ibid.

43. Interview with General Johnson, 23 April 1973, XII-25.

44. Interview with U. Alexis Johnson, 9 January 1979.

45. CIA/DIA/Department of State, Joint Memo, "Strength of Viet Cong Military Forces in South Vietnam," 17 March 1965, CMH, 2.

46. *Papers,* 3:468–69.

47. Cable, CINCPAC to JCS, "MEB Deployment to Da Nang," 192207Z, March 1965, CMH; *Papers,* 3:445.

48. ODCSOPS, Memo, DCSOPS to Chief of Staff, "Engineer Estimate, U.S. Army Corps Force, S.E.A. (U)," 26 April 1965, CMH; U.S. Army Corps of Engineers, Memo, Chief of Engineers to DCSOPS, "Engineer Estimate, U.S. Army Corps Force, S.E.A. (U)," 19 April 1965, CMH.

49. Cable, COMUSMACV to CINCPAC, "Commander's Estimate of the Situation," 271338Z, March 1965, CMH, 3–7, 9, 11.

50. Cable, Ambassador Maxwell D. Taylor through Secretary Dean Rusk to Ambassador U. Alexis Johnson and Gen. William C. Westmoreland, 30 March 1965, CMH, I.

51. Cable, COMUSMACV to CINCPAC, "MEB Deployment to Da Nang," 110123Z, April 1965, CMH; *Papers,* 3:407. The outcome was a provision for "mobile counterinsurgency" authorizing the Marines to operate out to fifty miles from their base in support of ARVN operations. Details of the president's decision can be found in NSAM 328.

52. NSAM 328, 6 April 1965, quoted in *Papers,* 3:702–3.

53. Interview with U. Alexis Johnson, 9 January 1979.

54. Cable, COMUSMACV to CINCPAC, "Additional Deployments and Command Concepts," 110825Z, April 1965, CMH, 1.

55. Cable, Ambassador Maxwell D. Taylor to Secretary of State, 120805Z, April 1965, CMH, 2.

56. Interview with Taylor, 17 June 1982; Cable, JCS to CINCPAC and CINCSTRIKE, "Deployment of 173d Airborne Brigade to Bien Hoa–Vung Tau Area," 140050Z, April 1965, CMH.

57. Cables, Ambassador Maxwell D. Taylor to Secretary of State, 140903Z and 141230Z, April 1965, CMH.

58. Memo, McGeorge Bundy to the President, 14 April 1965, CMH.

59. Interview with Taylor, 17 June 1982.

60. Interview with U. Alexis Johnson, 9 January 1979.

61. Cable, DOD to American Embassy, 160933Z, April 1965, CMH.

62. Cables, USARPAC to CINCPAC, "Deployment of CONUS Army Brigade TF to SVN (S)," 172112Z, April 1965; CINCPAC to JCS, "Deployment of ROK Division (S)," 140323Z, April 1965; and JCS to CINCPAC and COMUSMACV, "Concept of Operations (U)," 171847Z, April 1965—all CMH.

63. DA, Office of the Chief of Staff, Memo, Gen. Harold K. Johnson to JCS, "Actions Designed to Accelerate Stability in South Vietnam," 12 April 1965, CMH, 1.

64. Cables, CINCPAC to COMUSMACV, "Employment of MEB in Counterinsurgency (U)," 140830Z, April 1965, 1; and COMUSMACV to CG, 9th MEB, Da Nang, "Mission of the 9th MEB," 161400Z, April 1965, both CMH.

65. Interview with Taylor, 17 June 1982.

66. Memo, Robert S. McNamara to the President, 21 April 1965, CMH.

67. Ibid.

68. Provisions for the introduction of an ROK brigade and an Australian battalion were also discussed. The group also examined the possible introduction of the newly formed airmobile division, the remainder of the ROK division, and the final three MEF battalions at Da Nang.

69. Interview with Taylor, 17 June 1982.

70. Memo, McNamara to the President, 21 April 1965.

71. CIA, Office of National Estimates, Special Memorandum 12-65, "Current Trends in Vietnam," 30 April 1965, CMH, 1.

72. Westmoreland, *A Soldier Reports*, 135.

73. Rosson, "American Involvement in Vietnam," 190.

74. Cable, McGeorge Bundy to the President, 24 May 1965, CMH.

75. Clark Clifford to the President, 17 May 1965, CMH.

76. Cable, Ambassador Maxwell D. Taylor to Secretary of State, 031235Z, June 1965, CMH.

77. Cable, COMUSMACV to CINCPAC, "U.S. Troop Deployment to SVN (S)," 070340Z, June 1965, CMH, 1–3. It worked out to thirty-four U.S. battalions and ten allied (South Korean and Australian) battalions.

78. Ibid.; Westmoreland, *A Soldier Reports*, 140.

79. Cable, CINCPAC to JCS, "PACOM Watch Report No. 23-65," 081650Z, June 1965, CMH, 1.

80. Browley Smith, "Summary Notes of 552d NSC Meeting, 11 June 1965,

12:15 P.M.," CMH, 2; *Papers,* 3:468; Cable, CINCPAC to JCS, "Concept of Counterinsurgency Operations in South Vietnam (s)," 112210Z, June 1965, CMH, 1–3.

81. Smith, "Summary Notes of 552d NSC Meeting," 2; Cable, COMUSMACV to CINCPAC, "Tactical Employment of U.S./Allied Ground Forces in Support of RVN," 120838Z, June 1965, CMH, 2–3.

82. Cable, COMUSMACV to CINCPAC, "Concept of Operations—Force Requirements and Deployments, SVN," 131515Z, June 1965, CMH, 2.

83. Memo, George W. Ball to the President, "Keeping the Power of Decision in the Viet-Nam Crisis," 18 June 1965, CMH, 2, 4–6.

84. *Papers,* 3:414–15. On the day before Bundy's message, U. Alexis Johnson had informed McNaughton that in many respects the situation in South Vietnam was no worse than in 1964.

85. Memo, George W. Ball to McGeorge Bundy, 29 June 1965, CMH, 4–5, 7, 10.

86. Memo, Chester L. Cooper to McGeorge Bundy, "Comments on Ball Paper," 30 June 1965, CMH, 1.

87. Memo, William Bundy to Dean Rusk, "A 'Middle Way' Course of Action in South Vietnam," 1 July 1965, CMH, 1.

88. Memo, Robert S. McNamara to the President, "Program of Expanded Military and Political Moves with Respect to Vietnam," 26 June 1965, CMH, 1.

89. See above, n. 45; CIA, Intelligence Memo, "Developments in South Vietnam during the Past Year," 29 June 1965, CMH; Cable, William C. Westmoreland to Maxwell D. Taylor, "Allied vs. VC Force Ratios," 080250Z, June 1965, CMH, 1; and Cable, Maxwell D. Taylor to Secretary of State, 111239Z, July 1965, CMH.

90. Rosson, "American Involvement in Vietnam," 204.

91. See above, nn. 45 and 89; and Director of Intelligence and Research, Department of State, Thomas L. Hughes to Dean Rusk, "Giap's Third Phase in Prospect in South Vietnam?" 23 July 1965, CMH.

92. Interview with Westmoreland, 15 May 1982; Rosson, "American Involvement in South Vietnam," 204; Interview with Taylor, 16–17 February 1973, v-9; Interview with Kinnard, 21 June 1982. It would later be claimed that airmobility and firepower nullified the 15:1 ratio, even in phase 2 operations.

93. *Papers,* 4:291–94. At this time John McNaughton requested from Gen. Andrew J. Goodpaster, Wheeler's assistant, an evaluation of the "forces required to win in South Vietnam." Goodpaster reported back that thirty-five additional battalions (above the Westmoreland request) would be sufficient to achieve a 4:1 ratio over enemy forces.

94. Memo, Robert S. McNamara to the President, "Recommendations of Additional Deployments to Vietnam," 20 July 1965, CMH, 1.

95. Memo, McGeorge Bundy to the President, "Vietnam Planning at Close of Business, 19 July," 19 July 1965, CMH; Department of State, Policy Planning Council, Robert H. Johnson to W. W. Rostow, "Where Are We Going in Vietnam?" 22 July 1965, CMH.

96. See Memo, McNamara to the President, 20 July 1965, 4–6.

97. Johnson to Rostow, 22 July 1965; Hughes to Rusk, 23 July 1965.

98. Hughes to Rusk, 23 July 1965.

99. Ibid. (my emphasis).

100. Henry Cabot Lodge to the President, 20 July 1965, CMH, 2.

101. Memo, Chester L. Cooper to McGeorge Bundy, 21 July 1965, CMH (my emphasis).

102. Browley Smith, "Summary Notes of 553d NSC Meeting 27 July 1965—5:40 P.M.–6:20 P.M.," CMH, 3–4.

Chapter 6. A Strategy of Tactics

1. BDM, *Lessons Learned in Vietnam*, 3–25.

2. Interview with Brig. Gen. Edwin L. Powell by Col. Clyde H. Patterson, Jr., 4 March 1971, MHI.

3. Interview with Taylor, 17 June 1982.

4. Gen. William E. Depuy, "Department of History Colloquium," U.S. Military Academy, West Point, N.Y., 28 April 1982.

5. Henry Brandon, *Anatomy of Error* (Boston: Gambit, 1969), 29. As noted, the alternative approach to MACV's concept of operations was the enclave strategy. Yet they were but two sides of the same coin in MACV's eyes. The only question was whether U.S. or South Vietnamese forces would carry the burden of search-and-destroy operations.

6. Westmoreland, *A Soldier Reports*, 145.

7. Interview with Westmoreland, 13 March 1971, 11.

8. Westmoreland, *A Soldier Reports*, 146.

9. Gregory Palmer, *The McNamara Strategy and the Vietnam War* (Westport, Conn.: Greenwood Press, 1978), 122.

10. Westmoreland, *A Soldier Reports*, 146.

11. Wheeler, "From Marchiennes to Bien Hoa," 59–60.

12. Westmoreland, *A Soldier Reports*, 150, 153.

13. Ibid., 194.

14. MACV, Office of the Assistant Chief of Staff, Intelligence, "VC Tactics—Withdrawal," 18 March 1965, MHI, 1, 16.

15. Interview with Westmoreland, 15 May 1982.

16. Westmoreland, *A Soldier Reports*, 149; Adm. U.S.G. Sharp and Gen. William C. Westmoreland, *Report on the War in Vietnam* (Washington, D.C.: GPO, 1968), 117.

17. *Papers*, 4:300, 302; Alain C. Enthoven and K. Wayne Smith, *How Much Is Enough?* (New York: Harper Colophon Books, 1971), 299–300.

18. Sharp and Westmoreland, *Vietnam*, 99; Tolson, *Airmobility*, 83.

19. Interview with General Johnson, 23 April 1973, 55.

20. Starry, *Mounted Combat in Vietnam*, 143.

21. Westmoreland, *A Soldier Reports*, 178.

22. Starry, *Mounted Combat in Vietnam*, 84–85.

23. Col. Hugh T. Bartley, "Some Critical Notes," *Armor* 78 (November–December 1969): 36.

24. Gen. Earle Wheeler, "Vietnam—The Current Situation" (Address delivered to the Business Council, Hot Springs, Va., 16 October 1965), in *Addresses by General Wheeler*, 2:69.

25. Thompson and Frizzell, *Lessons of Vietnam,* 178; Thompson, *No Exit,* 136, 168–69.

26. Interview with Williams, 29 March 1978, 69–70.

27. Interview with General Johnson, 23 April 1973, 55.

28. Thompson, *No Exit,* 138.

29. Gen. Lewis W. Walt, *Strange War, Strange Strategy* (New York: Funk & Wagnalls, 1969), 29.

30. Ibid., 28–29.

31. Ibid., 42.

32. F. J. West, Jr., *The Enclave: Some Military Efforts in Ly Tin District, Quang Tin Province, 1966–68,* RM-5941-ARPA (Santa Monica, Calif.: RAND Corporation, December 1969), 3.

33. Lewy, *America in Vietnam,* 116–17.

34. HQ, III Marine Amphibious Force, "Force Order 31214A," 17 July 1967, CMH, 3.

35. Blaufarb, *Counterinsurgency Era,* 257.

36. OSD, Office of Systems Analysis (OSA) (hereafter cited as OSDSA), "Southeast Asia (SEA) Analysis Report," July 1967 (hereafter cited as "SEA Report").

37. R.U.S.I., *Lessons of the Vietnam War,* 19.

38. Walt, *Strange War,* 51–54.

39. R.U.S.I., *Lessons of the Vietnam War,* 19.

40. Robert D. Campbell, *Analysis of the Marine Pacification System* (Alexandria, Va.: Matrix Corp., April 1968), 39.

41. Interview with Kinnard, 21 June 1982.

42. Interview with Depuy, 26 March 1979, V-25.

43. R.U.S.I., *Lessons of the Vietnam War,* 18.

44. Westmoreland, *A Soldier Reports,* 164–65.

45. R.U.S.I., *Lessons of the Vietnam War,* 18.

46. Westmoreland, *A Soldier Reports,* 166.

47. OSDSA, "SEA Report."

48. MACV, Memo, Gen. William C. Westmoreland to CG, III MAF, "Operations in I Corps," 15 November 1965, MHI.

49. George W. Ball, "A Compromise Solution for South Vietnam," 1 July 1965, quoted in *Papers,* 3:415.

50. HQ, 173d Airborne Brigade, "Combat Operations After Action Report OPORD 25-65 (Iron Triangle)," 10 November 1965, CMH, 23.

51. MACV, Office of the Assistant Chief of Staff, Intelligence, "VC Tactics—Withdrawal," 18 March 1965.

52. Gen. Earle Wheeler, "Vietnam—Certain Military Aspects" (Address delivered to Calvin Bullock Forum, New York City, 17 March 1966), in *Addresses by General Wheeler,* 2:80.

53. William Bundy and John McNaughton, "1966 Program to Increase the Effectiveness of Military Operations and Anticipated Results Thereof," 8 February 1966, General Westmoreland Papers, Charleston, S.C.

54. *Papers,* 4:279, 316–17, 319.

55. Ibid., 320.

56. Interview with Kinnard, 31 March 1977, 36.
57. Westmoreland, *A Soldier Reports,* 271–72.
58. OSDSA, "SEA Report," 15.
59. Westmoreland, *A Soldier Reports,* 179.
60. *Papers,* 4:321.
61. Ibid., 100, 325.
62. Ibid., 2:576.
63. Ibid., 577.
64. Ibid., 576–78, 580.
65. DA, CDC, "Review and Analysis of the Evaluation of the US Army Mechanized and Armor Combat Operations in Vietnam," 15 May 1967, MHI, VIII-4, VIII-5.
66. *Papers,* 4:325; OSD, Memo, McNamara to JCS, "CINCPAC CY 1966 Adjusted Requirements & CY 1967 Requirements," 5 August 1966, quoted in ibid., 326.
67. OSD, DPM, McNamara to the President, "Trip Report, Actions Recommended for Vietnam," 14 October 1966, quoted in ibid., 348–51 (emphasis in the original).
68. Ibid.
69. William Corson, *The Betrayal* (New York: W. W. Norton, 1968), 78.
70. BDM, *Lessons Learned in Vietnam* 3–69, 3–70, 3–152.
71. *Papers,* 4:356–57.
72. Ibid.
73. Ibid., 379; Interviews with Taylor, 16–17 February 1973, V-27; and 17 June 1982. Incredibly, the CCP was generally ignored by the Army Staff in Washington. General Taylor, after several discussions with the Chiefs over the CCP, came away believing that "I was the only man in Washington that ever read it."
74. JCS 2343/855/27 (Program 4), 15 November 1966, quoted in "MACV Force Development Chronology," CMH.
75. OSD, DPM, McNamara to the President, "Recommended FY 67 Supplemental Appropriation," 17 November 1966, quoted in *Papers,* 4:365.
76. MACV, COMUSMACV Message 09101, Westmoreland to CINCPAC, 180403, March 1967, quoted in "MACV Force Development Chronology," CMH; *Papers,* 4:285, 409, 434–35, 460. Fifty of the ARVN's 120 infantry battalions were to be assigned to pacification in 1967.
77. Westmoreland, *A Soldier Reports,* 227; *Papers,* 4:442.
78. Sharp and Westmoreland, *Vietnam,* 134–35.
79. *Papers,* 4:440–41.
80. Thompson and Frizzell, *Lessons of Vietnam,* 148–49; Westmoreland, *A Soldier Reports,* 181–82; *Papers,* 4:415.
81. OSDSA, Memo for Secretary of Defense, "Force Levels and Enemy Attrition," 4 May 1967, quoted in *Papers,* 4:461.
82. OSDSA, "SEA Report," April 1967, 7.
83. Ibid., 8, 12.
84. *Papers,* 4:468.
85. OSDSA, Memo for Secretary of Defense, "Increase of SEA Forces," 1 May

1967, quoted in *Papers,* 4:463–66; OSDSA, Memo for Secretary of Defense, "Force Levels," 456–66.

86. DPM, OSD (ISA), to the President, "Future Actions in South Vietnam," 19 May 1967, quoted in *Papers,* 4:286.

87. Enthoven and Smith, *How Much Is Enough?* 293.

88. JCSM 288-67, "US Worldwide Military Posture," 20 May 1967, quoted in *Papers,* 4:286, 490.

89. OSDSA, DPM, John McNaughton to the President, "Alternative Military Actions against NVN," 12 June 1967, quoted in *Papers,* 4:287.

90. Douglas Kinnard, *The War Managers* (Hanover, N.H.: University Press of New England, 1977), 69.

91. Interview with Depuy, 26 March 1979, VI-21, VI-22.

92. Lt. Gen. Bernard W. Rogers, *Cedar Falls–Junction City: A Turning Point,* Vietnam Studies (Washington, D.C.: GPO, 1974), 74.

93. Sharp and Westmoreland, *Vietnam,* 137.

94. HQ, 1st Infantry Division, "After Action Report: Operation Junction City, 22 February 1967–15 April 1967," MHI, 1; Tolson, *Airmobility,* 128.

95. Rogers, *Cedar Falls–Junction City,* 157.

96. HQ, 1st Infantry Division, "After Action Report: Operation Junction City," 13, II-11.

97. Rogers, *Cedar Falls–Junction City,* 58.

98. *Papers,* 4:419, 421; Patrick J. McGarvey, "Visions of Victory: Selected Vietnamese Communist Military Writings, 1964–68" (Stanford University, 1969), 215; OSDSA, "SEA Report," January 1968, 19–20.

99. OSDSA, "SEA Report," February 1968, 7, 16–17; March 1968, 17. Other evidence confirmed that the Army was not providing an effective shield for pacification operations. For example, the VC assassinated more than twice as many GVN officials in 1967 as in 1966; they also killed and abducted 64 percent more Vietnamese in 1967 than in the previous year.

100. Ibid.

101. Despite the fixation with sanctuaries and infiltration, at the end of 1967 roughly 80 percent of the insurgent forces in South Vietnam consisted of locally recruited VC.

Chapter 7. Counterinsurgency American-Style

1. Cable, CINCPAC to JCS, "Command Arrangements in SEAsia," 312245Z, March 1965, CMH, 1–2.

2. BDM, *Lessons Learned in Vietnam,* vol. 6, bk. 2, pp. 11–34.

3. Rosson, "American Involvement in Vietnam," 196; "Discussion with General Harold K. Johnson, LTG K. K. Compton, MG J. B. McPherson, and Rear Admiral R. W. Mehle, 7 March 1965, Republic of Vietnam," MHI, 3. Quat's acquiescence stemmed from his desire to gain some control over his unruly generals.

4. Thomas C. Thayer, "How to Analyze a War without Fronts: Vietnam, 1965–1972," *Journal of Defense Research,* ser. B, *Tactical Warfare Analysis of Vietnam Data* 7B, no. 3 (1975): 811–12.

5. Rosson, "American Involvement in Vietnam," 198–99.

6. BDM, *Lessons Learned in Vietnam*, vol. 6, bk. 2; Functional Analyses, pp. 11–35.

7. Westmoreland, *A Soldier Reports*, 134.

8. Interview with Taylor, 17 June 1982.

9. Ibid.

10. Thayer, "How to Analyze a War," 811.

11. Thompson and Frizzell, *Lessons of Vietnam*, 272.

12. Gen. William E. Depuy, "Address to the Infantry Officer Advanced Course," Ft. Benning, Ga.; 1 November 1973, MHI, 11.

13. R.U.S.I., *Lessons of the Vietnam War*, 3.

14. Tolson, *Airmobility*, 117.

15. Thompson, *No Exit*, 127–28.

16. David R. Palmer, *Summons of the Trumpet* (San Rafael, Calif.: Presidio Press, 1978), 144. Palmer observed: "Colonel Berry also made frequent references to American units being pinned down. In spite of massive firepower, one searches in vain through all the literature of the war for an example of enemy units being pinned down!"

17. Gen. Earle Wheeler, "A Report on Armed Forces Day" (Address delivered to the Chamber of Commerce and Rotary Club, Houston, Tex., 19 May 1966), in *Addresses by General Wheeler*, 2.96.

18. Wheeler, "Vietnam—Certain Military Aspects," 81.

19. Interview with General Johnson, 22 January 1973, X-31.

20. R.U.S.I., *Lessons of the Vietnam War*, 7.

21. Kinnard, *The War Managers*, 54–55.

22. Richard A. Gabriel and Paul L. Savage, *Crisis in Command: Mismanagement in the Army* (New York: Hill & Wang, 1978), 234–44.

23. Khuyen, *The RVNAF*, 300.

24. Lewy, *America in Vietnam*, 71.

25. Ibid., 72.

26. Thayer, "How to Analyze a War," 827.

27. Konrad Keller, *Conversations with Enemy Soldiers in Late 1968/Early 1969: A Study of Motivation and Morale*, RM-6131-1-ISA/ARPA (Santa Monica, Calif.: RAND Corporation, September 1970), 85.

28. Lung, *Strategy and Tactics*, 108; CINCPAC, "An Appraisal of the Effectiveness of Arc Light Operations in SVN," Scientific Advisor Group Report 1-69, 1 February 1969, MHI, 3. The VC early-warning system monitored U.S. radio nets and watched for the departure of U.S. air activity in the areas to be hit by ARC LIGHT attacks.

29. Kinnard, *The War Managers*, 48.

30. Lt. Gen. Julian J. Ewell and Maj. Gen. Ira A. Hunt, Jr., *Sharpening the Combat Edge: The Use of Analysis to Reinforce Military Judgement*, Vietnam Studies (Washington, D.C.: GPO, 1974), 120.

31. Thayer, "How to Analyze a War," 828. Support from high-performance jets designed to combat sophisticated Soviet aircraft was notoriously inaccurate compared with the results achieved by slower, propeller-driven aircraft, yet over 90 percent of all sorties flown by the U.S. Air Force in Southeast Asia were by jets.

32. Ibid., 810.

33. Ott, *Field Artillery*, 187–88; Brig. Gen. S. L. A. Marshall, "Observations from a Vietnam Notebook," *Army* 16 (December 1966); 28.

34. Brig. Gen. S. L. A. Marshall, "On Heavy Artillery: American Experience in Four Wars," *Parameters* 8 (June 1978): 16–17; Thayer, "How to Analyze a War," 810; Kinnard, *The War Managers*, 47. Even after the VC retreated into phase 1 or low-level phase 2 operations after the Tet Offensive, and even with the gains made in pacification in 1969–70, there was no perceptible drop in the artillery consumption rate.

35. Interview with General Johnson, 21 May 1973, XIII-43; OSDSA, "SEA Report," July 1967, 19, 28. General Johnson admitted after the war that "far too much of our own artillery fire in Vietnam was unobserved fire [which was] not warranted in the preponderance in which it was fired."

36. OSDSA, "SEA Report," November 1967.

37. Enthoven and Smith, *How Much Is Enough?* 305–6.

38. Lewy, *America in Vietnam*, 100.

39. Ibid., 99.

40. Cincinnatus, *Self-Destruction* (New York: W. W. Norton, 1981), 83–84.

41. Interviews with General Johnson, 22 January 1973, X-32; 21 May 1973, XIII-43.

42. Interview with Taylor, 17 June 1982.

43. "Padded claims kept everyone happy; there were no penalties for overstating enemy losses, but an understatement could lead to sharp questions as to why US casualties were so high compared with the results achieved" (Enthoven and Smith, *How Much Is Enough?* 296).

44. Ibid., 295–96; Thayer, "How to Analyze a War," 846; Lewy, *America in Vietnam*, 81.

45. Douglas Robertson, "Enemy Deaths in 8 Days Put at 7,500," *New York Times*, 28 August 1968.

46. Ewell and Hunt, *Combat Edge*, 228.

47. Tolson, *Airmobility*, 181.

48. Ewell and Hunt, *Combat Edge*, 212.

49. DA, Office of The Adjutant General, "Lessons Learned, HQ, 9th Infantry Division," 18 September 1969, 27.

50. Confidential interview 3.

51. Ibid.

52. Interview with Lt. Gen. Julian J. Ewell, Officer Debrief, by Robert Crowley and Lt. Col. Norman M. Bissell, 10 April 1979, MHI, III-17.

53. See DA, Office of The Adjutant General, "Lessons Learned, HQ, 9th Infantry Division," 46.

54. Interview with Ewell, 10 April 1979, III-6.

55. Confidential interview 3.

56. Cables, COMUSMACV to JCS, "Tour Lengths," 161111Z, February 1965, CMH, 1; and JCS to CINCPAC, "Reevaluation of Tour Lengths (U)," 151349Z, May 1965, CMH.

57. Westmoreland, *A Soldier Reports*, 295.

58. Interview with Gen. Harold K. Johnson by Lt. Col. Rupert F. Glover, 21 May 1973, MHI, XII-39, XIII-44.

59. Interview with Westmoreland, 15 May 1982.

60. Cincinnatus, *Self-Destruction*, 155–57.

61. Thayer, "How to Analyze a War," 846.

62. Since factors such as promotion, relief, injury, and death were potential disruptions to the completion of command tours, the average length of command was somewhat *less* than six months.

63. See, for example, Lewy, *America in Vietnam*, 119; Yarmolinsky, *The Military Establishment*, 56; Vien et al., *The U.S. Advisor*, 70; and Donald B. Vought, "American Culture and American Arms," in Hunt and Schultz, *Lessons from an Unconventional War*, 170.

64. ODCSOPS, Summary Sheet, "Officer Counterinsurgency Assignments," 16 September 1963, CMH.

65. Peter M. Dawkins, "The United States Army and the 'Other War' in Vietnam: A Study of the Complexity of Implementing Organizational Change" (Ph.D. diss., Princeton University, 1979); Warren Graham and William L. King, *Military Advising in Vietnam, 1969–1970*, HumRRO Technical Report 73-24 (Alexandria, Va., November 1973).

66. Dawkins, "The 'Other War,' " 79.

67. DA, Office of the Under Secretary of the Army, Memo, Under Secretary of the Army David E. McGiffert to Secretary of the Army Stanley Resor, 26 July 1967, CMH.

68. MACV, MACJ12 Fact Sheet, "Prestige of Advisors," 9 August 1967, MHI, 1; Collins, *South Vietnamese Army*, 128.

69. Dawkins, "The 'Other War,' " 79.

70. Graham and King, *Advising in Vietnam*, 79.

71. Dawkins, "The 'Other War,' " 71; Confidential interview 4.

72. Vien et al., *The U.S. Advisor*, 70–71.

73. Graham and King, *Advising in Vietnam*, 89.

74. Gen. William C. Westmoreland to Province Senior Adviser Nominees, 9 March 1970, reproduced in Dawkins, "The 'Other War,' " 418–19. The incentive that Westmoreland offered prospective advisers basically involved a guarantee that their career would not be jeopardized by the assignment.

75. Norman and Spores, "Big Push on Guerrilla Warfare," 31.

76. National Research Council, *The Effects of Herbicides in South Vietnam* (Washington, D.C.: DOD, 1974), pt. A, "Summary and Conclusions," III-17.

77. MACV Chief of Staff to William C. Truehart, 29 September 1963, CMH.

78. Department of State, Memorandum of Conversation, "Situation in Vietnam," 22 May 1963, CMH, 2; Hilsman, *To Move a Nation*, 443.

79. Lung, *Strategy and Tactics*, 111–12; National Research Council, *Effects of Herbicides*, VII-57.

80. MACV, "Evaluation of the Defoliation Program," 18 October 1968, MHI.

81. Ibid.

82. Anthony J. Russo, *A Statistical Analysis of the US Crop Spraying Program in South Vietnam*, RM-5450-1-ISAARPA (Santa Monica, Calif.: RAND Corporation, October 1967), IX, 1.

83. Ibid., IX, 32.

84. U.S. Embassy, "Report of the Herbicide Policy Review," 28 August 1968, MHI, 18 (my emphasis).

85. Keller, *Conversations with Enemy Soldiers*, 16.
86. Lung, *Strategy and Tactics*, 113–14.
87. National Research Council, *Effects of Herbicides*, VII-48.

Chapter 8. The "Other" War

1. Thompson, *No Exit*, 151.
2. Sturdivant, *Pacification*, 1–2.
3. Marshall, "Observations," 26.
4. See Lewy, *America in Vietnam*, 189; and Thompson, *No Exit*, 153–54. The Army was left virtually untouched in the reapportionment of assets toward pacification. It has been suggested that McNamara, fearing an open rift with the Joint Chiefs, decided not to press the issue.
5. Thompson and Frizzell, *Lessons of Vietnam*, 191.
6. Scoville, "Pacification, Advice and Support," 2.
7. Thompson and Frizzell, *Lessons of Vietnam*, 215–16; Richard T. Schultz, "The Intellectual Origins and Development of Counterinsurgency Theory in American Foreign Policy Doctrine: The Vietnam Case Study" (Ph.D. diss., University of Miami, Miami, Fla., 1975).
8. Henry Kissinger, *White House Years* (Boston: Little, Brown & Co., 1979), 233.
9. See Collins, *South Vietnamese Army*, 72; and Col. John C. Burney, Jr., "So You're Going to Be an Advisor?" *Armor* 77 (May–June 1968): 53–54.
10. Maj. Gen. Charles J. Timmes, "Debriefing Report," [3?] June 1964, CMH, 12.
11. See, for example, Collins, *South Vietnamese Army*, 71; Vien et al., *The U.S. Advisor*, 131; Thayer, "How to Analyze a War," 883; Blaufarb, *Counterinsurgency Era*, 244; and Thomas C. Thayer, "Republic of Vietnam Armed Forces," in *A Systems Analysis View of the Vietnam War*, ed. Thomas C. Thayer (Columbus, Ohio: Battelle Columbus Laboratories, 1975), 6:90–91. By April 1969 the territorial forces had received enough M-16s to equip about half of their forces. A lack of radios, however, continued to hamper PF operations.
12. Thayer, *A Systems Analysis View*, 6:15.
13. OSDSA, "SEA Report," September 1967, 19; June 1968, 9.
14. Thayer, "How to Analyze a War," 887.
15. Thompson and Frizzell, *Lessons of Vietnam*, 259.
16. Ibid., 261. The measurements were obtained using the HES scores, the yardstick of measurement employed by CORDS to plot progress or regression in the pacification effort.
17. Robert W. Komer, *Impact of Pacification on Insurgency in South Vietnam*, P-4443 (Santa Monica, Calif.: RAND Corporation, August 1970), 13.
18. Lung, *Strategy and Tactics*, 52; Vien et al., *The U.S. Advisor*, 128; Lewy, *America in Vietnam*, 183; MACV, Office of the Assistant Chief of Staff (J-2), "Viet Cong Targeting of the People's Defense Forces," 10 March 1969, MHI, 1. At that time, many PF duties were assumed by the People's Self-Defense Forces (PSDF) as part of a program of national mobilization initiated after the Tet Offensive. The GVN claimed that between 3 million and 4 million men were in the PSDF by 1971, although this number is generally considered to be highly inflated. The rapid

growth of the PSDF program made it a prime target for VC infiltration and subversion.

19. See, for example, Thompson and Frizzell, *Lessons of Vietnam,* 260; Komer, *Impact of Pacification;* and Lewy, *America in Vietnam,* 182.

20. Interview with Ewell, 10 April 1979, III-28.

21. OSDSA, "SEA Report," December 1968, 45. The study covered the period February 1967–September 1968.

22. HQ, 1st Cavalry Division (Airmobile), Combat After Action Report, "Operation MASHER 25 Jan–3 Feb 66/Operation WHITE WING 4 Feb–6 Mar 66," 28 April 1966, MHI, 15, 23, 25, enclosure 16.

23. HQ, 1st Cavalry Division (Airmobile), "Lessons Learned," 27 October 1967, MHI, 4, 28, 31–32, 36–37, 49–51.

24. Ibid., 57–58.

25. Lewy, *America in Vietnam,* 59.

26. HQ, 1st Cavalry Division, "Lessons Learned," 36–37.

27. Gen. Earle Wheeler, "Vietnam—Certain Military Aspects" (Address delivered to the Ohio Staters, Inc., Symposium, 21 April 1966), in Wheeler, *Addresses by General Wheeler,* 2:90.

28. ODCSOPS, "A Program for the Pacification and Long Term Development of South Vietnam" (PROVN), 1 March 1966, CMH, 4–35; Lewy, *America in Vietnam,* 109.

29. See, for example, Jerry M. Tinker, *The Refugee Situation in Dinh Tuong Province* (McLean, Va., 1968), 14; and A. Terry Rambo, *The Causes of Refugee Movement in Vietnam: A Survey of Refugees in I and IV Corps* (McLean, Va., 1968), 7.

30. Melvin Gurtov, *The War in the Delta,* RM-5353-1-ISA/ARPA (Santa Monica, Calif.: RAND Corporation, September 1967), 25.

31. See also, Cable, U.S. Embassy to Department of State, "Joint GVN Security Council–U.S. Mission Council Meeting," 23 March 1965, CMH; and Lewy, *America in Vietnam,* 108.

32. Lung, *Strategy and Tactics,* 13, 20.

33. Memo, David McMeans to Mr. Calhoun, "Refugees in Region III," 2 January 1968, MHI, 1.

34. Lung, *Strategy and Tactics,* 46, 145.

35. Thayer, "How to Analyze a War," 913.

36. Blaufarb, *Counterinsurgency Era,* 247, 275.

37. Thayer, "How to Analyze a War," 914–15.

38. Interview with Yarborough, 15 April 1975, II-31.

39. Thompson and Frizzell, *Lessons of Vietnam,* 269–70.

40. Vien et al., *The U.S. Advisor,* 84.

41. U.S. Army, Vietnam (USARV), *Combat Operations: Concept of Employment for Long Range Patrol (LRP) Company,* USARV PAM 525-1, 30 November 1967, MHI, 2.

42. Col. John H. Speers, "Debriefing of Colonel John H. Speers," 15 July 1965, CMH, 10; Collins, *South Vietnamese Army,* 53–54, 80.

43. Kelly, *Special Forces,* 134; Collins, *South Vietnamese Army,* 74.

44. F. J. West, Jr., *The Strike Teams: Tactical Performance and Strategic*

Potential, P-3987 (Santa Monica, Calif.: RAND Corporation, January 1969), 12–13. West found that since strike teams operated as stripped-down, light infantry and comprised roughly a dozen men, the area blanketed by a given number of soldiers in strike teams substantially exceeded that obtained by the same number of men organized into main-force units.

45. In fact the Army (except for the Special Forces) was not training its people in strike team operations. A CDC report filed in May 1967 observed that "training in Long Range Reconnaissance Patrols is not currently being accomplished at Army training centers and service schools" (see DA, CDC, "USCONARC Comments of the Review and Analysis of the Evaluation of US Army Mechanized and Armor Combat Operations in Vietnam," 15 May 1967, 1-8).

Chapter 9. Tet: Defeat in Victory

1. See Lewy, *America in Vietnam,* 146–47; Herbert Y. Schandler, *The Unmaking of a President* (Princeton, N.J.: Princeton University Press, 1977), 68; and Col. Hoang Ngoc Lung, *The General Offensives of 1968–69,* Indochina Monographs (Washington, D.C.: CMH, 1981), 11.

2. Interview with Taylor, 16–17 February 1973, V-26.

3. Sharp and Westmoreland, *Vietnam,* 136; Westmoreland, *A Soldier Reports,* 381, 390.

4. Westmoreland, *A Soldier Reports,* 425–27. Wheeler had cabled Westmoreland asking, "Do you need reinforcements?" Wheeler had said that the United States "is not prepared to accept defeat in South Vietnam. In summary, if you need more troops, ask for them."

5. *Papers,* 4:542.

6. Interview with Gen. Earle Wheeler by Dorothy Pierce McSweeny, 21 August 1969, CMH, II-5.

7. Ibid., II-6.

8. Ibid.

9. *Papers,* 4:546–47.

10. Ibid., 548; interview with Wheeler, 21 August 1969, II-11.

11. *Papers,* 4:548–50.

12. Interview with Wheeler, 21 August 1969, II-9, II-11; Westmoreland, *A Soldier Reports,* 431–32; *Papers,* 4:556–57. Westmoreland contended that he and Wheeler had an understanding that only the first 108,000 men would be earmarked for Vietnam; the remainder of the 200,000 would be used to reconstitute the strategic reserve. Wheeler concurred that only the first increment was firm; the second and third would be dependent on the situation in Vietnam as time progressed. The 200,000 figure itself appears to have been based on MACV's unfulfilled request of May 1967 for 4⅔ divisions.

13. *Papers,* 4:556–57, 563; Schandler, *Unmaking of a President,* 127. Warnke had succeeded John McNaughton upon the latter's death in a commercial air crash in July 1967.

14. *Papers,* 4:564–65.

15. Schandler, *Unmaking of a President,* 156.

16. *Papers,* 4:568.

17. Ibid., 568–69.
18. Schandler, *Unmaking of a President*, 160–61; Don Oberdorfer, *Tet!* (Garden City, N.Y.: Doubleday & Co., 1971), 288.
19. *Papers*, 4:571–72 (my emphasis).
20. Interview with Clark Clifford by Paige Mulhollen, 2 July 1969, CMH, 16, 26; Clark Clifford, "A Vietnam Reappraisal," *Foreign Affairs* 47 (July 1969): 601–23.
21. *Papers*, 4:573.
22. Ibid., 580.
23. OSD, Memo, Secretary of Defense to Chairman, JCS, "SEA Deployments," 14 March 1968, quoted in *Papers*, 4:590–91.
24. Ibid.; Taylor, *Swords and Plowshares*, 386–88; Schandler, *Unmaking of a President*, 262–63. The briefings presented by Depuy and Carver brought out anew the dispute between the CIA and the military over enemy strength, the vital statistic in determining whether or not MACV had reached the crossover point. The military estimate, of course, was the lower of the two.
25. Schandler, *Unmaking of a President*, 262–63; *Papers*, 4:592.
26. *Papers*, 4:592. After the Wise Men departed, Johnson ordered his own briefings from Depuy, Habib, and Carver. Prior to that time he had been getting his picture of the war from reports presented by Walt Rostow.
27. DOD, Memo, Deputy Secretary of Defense to Secretaries of the Military Departments; Chairman, JCS; Assistant Secretaries of Defense, "SEA Deployment Program 6," 4 April 1968, quoted in ibid., 4:602.
28. Sharp and Westmoreland, *Vietnam*, 168; Westmoreland, *A Soldier Reports*, 321.
29. Sharp and Westmoreland, *Vietnam*, 170; Westmoreland, *A Soldier Reports*, 332; John Paul Vann to Lt. Gen. Fred C. Weyand, 29 February 1968, MHI.
30. Reflecting MACV's tendency to divorce military goals from political imperatives, the general once responded to the question of how the need to maintain popular support for the war in the United States impacted on his duties as COMUSMACV by stating, "It was none of my concern" (interview with Westmoreland, 15 May 1982).
31. Collins, *South Vietnamese Army*, 86–87; Gen. Matthew B. Ridgway, "Indochina: Disengaging," *Foreign Affairs* 49 (July 1971): 583–93; HQ, MACCORDS-PSG, "Dinh Binh Province—The Challenge, 1971," 12 June 1971, CMH; Lewy, *America in Vietnam*, 170–72.
32. John Paul Vann to Leroy Wehrle, Deputy Director, Vietnamese Bureau, AID, 7 March 1968.
33. HQ, MACV, "One War: MACV Command Overview, 1968–1972," CMH, 15.
34. Orientation courses in counterinsurgency at Forts Benning, Sill, and Rucker continued to feature large operations, heavy firepower, and digging in every night (see Ewell and Hunt, *Combat Edge*, 76).
35. HQ, MACV, Long Range Planning Task Group, Briefing for COMUSMACV, 20 November 1968, MHI, 20–21.
36. In three months the kill ratio leaped from 15.4:1 to 30.1:1 (see Ewell and Hunt, *Combat Edge*, 188).

37. HQ, 9th Infantry Division, "After Action Report: Operation SPEEDY EXPRESS," 1 December 1968, 32; DA, Office of the Chief of Staff, Memo for General Bartlett, 12 January 1972, CMH; Lewy, *America in Vietnam*, 142.

38. OSDSA, "SEA Report," September–October 1970, 17.

39. Ewell and Hunt, *Combat Edge*, 195.

40. OSDSA, "SEA Report," October 1968, 53, 5–55.

41. Quang Ngai Province Advisory Team, "Province Monthly Report," 31 March 1969.

42. Interview with Powell, 18 March 1978, II-9.

43. Thompson and Frizzell, *Lessons of Vietnam*, 79.

Chapter 10. Paths Untaken, Paths Forsaken

1. Kissinger, *White House Years*, 272–73, 307.

2. Kinnard, *The War Managers*, 1.

3. Interviews with Taylor, 17 June 1982; 16–17 February 1973, V-37.

4. Col. Harry G. Summers, *On Strategy: The Vietnam War in Context* (Carlisle Barracks, Pa.: U.S. Army War College, April 1981); Confidential interviews 1 and 6; Drew Middleton, "Colonel Cites Key Mistakes over Vietnam," *New York Times*, 7 February 1982. See also Gen. Bruce Palmer, *The Twenty-Five Year War* (Lexington: University of Kentucky Press, 1984).

5. Summers, *On Strategy*, 76–77.

6. Richard Halloran, "U.S. Will Not Drift into Combat Role, Weinberger Says," *New York Times*, 29 November 1984, idem, "Pentagon Chief Is Doubtful on GIS for Central America," ibid., 13 June 1983.

7. Ibid.

8. See, for example, Maj. Robert A. Doughty and Maj. Robert V. Smith, "The Command and General Staff College in Transition, 1946–1976" (Fort Leavenworth, Kans.), 56; Donald B. Vought, "Preparing for the Wrong War," *Military Review* 57 (May 1977): 16–34; and Dawkins, "The 'Other War,'" 437–38.

9. DA, *Command, Control and Support of Special Forces Operations*, FM31-22 (Washington, D.C.: GPO, 23 December 1981), 9-3, 9-4. See also Col. Robert J. Baretto's excellent article, "Special Forces in the 1980's: A Strategic Reorientation," *Military Review* 63 (March 1983).

10. Ibid.

11. DA, *Low Intensity Conflict*, FM100-20 (Washington, D.C.: GPO, January 1981), 162, 206, 211.

12. Alvin H. Bernstein and Col. John H. Waghelstein, "How to Win in El Salvador," *Policy Review* 17 (December 1984): 50–52.

13. ODCSOPS, "U.S. Army Operational Concept for Special Operations Forces," n.d., 12–13.

14. Ibid., 13.

15. ODCSOPS, Parker and Rosson to CG USCONARC, "Implementation of the U.S. Army Special Warfare Program, FY 1963–68 (U)," 25 October 1962; idem, "Implementation of the U.S. Army Special Warfare Program, FY 1963–68," n.d.,

CMH; ODCSOPS, "Special Warfare and Special Forces," 1; April 1965, ODCSOPS, Congressional Fact Paper, "Special Warfare Program," 1 April 1965.

16. DA, Briefing slides, *The United States Army Light Infantry Division: Improving Strategic and Tactical Flexibility.*

17. See Lt. Gen. James R. Hollingsworth (U.S. Army, Ret.), "The Light Division," *Army Forces Journal International,* October 1983, 84–92; Michael Duffy, "Army's New Light Tank," *Defense Week* 5 (16 July 1984): 1, 20; and idem, "9th Division Gets New Dune Buggy But an Old Tank," ibid. 5 (21 January 1985): 1–2.

18. See, for example, Lt. Col. John M. Oseth, "Intelligence and Low Intensity Conflict," *Naval War College Review* 37 (November–December 1984).

19. Interview with Yarborough, 15 April 1975, II-21.

Index

Abrams, Creighton W.: appointed COMUSMACV, 248, 252; and change in strategy, 252–55, 257

Advisers, Army, 5, 23–24, 76–77, 271; personnel policies, 207–10; and "revolt from below," 78–84, 259–60

Agrovilles, 216

Air assault exercises, 123–25

Airmobility, 112–27; competition of, with Air Force, 114, 121–24, 127; origins of, 113–15; and problems with insurgency, 170–71, 174, 266

Americal Division, 256

Ap Bac, battle of, 78–81

Armor, use of, 169–70, 182–83; and ARCOV Study, 188

Army Concept, 6, 7, 24, 34, 39, 65, 75, 79, 120, 127, 131, 141, 154, 156, 158, 161, 164, 167–68, 171–72, 186, 192, 194, 196, 203, 207, 213–14, 219, 221, 225, 233, 237, 245, 250, 253, 260–64, 268, 271; defined, 4–5; and flexible response, 29

Army Concept Team in Vietnam (ACTIV), 120–21

Army of the Republic of Vietnam (ARVN), 25, 62, 66, 74, 78, 158–59, 161, 196, 199, 219, 229, 238, 240, 251, 263–64; and attitude toward the population, 72; combat effectiveness, 56, 63, 65, 75–76, 78–79, 82–84, 91, 118, 131–32, 134, 151–52, 166–67; leadership of, 151–52; organization and training under MAAG, 20–24; and pacification, 68–69, 86, 185,

189, 216, 228; and Regional/Popular Forces, 220–21

Artillery, use of, 201–2, 222, 224, 226, 256

A Shau Valley, 239, 256

ATTLEBORO operation, 190–91

Attrition, strategy of, 164–68, 175–78, 182, 184–85, 190–92, 196–98, 221, 232, 241, 254–57, 259, 264, 266–67; and reappraisal after Tet, 242–48, 250

Australia, 160

Ball, George W., 133, 155–57, 247, 264

BARREL ROLL, 99

B-52 strikes (ARC LIGHT), 159, 190, 200, 224

Bien Hoa, attack on (1964), 97, 133

Binh Dinh Province, 166, 222–24, 256

Birrer, Ivan, 51

Body count, 222, 224, 239, 248, 252–56; command pressure for, 198–99, 202; and exaggeration of, 203

Bombing of North Vietnam, 97, 136–38, 141, 149, 154; BARREL ROLL, 99; FLAMING DART, 137; ROLLING THUNDER, 99, 146, 184; and Tonkin Gulf, 95

Booby traps, 201

Bradley, Omar N., 4, 16, 247

Buddhists, South Vietnamese, 86

Bundy, McGeorge, 31, 33, 35, 93, 134, 162, 247; and introduction of U.S. combat forces, 96, 98, 136, 148, 156–57